THE ELECTIONS OF 2024

Miller Center Studies on the Presidency

Guian A. McKee and Marc J. Selverstone, Editors

THE ELECTIONS OF 2024

Edited by Michael Nelson

University of Virginia Press • *Charlottesville and London*
Published in association with the University of Virginia's
Miller Center of Public Affairs

University of Virginia Press
© 2025 by the Rector and Visitors of the University of Virginia
All rights reserved
Printed in the United States of America on acid-free paper

First published 2025

9 8 7 6 5 4 3 2 1

LIBRARY OF CONGRESS CATALOGING-IN-PUBLICATION DATA
Names: Nelson, Michael, editor
Title: The elections of 2024 / edited by Michael Nelson.
Description: Charlottesville : University of Virginia Press, 2025. | Series: Miller
    Center studies on the presidency | Includes bibliographical references.
Identifiers: LCCN 2025003182 (print) | LCCN 2025003183 (ebook) |
    ISBN 9780813952840 hardback | ISBN 9780813952857 paperback |
    ISBN 9780813952864 ebook
Subjects: LCSH: Presidents—United States—Election—2024 | Trump, Donald,
    1946– | United States. Congress—Elections, 2024 | Elections—United States—
    History—21st century | United States—Politics and government—21st century
Classification: LCC JK1968 2024 .U55 2025 (print) | LCC JK1968 2024 (ebook) |
    DDC 324.973/0935—dc23/eng/20250320
LC record available at https://lccn.loc.gov/2025003182
LC ebook record available at https://lccn.loc.gov/2025003183

Cover photos: Portraits of Donald Trump and Kamala Harris. (Library of Congress, Prints and Photographs Division, LC-DIG-ppbd-00607 and LC-DIG-ppbd-01176)

Cover design: Cecilia Sorochin

CONTENTS

PREFACE

From the Vantage Point of 2021, when *The Elections of 2020*, the most recent of the eleven (and counting) postelection books in this series, was published, few things seemed less likely than that Donald Trump, the defeated forty-fifth president of the United States in 2020, would be inaugurated as the forty-seventh president in 2025. Unlike eight of the previous eleven incumbent presidents who ran, Trump lost. None of the three others who ran and lost (Gerald Ford, Jimmy Carter, and George H. W. Bush) ever again sought any office, much less the presidency. Trump also left Washington the only president ever to be impeached twice (tying the record for all forty-four of his predecessors combined) and the only one voted guilty in the Senate trial by any members of his own party. The second of these impeachments concerned Trump's conduct on January 6, 2021, when he incited a crowd of supporters to such an extent that many of them violently stormed the Capitol Building in an unprecedented effort to prevent Congress from certifying the results of the election.

Trump's fortunes did not seem to improve in 2022, when many politically weak but personally loyal Republican candidates whom he endorsed for election to the Senate and House of Representatives lost highly winnable elections, costing his party the opportunity that midterm elections usually afford to make substantial gains. As for 2023, during the spring and summer Trump was indicted in two federal courts and two state courts on a total of ninety-one criminal counts. In May 2024 a unanimous jury in the New York trial found him guilty on all thirty-four charges brought in that case.

All this and yet, in November 2024, Trump won the election, the first defeated president to attain a comeback victory since Grover Cleveland in 1892. He did so by securing a solid majority of electoral votes and a clear plurality of the national popular vote. In 2016, when he was first elected, all (including Trump) were surprised and many were shocked. In 2024 many were surprised but few were shocked. Republican primary voters already had made clear that none of Trump's unprecedented political liabilities would hurt him at the party's grassroots. He won all but two of fifty-six state and territorial contests, compiling 96 percent of Republican National Convention delegates. The New York case, which had nothing to do with his conduct in office, was generally judged the least politically damaging of the four, and the other three were delayed indefinitely. After an unprecedentedly early presidential debate in June, Trump's presumptive opponent in the general election, President Joe Biden, yielded to pressure from fellow Democratic leaders to drop out on the grounds of advanced age and apparent decline. Instead of Biden, Trump ended up running against Biden's vice president, Kamala Harris, who had barely three months to design and mount an effective campaign virtually from scratch.

Making sense of the 2024 presidential and congressional elections and their consequences is something the all-star team of political scientists assembled to write this book was both well equipped and eager to do. Some of the authors—notably Paul Quirk (on the presidency), Gary Jacobson (on Congress), and I (on the setting of the elections)—have been at this since our first such book on the 1984 contests. Others have contributed to one or more recent editions, including William Mayer (the nominations), Marc Hetherington (the election results), Marjorie Hershey (the media), Charles Hunt (campaign finance), and Andrew Rudalevige (the meaning of the election). Because of the various constitutional and legal issues that shadowed politics in 2024, John Maltese has added a chapter on the Supreme Court. Last, and far from least, Gerald Pomper, who organized the first postelection book by a team of political scientists in 1976, has authored the book's conclusion.

All of these scholars chronicle and analyze different aspects of what happened in 2024 while placing the year's events in historical and political context. Their purpose has been to shed the focused light of political science on developments that may otherwise appear to present a diffuse blur of confusing incidents and controversies. In every case, the authors' presentations offer clearly written accounts on complex topics.

As editor and coauthor, I have many thanks to offer to the talented members of the University of Virginia Press community who shepherded *The Elections of 2024* into being with consummate (and customary) professionalism and good grace. These include editor-in-chief Nadine Zimmerli, managing editor Ellen Satrom, project manager Erin Davis, acquisitions assistant Fernando Campos, production manager Joel Coggins, art director and cover designer Cecelia Sorochin, EDP coordinator Rachel Laney, and marketing associate Clayton Butler. On behalf of all the authors, I especially thank reviewers Bob Strong of Washington and Lee University and Richard Ellis of Willamette University for their timely and helpful comments on the manuscript.

Michael Nelson

The Setting

WHO CAN BE PRESIDENT?

The View from 2024

MICHAEL NELSON

DURING THE FOUR DECADES that have passed since *The Elections of 1984*, the first book in this postelection series, was published, the answer to the question posed in the title of this chapter has changed dramatically. In the forty-nine presidential elections that occurred before 1984, starting with George Washington's election in 1788–89, all ninety-five major party nominees for president and vice president were men. All were white. All avowed to be Christians. All were younger than seventy. All but one (James Buchanan, a bachelor) were married to women. All were experienced officeholders.[1]

To be sure, some barriers to entry into the presidential talent pool had already fallen by 1984. As recently as the eve of the 1960 election, political scientist Clinton Rossiter offered a then-accurate catalog of historically grounded "oughts" and "almost certainly musts" for would-be presidents that included the following: "lawyer," "more than forty-five years old," "Protestant," "a small-town boy," and "a self-made man."[2]

None of these barriers remained standing by year's end. In November 1960 forty-three- (not forty-five-) year-old John F. Kennedy, a rich (not self-made), urban (not small-town), Roman Catholic (not Protestant) candidate with no law degree, was elected president. Subsequently, in 1964 and 1976 Southerners Lyndon B. Johnson and Jimmy Carter were elected. Neither was a lawyer; nor was Ronald Reagan, who was elected in 1980 and reelected in 1984. As for the class backgrounds of the presidents elected by 1984, they could not have been more varied. Kennedy's parents were wealthy, but Johnson and Carter grew up in middle-class families. Richard Nixon, elected in 1968 and reelected in 1972; Bill Clinton, elected in 1992 and reelected in 1996; and Reagan were sons of the working class. And although

Geraldine Ferraro, the Democratic nominee for vice president in 1984, was not elected, she became the first woman (but not the last) ever to appear on a major party's national ticket.

Ferraro's nomination marked the first barrier to fall in the forty-year period covered by the eleven volumes of this series. Sarah Palin, the Republican nominee for vice president in 2008, was the second woman to appear on a national ticket, followed by Hillary Rodham Clinton's nomination for president in 2016 and Kamala Harris's election as vice president in 2020 and nomination for president in 2024. Harris also was the second African American (and the first Asian American) to be nominated after Barack Obama's nomination and election in 2008 and reelection in 2012. Joe Biden broke the age barrier in 2020, becoming the oldest person to be nominated and elected at age seventy-seven, and in 2024, Donald Trump rebroke it at age seventy-eight. In 2016 Trump had already become the first president in history to be elected with no previous experience in government.

Major parties have yet to nominate their first Hispanic, non-Christian, or LGBTQ candidates for president, but the field of serious contenders in recent elections has become remarkably diverse in matters of ethnicity, religion, and sexual identity. In 2016, Clinton's main rival for the Democratic nomination was Senator Bernie Sanders, who was bidding to become the first Jewish president. The GOP field included two Hispanics (Senators Marco Rubio of Florida and Ted Cruz of Texas), an Asian American (Louisiana Governor Bobby Jindal), and a Black surgeon (Ben Carson). It also included three candidates from the private sector (Carson and business leaders Trump and Carly Fiorina).

In 2020, Democrats offered an even broader range of candidates, accurately reflecting a party whose members were by then about 60 percent women, 40 percent people of color, and nearly 10 percent LGBTQ.[3] The field of twenty-eight candidates for the party's presidential nomination included six women, seven candidates of color, four candidates older than seventy, three younger than forty, two Jews, a Hindu, and a gay man. Among Biden's leading challengers were Elizabeth Warren, a seventy-one-year-old woman; Sanders and Mike Bloomberg, both of them seventy-eight-year-old Jewish men; Pete Buttigieg, a thirty-seven-year-old gay man; Kamala Harris, the daughter of a Black father and an Indian mother; and Andrew Yang and Tulsi Gabbard, two Asian Americans.

In terms of career background, the 2020 Democratic field was also pathbreaking. To be sure, it featured a vice president and multiple senators and governors, the traditional stepping-stone offices to a major party nomination for president. Specifically, the field included former senator (for thirty-six years) and vice president (for eight years) Biden, four governors, and seven senators. But it also contained candidates from nontraditional positions: seven members of the House of Representatives, five mayors, and three individuals from the private sector.

Although Biden broke the age barrier, his status as a white, male, married, Christian career politician made him an old-style candidate in every other way. Feeling compelled for political reasons to gesture in the direction of diversity, he pledged in March 2020 to "pick a woman to be vice president."[4] In the wake of massive protests following George Floyd's outrage-provoking murder by a police officer in May, many Democrats made clear that they would only be satisfied if the woman he chose was Black. Biden announced in July that he was considering four Black women, then tapped Harris.[5]

No Republican challenged Trump's bid for renomination in 2020, but the GOP field in 2024 included several traditional candidates, including former Vice President Mike Pence and current or former Governors Ron DeSantis of Florida, Asa Hutchinson of Arkansas, Doug Burgum of North Dakota, and Chris Christie of New Jersey. Trump, a nontraditionally credentialed candidate in 2016 because he lacked previous political experience, was now a traditional one because he had served as president for four years. The field also included the Asian American former governor of South Carolina, Nikki Haley, who emerged as Trump's main rival for the nomination; an African American senator from South Carolina, Tim Scott; another Asian American, biotech entrepreneur Vivek Ramaswamy, a Hindu; the Hispanic mayor of Miami, Francis Suarez; and an African American former member of the House of Representatives, Will Hurd. Haley sometimes gestured toward her gender as a reason to vote for her, often quoting former British Prime Minister Margaret Thatcher's gibe that "if you want something said, ask a man, but if you want something done, ask a woman."[6] Like all her rivals for the nomination, however, Haley downplayed her ethnicity.

Biden's renomination for president in 2024, like Trump's in 2020, Obama's in 2012, and those of most other incumbent presidents seeking a second term, faced only token opposition throughout the entire primary season. Some previous politically weak incumbents had to overcome serious challenges for renomination, notably Gerald Ford in 1976, Carter in 1980, and George H. W. Bush in 1992, but when all three were defeated in the general election, their parties seemed to learn that they would be better off standing with the president than dividing their supporters by trying to replace him. But even though President Biden's one declared rival in 2024, Rep. Dean Phillips of Minnesota, failed to gain traction, the concerns Phillips raised about Biden's age-related decline became decisive after the president's muddled performance in his debate with Trump on June 27, 2024. Much to the Trump campaign's dismay, pressures from fellow Democrats forced Biden to withdraw on July 21, less than a month later.[7] In the course of withdrawing, he urged the Democratic National Convention to nominate Vice President Harris in his stead. When no rivals arose to challenge her, Harris became the party's consensus choice for president.

To demonstrate just how remarkable the 2024 election and its recent predecessors were in the breadth and variety of their pools of candidates, I review the record of the previous 235 years of presidential elections to see what answers history long provided to the question of who can be president— that is, what kinds of people have any realistic chance of being elected to the office. I also describe and analyze how that record has been transformed by recent social and political developments. Finally, I assess the ways in which the broadening of the presidential talent pool contributes to and detracts from the presidency as a governing institution.

Who Can Be President? The Constitutional Answer

The first answer to the question of who can be president is in the original constitution. Article II, section 1, paragraph 5, states, "No person except a natural born Citizen, or a Citizen of the United States, at the time of the Adoption of this Constitution, shall be eligible to the Office of President; neither shall any Person be eligible to that Office who shall not have attained to the Age of thirty five Years, and been fourteen Years a Resident within the United States."

Why the Framers chose to include this list of qualifications—thirty-five years or older, natural-born citizen, and at least fourteen years a resident— is far from obvious.[8] The recorded debates on presidential qualifications at the Constitutional Convention of 1787 are meager. Even so, the delegates' actions throughout the convention manifested a consistent principle: When the Constitution states qualifications for those who fill an office, then it need not state qualifications for the office itself, but when the Constitution states no qualifications for those who fill an office, then it must do so for the one who is selected. In the case of Congress, the need for a qualifications clause for members was agreed on from the beginning. Conversely, in the case of judges, department heads, and other public officials mentioned in the Constitution, no qualifications ever were stated or even proposed. None were needed, the delegates seemed to assume, because these individuals would be selected by constitutional officials for whom qualifications had been established.

Qualifications did need to be stated, however, for the president, who is chosen by the Electoral College. (The only qualification for electors stated in the Constitution is that they cannot be members of Congress or hold other federal offices.) Such qualifications would have to be high, in the delegates' minds, because of a second principle they deemed relevant: The greater the powers of an office, the higher the qualifications for holding that office must be. Just as senators had to satisfy stiffer age, residency, and citizenship requirements than representatives, so would the president have to be more qualified in these ways than senators. Regarding the requirement that the president be a natural-born citizen, it was not only steeper than the unadorned citizenship requirement for legislators, but it also helped to solve a political problem that the delegates anticipated as they considered how to get the Constitution ratified by the states.

The Framers realized that the presidency they were creating was the closest thing in the new constitution to a British-style king. During the summer, rumors spread across the country that the delegates were plotting to import a foreign prince—perhaps Frederick, Duke of York, the second son of King George III, or Prince Henry of Prussia, the younger brother of Frederick the Great—to rule the United States. So vexing was this rumor that the delegates momentarily lifted the convention's veil of secrecy with a statement to *The Pennsylvania Journal* affirming that, "though we cannot, affirmatively, tell you what we are doing, we can, negatively, tell you what we are not doing—we never once thought of a king."⁹

However effective the delegates' attempt to squelch this rumor may have been, they knew that the mere presence of an independent, one-person executive in the Constitution would prompt further attacks on the presidency's latent monarchical character during the ratification process. If nothing else, they could at least defuse the foreign-king issue by requiring that the president be a natural-born citizen.

The final reason for setting a natural-born citizenship requirement for the president was the office's power as commander in chief. With troops at the president's disposal, it was feared that a foreign agent who occupied the office might seize tyrannical power or lay down American arms before an invading army. In late July 1787, John Jay of New York sent a letter to this effect to George Washington, the president of the convention, urging that the delegates "declare expressly that the commander in chief of the American Army shall not be given to, nor devolve upon, any but a natural born citizen."¹⁰ Interestingly, one widely circulated post-2024 election explanation of why a woman has yet to be chosen as president was that voters have a hard time imagining a woman as commander in chief, never having seen even a female secretary of defense or chair of the Joint Chiefs of Staff.[11]

One cannot be certain what effect Jay's letter had. The record shows, however, that on September 2 Washington replied to him, "I thank you for the hints contained in your letter."[12] Two days later, the convention's Committee on Postponed Matters recommended that the president be "a natural born citizen or a citizen of the US at the time of the adoption of this Constitution."[13]

How does the Constitution's presidential qualifications clause affect the nation's choice of its president? Chiefly by eliminating about 60 percent of the current population of about 335 million from eligibility: the approximately 150 million people who are younger than thirty-five and the roughly 47 million who are not natural-born citizens.[14] Partly, too, by muddying the waters of presidential eligibility. "Natural-born citizen" is an especially murky term. At the time the Constitution was written, two meanings could be found in the English common law from which the term was borrowed: jus sanguinis, which held that anyone whose parents were citizens was a natural-born citizen, and jus soli, which held that one had to be born on the nation's soil to gain this status. Subsequently enacted American laws brought some clarity. The Naturalization Act of 1790 provided that "the children of the United States that may be born beyond the sea, or out of the limits of the United States, shall be considered as natural-born citizens." As for children of noncitizens born on American soil, the Fourteenth Amendment, which was added to the Constitution in 1868, stated that "all persons born or naturalized in the United States . . . are citizens of the United States."

Thanks to Trump, the political effects of the qualifications clause were felt in every election from 2012 to 2024. Trump rose to national political notoriety in 2011 by challenging Obama's status as a natural-born citizen and demanding to see his birth certificate, fueling the "birther" lie that Obama was actually born in Kenya. Even though Obama found and released the document, the doubts raised by Trump's charges continued. In a YouGov poll, 53 percent of Republicans answered *not* when asked if "Obama was born in the United States, or not."[15] Four years later, Trump raised questions during the 2016 Republican nomination campaign about Senator Cruz's eligibility to be president. Although anyone born to a U.S. citizen is automatically a citizen by birth, Trump argued that because Cruz was born in Canada and only his mother was a U.S. citizen, Cruz's eligibility was "very precarious."[16]

In 2020, while seeking a second term, Trump reacted to Biden's August 12 announcement of Harris's selection as his vice-presidential running mate by questioning her status as a natural-born citizen, which, under the Twelfth Amendment, the vice president also must be. "I heard it today that she doesn't meet the requirements," Trump said the day after her selection.[17] Harris's Jamaican father and Indian mother were working in California when she was born in 1964, several years after their arrival in the United States. In 2024, Trump claimed that despite being born in the United States, Nikki Haley also was ineligible to be president because her parents weren't citizens at the time of her birth.[18] Harris and Haley were so-called birthright citizens, a legal status defined by the Fourteenth Amendment's provision that anyone born in the United States is a citizen and affirmed by the Supreme Court in the 1898 case of *United States v. Wong Kim Ark*.[19] In every instance, constitutional scholars found no validity in Trump's insinuations, which appeared to reflect his desire to rouse animus toward immigrants and people of color more than any serious legal understanding.[20] Yet with regard to birthright citizenship, he fulfilled his campaign promise to "end that because it's ridiculous" by issuing an executive order on the first day of his second term, an action that triggered multiple successful challenges in federal court.[21]

Constitutional matters relating to eligibility for the presidency arose in an additional form in 2024. On January 6, 2021, the day Congress met to count the electoral votes cast in the 2020 election and formally declare Biden the winner, Trump urged a large crowd of supporters to march on the Capitol and "fight like hell" in protest. Members of the crowd took him literally and violently stormed the building in hope of preventing Congress from completing its task. As a result, in December 2023 the Colorado Supreme Court struck Trump's name from the state's Republican primary ballot, ruling that his actions on January 6 constituted an incitement to insurrection, thereby making him constitutionally ineligible to become president. A few days later, Maine's secretary of state announced that she was barring Trump from her state's primary ballot as well. Litigants in other parts of the country filed similar cases in hope of having Trump kept off the ballot in their states.[22]

The issue arose because of a newly circulated law review article that drew attention to section 3 of the Fourteenth Amendment, enacted in the aftermath of the Civil War. The amendment states that "no person shall . . . hold any office . . . who, previously having taken an oath . . . as an officer of the United States . . . to support the Constitution of the United States, shall have engaged in insurrection or rebellion." The authors of the article, both of them conservative legal scholars, said that, having "taken the oath" of office as president and "engaged in insurrection" on January 6, Trump had made himself constitutionally unqualified to "hold any office" in the future, much less president.[23] Some, but not all, other legal scholars agreed.[24] The Supreme Court did not. On March 4, 2024, the eve of the Colorado primary, it ruled unanimously in *Trump v. Anderson* that a state cannot prevent candidates for federal office from running based on a claim that they are insurrectionists.[25] The court grounded its ruling in section 5 of the Fourteenth Amendment, which designates Congress as the body that "shall have power to enforce, by appropriate legislation, the provisions of this article."[26]

A final constitutional answer to the question of who can be—or in this case who cannot be—elected president became part of the document in 1951. According to the Twenty-Second Amendment, "No person shall be elected to the office of the President more than twice." Unfazed, and in contradiction to the plain language of the amendment, Trump supporter Steve Bannon falsely claimed that "since it doesn't actually say 'consecutive'" in the amendment, Trump was only barred from serving more than two terms in a row.[27] Representative Andy Ogles of Tennessee then introduced a constitutional amendment that would allow Trump to seek a third, nonconsecutive third term in 2023 while (intentionally, Ogles said) barring Obama, whose two terms came back to back.[28] Others floated the idea of electing Trump not as president but as vice president in 2028 with the understanding that he would succeed to the presidency when the elected president, by prearrangement, resigned.[29] In a kidding-not-kidding way, Trump himself floated the third-term idea as early as 2020 and, after his election in 2024, told a gathering of House Republicans that he "won't be running again unless you say, 'He's so good we've got to figure something else out.'"[30] "Should I run again? You tell me," he asked a cheering crowd at a Black History Month event in the White House on February 20, 2025, one month into his second term.[31]

Who Can Be President? Career Background

The answer the Constitution provides to the question of who can be president is wildly incomplete. In any election year, more than one hundred million people are eligible, but fewer than one hundred have any realistic chance even to mount a campaign, much less be nominated or elected. Far more important historically has been an unwritten career requirement that centers on recent, prominent service in government. Nearly everyone elected or even nominated by a major party for president since the founding has been a current or former senator, governor, vice president, general, or cabinet member.[32] Unlike the constitutional qualifications, this requirement emerged over time in the habits and preferences of the political parties and voters.

These habits and preferences were modified in 2016 by the Republicans, who rejected multiple senators and governors and nominated the celebrity businessman Trump. As a candidate, Trump actively disdained the value of governmental experience, claiming repeatedly that his time in business was better preparation for the presidency. He asked, "Do you want someone who gets to be president and that's literally the highest-paying job he's ever had?" as well as bragging, "I deal with killers that blow these [politicians] away. It's not even the same category. This [governing] is a category that's like nineteen levels lower."[33]

As the party most supportive of government, Democrats have never shown any inclination to nominate candidates for president or vice president who lacked extensive experience in office. Although hedge-fund billionaire Tom Steyer and New Age spiritualist Marianne Williamson jumped into the 2020 race, neither got very far, despite Steyer's massive spending and Williamson's celebrity status. Democrats instead chose Biden, who, after nearly a half-century in high office, was by far the most experienced presidential nominee in history. With the exception of Buttigieg, all of Biden's leading rivals for the nomination—Sanders, Warren, Harris, Amy Klobuchar, and Cory Booker—had Senate experience as well.

The relative value of each of the traditional career credentials to would-be presidents has varied over the years in response to changing public expectations. In the early nineteenth century, secretary of state was the leading stepping stone to the Executive Mansion. Starting with Thomas Jefferson, four consecutive presidents held this office between 1801 and 1829. From then until 2012, however, only three secretaries of state were even nominated by a major party, and none after 1884.[34] Indeed, the only cabinet members of any kind to be nominated for president after that were chosen about a century ago: Secretary of War William Howard Taft in 1908 and Secretary of Commerce Herbert Hoover in 1928. Democratic nominee Hillary Clinton's experience as Obama's first-term secretary of state ended well before the 2016 election and, like that of Jefferson and the other early occupants of that position, was preceded by several years in elected office, in her case as a twice-elected senator from New York.

Wartime general was another much-valued credential for candidates seeking the presidency before the twentieth century. Washington, Andrew Jackson, William Henry Harrison, Zachary Taylor, and Ulysses S. Grant all earned national fame as victorious generals. After that, only World War II Supreme Allied Commander Dwight D. Eisenhower successfully used his army service as a presidential springboard. General Wesley Clark sought the Democratic nomination in 2004, but his bid foundered in the primaries.

What modern cabinet members and generals have in common is that they are unelected officials, most of them inexperienced and often uninterested in political campaigning. This was no barrier in the eighteenth and nineteenth centuries, when party leaders controlled the presidential nominating process and nominees were not expected to campaign. Subsequently, the rise of primaries, joined to new public expectations that candidates run rather than stand for office, placed cabinet members and generals at a disadvantage. Even former General Colin Powell, who was enormously popular in 1996, chose not to undergo the ordeal of a modern presidential campaign. "I never woke up a single morning saying, 'Gee, I want to go to Iowa,'" Powell told an interviewer.[35]

Except for Taft, Hoover, and Eisenhower, every president elected from 1884 to 2012 was a current or former senator, governor, or vice president. Each of these offices allows candidates to make a distinctive claim about their qualifications for the presidency. Governors, like presidents, have been chief executives. Senators, like presidents, have dealt with national and international issues. Vice presidents, although lacking independent responsibilities, have stood first in the line of presidential succession and, in most cases, were senators or governors before they became vice president.

Over the years, the persuasiveness of the competing claims of senators, governors, and vice presidents has waxed and waned. Governors dominated presidential elections in two periods: 1900–1932, when four of seven presidents were governors, and 1976–2004, when four of five presidents were. Compared with state governments, the government in Washington was relatively unimportant during the first period, which preceded the federal government's rise to prominence after the New Deal, and was unpopular during the second, in the aftermath of the Vietnam War and Watergate crisis. Senators, in contrast, dominated the post–New Deal, post–World War II era. In the twelve-year stretch from 1960 to 1972, all eight major party nominees for president were either senators or vice presidents who had served in the Senate. In 2008, a time of war in Afghanistan and Iraq as well as against terrorists around the globe, both major parties nominated senators for president: Democrat Barack Obama of Illinois and Republican John McCain of Arizona.

In 2020 Biden not only proclaimed his deep Washington experience but featured it in his campaign. Four years later, Harris offered voters an interesting mix of career-based appeals. Although she served four years in the Senate and another four as vice president, her campaign emphasized her previous work in state and local government as attorney general in California and district attorney in San Francisco. After stumbling a bit in her early months as vice president, Harris found her footing as a champion of abortion rights in the aftermath of the Supreme Court's June 2022 *Dobbs* decision, which overturned forty years of rulings in defense of a woman's constitutional right to choose whether to carry a pregnancy to term.[36]

The vice presidency became an especially valuable stepping stone to a presidential nomination after the Twenty-Second Amendment was added to the Constitution. By imposing a two-term limit on presidents, the amendment freed second-term vice presidents to campaign actively for president themselves. Richard Nixon in 1960, George H. W. Bush in 1988, and Al Gore in 2000 each won their party's presidential nomination at the end of their second term as vice president. That pattern was interrupted when George W. Bush and Obama chose vice presidents whose presidential ambitions were thought to be in the past and who therefore could serve them free from political distraction. "When you're getting advice from somebody . . . ," said Bush, explaining his choice of Vice President Richard B. Cheney, "if you think deep down part of the advice is to advance a personal agenda, . . . you discount that advice."[37] Obama told Biden that he wanted him to view the vice presidency "as the capstone of your career."[38]

In preparation for the 2016 election, Biden surprised Obama by saying that he wanted to seek their party's presidential nomination a third time. (His previous efforts in 1988 and 2008 were conspicuous failures.) But Biden badly trailed Clinton and Sanders in fall 2015 polls and was actively discouraged from entering the race by most party leaders, including Obama. When Biden was slow to take the hint, Obama sent campaign aide David Plouffe to tell the vice president he did not want to see his career "end in some hotel room in Iowa with you finishing third behind [Clinton and] and Bernie Sanders."[39] Soon afterward, Biden reluctantly announced that he would not run.

Clinton's defeat in 2016 opened the door to another Biden candidacy four years later. His long record in the Senate proved an occasional obstacle in his campaign, especially for his party's nomination. Although Biden's opposition to busing students to achieve school integration in the 1970s and his votes in favor of measures such as the 1994 crime bill, the 1996 welfare reform act, and the 2002 Iraq war resolution were popular at the time, even among many Democrats, the party's primary electorate had recently become much more liberal. In 1994, 25 percent of Democrats identified as liberals, the same percentage that said they were conservatives. By 2018, the liberals' share had doubled to 51 percent and the conservatives' share had dwindled to 13 percent.[40] The party's leftward movement and critical stance toward items in Biden's voting record were even more pronounced among grassroots party activists.[41]

Working entirely in Biden's favor as he sought the Democratic nomination in 2020 were his two terms as vice president. They allowed him to identify with the popular Obama in a way no other candidate could. Biden often spoke of his service in the "Obama–Biden administration" and proclaimed himself an "Obama–Biden Democrat." Nothing did more to solidify Biden's popularity among African American Democrats than his close personal and professional association with the first Black president. After Biden suffered humiliating defeats in the overwhelmingly white Iowa caucuses and New Hampshire primary, African American voters propelled him to a landslide victory in the majority-Black South Carolina Democratic primary on February 29 and, three days later, to a near sweep of the mostly Southern Super Tuesday contests, whose Democratic primary electorates also were majority or near-majority Black. Having established a commanding lead against his rivals, Biden cruised to the nomination.

In contrast to the success Biden had translating his vice-presidential experience into his party's presidential nomination, Trump's first-term vice president, Mike Pence, got nowhere when he sought the Republican nomination in 2024. Pence caught it from both sides of his party. Anti-Trump Republicans disdained him for the unflagging loyalty and devotion he displayed toward Trump during his first three years and fifty weeks as vice president. Pro-Trump Republicans blamed him for not supporting the president during his final two weeks by tossing out legally cast electoral votes for Biden when presiding over Congress during the official count. Pence ended his campaign for the GOP's 2024 nomination on October 28, 2023, less than five months after it began.[42] The normal vice-presidential pattern was restored in July 2024 when Biden's endorsement of Harris as his successor cleared her path to an uncontested Democratic nomination for president.

Historically, presidential candidates from outside government made only an occasional appearance on the national scene. In 1940, seeking to thwart Franklin D. Roosevelt's quest for a third term, the Republicans nominated business executive Wendell Willkie. In both 1984 and 1988, civil rights leader and ordained minister Jesse Jackson made a determined run for the Democratic nomination. In 1992 and 1996, another well-known business leader, Ross Perot, ran strongly as an independent candidate. None were elected, but a certain *Mr. Smith Goes to Washington*–style aura seemed to attach to the idea of finding a president outside the usual political channels.

In 2016, the Democrats followed the traditional pattern, limiting their choice to two high-ranking government officials—Clinton and Sanders. The GOP went in an entirely different direction. None of the nine former or current governors in the race gained much traction in the competition for the party's presidential nomination. Of the five current or former senators who ran, only Cruz remained in the contest as late as March 16.

Trump's candidacy was initially regarded as a "sideshow" by mainstream media outlets. The *Huffington Post*, for example, refused for months to "report on Trump's campaign as part of [our] political coverage. Instead we will cover his campaign as part of our entertainment section."[43] Yet his attractiveness as a candidate in 2016 stood squarely at the confluence of two roaring political streams: the mood at his party's grass roots, which was intensely antigovernment, and his iconoclastic, celebrity-based personal popularity. As someone who had never held public office, Trump could appeal to GOP primary voters as a complete outsider committed to cleaning up "the mess in Washington." Trump was already well known as a best-selling author of braggadocious business books, a frequent talk show guest, and the host of the popular NBC television series *The Apprentice*. On the eve of the campaign, 58 percent of Republicans in a September 2015 *Washington Post* / ABC News poll said they would prefer "someone from outside the existing political establishment" to "someone with experience in how the political system works."[44]

Trump's inexperience as a candidate who had not been vetted in previous campaigns was tested in the general election when the electorate included Democrats and independents as well as Republicans. Only 23 percent of Democratic voters and 40 percent of independent voters said they preferred "outside" status to governing "experience." But despite losing the national popular vote to Hillary Clinton's by a 2.9-million-vote margin, Trump won the election with a solid 304–227 majority in the Electoral College. Remarkably, Trump maintained his outsider demeanor while serving as president. He did so by refusing to conform to long-standing norms of appropriate presidential conduct and by continuing to portray himself as someone whose main purpose in Washington was to "drain the swamp," which he saw as infested with hostile legislators, bureaucrats, lobbyists, and reporters.[45]

In 2020 voters faced an unusual choice when considering the career backgrounds of the two major party candidates. Although Trump had been president for nearly four years, Biden had considerably more experience in Washington and knew much more about its programs and processes. The choice for voters in 2024 seemed even more atypical. Only once in history had a president defeated for reelection come back four years later and been chosen by his party to run again.[46] Grover Cleveland, defeated by Benjamin Harrison in his bid for a second term in 1888, challenged Harrison's campaign for reelection in 1892 and won. Other nineteenth- and early twentieth-century former presidents, notably Martin Van Buren, Millard Fillmore, and Theodore Roosevelt, ran but were defeated. For more than a century, most presidents who lost their bids for reelection (notably Ford, Carter, and George H. W. Bush) withdrew from presidential politics, signed multimillion-dollar contracts to write their memoirs, and focused on raising funds to build their presidential library. Not Trump, who made clear that he would run again. A Cleveland–Harrison–style rematch seemed likely to be repeated in 2024 when President Biden and former President Trump each swept through the primaries en route to renomination by their parties. But when Biden withdrew, Trump found himself facing Harris, a different opponent. This was not merely an unusual turn of events, it was unprecedented.

Moreover, as Election Day 2024 loomed, voters had to decide whether another unique aspect of Trump's career background was disqualifying: his status as the first major party presidential candidate in history with a criminal record. In spring 2023, Trump was indicted in four different state and federal cases on ninety-one counts for offenses allegedly committed during his business and political career. In May 2024, a unanimous jury in New York City found him guilty on thirty-four of these counts in the one case that came to trial before the election. All this was on top of the more than half-billion dollar civil suits he and his main business operation lost involving fraud and sexual abuse. In 1974 voters had turned against President Nixon when his Watergate-related crimes were revealed, forcing him to resign or face certain impeachment and removal. Unlike Nixon, Trump did not assume that criminal conduct was an insurmountable barrier to election. Instead he consistently charged that his opponents were abusing the criminal justice process to persecute, not prosecute, him. (This was the same Trump who in 2016 said, "I could stand in the middle of Fifth Avenue and shoot somebody, and I wouldn't lose voters.")[47] In 2024, with real, not hypothetical, felonies as part of his record, enough voters either agreed or were willing to place their concerns aside for him to be elected.

Who Can Be President? Social Characteristics

Among potential presidential candidates with the requisite career background to be taken seriously by voters, a further set of criteria has long defined the field of eligible contenders: the social characteristics traditionally associated with presidents. In recent decades, most but not all social barriers to the presidency have fallen, usually in one of four ways: vice-presidential succession, changing public attitudes, facing the issue, and, sometimes but not always, positive bias.

VICE-PRESIDENTIAL SUCCESSION

Historically vice-presidential succession to the presidency has been one means of toppling social barriers to the presidency. After Whig Party nominee Zachary Taylor of Louisiana was elected in 1848, no Southerner was nominated for president by a major party for more than a century. Intense opposition among Southern whites to the civil rights movement of the 1950s and 1960s made it seem even less likely that either party would nominate a Southerner. The vice presidency, however, was a different matter. Kennedy of Massachusetts added Johnson of Texas to the ticket in 1960 to help carry the South. Three years later Johnson succeeded to the presidency when Kennedy was assassinated. Defying regional stereotypes, the new president became an ardent champion of civil rights and other liberal causes. By the time Johnson ran for a full term in 1964, anti-Southern prejudice had nearly vanished from the electorate. Johnson, Jimmy Carter of Georgia, Bill Clinton of Arkansas, and the two Bushes of Texas won seven of the eleven presidential elections between 1964 and 2004.

Since Johnson, no vice president has succeeded to the presidency as the result of a presidential death—a remarkable record considering that from 1841 to 1963 presidents died in office an average of once every fifteen years, four times by assassination and four times of natural causes. On October 28, 2015, the previous record for the longest period in American history without a presidential death (fifty-one years, eleven months, and five days, set during the founding era) was broken.[48] It remained unbroken for another decade—and counting.

What accounts for the current period of presidential longevity? The ever-tighter security that surrounds modern presidents may not render assassinations impossible—a bullet fired at Trump at an outdoor rally on July 13, 2024, would have entered his skull had he not suddenly turned his head—but it does make them much more difficult. Regarding natural death, the marathon nature of the modern election process all but guarantees that whoever wins is in good health. During the 2020 Democratic nomination campaign, Trump tried to persuade voters that Biden was "a tired, exhausted man," and Democrats spread rumors that Trump had suffered a series of ministrokes in 2019.[49] Despite the charges and counined charges—"He's shaky, weak, trouble speaking, trouble walking," intoned an anti-Trump ad; "Joe Biden is slipping . . . is clearly diminished," retorted the Trump campaign—the voters of each party seemed to regard their candidate as an exception to the rule that advanced age is a political liability.[50]

As discussed later, age seems to have caught up with Biden sometime after he turned eighty in late 2022, but he persisted in his bid for reelection well into 2024. An unprecedented form of vice-presidential succession took place when Biden, after ending his campaign in late July, anointed Harris as his choice to replace him as their party's nominee.

Although experience as vice president sometimes serves as a stepping stone to the presidency either directly (through succession) or indirectly (through election), it is far from an unalloyed political blessing. Vice presidents must work hard to gain even a small share of credit for the successes of the administration in which they serve, but they can count on being attacked for all of its shortcomings. A vice president who tries to stand apart may alienate the president and cause voters to wonder why these concerns were not voiced earlier, when they might have made a difference. The vice president can always say that loyalty to the president forecloses public disagreement, but that course is no less perilous. The voters who value loyalty in a vice president value strength, vision, and independence in a president, qualities that the vice president almost never gets a chance to display.

After coasting to her party's presidential nomination in 2024, Harris was plagued by all of the political problems inherent in the office. Although she declared, "My presidency will not be a continuation of Joe Biden's presidency," she faltered when asked if she would have done "anything . . . differently from President Biden during the last four years." Her reply— "There is not a thing that comes to mind"—was an understandably failed attempt to walk the narrow path between loyalty and independence. The lateness of her nomination denied Harris the opportunity that George H. W. Bush—the only sitting vice president to be elected president since 1836—seized in 1988 to simultaneously demonstrate loyalty to President Reagan and establish his own leadership qualities by promising to be an "education president" and an "environmental president." It also helped that Reagan was popular in 1988 in ways that Biden was not in 2024.

CHANGING PUBLIC ATTITUDES

The second way social barriers have fallen is through growing public acceptance. Like being a Southerner, being divorced was long considered a disqualifier for the presidency. In the 1950s, when Illinois Governor Adlai

Stevenson was the twice-defeated Democratic nominee, and the 1960s, when Governor Nelson Rockefeller of New York unsuccessfully sought the Republican nomination two times, divorce proved an insuperable political obstacle. In 1980, however, Reagan was elected president with scarcely a whisper that his divorce from actress Jane Wyman should be held against him. Society's tolerance for divorce had grown so great during the 1970s that it was no longer a barrier to the presidency by the time Reagan ran. Trump's path to the White House in 2016 was unobstructed by his two divorces and multiple, much-publicized extramarital affairs.

Concerning religion as a social barrier, in 2000 Democratic presidential candidate Al Gore chose Senator Joseph Lieberman of Connecticut as the first non-Christian nominee for vice president. In Election Day exit polls, 72 percent of voters said they thought Lieberman's Jewish religion would make him neither a better nor a worse vice president, and of the remaining 28 percent, twice as many thought it would make him a better one.[51] By January 2024, less than 10 percent of respondents to a Gallup poll said that they would not vote for "a generally well-qualified person for president who happened to be Jewish," but when the Harris campaign revealed that Governor Josh Shapiro of Pennsylvania, an observant Jew, might be her choice for vice president, pro-Palestinian progressive Democrats successfully urged her to "say no to Genocide Josh Shapiro for vice president."[52] Regarding other religions, 71 percent told Gallup in 2024 they were willing to vote for a Muslim. But more than one-third—36 percent—said they would not vote for an atheist.[53]

In 2016 Sanders became the first Jewish candidate ever to win a presidential primary or caucus by sweeping to victory in New Hampshire and going on to prevail in twenty-two more contests, finishing a strong second in the battle for the Democratic nomination. Sanders's Jewish identity proved no obstacle among Democrats either then or in 2020, when he again finished second in the nominating contest. Nor was his decision not to be "not actively involved in organized religion" in any form as an adult a political liability within the party.[54] But in a general election that also included independent and Republican voters less indifferent to the religious beliefs of their presidents than many white Democrats professed to be, Sanders's self-identification as a strongly secular person might have cost him substantially more votes than his Jewish upbringing.

In 2020 Sanders was far from alone in downplaying any claim to a religious identity. Of the more than two dozen candidates who sought the Democratic nomination, only Buttigieg, an Episcopalian; Booker, a

Baptist; Warren, a Methodist; and Biden, a Roman Catholic who said that faith is the "bedrock foundation of my life," talked much about their religious beliefs.[55] For "Mayor Pete," this was part of a broader effort to show that although he was a highly nontraditional candidate in terms of career background, youth, and sexual identity, he was also highly traditional in his religion, wartime military service, and marital status. As for Biden's bidding to become only the second Catholic president in history, this historic aspect of his candidacy was barely mentioned by him or anyone else.

Trump consistently claimed to be a Christian and in 2024 actually marketed a "God Bless the USA Bible." The so-called Trump Bible came in various editions, including a "The Day God Intervened Edition" marking the failed attempt on his life on July 13, and a $1,000 "signature edition" autographed by Trump. Although Trump's behavior showed little personal engagement with religion of any kind, marked instead by minimal church attendance and maximal ignorance about basic tenets of the faith such as the centrality of the Eucharist ("my little cracker") and the need for forgiveness ("Why do I have to repent or ask for forgiveness if I'm not making mistakes?"), evangelical Christians supported him overwhelmingly in all three of his campaigns.[56] Some compared him to Cyrus the Great, the Persian emperor mentioned in the Old Testament who, although not a believer himself, was chosen by God to liberate the Jewish people from captivity in Babylon.[57] Trump even referred to himself as "the chosen one," looking heavenward while he said it.[58] As for Harris, although a longtime member of a Black church in San Francisco, she seldom talked about her faith during the campaign, and only in the most general terms.[59]

By the 2020s additional social barriers to a major party nomination for president appeared to be cracking in the face of changing social attitudes. In a 2024 survey, 74 percent of Americans, up from 26 percent as recently as 1978, said they were willing to vote for a "gay or lesbian" candidate for president.[60] Three openly LGBTQ senators and nine representatives were already serving in Congress, and on Election Day Delaware voters elected Sarah McBride, Congress's first transgender member, to the House. In the previous decade, voters in Oregon, Massachusetts, and Colorado elected LGBTQ governors. Biden appointed Buttigieg as secretary of transportation in his administration. All of these officials have been Democrats.

Looking ahead, one might reasonably forecast that if present trends continue (always a dangerous assumption), then as younger cohorts replace older ones in the electorate and more members of these historically disfavored

groups win prominent elective office, the nation may regard without prejudice its first atheist, Muslim, and LGBTQ candidates for president.

FACING THE ISSUE

Facing public prejudices squarely was the strategy John F. Kennedy
employed to overcome widespread bias against Roman Catholics in 1960.
Although adherence to Protestant Christianity was a legal requirement for
office in several states at the time of the nation's founding, the Constitutional Convention voted unanimously that "no religious Test shall ever be
required as a Qualification to any Office or public Trust under the United
States." In practice, however, all thirty-three presidents from Washington
to Eisenhower were Protestants of one sort or another.

Kennedy's strategy, unusual in an era when competing in presidential
primaries was generally regarded as a sign of political weakness, was to
enter several contests in order to convince the leaders of his party (many of
them Catholics themselves) that a Catholic could win. In the midst of his
crucial primary campaign in overwhelmingly Protestant West Virginia,
Kennedy told a television audience, "When any man stands on the steps
of the Capitol and takes the oath of office as President, he is swearing to
support the separation of church and state."[61] In September, again with
cameras rolling, he addressed the Greater Houston Ministerial Association, declaring, "I do not speak for my church on public matters; and the
church does not speak for me."[62] In 1958, 24 percent of Americans said they
would not vote for a presidential candidate "who happened to be Catholic." Soon after Kennedy was elected, that number fell to 13 percent and, by
1969, to 8 percent, where it has remained.[63]

The candidate who faced the most difficult religious challenge after Kennedy was former Republican Governor Mitt Romney of Massachusetts,
who first sought his party's nomination in 2008 and won it in 2012. In a
2007 Gallup poll, 24 percent said they would not vote for a Mormon, with
fewer Mormons to offset them than Kennedy had Catholics in 1960. Kennedy's mission had been to convince voters that his religion did not matter.
Romney's challenge was different: to persuade white evangelical Christians
that he was one of them. In a much-publicized speech in December 2007,
Romney declared, "I believe that Jesus Christ is the Son of God and the
Savior of mankind."[64] Still, Romney fared badly in Republican primaries
in the heavily Christian South both times he ran.

Advanced age has been another unwritten barrier to the presidency. The
Constitution includes a minimum age requirement for the presidency but

places no limit on how old a president can be. The voters have expressed preferences of their own on this matter. An August 2007 Gallup poll offered a cross section of Americans a long and varied list of social and career characteristics of potential presidential candidates and asked if each "would be a desirable characteristic for the next president to have, an undesirable characteristic, or if it wouldn't matter much to you either way." Of the twenty characteristics on the list, a majority of voters identified only two as undesirable. One was employment as a "government lobbyist." The other was being "70 years of age or older."[65]

Unlike other social characteristics, a candidate's age is a factor about which commentators have felt comfortable raising doubts. Political pundits branded the Republican nominee in 1996, seventy-three-year-old Bob Dole, as past his prime. In 2008 "McCain's Age Is a Legitimate Issue" was the headline of one typical article about the seventy-two-year-old senator; another was titled "Is McCain Too Old to Be President?"[66]

Through words and actions, Dole and McCain worked hard to overcome the political stigma of age. Dole joked that some people thought his campaign slogan "Dole in '96" actually meant "Dole is 96." McCain declared, "I'm not the youngest candidate, but I am the most experienced."[67] In the end, both candidates were handily defeated by much younger opponents: Bill Clinton (age fifty) and Obama (age forty-seven), respectively.

In 2016 both Trump (seventy) and Hillary Clinton (sixty-nine) were older than almost any previous newly elected president (Reagan, also sixty-nine, was the only exception). Clinton avoided the topic, allowing Trump to make an issue of it. Clinton, Trump claimed, lacked the "stamina" to be president, repeating the charge in four consecutive sentences during their first televised debate and then, days before their third debate, insisting that both candidates "take a drug test," the implication being that Clinton needed to rely on performance-enhancing drugs.[68]

By 2019 public attitudes concerning the appropriate age of presidents had modestly changed. Sixty-three percent of voters said they would be open to voting for a candidate over the age of seventy, a somewhat low figure considering that the leading contenders for both parties' 2020 nominations were already in their seventies: Trump for the GOP and Biden and Sanders for the Democrats. Former President Jimmy Carter, who turned ninety-five in 2019, said, "If I were eighty years old, . . . I don't believe I could undertake the duties I experienced when I was president."[69]

Unwilling to make Clinton's mistake of trying to brush off the age issue, Sanders, Biden, and Trump addressed it in varying ways in 2020. Sanders, who suffered a minor heart attack in October 2019, came back energetically after stents were inserted into a previously blocked artery. As in 2016, he emerged as the most popular candidate among younger Democratic voters. "I am old," declared Sanders. "But there are advantages to being old. The ideas that I am fighting for now didn't come to me yesterday."[70] Biden often said, "Watch me," in 2020 as he jogged from one side of the street to the other when marching in parades. In a bit of overreach, he even challenged skeptics to push-up and IQ contests while claiming that, "with experience, hopefully, comes judgment and a little bit of wisdom."[71] Campaign aides found that ads that showed him speaking directly to the camera about issues were even more effective in muting voters' age-related concerns than footage of him doing physically energetic things.[72] Nevertheless, Biden described himself as "a bridge, not anything else"—a "transition candidate" to "newer, younger people" in the Democratic Party, which many interpreted to mean he would not seek a second term in 2024 at age eighty-two.[73]

No sooner did Biden become president than he changed his mind, regarding himself as the only Democrat capable of preventing Trump from being elected in 2024 and, like all modern presidents, unwilling to let go the reins of power if he thought there was any chance of remaining in office for another term. Voters' concerns about Biden's age, never absent, accelerated after he turned eighty on November 20, 2022. In early 2024, only 31 percent of voters said they would consider voting for a candidate "over the age of 80."[74]

Rather than face the issue, Biden endlessly repeated his "watch me" mantra, even as Americans witnessed his stride become a shuffle and his speech become halting and slurred. Biden compounded these concerns by denying them. When special counsel Robert Hur reported on February 8, 2024, that the president had seemed a "well-meaning, elderly man with a poor memory" in a series of interviews, Biden went on television to angrily declare that he was "well-meaning and I'm an elderly man—and I know what the hell I'm doing." Minutes later, he referred to the president of Egypt as "the president of Mexico."[75]

As voters' age-related concerns grew, Biden continued to amass delegates in the nearly uncontested 2024 Democratic primaries and appeared unstoppable in his bid for renomination. Perhaps in response to Trump's relentless ridiculing of Biden's diminishing capacities ("Sleepy Joe" was the mildest of his insults), Democrats bent over backward to deny that the president was experiencing decline. Biden himself assumed and party leaders hoped that by scheduling an unprecedentedly early June 27 debate with Trump, he could show the doubters that he remained physically and mentally sharp. Instead, in one meandering and sometimes incoherent answer after another, he transformed doubts into certainty that he needed to withdraw from the election. Even as Biden insisted that he would remain in the race unless the "Lord almighty" told him to quit, pressures to abandon his candidacy mounted from Democratic leaders who previously had blindly defended and supported him. Polls showed that a strong majority of voters wanted Biden to drop out.[76] On July 21, he announced his withdrawal from the race and endorsed Harris.

Attention now turned to Trump, who, instead of being three years younger than his opponent, suddenly was nearly twenty years older (Harris was fifty-nine). Biden's presence in the race, along with Trump's artfully polished physical appearance and displays of stamina at campaign events, had long distracted many voters from the fact that, if elected, Trump would be older at the time of his inauguration than any president in history, including Biden. Trump made his own share of verbal miscues, which took on new significance now that voters were comparing him with a much younger opponent. In his acceptance speech at the Republican National Convention, Trump warned that America was now "teetering on the edge of World War III."[77] Arguing that Biden "should take a cognitive test like I did," he cited "Doc Ronny Johnson," whom Trump claimed had described him as "the heathiest president in history." (Doc Ronny's name is Jackson, not Johnson.)[78] In another speech, Trump confused Nikki Haley with Nancy Pelosi.[79] Some recalled that Haley, who now endorsed Trump, had called for "mandatory mental competency for politicians over seventy-five years old" during her bid for the GOP nomination.[80]

In the fall campaign, Harris described Trump as "weak," "unstable and unhinged," and former President Obama called him "an older, loonier Donald Trump."[81] The share of voters who thought Trump was too old to be president—roughly 40 percent before Biden dropped out—rose to 47 percent in Election Day exit polls.[82] But discounting that concern, 52 percent of voters agreed that Trump "has the mental capacity to serve effectively as president," 54 percent said he "is capable of handling a crisis," and 55 percent said he "is a strong leader."[83]

Harris faced issues not of age but of race and gender. The racial barrier to the presidency was breached in 2008, when Obama was elected (and then reelected four years later). A solid white majority of Illinois voters had already sent him to the Senate in 2004 with 70 percent of the vote, and a February 2007 Gallup poll found 94 percent of voters nationwide saying they were willing to support a "generally well-qualified" Black candidate for president, a number that had risen sharply since 1937, when only 33 percent said that.[84] In the November 2008 election, Obama won 44 percent of the white vote, considerably better than the average of 39 percent that white Democratic nominees won from white voters in the ten elections from 1968 to 2004.[85] By 2020, openness to Black nominees and other candidates of color had grown even more. Ninety-six percent of voters professed their willingness to vote for a Black nominee for president, and 95 percent for a Hispanic one.[86]

Harris deemphasized her race as well as her gender, almost never mentioning them in campaign ads and appearances, except to say, "I will never assume that anyone should elect a leader based on their gender or their race."[87] In contrast, Trump repeatedly alluded to Harris's gender and race in barely coded language. She was "weak," Trump said, and other world leaders would treat her "like a play-toy."[88] She was "a low-IQ person," "retarded," "lazy as hell," "dumb as a rock," a "stupid person," a "dummy."[89] On Election Day Trump, who already had faced down the issue of criminal conduct as an insurmountable barrier to the presidency, prevailed among white men by 59 percent to 39 percent. Harris, not having faced the issue of gender and racial bias in her campaign, actually received less support from women and voters of color than Biden, a white man, had in 2020.[90]

POSITIVE BIAS?

A fourth historical barrier-buster in presidential elections has been positive bias. Although Kennedy's religion hurt him with anti-Catholics in 1960, it also won him support among the roughly 25 percent of voters who were Catholics and proud to see one of their own contending for the presidency. In general, anti-Catholic voting hurt Kennedy in the South, and pro-Catholic voting helped him in the much larger and more populous North.[91] In 2020 Trump—who had won the Catholic vote by 4 percentage points against Hillary Clinton, a Methodist, in 2016—lost it to Biden, a Catholic, by 5 points.[92]

As the first African American major party nominee for president in 2008, Obama secured 95 percent of the Black vote, up from Senator John F. Kerry's 88 percent share in 2004. This prize turned out to be all the more valuable because Black turnout surged from 11 percent of the electorate in 2004 to 13 percent in 2008. Obama also won 66 percent of Hispanic votes, a 13-point improvement over Kerry's 53 percent showing. The pattern was repeated when Obama sought reelection in 2012 and won 93 percent of the Black vote and 71 percent of the Hispanic vote.[93]

As was true of Harris in 2024, Hillary Clinton's campaigns for her party's presidential nomination—nearly successful in 2008 and entirely successful in 2016—were distinctive because she is a woman. In surveys taken from 1937 to 2007, the Gallup poll found that Americans had become increasingly willing to vote for a "generally well-qualified" woman for president. As recently as 1945, only 33 percent said they would consider doing so, but that number rose to 88 percent in 2007 and 93 percent in 2024.[94] In part, this was because the ranks of women meeting the public's career background criteria for president had grown. In 1976, no women served in the Senate and only one was a governor. By 2008 there were nine woman governors and sixteen woman senators—numbers that rose to thirteen and twenty-five, respectively, by 2024, when Harris also had been vice president for the previous four years.

As the first woman ever to stand center stage in a presidential election, Clinton employed different strategies in 2008 and 2016. In her first campaign, she downplayed gender-based appeals by claiming leadership qualities traditionally associated with men, especially strength. In her second bid, she chose to emphasize her gender, declaring, "This really comes down to whether I can encourage and mobilize women to vote for the first woman president."[95] In campaign speeches, she argued, "One of my merits is I'm a woman," weaving so-called women's issues into most elements of her policy agenda, including paid leave for new mothers and equal pay for women in the workforce.[96]

By 2020, voters were more open than ever to the possibility of electing a woman as president. The 6 percent who said they would not vote for one were more than outnumbered by the 10 percent who said it was "very important" that the Democrats nominate a woman.[97] But with six women (four of them senators) seeking the Democratic nomination, it was hard for any of them to become, as Clinton was in 2016, the party's consensus female candidate. All six eventually dropped out in favor of Biden.

Harris did not have to fight for the Democratic presidential nomination after Biden withdrew in late July 2024, in part because none of the other potentially viable contenders, including Governor Gretchen Whitmer of Michigan (whose entry into the race Trumped feared), saw anything to be gained from challenging the first Black, Asian American, and female vice president's campaign to lead a major political party.[98] In that sense, positive bias in a party that places a premium on diversity worked in Harris's favor.

Less certain was how Harris's unique identity would play out in the general election. Trump greeted her candidacy by telling a convention of Black journalists that until recently Harris "was Indian all the way, and then all of a sudden she made a turn and became a Black person."[99] This was absurd: While embracing her identity as the daughter of a Jamaican father and Indian mother, Harris had always presented herself as Black.

(She went to historically Black Howard University and joined Alpha Kappa Alpha, a Black sorority.) Harris tried to brush off Trump's comment, responding, "Same old, tired playbook."[100] Unlike Clinton in 2020, Harris assumed that the history-making nature of her candidacy would speak for itself without her having to draw attention to it. "Well, I'm clearly a woman," she told a persistent questioner. "I don't need to point that out to anyone."[101] During her career, when asked to talk about women's issues, she often would reply, "Oh, you want to talk about the economy? You want to talk about climate change?"[102]

To turn positive in a candidate's favor, however, a negative bias among voters must be addressed by the candidate; if left unaddressed, it will remain unchanged. Harris's vice-presidential running mate, Governor Tim Walz of Minnesota, highlighted her identity, urging voters to "put that fist through the glass ceiling" that kept women out of the Oval Office.[103] So did Barack Obama, who chastised Black men who "aren't feeling the idea of having a woman as president."[104] (Obama also joked about Trump's masculine obsession with "size," glancing below his waist as he did so.)[105] But Harris herself, by failing to stress to women that they could help elect the nation's first female president, ceded the discussion to Trump. On Election Day, only 36 percent of voters said that electing the first woman president was a significant factor in their decision.[106] Even more important, with the exception of college-educated white women, all other categories of female voters (and therefore women as a whole) gave Harris less support in 2024 than they gave Obama in 2008 and 2012, Hillary Clinton in 2016, or Biden in 2020.[107]

A Note on Presidential Dynasties

Asked after the election if he thought his victory marked the beginning of a "Trump dynasty," the president-elect mentioned several of his children and their spouses, then said, "I think there could be, yeah."[108] He was not the first president in history to consider the possibility of a future president who shared his last name.

Family "dynasties" have mattered in presidential politics from the beginning, as witnessed by the two Adams presidents, the two Harrisons, the two Roosevelts, and the two Bushes. All twelve late twentieth- and twenty-first-century presidential elections have featured at least one Bush (five for George H. W. and two for George W.), Clinton (two each for Bill and Hillary), or Biden (six for Joe, whose son Beau was a rising political star before dying at age forty-six). Three Kennedys have either been elected president

(John) or come close (Robert and Ted); and since 1947 at least one Kennedy has held federal office in all but two years.

No dynastic candidates appeared on the 2024 ballot after Biden withdrew, but Robert F. Kennedy Jr. commanded broad national support for a time by running as the self-declared political heir to his father and uncle. Kennedy's campaign foundered when his many siblings and cousins disavowed his candidacy; in the end, he endorsed Trump, who revived Kennedy's political viability by appointing him to head the Department of Health and Human Services. Trump himself promoted Donald Trump Jr. as a national figure in the Republican Party and appointed daughter Ivanka and son-in-law Jared Kushner to his first-term White House staff; he then named Lara Trump cochair of the Republican National Committee. Even Barron Trump, an eighteen-year-old college freshman in 2024, dipped his toe into the political waters when he persuaded his father to appear on multiple podcasts that appeal to young male voters.[109]

During his first term, Trump declared that he had "the right to do anything I want as president," a kingly claim reinforced by his frequent use of the ultimate royal power to grant pardons to political allies. In his second-term inaugural address, delivered hours before he issued sixteen hundred pardons to January 6, 2021, rioters, Trump implied that he ruled by divine right, declaring he "was saved by God to make America great again." "LONG LIVE THE KING!" the White House posted on Truth Social one month later, accompanied by a post on X of a fake *Time* magazine cover showing Trump wearing a crown.[110] These followed shortly on the heels of another Trump post on Truth Social: "He who saves his Country does not violate any law," a statement usually attributed to the Emperor Napoleon.[111]

The tendency for members of the same family to succeed in politics from generation to generation is deeply ingrained in American political history, something that Benjamin Franklin and Thomas Jefferson would not have found surprising. "There is a natural inclination in mankind to Kingly Government," Franklin observed at the Constitutional Convention.[112] Jefferson, writing from Paris to John Adams in London soon after the convention, described the presidency as a "bad edition of a Polish king."[113] One explanation for this tendency is that being the son or daughter of a prominent leader gives one a famous name, access to a network of political and financial supporters inherited from one's parent, and the ability to learn about politics at the feet of a master. Another seems ingrained in a sort of royalist strain in the nation's political culture, a carryover from the original colonies' nearly two-century-long dependency on a series of British monarchs and Americans' continuing obsession with the British royal family.

Ironically, although George Washington regretted not having children for personal reasons, he recognized from the beginning that it was good for the country not to be tempted to turn the first president's family into a kind of de facto royal family. "I have no child for whom I could wish to make a provision—no family to build in greatness upon my country's ruin," he wrote.[114] Only one of the first five presidents had a son, and the eldest son of that president, John Adams, became President John Quincy Adams.[115]

Conclusion

Kamala Harris's election as the first woman and the first Black vice president in 2020 was historic. So was Harris's selection as the first Black woman to be nominated for president by a major party in 2024. Like the election of the first Catholic president in 1960, the first Southern president in more than a century in 1964, the first divorced president in 1980, the first African American president in 2008, and the first major party nomination of a woman for president in 2016, Harris's candidacy represented an altogether sensible broadening of the talent pool from which the United States draws its chief executives. Far from demonstrating that a woman cannot be elected president, as some Democrats bewailed after the 2024 results were tabulated, the women nominated by their party in two of the last three presidential elections (Clinton and Harris) actually outpolled Trump, their male opponent, by 140.9 million to 140.3 million popular votes.

The same openness to nontraditional candidates is apparent in public opinion polls and elections to other prominent political offices, without regard to their religion, race and ethnicity, or sexual identity. Historically, these and other artificial barriers excluded massive numbers of potentially excellent presidents from consideration on the basis of social characteristics unrelated to their ability to do the job. Vice-presidential succession, changing public attitudes, positive bias, and facing the issue—sometimes in combination—seem likely to be the vehicles of change in the future, just as they have in the past.

In other ways, the falling of social barriers to the presidency remains a journey in progress. No woman, Hispanic, Asian, Jewish, Muslim, or LGBTQ American has ever been elected president, although Sanders and Bloomberg (Jewish), Buttigieg (gay, young), and Klobuchar and Warren (women) ran strong races for their party's nomination in 2020 and Harris's election as vice president made her the obvious Democratic choice after Biden dropped out in 2024. That said, polls asking people if "their neighbors" would be comfortable with various nontraditional kinds of candidate find lower levels of support than they themselves purport to hold, which may indicate a shallower openness than indicated by the more direct questions.[116]

Not age per se, but vitality, is a different matter. While in their seventies, Biden in 2020 and Trump in all three of his campaigns displayed the energy that Americans understandably want in their president. In 2024, as in 1996 with Dole and in 2008 with McCain, many voters lacked that confidence in Biden. Perversely, he confirmed their doubts in the course of seeking to allay them. Insisting on a debate with Trump months earlier than usual, Biden intended to show voters he still was up to the job. Instead he showed them the opposite. Astonishingly, even as he claimed after the election that he would have won if he had stayed in the race, he answered, "I don't know," when asked if he would have had the "vigor" to serve the full term.[117]

The recent broadening of the presidential talent pool to include candidates lacking in governing experience is more worrisome. Virtually without precedent in American history, the public's growing openness to political novices in the presidency originated in the late twentieth century, when frustration with government led many voters first to devalue service in Washington and then to look askance at any experience in governing at all. Reforms of the political parties that devolved control of nominations from party leaders and officeholders to primary and caucus voters accelerated this process.

Trump's candidacy for the Republican nomination in 2016 came less than a quarter century after the independent campaigns launched in the 1990s by another celebrity business leader, Ross Perot. Perot led in the polls for a period of time, and won 19 percent of the national popular vote on Election Day in 1992, the highest vote for a third-party candidate since former President Theodore Roosevelt ran in 1912. Trump won, but the shallowness of his understanding of the challenges a president must address, as well as the laws and Constitution under which presidents must govern, was all too apparent in 2016 and, despite four years of experience in the office, in 2020 and 2024. Even his understanding of royalty is dimly informed, focused on the trappings and powers of kingship but blind to its duties and constraints.

Trump's first term was flawed by many things, but among them was his lack of understanding of the presidency's constitutional foundation. This was no less true at the end of his term, when he refused to accept that he had lost the election to Biden and on January 6, 2021, rallied a large crowd of supporters to thwart the official counting of electoral votes by Congress. Two years later, he said that if he thought the 2024 election was unfair, he would call for the "termination of all rules, regulations and articles, even those found in the Constitution."[118] Trump also repeatedly threatened to bring criminal prosecutions and other forms of "retribution" against rivals and critics ranging from former President Obama and former Joint Chiefs of Staff Chair Mark Milley to Facebook founder Mark Zuckerberg, even as he pardoned personal courtiers and politically supportive violent offenders.[119]

Apart from an understanding of constitutional laws and norms, presidents also need certain skills if they are to lead effectively.[120] To be sure, skills of political rhetoric and communication are demonstrated (or not) in the election campaign. Trump showed a capacity to hold audiences spellbound for ninety minutes at a time and to make pathbreaking use of new forms of media, especially Twitter in 2016 and podcasts in 2024. But skills directly related to governing were undeveloped during his business career, one devoid of experience in political office. Bargaining with a Congress whose existence and influence are mandated by the Constitution is different from making deals with contractors or developers who can readily be replaced. The same can be said of the subtle but vital capacity to sense the broader public's willingness to be led in different directions at different paces at different times, as opposed to inhabiting, as Trump did, an echo chamber of supportive news outlets and social media within an established base of devoted supporters. The challenges of administrative management are also different in government from those in the corporate world, much less in the small-scale style of private companies that Trump long led without ever having to share power with a board of directors. The managerial culture clash between business (create new products) and government (provide legally mandated services) accelerated at the start of Trump's second term, when he brought in Space X founder Elon Musk to apply his company's "fail fast, learn faster" approach to the federal government's administrative operations. But even putting Trump aside, it remains the case that although success in the private sector may speak well of a person and usually requires some of these skills, only politics and government require all of them.[121]

Notes

1. George Washington ran unopposed in 1788–89 and 1792, as did James Monroe in 1820. Grover Cleveland, unmarried at the time of his election, got married fifteen months into his first term.
2. Clinton Rossiter, *The American Presidency*, rev. ed. (New American Library, 1960), 193–194.

3. Bill Scher, "How Does a Straight White Male Democrat Run for President?," *Politico*, February 17, 2019, https://www.politico.com/magazine/story/2019/02/17/white-male-democrats-2020-225101; Jocelyn Kiley and Shiva Maniam, "Lesbian, Gay and Bisexual Voters Remain a Solidly Democratic Bloc," Pew Research Center, October 25, 2016, https://www.pewresearch.org/fact-tank/2016/10/25/lesbian-gay-and-bisexual-voters-remain-a-solidly-democratic-bloc/.

4. Matt Stevens, "Joe Biden Commits to Selecting a Woman as Vice President," *New York Times*, March 15, 2020.

5. Katie Sullivan and Sarah Mucha, "Joe Biden Says He Is Considering Four Black Women to Be His Running Mate," CNN, July 21, 2020, https://www.cnn.com/2020/07/21/politics/joe-biden-four-black-women-vice-president/index.html. Of these four, Harris was the only one to have been elected to a statewide office.

6. Jazmine Ulloa, "Nikki Haley Aims to Turn Her Debate Moment into Momentum," *New York Times*, August 24, 2023.

7. Michael Wolff, *All or Nothing: Hoe Trump Recaptured America* (Crown, 2025), 268–269.

8. A fuller account of the argument that follows may be found in Michael Nelson, "Constitutional Qualifications for President," in *Inventing the Presidency*, ed. Thomas E. Cronin (University Press of Kansas, 1989).

9. Quoted in Cyril C. Means Jr., "Is Presidency Barred to Americans Born Abroad?," *U.S. News and World Report*, December 23, 1955, 28.

10. John Jay to George Washington, July 25, 1787, Founders Online, National Archives, https://founders.archives.gov/documents/Washington/04-05-02-0251.

11. Anne-Marie Slaughter, "The United States Is Not Ready for a Woman President," *Politico*, November 15, 2024, https://www.politico.com/news/magazine/2024/11/15/us-woman-president-expert-roundup-00189718.

12. George Washington to John Jay, September 2, 1787, Founders Online, National Archives, https://founders.archives.gov/documents/Washington/04-05-02-0282.

13. "Madison Debates, September 4," Avalon Project, Lillian Goldman Law Library, Yale Law School, accessed March 11, 2025, https://avalon.law.yale.edu/18th_century/debates_904.asp.

14. Calculated from data at "National Population by Characteristics: 2020–2023," U.S. Census Bureau, December 2024, https://www.census.gov/data/tables/time-series/demo/popest/2020s-national-detail.html; and Mohamad Moslimani and Jeffrey S. Passel, "What the Data Says About Immigrants in the US," Pew Research Center, July 22, 2024, https://www.pewresearch.org/short-reads/2024/07/22/key-findings-about-us-immigrants/.

15. Charles M. Blow, "Trump: Grand Wizard of Birtherism," *New York Times*, September 19, 2016.

16. Robert Costa and Philip Rucker, "Trump Says Cruz's Canadian Birth Could Be 'Very Precarious' for GOP," *Washington Post*, January 5, 2015.

17. Katie Rogers, "Trump Encourages Racist Conspiracy Theory About Kamala Harris," *New York Times*, August 13, 2020.

18. David Jackson, "Trump Shares False Claim Haley Isn't Eligible to Be President," *USA Today*, January 11, 2024.

19. United States v. Wong Kim Ark, 169 U.S. 469 (1898).

20. See, for example, Paul Clement and Neal Katyal, "On the Meaning of 'Natural Born Citizen,'" *Harvard Law Review Forum* 128, no. 5 (2015): 161–164; and Jack Maskell, *Qualifications for President and the "Natural Born" Citizenship Eligibility Requirement* (Congressional Research Service, 2011). Reportedly, Biden eliminated Senator Tammy Duckworth of Illinois from consideration as vice president, in part because he feared similar legally groundless challenges based on her birth in Bangkok to an American military veteran and a Thai mother. Alexander Burns et al., "How Biden Chose Harris," *New York Times*, August 13, 2020.

21. Rebecca Santana, "Trump Promises to End Birthright Citizenship," Associated Press, December 9, 2014, https://apnews.com/article/birthright -citizenship-immigration-trump-20919d26029cf0f98ecb0dc7f90a066b.

22. Jenna Russell et al., "Maine Joins Colorado in Finding Trump Ineligible for Primary Ballot," *New York Times*, December 28, 2023.

23. William Baude and Michael Stokes Paulsen, "The Sweep and Force of Section Three," *University of Pennsylvania Law Review* 172, no. 3 (2024): 605–744. Although unpublished at the time, a draft of the article circulated widely in August 2023.

24. See, for example, J. Michael Luttig and Laurence H. Tribe, "The Constitution Prohibits Trump from Ever Being President Again," *Atlantic*, August 19, 2023. In contrast, Michael McConnell warned that "this approach could empower partisans to seek disqualification every time a politician speaks in support of the objectives of a political riot." Quoted in David French, "Appeasing Trump Won't Work," *New York Times*, August 20, 2023.

25. Trump v. Anderson, 601 U.S. 100 (2024).

26. A constitutional quirk, the requirement that electors not vote for both a president and vice president from their own state, may have cost Senator Marco Rubio of Florida the 2024 Republican vice-presidential nomination. Rubio and Trump were both registered to vote in Florida, which means one of them would have had to move to another state to avoid forfeiting Florida's thirty electoral votes.

27. Emmy Martin, "Steve Bannon Floats an Unconstitutional Candidate: Trump in 2028," *Politico*, December 16, 2024, https://www.politico.com /live-updates/2024/12/16/congress/trump-2028-00194535.

28. James Romoser, "How Trump Could Defy the Constitution—or Find a Loophole—and Seize a Third Term," *Politico*, January 31, 2025, https:// www.politico.com/news/magazine/2025/01/31/trump-defy-constitution -third-term-00200239.

29. Many other national leaders have resorted to similar subterfuges to evade term limits, including Vladimir Putin of Russia, who supported the election of a figurehead president while holding a different office while reserving presidential power for himself. See Mila Versteeg et al., "The Law and Politics of Presidential Term Limit Evasion," *Columbia Law Review* 2020 (March 27, 2019), https://papers.ssrn.com/sol3/papers.cfm?abstract_id=3359960.

30. Neil Vigdor, "No, Trump Cannot Run for Re-Election Again in 2028," *New York Times*, November 18, 2024.

31. Brakkton Booker, "Trump Talks of a Third Term amid Growing Concerns About a Constitutional Crisis," *Politico*, February 21, 2025, https://www .politico.com/news/magazine/2025/01/31/trump-defy-constitution-third -term-00200239.

32. The exception was Abraham Lincoln, whose previous political experience consisted of several terms in the Illinois legislature and a single two-year term in Congress.

33. Michael Nelson, *Trump: The First Two Years* (University of Virginia Press, 2019), 14, 146–147.

34. They were Martin Van Buren, James Buchanan, and James Blaine.

35. Quoted in David Remnick, "The Joshua Generation," *New Yorker*, November 17, 2008.

36. Dobbs v. Jackson Women's Health Organization, 597 U.S. 215 (2022).

37. Stephen F. Hayes, *Cheney: The Untold Story of America's Most Powerful and Controversial Vice President* (HarperCollins, 2007), 307.

38. Matt Flegenheimer, "Joe Biden's Time in Sarah Palin's Shadow," *New York Times*, May 11, 2020.

39. Janet Hook and Colleen McCain Nelson, "WSJ Poll: Hillary Clinton Widens Lead in Primary Race," *Wall Street Journal*, October 20, 2015; Glenn Thrush, "Party of Two," *Politico Magazine*, July/August 2016, http:// www.politico.com/magazine/story/2016/07/2016-barack-obama-hillary -clinton-democratic-establishment-campaign-primary-joe-biden -elizabeth-warren-214023.

40. Janie Valencia, "Most Democrats Now Identify as Liberal," Five-ThirtyEight, January 11, 2019, https://fivethirtyeight.com/features/most -democrats-now-identify-as-liberal/.

41. Alan I. Abramowitz, *The Disappearing Center: Engaged Citizens, Polarization, and American Democracy* (Yale University Press, 2010), chap. 3.

42. Jill Colvin, "Pence Ends White House Campaign After Struggling to Gain Traction," Associated Press, October 28, 2023, https://apnews.com/article /mike-pence-2024-president-campaign-republican-trump-0ec44fc2a5b 8683f34883e0ea72b2ab2.

43. Ryan Grim and Danny Shea, "A Note About Our Coverage of Donald Trump's 'Campaign,'" *Huffington Post*, July 17, 2015, http://www.huffing tonpost.com/entry/a-note-about-our-coverage-of-donald-trumps -campaign_us_55a8fc9ce4b0896514d0fd66.

44. "Rise of the Anti-Establishment Presidential Candidates," *Washington Post*, September 14, 2015.

45. Nelson, *Trump*.

46. Martin Van Buren, Ulysses S. Grant, Theodore Roosevelt, and Herbert Hoover sought but failed to regain their party's presidential nomination.

47. Jeremy Diamond, "Trump: I Could 'Shoot Somebody and I Wouldn't Lose Voters,'" CNN, January 24, 2016, https://www.cnn.com/2016/01/23/politics /donald-trump-shoot-somebody-support/index.html.

48. Michael Nelson, "A New Record for Presidential Longevity," *Cook Political Report*, October 22, 2016, http://cookpolitical.com/story/8954.

49. Peter Baker, "As He Questions His Opponent's Health, Trump Finds His Own Under Scrutiny," *New York Times*, September 2, 2020.

50. Ashley Parker and Josh Dawsey, "Trump Is Increasingly Preoccupied with Defending His Physical and Mental Health," *Washington Post*, June 22, 2020.

51. Michael Nelson, "The Election: Ordinary Politics, Extraordinary Outcome," in *The Elections of 2000*, ed. Michael Nelson (CQ Press, 2001), 75.

52. Kaitlin Lewis, "'No Genocide Josh' Campaign Doubles Down as Shapiro VP Speculation Grows," *Newsweek*, August 2, 2024.

53. Lydia Saad, "Felonies, Old Age Heavily Count Against Candidates," Gallup, January 26, 2024, https://news.gallup.com/poll/609344/felonies-old -age-heavily-count-against-candidates.aspx.

54. Aaron Blake, "Bernie Sanders: Our First Non-Religious President?," *Washington Post*, January 27, 2016.

55. E. J. Dionne, "Joe Biden Can't 'Hurt God.' He Can End the Catch-22 Around Religion," *Washington Post*, August 9, 2020.

56. Eugene Scott, "Trump Believes in God, but Hasn't Sought Forgiveness," CNN, July 18, 2015, https://www.cnn.com/2015/07/18/politics/trump-has -never-sought-forgiveness/index.html; "Election 2024: Exit Polls," CNN, last updated December 13, 2024, https://www.cnn.com/election/2024/exit -polls/national-results/general/president/0.

57. Katherine Stewart, "Why Trump Reigns as King Cyrus," *New York Times*, December 31, 2018.

58. Chris Cillizza, "Yes, Donald Trump Really Believes He Is 'the Chosen One,'" CNN, August 24, 2019, https://www.cnn.com/2019/08/21/politics/donald-trump-chosen-one/index.html.

59. Ruth Graham and Clyde McGrady, "Harris's Faith, Inside and Outside the Black Church," *New York Times*, October 21, 2024.

60. Saad, "Felonies, Old Age."

61. Quoted in Theodore H. White, *The Making of the President 1960* (Pocket Books, 1961), 128–129.

62. John F. Kennedy, "Address to the Greater Houston Ministerial Association," delivered September 12, 1960, at the Rice Hotel in Houston, TX, https://www.americanrhetoric.com/speeches/jfkhoustonministers.html.

63. George H. Gallup, *The Gallup Poll: Public Opinion, 1935–1971* (Random House, 1971), 3:1605, 1735, 2190; Saad, "Felonies, Old Age." By 2024, the number of anti-Catholic voters was 6 percent. Saad, "Felonies, Old Age."

64. "Romney's Speech Addresses His Mormon Faith," *Talk of the Nation*, NPR, December 6, 2007, https://www.npr.org/2007/12/06/16978445/romneys-speech-addresses-his-mormon-faith.

65. Joseph Carroll, "Which Characteristics Are Most Desirable in the Next President?," Gallup, September 17, 2007, https://www.gallup.com/poll/28693/Which-Characteristics-Most-Desirable-Next-President.aspx.

66. Bud Jackson, "McCain's Age Is a Legitimate Issue," *Politico*, May 22, 2008, https://www.politico.com/story/2008/05/mccains-age-is-a-legitimate-issue-010529; Steve Chapman, "Is McCain Too Old to Be President?," RealClearPolitics, September 9, 2007, https://www.realclearpolitics.com/articles/2007/09/is_mccain_too_old_to_be_presid.html.

67. Alexander Burns, "McCain and the Politics of Mortality," *Politico*, September 3, 2008, https://www.politico.com/story/2008/09/mccain-and-the-politics-of-mortality-013096.

68. "The First Trump-Clinton Presidential Debate Transcript, Annotated," *Washington Post*, September 26, 2016; Jeremy Diamond, "Trump Calls for Drug Rest Ahead of Next Debate," CNN, October 16, 2016, https://www.cnn.com/2016/10/15/politics/donald-trump-hillary-clinton-drug-test/index.html.

69. John Wagner, "'I Hope There's an Age Limit': Jimmy Carter Questions Whether He Could Have Handled the Presidency at 80," *Washington Post*, September 18, 2019.

70. Sean Sullivan, "Bernie Sanders, 78, Declares His Age Is an Asset," *Washington Post*, October 25, 2019.

71. Matt Viser and Cleve R. Wootson Jr., "Joe Biden Is a 'Healthy, Vigorous' 77-Year-Old, His Doctor Declares," *Washington Post*, December 17, 2019; Frank Bruni, "Give Joe Biden His Due," *New York Times*, December 20, 2019.

72. Sasha Issenberg, "In 2020, the Biden Campaign Knew Age Was His Achilles' Heel. Here's What They Did," *Politico*, March 12, 2020, https://www.politico.com/news/magazine/2024/03/12/biden-age-issue-2020-00146296.

73. Evan Osnos, *Joe Biden: The Life, the Run, and What Matters Now* (Scribner, 2020), 18; Ezra Klein, "The Democratic Party Is Having an 'Identity Crisis,'" *New York Times*, February 2, 2024.

74. Kaleigh Rogers, "Americans Were Worried About Biden's Age Long Before the Debate," ABC News, July 12, 2024, https://abcnews.go.com/538/americans-worried-bidens-age-long-debate/story?id=111858302.

75. Matt Viser and Tyler Pager, "Biden Responds Angrily to Special Counsel Report Questioning His Memory," *Washington Post*, February 8, 2024.

76. Shane Goldmacher, "Trump Widens Lead After Biden's Debate Debacle, Times/Siena Poll Finds," *New York Times*, July 3, 2024.

77. "Trump at RNC: 'Our Planet Is Teetering on the Edge of World War III,'" WSJ Video, 3 min., 5 sec., July 18, 2024, https://www.wsj.com/video/trump-at-rnc-our-planet-is-teetering-on-the-edge-of-world-war-iii/3CCADAC9-7345-47D1-9B1E-2F22642CF5DE.

78. Megan Lebowitz, "Trump Confuses the Names of His Doctor When Bragging About Taking a Cognitive Test," NBC News, June 16, 2024, https://www.nbcnews.com/politics/donald-trump/trump-confuses-ronny-jacksons-name-bragging-taking-cognitive-test-rcna157432.

79. Dylan Wells, "Haley Questions Trump's Mental Fitness, Citing New Hampshire Rally Flub," *Washington Post*, January 20, 2024.

80. Kelly Garrity, "Nikki Haley Calls for Competency Tests for Politicians over 75 During Campaign Launch," *Politico*, February 15, 2023, https://www.politico.com/news/2023/02/15/nikki-haley-competency-tests-00083018.

81. Jennifer Rubin, "Unstable and Unhinged," *Washington Post*, October 18, 2024; "Obama Warns of 'Older, Loonier' Donald Trump During Wisconsin Rally," ABC News, October 22, 2024, https://abcnews.go.com/Politics/video/obama-warns-older-loonier-trump-wisconsin-rally-115041676.

82. Goldmacher, "Trump Widens Lead"; "Election 2024: Exit Polls."

83. "2024 Fox News Voter Analysis," Fox News, accessed February 11, 2025, https://www.foxnews.com/elections/2024/general-results/voter-analysis.

84. Jeffrey M. Jones, "Some Americans Reluctant to Vote for Mormon, 72-Year-Old Presidential Candidates," Gallup News Service, February 20, 2007, www.gallup.com/poll/26611/Some-Americans-Reluctant-Vote-Mormon-72YearOld-Presidential-Candidates.aspx; Linda Feldman, "In 2008, Many Presidential 'Firsts' Are Possible," *Christian Science Monitor*, February 16, 2007.

85. All 2008 exit poll results are from "Election Results 2008: National Exit Poll Tables," *New York Times*, November 5, 2008, https://archive.nytimes

.com/www.nytimes.com/elections/2008/results/president/national-exit
-polls.html?ref=quillette.com.

86. Justin McCarthy, "Less Than Half in U.S. Would Vote for a Socialist for
President," Gallup, May 9, 2019, https://news.gallup.com/poll/254120/less
-half-vote-socialist-president.aspx.

87. Kaleigh Rogers, "Is Harris's Race or Gender Affecting Her Support?," *New
York Times*, October 26, 2024.

88. Summer Concepcion, "Trump Says Harris Would Be 'Like a Play Toy' to
World Leaders If Elected," NBC News, July 31, 2024, https://www.nbcnews
.com/politics/2024-election/trump-says-harris-play-toy-world-leaders
-elected-rcna164483.

89. Ashley Parker, "Trump Keeps Calling Harris 'Stupid,' Offending Many
Voters," *Washington Post*, October 21, 2024; Maureen Dowd, "It's a Man's,
Man's, Man's World," *New York Times*, November 6, 2024.

90. "Election 2024: Exit Polls."

91. Philip E. Converse et al., "Stability and Change in 1960: A Reinstating
Election," in *Elections and the Political Order*, ed. Angus Campbell et al.
(John Wiley and Sons, 1966).

92. Andrew E. Busch and John J. Pitney Jr., *Divided We Stand: The 2020 Election and American Politics* (Rowman and Littlefield, 2021), 130.

93. Michael Nelson, "The Setting: Who Can Be President?" in *The Elections
of 2020*, ed. Michael Nelson (University of Virginia Press, 2021), 22.

94. Jones, "Some Americans Reluctant."

95. Nicholas Kristof, "Clinton, Trump and Sexism," *New York Times*, January 23, 2016.

96. Peter Nicholas, "Clinton Steps Up Efforts to Woo Women Voters," *Wall
Street Journal*, September 11, 2015.

97. McCarthy, "Less Than Half."

98. Wolff, *All or Nothing*, 276.

99. Eric Bradner and Aaron Pellish, "Donald Trump Falsely Suggests Kamala
Harris 'Happened to Turn Black,'" CNN, July 31, 2024, https://www.cnn
.com/2024/07/31/politics/donald-trump-kamala-harris-black-nabj
/index .html.

100. Karen Tumulty, "Harris Is Freaking Trump Out by Shrugging Him Off,"
Washington Post, August 30, 2024.

101. Sudiksha Kochi and Savannah Kuchar, "Harris Pressed on Transgender
Rights," *USA Today*, October 23, 2024.

102. Maeve Reston, "Harris Has Largely Stayed Away from Embracing the
'First Woman' Rallying Cry," *Washington Post*, August 19, 2024. When
Harris became vice president, she told Biden that "she didn't want to work
on women's issues or anything to do with race." Franklin Foer, *The Last
Politician: Inside Joe Biden's White House and the Struggle for America's
Future* (Penguin, 2023), 113.

103. Kellen Browning, "Harris Often Sidesteps Her History-Making Potential. Walz Doesn't," *New York Times*, October 7, 2024.
104. Yasmeen Abutaleb, "Obama Admonishes Black Men for Hesitancy in Supporting Harris," *Washington Post*, October 10, 2024.
105. "Obama Mocks Trump About His 'Weird Obsession with Crowd Sizes,'" CNN, August 21, 2024, https://www.cnn.com/2024/08/21/politics/video/barack-obama-donald-trump-crowd-size-dnc-digvid.
106. "2024 Fox News Voter Analysis."
107. Zachary B. Wolf et al., "Anatomy of Three Trump Elections," CNN, November 6, 2024, https://www.cnn.com/interactive/2024/politics/2020-2016-exit-polls-2024-dg/.
108. "Read the Full Transcript of Donald Trump's Person of the Year Interview with *Time*," *Time*, December 12, 2024, https://time.com/7201565/person-of-the-year-2024-donald-trump-transcript/.
109. John Santucci and Sean Keene, "Donald Trump's Gen Z Son Is Serving as His Unofficial Podcast Adviser," ABC News, October 25, 2024, https://abcnews.go.com/Politics/donald-trumps-gen-son-barron-serving-unofficial-podcast/story?id=115067138.
110. Drew Harwell and Sarah Ellison, "Inside the White House's New Media Strategy to Promote Trump as 'KING,'" *Washington Post*, March 6, 2024.
111. Doina Chiacu, "Trump: If It Saves the Country, It's Not Illegal," Reuters, February 16, 2025, https://www.reuters.com/world/us/trump-if-it-saves-country-its-not-illegal-2025-02-16/.
112. "Madison Debates, June 2," Avalon Project, Lillian Goldman Law Library, Yale Law School, accessed March 11, 2025, https://avalon.law.yale.edu/18th_century/debates_602.asp.
113. "From Thomas Jefferson to John Adams, 13 November 1787," Founders Online, National Archive, accessed March 11, 2025, https://founders.archives.gov/documents/Jefferson/01-12-02-0342. At the time, Polish kings typically were reelected again and again, thereby serving until they died.
114. George Washington, "Undelivered First Inaugural Address: Fragments, 30 April 1789," Founders Online, National Archives, https://founders.archives.gov/documents/Washington/05-02-02-0130-0002.
115. The unwritten rule that presidents should be married raised questions about Senator Tim Scott's candidacy for the Republican nomination in 2024. Scott responded in two contradictory ways: by saying that as a single man he would have "more time, more energy, and more latitude to do the job" and announcing that he had a girlfriend and that they were engaged. He married in August. Ben Terris, "Tim Scott's Girlfriend," *Washington Post*, September 22, 2023.
116. See, for example, Ledyard King et al., "Elizabeth Warren's Latest Hurdle to the Presidency," *USA Today*, September 10, 2019.

117. "Read What Joe Biden Said During His Exclusive Interview with *USA Today*: Transcript," *USA Today*, January 8, 2025.

118. Kristen Holmes, "Trump Calls for the Termination of the Constitution in Truth Social Post," CNN, December 4, 2022, https://www.cnn.com/2022/12/03/politics/trump-constitution-truth-social/index.html.

119. Summer Concepcion, "Trump Suggests That, If Re-Elected, He Would Have Biden Indicted," NBC News, January 8, 2024, https://www.nbcnews.com/politics/donald-trump/trump-suggests-re-elected-biden-indicted-rcna132810; Shawn McCreesh, "Trump's Latest Photo Book Offers Gossip, Boasting, and a Threat," *New York Times*, September 9, 2024.

120. Erwin C. Hargrove and Michael Nelson, *Presidents, Politics, and Policy* (Johns Hopkins University Press, 1984), chap. 4.

121. Michael Nelson, "Who Vies for President?," in *Presidential Selection*, ed. Alexander Heard and Michael Nelson (Duke University Press, 1987).

The Presidential Nominations

RERUN INTERRUPTED

WILLIAM G. MAYER

THROUGH 2023 AND THE FIRST HALF of 2024, the 2024 presidential nomination races looked to be the least interesting contests since 1900, when William McKinley and William Jennings Bryan were both unanimously nominated by their party's national conventions. In another parallel with 2024, McKinley and Bryan had been the major party nominees four years earlier, just like Joseph Biden (or so it seemed) and Donald Trump. And then, starting in late June 2024, things got a lot more interesting.

The Democratic Nomination: Phase 1

From the moment that Joe Biden was sworn into office in early 2021, it was widely assumed that, like all of his predecessors since Calvin Coolidge, he would run for reelection.[1] Born in 1942, Biden would have been eighty-two at the start of his second term, eighty-six when it ended. Before him, the oldest sitting president had been Ronald Reagan, who was seventy-seven when he left office—and many commentators thought that the Gipper was showing signs of senility during his final years as president. But it wasn't just Biden's numerical age that caused concern. During his 2020 campaign and throughout his presidency, Biden's advisers and handlers seemed determined to shield him from public exposure: to limit the number of his press conferences and any other situations in which he was required to do something more than read a speech on a teleprompter. Even with such precautions, Biden sometimes garbled the text he was given or decided to go ex tempore, with the result that his remarks, especially when transcribed, gave new and vivid currency to the term *word salad*.[2] Fortunately for Biden, the major media made little attempt to raise or investigate questions about his mental fitness during his first three and a half years in office. In the wake of his disastrous performance in his debate with Trump, a second and more extended debate would take place as to whether and why the media had previously given Biden's problems a pass.[3]

In a further effort to discourage intraparty opposition, Biden made every effort to protect his left flank. Gerald Ford in 1976 and Jimmy Carter in 1980 had both failed to mollify their party's dominant ideological wing—and had thus endured a very hard-fought battle for renomination, then lost the subsequent general election. Pat Buchanan's challenge to George H. W. Bush's renomination in 1992 was much less threatening—yet Bush too lost his bid for reelection. Though it is far from clear that a contested nomination race causes a poor showing in the general election, some political scientists—and lots of politicians and political consultants—believe that it does.[4]

Biden seemed to be in a particularly vulnerable position in this respect. The party's hardcore left had shown little enthusiasm for Biden in the first three events of the 2020 delegate selection season. He came in fourth in the Iowa caucuses, fifth in the New Hampshire primary, and a distant second in the Nevada caucuses, 21 percentage points behind the winner. The only major voting bloc that strongly supported him in the early going was Black people, which was the principal reason he posted a decisive win in the next major contest, the South Carolina primary. After that, he swept through the remaining primaries and caucuses largely because he was seen as the only real alternative to the nomination of Bernie Sanders, whom many Democrats feared would lose to Trump.[5] Against that background, Biden was determined to make sure that his party's liberal wing had no major causes for grievance. In 1992, Bill Clinton, speaking in front of a meeting of Jesse Jackson supporters, had famously criticized a Black rap artist named Sister Souljah for making favorable comments about Black-on-white violence. It is difficult to think of anything similar that Joe Biden did during his presidency.

Already during the 2020 campaign, Biden had moved away from some of the comparatively centrist parts of his record, a trend that continued when he assumed office in 2021.[6] One of those new positions, his policies on immigration, would cause him and then Vice President Kamala Harris considerable difficulties in the 2024 general election. In terms of his immediate needs, however, Biden's move to the left worked. In January 2024, just before the start of the delegate selection season, a Gallup poll found that Biden had an overall approval rating of just 41 percent, significantly below the level normally needed to win a general election. But his performance was approved by 83 percent of the nation's Democrats.

The bottom line was that, until quite late in the 2024 election cycle, Biden faced little opposition in his quest for renomination. The political rumor mills suggested that several major Democrats were poised to enter the 2024 nomination race if Biden decided not to run or appeared hopelessly weak. California Governor Gavin Newsom, Illinois Governor J. B. Pritzker, and Secretary of Transportation Pete Buttigieg were three names often mentioned in this regard. But in the end, none of them pulled the trigger. As of fall 2024, 224 people had filed a form with the Federal Election Commission (FEC) announcing that they were seeking the Democratic presidential nomination.[7] But 208 of these would-be presidents never reported spending a single cent in pursuit of that goal. Only 6 spent more than $100,000—and 1 of the 6, a progressive political activist named Cenk Uygur, was born in Turkey and thus constitutionally ineligible to become president. (One name that wasn't on the FEC list was Robert F. Kennedy Jr.: By the time I checked the FEC website, he had decided to run as an independent.)

Table 1 lists the six candidates who were treated as at least somewhat serious by most media outlets, along with their announcement and withdrawal dates. Of the six, the only one who attracted a modest amount of media attention was Kennedy, and that, of course, was primarily due to his ancestry. The Kennedy name had once been the most potent in all of American politics, but memories fade and older voters who idolized the Kennedys gradually died off and were replaced by younger voters who knew the Kennedys—if they knew them at all—only through the history books. As Robert's uncle Ted learned in 1980, his last name was not enough to guarantee victory in a Democratic presidential nomination contest, even against a fairly weak opponent. Indeed, as Joseph P. Kennedy III would learn in 2020, it didn't even guarantee victory in a Massachusetts primary.[8]

To give him his due, Robert Kennedy Jr. had once been a highly regarded environmental lawyer and activist, but he had increasingly been consigned to the political fringe because of his opposition to vaccination and support for a variety of conspiracy theories. His personal life included both a lengthy addiction to heroin and a reputation as a compulsive philanderer. As Kennedy himself said, "I have so many skeletons in my closet that if they could all vote, I could run for king of the world."[9]

The other Biden challengers were even less formidable. Marianne Williamson, a self-help guru and onetime spiritual adviser to Oprah Winfrey, had first run for the Democratic nomination in 2020, when her candidacy, as one reporter put it, "featured more quirky calls for spiritual healing than actual voter support."[10] Jason Palmer, a little-known businessman and entrepreneur, at least had the advantage of being able to finance his campaign largely out of his own pocket. Dean Phillips was the only Biden challenger who had actually been elected to public office; he was a

TABLE 1. Major candidates for the 2024 Democratic and Republican presidential nominations

Candidate	Announcement date	Withdrawal date
Democrats		
Marianne Williamson[a]	March 4, 2023	February 7, 2024
	February 28, 2024	June 11, 2024
	July 2, 2024	July 29, 2024
Robert F. Kennedy Jr.[b]	April 19, 2023	October 9, 2023
Joseph Biden	April 25, 2023	July 21, 2024
Jason Palmer	October 22, 2023	May 15, 2024
Dean Phillips	October 26, 2023	March 6, 2024
Kamala Harris	July 21, 2024	—
Republicans		
Donald Trump	November 15, 2022	—
Nikki Haley	February 14, 2023	March 6, 2024
Vivek Ramaswamy	February 21, 2023	January 15, 2024
Perry Johnson	March 2, 2023	October 20, 2023
Larry Elder	April 20, 2023	October 26, 2023
Asa Hutchinson	April 26, 2023	January 16, 2024
Tim Scott	May 19, 2023	November 12, 2023
Ron DeSantis	May 24, 2023	January 21, 2024
Mike Pence	June 5, 2023	October 28, 2023
Chris Christie	June 6, 2023	January 10, 2024
Doug Burgum	June 7, 2023	December 4, 2023
Francis Suarez	June 14, 2023	August 29, 2023
Will Hurd	June 22, 2023	October 9, 2023

[a]Having initially withdrawn on February 7, 2024, Williamson reentered the race three weeks later, withdrew for a second time in June, got back in the race after Biden's withdrawal, then withdrew for a third and final time in late July.

[b]Kennedy withdrew from the Democratic nomination race in order to run as an independent. He ended his independent bid in August 2024 and endorsed Donald Trump.

three-term member of the U.S. House of Representatives from Minnesota, though not an especially visible member of that body.

Throughout Biden's presidency, polls regularly showed that most Americans did not want him to run for a second term. On eleven occasions between February 2022 and July 2023, three different survey organizations posed a straightforward question to national samples of Americans: "Would you like to see Joe Biden run for president in 2024, or not?"[11] On average, with relatively little variation, 28 percent said yes, 69 percent said no. More strikingly, a sizable majority of Democrats took the same position. On four occasions between September 2022 and September 2023, ABC News and *The Washington Post* asked the country's Democrats if their party should "nominate Biden to run for a second term" or if it should "nominate someone other than Biden." No more than 36 percent wanted to renominate Biden, while no less than 56 percent preferred nominating someone else.

While such questions clearly showed a substantial level of dissatisfaction with Biden, they were a problematic way of assessing how he would fare in a contested nomination race, since they effectively pitted Biden against an ideal opponent. When survey questions matched Biden against his actual nomination opponents, he fared much better. According to the Roper Center's iPoll database, fifteen national polls were conducted between April and September 2023 in which the nation's Democrats were asked whom they would vote for if the candidates were Biden, Kennedy, and Williamson. (Phillips and Palmer hadn't entered the race yet and therefore weren't included in these questions.) On average, the results were Biden, 64 percent; Kennedy, 15 percent; Williamson, 7 percent. On October 9, 2023, realizing that he had little support within the Democratic Party, Kennedy announced that he would run as an independent. After Kennedy's withdrawal, nine national polls asked Democrats to choose among Biden, Williamson, and Phillips (Palmer's name was never included in these or any other polls I could find). The average result was Biden, 73 percent; Williamson, 10 percent; Phillips, 4 percent.

In the end, the Democratic primary and caucus season was even less competitive than the polls had suggested. Biden won 87 percent of the votes cast (table 2). Palmer, who won just 0.1 percent of the total vote, nevertheless managed to win the caucuses held in American Samoa, the only contest Biden lost or even came close to losing. Palmer's victory was less impressive than it might appear, however: Just ninety-one people took part in those caucuses, fifty-one of whom voted for Palmer. By the night of March 12, Biden had won enough delegates to clinch the Democratic nomination.

The Republican Nomination

The race for the 2024 Republican nomination really began on election night 2020, when Donald Trump claimed that he had actually won the election by a "landslide" but was denied his rightful victory by Democratic vote fraud. It was a boldface lie, utterly bereft of solid evidence. But its morality

TABLE 2. Total votes in the 2024 Democratic presidential primaries

	Total votes	Percentage
Joseph Biden	14,183,228	87.0
Dean Phillips	529,486	3.2
Marianne Williamson	473,463	2.9
Uncommitted	349,281	2.1
Jason Palmer	20,939	0.1
Total	16,302,264	100.0

Source: "Democratic Convention 2024," Green Papers, accessed December 2, 2024, https://www.thegreenpapers.com/P24/D.

Note: The numbers presented here do not include votes for other candidates, write-ins, or similar, so do not add to 100 percent.

aside, the claim was a clever political move. It neutralized what might otherwise have been one of the strongest arguments against renominating him in 2024: that he was a weak candidate, who had lost one presidential election and had been the principal reason why the Republicans lost so many House seats in 2018. Most of the Senate candidates he endorsed in 2022 also fared poorly. In a further attempt to discourage intraparty opposition, Trump announced his 2024 candidacy on November 15, 2022, just seven days after the midterm election, at a time when several congressional races were still undecided.

There is no single criterion or a widely agreed-on set of criteria that allows analysts to say who is and who is not a "serious candidate" for a major party presidential nomination. Anyone who has previously been elected to a governmental office almost always makes the list, even if the office is a relatively low-level one.[12] Wealthy businesspeople without previous governmental experience generally did not make the grade at one time, but after the success of Steve Forbes in 1996 and Donald Trump in 2016, now they do. Much like the Democrats, there were a lot of frivolous Republican candidates in 2024: 439 registered with the FEC, but 400 spent no money at all and just 17 spent more than $100,000. By most counts, there were 13 Republican presidential candidates in the 2024 race, listed in table 1 along with their announcement and withdrawal dates. In addition to Trump, they included a number who, in a different year, might have been formidable contenders, such as Florida Governor Ron DeSantis, U.S. Senator Tim Scott (SC), former Trump Vice President Mike Pence, and former South Carolina Governor and UN Ambassador Nikki Haley.

Table 3 shows the results of eight national polls of Republican or likely Republican primary voters conducted between mid-July 2022 and the first two months of 2023. Through October 2022, Trump had a sizable though by no means insuperable lead over DeSantis, with all the other candidates mired in single digits. In early November, however, DeSantis trounced his opponent in the Florida gubernatorial election, beating Democrat Charlie Crist by 19 percentage points. Though it wasn't widely noted in contemporary press coverage, Crist was not a particularly strong opponent. A former Republican governor of Florida (2007–11), Crist ran for the U.S. Senate in 2010 but lost the GOP primary to Marco Rubio. In 2012, he switched parties, won the 2014 Democratic gubernatorial primary, and lost the general election to Rick Scott. But such details were largely ignored in the flood of stories that suggested that DeSantis was a candidate who was unafraid

TABLE 3. Polls of the 2024 Republican nomination race, July 2022–February 2023 (in percentages)

Survey organization	Date	Trump	DeSantis	Pence	Haley	Pompeo
NYT/Siena[a]	July 5–7, 2022	49	25	6	6	2
USA Today/Suffolk[b]	July 22–25, 2022	43	34	7	3	1
Ipsos/ReconMR[a]	October 9–12, 2022	49	26	6	3	2
538/Ipsos[a]	November 9–21, 2022	25	37	6	3	n/a
Monmouth[c]	December 8–12, 2022	26	39	2	1	*
Monmouth[d]	January 26–February 2, 2023	33	33	2	1	1
Quinnipiac[d]	February 9–14, 2023	42	36	4	5	4
Fox/Beacon Research[a]	February 19–22, 2023	43	28	7	7	1

Note: Question wordings sometimes included other candidates, declared and undeclared, who rarely received more than 2 percent of the vote. An asterisk (*) means the candidate received less than 0.5 percent.

[a] Asked of registered voters who say they are likely to vote in the Republican primary.

[b] Asked of registered voters who identify as Republicans and independents who tend to vote in Republican primaries.

[c] Asked of Republican identifiers, including leaners.

[d] Asked of registered voters who identify as Republicans, including leaners.

TABLE 4. Polls of the 2024 Republican nomination race, February–December 2023 (in percentages)

Date	Trump	DeSantis	Haley	Ramaswamy	Christie	All others
February 19–22, 2023	43	28	7	n/a	*	16
March 24–27, 2023	54	24	3	1	1	16
April 21–24, 2023	53	21	4	3	1	16
May 19–22, 2023	53	20	4	4	*	11
June 23–26, 2023	56	22	3	5	1	9
August 11–14, 2023	53	16	4	11	3	10
September 9–12, 2023	60	13	5	11	2	6
October 6–9, 2023	59	13	10	7	3	2
November 10–13, 2023	62	13	10	7	3	4
December 10–13, 2023	69	12	9	5	2	1

Source: All polls were conducted by Beacon Research for Fox News.
Note: Question was asked of registered voters who said they were likely to vote in the Republican primary or caucus in their state. An asterisk (*) means the candidate received less than 0.5 percent.

to take a stand against political correctness and still win a crushing victory in a competitive state.

For the next two months, DeSantis had a comfortable lead over Trump in the polls. But it didn't last. By February 2023 Trump had regained his lead, a lead that, as shown in table 4, grew steadily larger through the rest of the year. It is unclear whether Trump's numerous legal troubles actually helped his campaign, as he often claimed, but they certainly didn't hurt it. By December 2023, a month before the Iowa caucuses and the start of the delegate selection season, 69 percent of likely Republican primary voters supported Trump versus just 12 percent for DeSantis and 9 percent for Nikki Haley.

The 2024 Republican nomination race, like almost every contested nomination race since the 1960s, featured a series of debates between the major Republican candidates. Though candidate debates have rarely played a significant role in presidential general elections,[13] they have sometimes been very important in nomination races. George H. W. Bush's unwillingness to allow four other Republican candidates to be included in a 1980 debate with Ronald Reagan turned what had been a close New Hampshire primary—some predebate polls showed Bush slightly ahead—into an overwhelming Reagan victory. The Bush campaign never recovered. Walter

Mondale's "Where's the beef?" riposte to Gary Hart allowed him to halt Hart's momentum, win two of the seven contests on 1984's Super Tuesday, and then go on to win the Democratic nomination.[14] Rubio's failure to answer Chris Christie's challenge to his capacity to handle the responsibilities of the presidency doomed Rubio's candidacy in 2016.[15] And Elizabeth Warren's sharp takedown of Michael Bloomberg in a 2020 debate effectively spelled the end of Bloomberg's candidacy. But the Republican debates of the 2024 election cycle seem not to have mattered much at all.

The Republican Party sponsored four debates in the 2024 nomination contest, held, respectively, on August 23, September 27, November 8, and December 6, 2023. Perhaps the most noteworthy feature of these debates was that Trump didn't participate in any of them. In a reasonable attempt to limit the number of participants, the Republican National Committee had established a list of qualifications a candidate had to meet in order to participate. To be included in the first debate, for example, a candidate had to

- be constitutionally eligible for the office;
- have polled at least 1 percent in three national polls or two national polls and one poll in two of the early primary or caucus states;
- have attracted donations from at least forty thousand individuals, with at least two hundred contributors in each of twenty states or territories; and
- sign a pledge indicating that he or she would not take part in any debate that had not been sanctioned by the Republican National Committee and *would support the eventual nominee* [emphasis mine].

(These qualifying standards became more stringent in later debates.) In 2024, as in the 2016 nomination contest, Trump refused to say that he would support the eventual nominee—which gave him an excuse for saying that he would not participate. The Republican National Committee might have waived this requirement in one or more of the later debates in order to pressure Trump to take part and thus open himself to greater scrutiny, but for whatever reason it made no effort to do so.

One might have expected the other candidates to attack Trump for such high-handed behavior. In fact, Christie was the only debate participant who was willing to offer sustained criticism of Trump. Mike Pence did so when asked specifically about his decision not to challenge many states' electoral votes when those votes were counted on January 6, 2021. Other than that, he consistently praised the record of the "Trump–Pence" administration. Most of the other candidates, DeSantis in particular, apparently believed that attacking Trump would only alienate his supporters. This might have been a reasonable strategy if Trump had been sitting at 20 or 25 percent in the polls. But by mid-August 2023, when the first debate was held, more than 50 percent of likely Republican primary voters said they would vote for Trump, while DeSantis had the support of only about 15 percent. Though an attack strategy might have backfired, refusing to criticize Trump would almost certainly guarantee his renomination.

While the Republican electorate probably didn't want to hear that Trump had really lost the 2020 election, there were a number of issues one of the other candidates might have exploited. For all his claims to be an effective leader who had accomplished great things in his first term, there were a number of major discrepancies between what Trump had promised and what he had actually achieved. The greatest such discrepancy involved that celebrated border wall he had repeatedly promised to build—and make Mexico pay for—during his 2016 campaign. The border between the United States and Mexico is 1,954 miles long; by the end of his term, Trump had managed to build a wall of only about 450 miles—and, of course, Mexico had paid for not a dime of it. An effective ad might have been made showing a candidate standing along the Rio Grande River, with not a bit of wall in sight. The annual U.S. trade deficit, which Trump promised to close, actually grew during his time in office, from $481 billion in 2016 to $679 billion in 2020. Though Trump had promised to weed out "waste, fraud, and abuse" in federal spending, the budget deficit increased significantly during his presidency, from $584 billion in 2016 to $983 billion in 2019. (This was before the massive increases in spending both parties believed were necessary in 2020 due to the COVID-19 pandemic.) When George H. W. Bush initially declined to debate Bill Clinton in 1992, the Clinton campaign had a series of men wearing a chicken costume, dubbed Chicken George, follow Bush around until Bush finally agreed to a series of debates. So far as I can determine, none of Trump's Republican opponents tried to copy this stratagem.

Meanwhile, in what has become a regular feature of contemporary presidential nomination races, many of the Republican candidates ended their campaigns before a single delegate had been chosen. Between late August and mid-November 2023, six GOP candidates folded their tents: Francis Suarez, Will Hurd, Perry Johnson, Larry Elder, Mike Pence, and Tim Scott. Johnson and Elder both endorsed Trump when announcing their withdrawal; Suarez and Scott would endorse the former president later, during the primary season. Hurd announced that he was supporting Nikki Haley; Pence never endorsed anyone. Doug Burgum exited the race on December 4; he too endorsed Trump.

With a large lead among the nation's Republican voters and no significant criticism from many of his leading opponents, the 2024 Republican
primaries were all but certain to be a pretty dull affair. As shown in tables 5
and 6, Trump won every primary and caucus except the primaries held in
the District of Columbia and Vermont. In a substantial majority of cases,
Trump won at least 70 percent of the votes cast.

Trump's last remaining opponent was Nikki Haley. The closest she came
to an important and possibly game-changing victory was in New Hampshire. Eight days earlier, Trump had posted a solid win in the Iowa caucuses,
but the size of his victory margin owed much to the fact that the anti-Trump
vote was divided among his two major opponents: Haley and DeSantis. But
DeSantis, who finished narrowly ahead of Haley in Iowa, dropped out of
the race two days before the New Hampshire vote, meaning that Haley
finally had the chance to face Trump one-on-one, in a state that had often
shown a fondness for underdogs. And unlike many later primaries, the
results in New Hampshire are heavily covered by the media—overcovered,
many would argue—and thus have the potential to upend the whole race,
as they did for the Democrats in 1968 and 1984 and for the Republicans in
2000 and 2008. In the end, Haley came moderately close (at least as compared with the results in most other states) but fell short of victory: She
received 43 percent of the vote, to 54 percent for Trump.

Table 7 shows some of the most important results from the New Hampshire primary exit poll. In general, Haley did well among all of the numer-
ically least significant groups in the Republican electorate. She won
substantial majorities of the votes cast by self-identified Democrats and
independents, while Trump won the Republican vote by a three-to-one
margin. She won a whopping majority of the votes cast by liberals and moderates, but lost the conservative vote by 54 percentage points. Haley also
ran very well among the few Republicans who thought the nation's economy was excellent or good; among those who were enthusiastic or satisfied
with the "way things are going in the U.S."; among those who never go to
church services; among voters who wanted to offer undocumented immigrants a chance for legal status; and among non–gun owners.

The third and fourth questions in table 7 suggest further reasons for
Trump's victory. Republican voters seem to have thought that Trump would
do particularly well in handling two issues: the economy and especially
immigration. Those who wanted a candidate with the "right temperament"
voted for Haley. But as in 2016, many voters favored Trump because he
would "fight for people like me." Trump's remarkable ability to get his beliefs
and opinions accepted by the Republican rank and file is shown in two other

TABLE 5. 2024 Republican presidential primary results (in percentages)

State	Date	Trump	Haley
New Hampshire	January 23	54.3	43.3
South Carolina	February 24	59.8	39.5
Michigan	February 27	68.1	26.6
District of Columbia	March 1–3	33.3	62.8
Alabama	March 5	83.2	13.0
Alaska	March 5	87.6	12.0
Arkansas	March 5	76.9	18.4
California	March 5	79.2	17.4
Colorado	March 5	63.5	33.3
Maine	March 5	71.9	25.4
Massachusetts	March 5	59.6	36.7
Minnesota	March 5	68.9	28.8
North Carolina	March 5	73.8	23.3
Oklahoma	March 5	81.8	15.9
Tennessee	March 5	77.3	19.6
Texas	March 5	77.8	17.4
Virginia	March 5	63.0	35.0
Vermont	March 5	45.1	49.3
Georgia	March 12	84.5	13.2
Mississippi	March 12	92.5	5.4
Washington	March 12	76.4	19.3
Arizona	March 19	78.8	17.8
Florida	March 19	81.2	13.9
Illinois	March 19	80.5	14.5
Kansas	March 19	75.5	16.1
Ohio	March 19	79.2	14.4
Louisiana	March 23	89.8	6.8
Connecticut	April 2	77.9	14.0
Delaware	April 2	Canceled	
New York	April 2	81.1	13.0
Rhode Island	April 2	83.7	10.5
Wisconsin	April 2	79.0	12.7
Pennsylvania	April 23	83.4	16.6
Indiana	May 7	78.3	21.7
Maryland	May 14	77.3	22.7
Nebraska	May 14	79.9	18.2
West Virginia	May 14	88.4	9.4
Kentucky	May 21	85.0	6.4
Oregon	May 21	91.6	0.0
Montana	June 4	90.9	0.0

(continued)

TABLE 5 *(continued)*

State	Date	Trump	Haley
New Jersey	June 4	97.1	0.0
New Mexico	June 4	84.5	8.6
South Dakota	June 4	Canceled	
Total		76.4	19.7

Sources: Most results were taken from "Republican Convention," The Green Papers: 2024 Presidential Primaries, Caucuses, and Conventions, accessed March 11, 2025, https://www.thegreenpapers.com/P24/R. Where that source reported only preliminary results, I tried to get final figures from the website of the state agency responsible for counting and reporting election results.

Note: The Delaware and South Dakota primaries were not held because they were uncontested—that is, Trump was the only candidate.

TABLE 6. 2024 Republican presidential caucus results (in percentages)

State	Date	Trump	Haley	DeSantis
Iowa	January 15	51.0	19.1	21.3
Nevada	February 8	99.1	0.0	0.0
Idaho	March 2	84.9	13.2	1.4
North Dakota	March 4	84.4	14.1	0.0
Utah	March 5	56.4	42.7	0.0
Hawaii	March 12	97.1	1.5	0.6

Notes: Some results are based on media reports and are thus unofficial. Since caucuses are generally run by state parties, no agency compiles an official set of results. Unlike Democratic caucuses, there is no requirement in Republican caucuses that delegates to the next round of meetings be awarded in proportion to the candidates' support in the caucuses and thus no requirement that the presidential preferences of caucus attendees be measured. There appears to be no measure of the preferences of caucus attendees in the Missouri, Montana, and New Mexico caucuses.

questions from the New Hampshire exit poll that are not included in table 7. Fifty-four percent of the voters said that Trump would be "fit for [the] presidency" even "if convicted of a crime." And 51 percent thought Biden had not legitimately won the 2020 election.

Similar results show up in the small number of other states in which the major media organizations conducted exit polls.[16] Of the fourteen primaries held on March 5, Super Tuesday, Haley won just one (Vermont) and held

TABLE 7. Factors affecting the vote in the 2024 New Hampshire Republican presidential primary

Survey question	Percentage of New Hampshire primary voters	Trump	Haley
Party identification			
Republican	50	74	25
Independent	44	39	58
Democrat	6	5	86
Ideology			
Conservative	67	71	27
Moderate	28	25	72
Liberal	6	8	85
Most important issue			
Foreign policy	15	37	62
Abortion	12	26	66
Immigration	30	79	20
Economy	37	55	43
Which candidate quality mattered most?			
Shares my values	30	56	40
Has right temperament	21	14	84
Fights for people like me	31	86	13
Can defeat Biden	14	59	39
Condition of nation's economy			
Excellent/good	25	17	79
Not good/poor	74	68	30
Feeling about way things are going in United States			
Enthusiastic/satisfied	19	24	71
Dissatisfied/angry	79	62	37
Most undocumented immigrants in the United States should be:			
Offered chance at legal status	42	28	68
Deported	55	76	23
Does anyone in your household own a gun?			
Yes	55	62	36
No	45	43	53

(continued)

TABLE 7 *(continued)*

Survey question	Percentage of New Hampshire primary voters	Trump	Haley
How often do you attend religious services?			
Weekly or more	27	62	35
Occasionally	38	56	43
Never	33	47	50
Education			
Never attended college	16	76	22
Some college	19	61	37
Associate's degree	17	64	34
Bachelor's degree	28	45	53
Advanced degree	20	36	60

Source: Edison Research New Hampshire Primary Exit Polls, as reported in "Exit Polls: Exit Poll Results for 2024 Presidential Primaries and Caucuses," CNN, last updated January 26, 2025, https://edition.cnn.com/election/2024/primaries-and -caucuses/exit-polls/new-hampshire/republican-primary/president/0.

Trump below 60 percent in one other (Massachusetts). One day later she suspended her campaign, and Trump clinched the nomination on March 12.

Trump Versus Biden, and Then Harris

By March 12, then, both major party presidential nominations appeared to be set. It would be Biden versus Trump, just as in 2020. But there was one notable difference between the two elections. In 2020, polls that pitted Biden against Trump had always shown Biden with a sizable lead. In the 2024 polls, by contrast, Trump was ahead.

According to the RealClear Polling website, which collects polling results from a large number of polling organizations and computes a running average, at no time between September 1, 2019, and Election Day 2020 did Trump lead Biden. Biden's lead varied from about 4 percentage points to 10 percentage points, but of all the hundred or so national polls conducted after April 2020, exactly one showed Trump ahead.[17] (Four percentage points might not be statistically significant if that number came from just one poll, but since it represents an average of six or eight or a dozen polls, it almost certainly does pass that threshold.) The polls in 2016 told pretty much the same story. There were two brief moments when Trump had a small lead: in May, when he clinched the Republican nomination, and right after the Republican National Convention in July.[18] But the 2024 polls were different. Again using data from RealClear Polling, the last time the polls showed Biden in the lead was in mid-September 2023. Trump's lead after that was less than Biden's had been during the 2020 election cycle—rarely more than 4 percentage points. And polls conducted during the first half of an election year are not a reliable predictor of how the vote will turn out in November. But the polls were enough to make Democrats worry.

Whatever reservations many Democrats had about Biden, the key event that upended the race was his June 27 debate with Trump. Given concerns about Biden's age, every one of his major public appearances was eagerly watched to see if the president appeared capable of performing his duties with a minimum level of competence. In his 2024 State of the Union address, delivered in early March, Biden had clearly passed this admittedly low bar. In the debate, he just as clearly failed. His voice was hoarse and raspy, he sometimes seemed to lose his train of thought, and he failed to rebut many of Trump's more controversial or dubious assertions. Normally when two candidates debate, their partisans and supporters each claim that their side won; and many journalists are reluctant to pronounce a clear winner. In the aftermath of the Biden–Trump skirmish, even the most hardcore liberal commentators said that Biden had looked and sounded awful. In the next few days, columnists at *The Hill*, CNN, *Politico*, *The New York Times*, *USA Today*, and *Vox* all said that Trump won the debate.[19] While other commentators were reluctant to declare Trump the winner given how many lies he had told, they did say that Biden had lost.[20] Even ardent Biden supporters acknowledged that he had had a "bad night."

The chorus of people and organizations that wanted Biden to get out of the race now became louder and more insistent. Within days after the debate, a number of major newspapers—including most prominently *The New York Times*—published editorials urging his withdrawal.[21] Initially, Biden showed no inclination to accept their recommendation. Few politicians are wont to admit that their time has passed, that they are no longer capable of performing effectively. Moreover, Biden had overcome a number of other crises in his political career, including the death of his wife and daughter shortly after he was first elected to the U.S. Senate in 1972 and a plagiarism scandal that forced him out of the presidential nomination contest in 1987. Surely, he seems to have believed, his performance in one debate was just a "Beltway" issue, a concern only to political insiders that failed to register with ordinary voters. Biden also had long believed that he failed to receive proper credit for a number of major achievements during his presidency and hence longed for a chance to make his case to the voters and then "finish the job."[22]

While all of the details surrounding Biden's withdrawal probably won't be known until some of his aides and supporters write their memoirs, a steady drumbeat of criticism and bad news seems to have gradually worn him down.[23] Prominent Democratic campaign "donors canceled fund-raisers and stopped giving money."[24] The media, having largely failed to cover concerns about his mental health before the June 27 debate, now gave the matter such heavy coverage as to crowd out the many issues Democrats thought were more important. The campaign's own polls showed him slipping further behind Trump, both nationally and in the major battleground states. When Richard Nixon was unwilling to resign from the presidency in 1974 even though it was clear that he had virtually no support in Congress, what finally pushed him to accept the inevitable was meetings with major Republican Party leaders like Barry Goldwater. In similar fashion, Democratic leaders like Senate Majority Leader Charles Schumer and former House Speaker Nancy Pelosi conveyed to Biden the worries of many Democratic House and Senate candidates that having him at the top of the ticket might weaken everyone lower on the ballot.

Having insisted for more than three weeks that he would not withdraw, Biden apparently changed his mind late on July 20. On July 21, he released two statements on his X account (the former Twitter). The first said, "I believe it is in the best interests of my party and the country for me to stand down." The second, equally significant announcement read, "Today I want to offer my full support and endorsement for Kamala [Harris] to be the nominee of our party this year."[25] In an interview in August, Biden said his principal reason for withdrawing was that "a number of my Democratic colleagues in the House and Senate thought that I was going to hurt them in the races. And I was concerned if I stayed in the race, that would be the topic. . . . I thought it'd be a real distraction."[26]

If Democratic leaders had any ideas about holding a new nomination contest, Biden's second statement effectively foreclosed that possibility. In fact, just two days later, an Associated Press survey showed that virtually all the convention delegates wanted to nominate Harris for president. In order to comply with Ohio election law, which might otherwise have prevented the Democratic presidential nominee from being listed on that state's general election ballot, the Democrats already had decided to conduct a "virtual roll call" in advance of their convention. To be listed on the virtual roll call ballot, a candidate had to obtain, by July 30, signatures from at least 300 delegates, with no more than 50 from any one state.[27] To no one's surprise, Harris was the only person who qualified, and she then received 4,563 votes out of 4,615 cast (98.9 percent). The other 52 voted "present," the only alternative listed on the virtual ballot.[28]

Grading the Democrats

In evaluating what the Democrats did in 2024, it is important to note that there was no precedent for the situation the party confronted. A number of presidents have announced that they would not seek another term even though they were constitutionally and perhaps politically eligible to do so, but never so late in the election year.[29] Calvin Coolidge, who became president in August 1923 on the death of Warren Harding and was then elected to a full four-year term in 1924, might reasonably have claimed that running again in 1928 did not violate the precedent set by George Washington that no president should serve more than two terms. Instead, Coolidge issued his famous statement that he did "not choose to run for President in nineteen twenty eight." But this statement was released to reporters on August 2, 1927—well before the 1928 presidential nomination races got going (the first primary that year was on March 6, 1928). Harry Truman in 1952 and Lyndon Johnson in 1968 both waited until the primary season had started before withdrawing—but their withdrawal announcements took place at the end of March (March 29 in Truman's case, March 31 in Johnson's), leaving more than enough time for a contested nomination race to take place. In 1972, Democratic vice-presidential nominee Thomas Eagleton had to withdraw from the election after he acknowledged that he had twice received electroshock therapy for clinical depression. But Eagleton's withdrawal occurred nineteen days after the conclusion of the Democratic National Convention. And the problem the Democrats faced that year was to fill the vice-presidential slot, a task that was by then almost entirely at the discretion of the presidential nominee. The official confirmation of George McGovern's selection of Sargent Shriver occurred at a meeting of the Democratic National Committee. When the Democrats created a party "charter" in 1974, that procedure was formalized by a provision that specifically allowed the national committee to fill "vacancies in the nominations for the office of President and Vice President."[30]

But what if the all-but-certain nominee, who had won a clear majority of the primary votes and delegates, as Biden did in 2024, chose to withdraw after the end of the primary season but before the start of the national convention? There is, so far as I can tell, nothing in the party rules that deals with such a situation.

Nothing that the Democrats did in 2024, it should be noted, explicitly violated a state or national party rule. Many states have provisions in their election laws that require delegates elected in the state's presidential primary to vote for the candidate whom they were pledged to support when elected, at least on the first convention ballot. But every such state law that I am aware of specifically says that such a pledge no longer applies if the presidential candidate has ended his or her campaign, as Biden had by withdrawing. Moreover, since 1984 the Democratic Party's delegate selection rules have included a specific provision that reads, "Delegates elected to the national convention pledged to a presidential candidate shall in all good conscience reflect the sentiments of those who elected them."[31] Though it may not be obvious at first reading, this rule was adopted to supersede a 1980 rule that allowed presidential candidates to replace any delegates elected in their name who had changed their minds and decided not to vote for them.[32] In that context, it is clear that while the revised rule encouraged the delegates to honor their pledges, it did not require them to do so. And even if states quixotically required delegates to vote for a candidate even after he or she had withdrawn from the race, the Supreme Court had made clear in several different cases that the national conventions were not required to obey state laws when they conflicted with convention rules.[33]

A case can be made, however, that Harris's nomination violated the spirit of the Democratic rules. The McGovern–Fraser Commission, which rewrote the Democrats' delegate selection rules between 1969 and 1972, had clearly intended to devise a presidential nomination process in which the choice would be made by ordinary voters participating in primaries and caucuses, not by party leaders.[34] This was why the commission issued a series of detailed "guidelines" that all state parties were required to abide by, including a ban on ex officio delegates. A variety of other rules were plainly designed to facilitate popular participation.[35] The McGovern–Fraser guidelines also included a "timeliness" requirement that prevented states from starting their delegate selection processes before the election year. (The so-called window would be tightened in subsequent years.) Before adopting this rule, national convention delegates were chosen by party officials in a number of states who had been chosen in the preceding *midterm* election, before the vast majority of candidates had launched their campaigns and the major issues at stake had been clearly defined. Though this rule said nothing about what would happen after the delegates were chosen, the clear implication was that the delegates would be selected at a time when ordinary voters knew who the candidates were and what policies they were advocating. That said, any reasonable presidential nomination process has to handle not just the typical situation but also unexpected circumstances—and it was just this sort of exceptional case that the Democrats faced in 2024.

Could the Democratic Party have devised a different process for nominating its presidential candidate after Biden withdrew in 2024? It is difficult to think how such a process could have worked, given the highly compressed timetable. To repeat the key dates, Biden announced his withdrawal on July 21; the Democratic National Convention was scheduled to start on August 19, just four weeks later. And the relevant time period for conducting an alternative process was probably even narrower, due to the previously mentioned provision in Ohio election law. That provision required that in order to be listed on the state's general election ballot, the major parties had to have named their presidential and vice-presidential candidates ninety days before the November election day—in 2024, that meant by August 7. (Faced with criticism, the Ohio legislature had passed a law changing the date of candidate certification, but it was unclear whether the new law applied to the 2024 election.)[36] The only alternative I am aware of to the process the Democrats followed was proposed by erstwhile presidential candidate Dean Phillips. He wanted to hold a straw poll of the national convention delegates to determine the party's four top presidential aspirants. Those four candidates would then take part in four forums in which they would lay out their qualifications and policy positions. The choice among these four candidates would then be made by the delegates at the national convention.[37] (How Phillips proposed to deal with the Ohio law is unclear.) One final constraint on the Democrats' options was that although Harris had many weaknesses as a presidential candidate, any attempt to deny her the nomination would almost certainly have stirred up the fervent opposition of two important Democratic constituency groups: Black voters and women.[38] In the end, the Democrats decided to handle the 2024 nomination in the least chaotic way possible, by nominating Biden's vice president, who would have been his running mate again in 2024 and thus would have become president if Biden died or resigned after being reelected. Anyone who voted for Biden in the primaries or caucuses presumably would have known that.

But if the "process" by which Harris was nominated cannot be faulted on legal or rule-based grounds, there are ample grounds for thinking that the Democratic Party was ill served by it. In nominating Harris, the Democrats had someone at the head of their ticket who was not well regarded by the American public and had never demonstrated the ability to wage an effective national campaign. Through most of the Biden presidency, her favorability ratings were lower than those of Biden and Trump. Her short-lived campaign for the Democratic presidential nomination in

2020 had been distinctly unimpressive. Her one great moment, ironically, had been in a debate in which she criticized Joe Biden for saying that he got along with pro-segregation Southern senators. In a Quinnipiac poll conducted shortly after that debate, Harris was supported by 20 percent of the nation's Democrats, a statistical tie with Biden. But she was unable to follow up on this opening: One month later, her support had fallen to 7 percent.[39] She ended her candidacy on December 3, 2019, two months before the start of the delegate selection season.

Harris's selection as Biden's running mate was testimony to her résumé— her experience as San Francisco district attorney and California attorney general, her four years in the U.S. Senate—but also to the Democratic Party's preoccupation with identity politics. In March 2020, after he was already the all-but-certain Democratic nominee, Biden had explicitly committed himself to picking a woman as his vice-presidential candidate, apparently in the belief that doing so would help unify the party. Over the next several months, pressure grew for Biden to pick a Black woman running mate. And if he was determined to do so, Harris was the almost prohibitive choice: She was the only Black woman in the Senate at the time, and there were no Black women serving as governors.

The Democratic Party might have been better served in 2024 if Harris had been required to fight for her nomination rather than having it given to her by default. As a columnist for *The Boston Globe* observed several days after Trump's general election victory, "Being forced to compete for the support of primary voters or even convention delegates would have made Harris or another Democrat much stronger—more adept at differentiating their candidacy from Biden's unpopular policies and fleshing out their own. But that would have required Biden to decline a second term far earlier than he did—by the summer of 2023 at the latest, rather than the summer of 2024." Or as this columnist summed up the situation in pithier terms, "If this election had a box score, Biden would be the losing pitcher."[40]

Vice-Presidential Selections and the National Conventions

Two final tasks remained that are part of the presidential nomination process: choosing the vice-presidential candidates and holding the national conventions.

As the out-party, the Republicans went first. The Republican National Convention was held in Milwaukee on July 15–18, and on the first day, Trump announced that he had selected Ohio Senator J. D. Vance as his running mate. As many Democrats pointed out, Vance had once been a sharp critic of Trump's. During the 2016 campaign, Vance told his former law school roommate that he went "back and forth between thinking" that Trump was either a "cynical asshole like Nixon" or "America's Hitler." Of Trump's policies, he wrote, "To every complex problem, he offers a simple solution. . . . He never offers details for how these plans will work, because he can't." In one 2016 interview, Vance described himself as a "'Never Trump' guy. I never liked him." In another interview, he said he would probably vote for a third-party candidate because he "can't stomach Trump."[41] As of early 2020, Vance showed no signs of having changed his mind, saying that Trump had "just so thoroughly failed to deliver on his economic populism."[42]

But Vance changed his tune when he decided to run for an Ohio Senate seat in 2022, offering praise for Trump's presidency, seeking and eventually getting Trump's endorsement. As a senator, Vance soon emerged as one of Trump's strongest and most articulate defenders, echoing Trump's claims that the 2020 election had been stolen and standing "by [his] side at the New York courthouse during his criminal hush money trial." Besides his media skills, probably his principal appeal to Trump was that as someone who grew up in a blue-collar family and now represented an important swing state, Vance might attract votes from a number of groups that Trump saw as central to victory in the 2024 campaign. In announcing Vance's selection on his Truth Social account, Trump said that "during the Campaign, [he] will be strongly focused on the people he fought so brilliantly for, the American Workers and Farmers in Pennsylvania, Michigan, Wisconsin, Ohio, Minnesota, and far beyond."[43] Vance also was aligned with Trump on all of his major campaign themes: He favored protectionism and a stronger effort to curb illegal immigration, and he opposed military aid to Ukraine.

Two days before the Republican convention opened, at a rally in Pennsylvania, Trump was hit in the ear and almost killed by an AR-15-wielding gunman shooting from a nearby rooftop. After initially crouching behind his podium to protect himself from further shots, Trump eventually stood up, raised his fist, and seemed to shout the word "fight" twice. Trump as a heroic fighter thus became a major theme of the Republican convention. His acceptance speech lasted ninety-three minutes, the longest such speech in American history. For anyone who has followed Trump's political career, one of the more striking aspects of the speech was his pledge, "The discord and division in our society must be healed. . . . I am running to be president for all of America, not half of America, because there is no victory in winning for half of America."[44]

The Democratic National Convention was held in Chicago from August 19 to 22, but to make sure that their names were listed on the Ohio ballots, Harris's choice for the party's vice-presidential candidate was

announced on August 6: Minnesota Governor Tim Walz. Given the truncated process by which she had won the Democratic presidential nomination, Harris was clearly concerned that her choice help unify the party. Walz
was a former teacher and a strong union supporter, who as governor had
pushed the state to adopt what were called "sweeping protections" for
abortion rights. Two items on his résumé might have been seen as broadening the party's appeal to men (though hopes that a vice-presidential candidate will attract votes based on his or her personal characteristics rarely
work out). Walz had served twenty-four years in the Army National Guard
and had once been a football coach. In light of Harris's inability to carry
any of the major swing states, it is worth noting that she personally inter-
viewed three potential running mates before making her final choice: Arizona Governor Mark Kelly, Pennsylvania Governor Josh Shapiro, and Walz.
Though most studies have found that vice-presidential candidates add few
votes to their party's ticket—people vote for president, not vice president—
one of the few exceptions to that generalization is that vice-presidential
nominees can increase a party's vote by a small but potentially significant
margin in the candidate's own home state. Arizona and Pennsylvania were
on everybody's list of swing states in 2024; solidly blue Minnesota was not.

Though the Democratic convention was generally rated as a political
success—the party was clearly united, both Walz and Harris gave well-
regarded acceptance speeches—it is surprising that the Democrats didn't
give great visibility to the significant number of Republicans and former
Trump administration officials who had announced their unwillingness to
vote for him in 2024. In most recent conventions, both parties have tried to
feature at least one person from the opposite party who was declining to support his or her party's presidential nominee. At the 2004 Republican convention, for example, the keynote speech was given by Democratic Senator Zell
Miller of Georgia. The Democratic convention that year gave a prime-time
speaking slot to Ron Reagan, the former president's son, who criticized President George W. Bush for the restrictions he had placed on federally funded
embryonic stem cell research. The only speaker of this kind at the 2024
Democratic convention was former Rep. Adam Kinzinger, hardly a household
name or a person with special expertise for assessing Trump's presidency.

Conclusion

A recurrent feature of contemporary American presidential nominations is
that large numbers of the potential electorate are dissatisfied with both of the
major party choices. According to the general election exit polls, a majority of

the 2024 voters had unfavorable opinions of both Trump and Harris. This undoubtedly is, to some extent, a reflection of the highly polarized state of American politics. If you liked Trump, it was unlikely that you liked Harris, and vice versa. (A scant 2 percent of voters had a favorable opinion of both.)[45] Though Trump will no doubt operate as if he received a decisive mandate from the voters, there is ample evidence in the exit polls to think otherwise. Just 22 percent of the voters said they were "excited" about the prospect of a Trump presidency; 35 percent were "scared," another 14 percent "concerned." Perhaps the biggest factor working in Trump's favor was dissatisfaction with the Biden presidency: 59 percent of general election voters disapproved of Biden's performance, with 45 percent saying they "strongly disapproved." Sixty-eight percent of voters said that the condition of the economy was "not good" or "poor," versus 5 percent who thought it was "excellent."

Perhaps if Biden had withdrawn earlier, the Democrats might have nominated someone else, or they would have nominated a more battle-tested version of Harris, one who had a better sense of how to run a national campaign and who would have had a greater opportunity to define some of her policy views and put at least a bit of distance between Biden and herself. Given when he did bow out, Harris was the party's overwhelming choice to succeed him. On the Republican side, one can tell a lot of "what if" stories about Trump's path to victory in the 2016 nomination contest. But by 2024, he was undeniably the favorite choice of most Republicans. Though a sizable number of conservative and Republican (or ex-Republican) intellectuals are appalled by Trump, their opinion is plainly not shared by very many ordinary voters. In 2024, Trump won 90 percent of the votes cast by self-identified conservatives, 94 percent by Republican identifiers. Though 54 percent of all voters said that Trump's views were "too extreme," it is unlikely that this will persuade him to modify his views, especially given that he has, at least for the next two years, supportive majorities in the House and the Senate. The good news for Democrats is that by 2026, he won't have Joe Biden to kick around anymore.

Notes

1. As discussed later, Lyndon Johnson eventually chose not to run for reelection in 1968, but not until March 31, two and a half weeks after he almost lost the New Hampshire primary to Eugene McCarthy. Harry Truman chose not to run for what would have been a third term in 1952 (at least as a term is defined in the Twenty-Second Amendment), but he did run for a second term in 1948.

2. Transcribed speech often includes a significant number of "uhs" and "ers" that are less noticeable when listening to the same content.

3. For various perspectives on this issue, see, among others, Jill Filipovic, "The Biden Blame Game," *Slate*, July 8, 2024, https://slate.com/news-and -politics/2024/07/joe-biden-debate-the-media-did-not-cover-up-aging -problems.html; Jeffrey M. McCall, "Why Didn't the Media Question Biden's Fitness for Office Until Now?" *Hill*, July 10, 2024, https://thehill .com/opinion/campaign/4762423-media-omission-biden-cognitive -challenges; Francine Kiefer, "Reporting on the President's Acuity: It's Harder Than It Looks," *Christian Science Monitor*, July 24, 2024, https:// www.csmonitor.com/USA/Politics/2024/0712/biden-age-white-house -media-mental; Brian Stelter, "Did the Media Botch the Biden Age Story?," *Vox*, July 3, 2024, https://www.vox.com/politics/358877/biden-age-debate -media-coverage; David Bauder, "Why Was It a Surprise? Biden's Debate Problems Leave Some Wondering If the Press Missed the Story," Associated Press, July 3, 2024, https://apnews.com/article/biden-media-condition -late-b8f568526dda9a66f2af9806903e76fa; and Hadas Gold, "Biden's Mental Fitness Could Have Been Better Covered Leading Up to the Debate, Some White House Reporters Acknowledge," CNN, July 2, 2024, https://www.cnn.com/2024/07/02/media/biden-mental-fitness /index.html.

4. In the academic literature, this is generally known as the divisive primary hypothesis. For arguments and evidence in support of this hypothesis, see, among others, Martin P. Wattenberg, "The Republican Presidential Advantage in the Age of Party Disunity," in *The Politics of Divided Government*, ed. Gary W. Cox and Samuel Kernell (Westview, 1991); Robert A. Bernstein, "Divisive Primaries Do Hurt: U.S. Senate Races, 1956–1972," *American Political Science Review* 71 (June 1977): 540–545; James I. Lengle, "Divisive Presidential Primaries and Party Electoral Prospects, 1932– 1976," *American Politics Quarterly* 8 (July 1980): 261–277; and Patrick J. Kenney and Tom W. Rice, "The Relationship Between Divisive Primaries and General Election Outcomes," *American Journal of Political Science* 31 (February 1987): 31–44. For my own critique of this literature, see William G. Mayer, *The Divided Democrats: Ideological Unity, Party Reform, and Presidential Elections* (Westview, 1996), chap. 3.

5. For a detailed demonstration of the points made here, see William G. Mayer, "The Presidential Nominations," in *The Elections of 2020*, ed. Michael Nelson (University of Virginia Press, 2021).

6. See Ben Mathis-Lilley, "Joe Biden Is Pivoting to the Left. What? Why?," *Slate*, May 15, 2020, https://slate.com/news-and-politics/2020/05/joe-biden -is-pivoting-to-the-left-what-why.html; and Hans Nichols, "Biden's Centrist Mirage," *Axios*, September 4, 2020, https://www.axios.com/2020/09 /04/joe-biden-shifting-center.

7. Federal law requires "an individual running for federal office [to] register . . . when he or she raises or spends more than $5,000 in contributions or expenditures." "Registering as a Candidate," Federal Election Commission, accessed November 4, 2024, https://www.fec.gov/help -candidates-and-committees/registering-candidate/. Nevertheless, every four years hundreds of Americans who have no chance of getting nominated, appearing in a debate, or getting one line of media coverage file forms with the FEC, apparently because they like the cachet of claiming that they are "official" presidential candidates.

8. In 2020, Joseph P. Kennedy III, then a four-term member of the U.S. House of Representatives, decided to challenge incumbent Senator Edward Markey in the Democratic primary. Markey handily beat Kennedy, 55 percent to 45 percent.

9. Quoted in Mike Wendling, "'I Am Not a Church Boy': RFK Jr Responds to Sex Assault Allegation," BBC, July 2, 2024, https://www.bbc.com/news /articles/c6p27evjz49o.

10. Will Weissert, "Marianne Williamson Begins Longshot 2024 Challenge to Biden," Associated Press, March 4, 2023, https://apnews.com/article /marianne-williamson-president-2024-biden-democratic-primary -14e59754bed9e0c54dad4fdfbbc1fa6b.

11. The three survey organizations were Quinnipiac, Marquette Law School, and Fox News / Beacon Research.

12. This explains why many media organizations included Wayne Messam, mayor of Miramar, Florida, and Richard Ojeda, a West Virginia state senator, whenever they published a list of the candidates for the 2020 Democratic presidential nomination.

13. One general election in which the debates are widely believed to have made a large difference is the Kennedy–Nixon contest in 1960. In fact, however, polls indicate that the race was essentially tied before the debates: In the Gallup polls, for example, Nixon had a statistically insignificant 1 percentage-point lead in the final poll before the debates. And the final vote showed the popular vote to be tied. Indeed, if the votes in Alabama are counted correctly, Nixon actually won a small plurality. As Irwin Gellman has concluded in the most recent academic book on the election, "The Kennedy proposition that the debates were the deciding factor in the election seems an exaggeration. . . . Even given his [Kennedy's] superior performance in the first round—the one enshrined in the JFK legend— there is no plausible argument that the debates decided the election. Other factors were far more important." Irwin F. Gellman, *The Campaign of the Century: Kennedy, Nixon, and the Election of 1960* (Yale University Press, 2021), 216.

14. On the Atlanta debate and Mondale's "Where's the beef?" line, see Jack W. Germond and Jules Witcover, *Wake Us When It's Over: Presidential*

Politics of 1984 (Macmillan, 1985), 187–190. On the 1980 Nashua debate, see Jack W. Germond and Jules Witcover, *Blue Smoke and Mirrors: How Reagan Won and Carter Lost the Election of 1980* (Viking, 1981), 125–130; and Michael J. Birkner, "That Defining Moment: The 1980 Nashua Debate," *Historical New Hampshire* 42 (Fall 1987): 283–296, https:// cupola.gettysburg.edu/cgi/viewcontent.cgi?referer=&httpsredir =1&article=1013&context=histfac.

15. For a detailed account of this debate, see William G. Mayer, "The Nominations: The Road to a Much-Liked General Election," in *The Elections of 2016*, ed. Michael Nelson (CQ Press, 2018), 49.

16. Normally, the major networks conduct exit polls in conjunction with every primary and caucus until the race is settled. In 2024, they seem to have concluded that the race was over after New Hampshire and South Carolina, even though Trump had by then accumulated only a fraction of the delegates needed for nomination. The result was that exit polls were conducted in just three of the fourteen states that held primaries or caucuses on Super Tuesday (California, North Carolina, and Virginia). For reasons that are far from clear, the media consortium that sponsors the exit polls also decided to conduct a poll for the Ohio primary, which was held on March 19, by which time all of Trump's opponents had withdrawn from the race and he did have a majority of the delegates.

17. The outlier was a Rasmussen poll of September 9–15, 2020. For the full data, see "2020 General Election: Trump vs Biden," RealClear Polling, accessed November 13, 2024, https://www.realclearpolling.com/polls /president/general/2020/trump-vs-biden.

18. "2016 General Election: Trump vs Clinton," RealClear Polling, accessed November 19, 2024, https://www.realclearpolling.com/polls/president /general/2016/trump-vs-clinton.

19. Based on the list compiled in "Withdrawal of Joe Biden from the 2024 United States Presidential Election," Wikipedia, accessed November 12, 2024, https://en.wikipedia.org/wiki/Withdrawal_of_Joe_Biden_from _the_2024_United_States_presidential_election. In every case, the news outlet named was linked to an article on the web.

20. Ibid.

21. For a sampling of early newspaper editorials on this topic, see Nick Robertson, "These Major Media Outlets Have Called for Biden to Drop Out," *Hill*, June 30, 2024, https://thehill.com/homenews/media/4748637-biden -debate-step-aside-newspapers. The *New York Times* editorial is "To Serve His Country, President Biden Should Leave the Race," June 28, 2024.

22. The quoted phrase was used several times by Biden when he announced his reelection bid in April 2023.

23. My discussion of Biden's withdrawal draws on Eli Stokols et al., "Why Biden Finally Quit," *Politico*, July 21, 2024, https://www.politico.com/news

/2024/07/21/why-biden-dropped-out-00170106; Michael D. Shear et al., "He Still Thought He Could Win: Inside Biden's Decision to Drop Out," *New York Times*, August 15, 2024; Mike Wendling, "Biden Explains Why He Dropped Out of White House Race," BBC, August 11, 2024, https://www.bbc.com/news/articles/c1l5n2gy74vo; and Brian Bennett and Philip Elliott, "Why Joe Biden Dropped Out," *Time*, July 21, 2024.

24. Shear et al., "He Still Thought."

25. For the full text of both announcements, see Jeongyoon Han, "Want to Know What Biden Said When He Dropped Out? The Full Letter Is Here," National Public Radio, July 21, 2024, https://www.npr.org/2024/07/21/g-s1 -12544/biden-letter-withdraw-harris-endorsement.

26. Quoted in Shear et al., "He Still Thought."

27. Details on the Democrats' virtual roll call are taken from Aaron Navarro, "The DNC's Virtual Roll Call to Nominate Kamala Harris Started August 1. Here's How the Vote Works," CBS News, August 2, 2024, https://www.cbsnews.com/news/dnc-virtual-roll-call-2024-how-it-works.

28. These results are taken from Robert Yoon, "Harris Wins Democratic Presidential Nomination in Virtual Roll Call. Here's How the Process Worked," Associated Press, August 6, 2024, https://apnews.com/article /kamala-harris-nomination-virtual-roll-call-explainer-c42bbf87ac85f359 b84607ea55d1ca4a.

29. The Twenty-Second Amendment to the Constitution was ratified in 1951 and thus did not apply to Coolidge. It also specifically did not apply to "any person holding the office of President when this Article was proposed by the Congress." Having been proposed by Congress in 1947, the amendment thus exempted Truman. And since it counted as a term only an instance when a person had succeeded to the presidency for "more than two years," it didn't apply to Lyndon Johnson in 1968.

30. "The Charter and Bylaws of the Democratic Party of the United States," as amended September 10, 2020, art. 3, sec. 1(c), https://democrats.org/wp -content/uploads/2024/12/DNC-Charter-Bylaws-09.10.1022.pdf.

31. Democratic National Committee, "Delegate Selection Rules for the 2024 Democratic National Convention," accessed November 5, 2024, rule 13J, democrats.org/wp-content/uploads/2024/07/2024-Delegate-Selection -Rules.pdf.

32. The 1980 rule had been a major source of contention between the Carter and Kennedy forces at the 1980 convention. See Germond and Witcover, *Blue Smoke and Mirrors*, 199–202.

33. The seminal cases on this issue are *Cousins v. Wigoda*, 419 U.S. 477 (1975); and *Democratic Party of the United States v. Wisconsin ex rel. LaFollette*, 450 U.S. 107 (1981).

34. The best account of what the McGovern–Fraser Commission did and why it did it is now (and probably will continue to be for the next century)

Byron E. Shafer, *Quiet Revolution: The Struggle for the Democratic Party and the Shaping of Post-Reform Politics* (Russell Sage, 1983).

35. For the full set of guidelines, see Commission on Party Structure and Delegate Selection, *Mandate for Reform* (Democratic National Committee, 1970), 38–48. The ban on ex officio delegates is guideline C-2.

36. The Ohio law and the Democrats' plan to deal with it are discussed in Sam Cabral, "Democrats Unveil Plan to Get Biden on the Ohio Ballot," BBC, May 28, 2024, https://www.bbc.com/news/articles/crggxmord230; and Navarro, "DNC's Virtual Roll Call."

37. The Phillips proposal is discussed in Mark Zdechlik, "Rep. Phillips Backs Harris for President but Wants Other Contenders Heard," Minnesota Public Radio News, July 22, 2024, https://www.mprnews.org/story/2024/07/22/rep-dean-phillips-backs-harris-for-president-wants-other-contenders-heard.

38. The efforts of a group of Black women to make sure that Harris was nominated are reported in Errin Haines, "How Kamala Harris Earned the Nomination," 19th, August 7, 2024, https://19thnews.org/2024/08/errin-haines-the-amendment-how-kamala-harris-earned-the-nomination.

39. For the data, see Mayer, "Presidential Nominations," 38–39.

40. Brian Bergstein, "Biden Blew It," *Boston Globe*, November 10, 2024.

41. All quotations are taken from Amy B. Wang and Meryl Kornfield, "The Not-So-Kind Things J.D. Vance Said About Trump Before He Was VP Pick," *Washington Post*, July 15, 2024.

42. Peter Jamison, "JD Vance, in 2020 Messages, Said Trump 'Thoroughly Failed to Deliver,'" *Washington Post*, September 27, 2024.

43. For the full text of Trump's announcement, see "Statement by Donald Trump Announcing the Selection of J.D. Vance as the Republican Vice Presidential Nominee," American Presidency Project, July 15, 2024, https://www.presidency.ucsb.edu/documents/statement-donald-trump-announcing-the-selection-jd-vance-the-republican-vice-presidential.

44. For the full text of Trump's speech, see "Read the Transcript of Donald J. Trump's Convention Speech," *New York Times*, July 19, 2024.

45. All results cited here are taken from "Election 2024: Exit Polls," CNN, last updated December 13, 2024, https://edition.cnn.com/election/2024/exit-polls/national-results/general/president/0.

The Presidential Election

THE EMPIRE STRIKES BACK

MARC J. HETHERINGTON

NEARLY EVERY RECENT presidential election has featured something unprecedented—the first in which the Supreme Court intervened, thereby deciding the winner (2000), the first with a Black major party nominee and election winner (2008), the first with a woman major party nominee (2016), and the first contested during a pandemic with significant voting done by mail (2020). The election of 2024 was no exception, only with many unprecedented features. Never before had a party's presumptive nominee been convicted of multiple felonies the summer before the general election, as Donald Trump was in May 2024 for falsifying business records to cover up hush money payments made to Stormy Daniels, who alleged having an affair with him. Never before had a party's presumptive nominee withdrawn from the race so close to the general election, as Joe Biden did in late July after a disastrous debate performance. Kamala Harris then became the presumptive nominee a mere one hundred days before Election Day, another unprecedented development in the modern era. And never before had a major party candidate survived an assassination attempt during the campaign,[1] as Trump did at a rally in Butler, Pennsylvania, weeks before the Republican National Convention. Trump was targeted a second time at a golf course in Florida, although the would-be assassin was discovered before firing his weapon.

In a less polarized time, when voting decisions were not so tightly tied to people's partisanship, Trump's felony convictions, Biden's historically bad debate, Harris's introduction as his replacement, and Trump's near-death experience would have led to wide swings in pre-election polls. Big events or campaign tactics like those during the presidential campaign used to sometimes move a substantial number of voters from one camp into the other. In 1988, for example, Michael Dukakis, the Democratic nominee, led George H. W. Bush by 17 points after his party's convention but ended up losing the election by 7 points. Polarization has made wide swings like that a thing of the past. Because most partisans absolutely despise the other party these days, defecting from their own party's presidential candidate no longer feels like an option even if they might think that candidate is flawed.

Strong partisanship in the electorate reduces the number of people who change their vote intention over the course of the campaign. Based on the Cook Political Report's aggregated average of all available national surveys from January through November 2024, Trump never led by more than 3 points, and even that margin appeared only briefly in the days directly after a Biden debate performance that left many seriously wondering whether the president suffered from dementia.[2] In another era, a debate disaster of that magnitude would have led to a swing of 10 points or more. Similarly, Harris never led by more than 3 points even after the remarkably successful Democratic National Convention in August and a seeming thirst in the electorate for something different from two old white men who'd been duking it out for most of the year.

Despite 2024's many unprecedented developments, it is perhaps predictable that the popular vote margin and Electoral College margin ended up being close—very much like almost every election since 2000. For the sixth time in seven elections, the popular vote margin was less than 4.5 percentage points, with Trump ahead by 1.55 percentage points at the time of this writing. The only other string of American presidential elections that were similarly close in the popular vote occurred between 1876 and 1896. As for the Electoral College, fully thirty-five states and the District of Columbia have now voted for the same party's presidential candidate in every election since 2000, and another six have voted the same way in six of these seven elections.

Trump's Electoral College map in 2024 (map 1) is almost precisely the same as it was in 2016, with Nevada the only state that voted for him in 2024 but not the first time he ran in 2016. Modern Democrats always dominate in New England, most of the middle Atlantic region, and along the Pacific coast. Modern Republicans always dominate in the South and the Great Plains. The Rust Belt—industrial states running from Pennsylvania in the East to Wisconsin in the West—and the desert Southwest are more up for grabs. As I will develop later, the difference between Trump winning in 2016 and 2024 but losing in 2020 can be boiled down to the outcomes in three states—Wisconsin, Michigan, and Pennsylvania. A shift of a little more than 230,000 across those three states in 2024 would have delivered the White House to Harris. Table 1 includes the percentage vote for both major party candidates across all states.

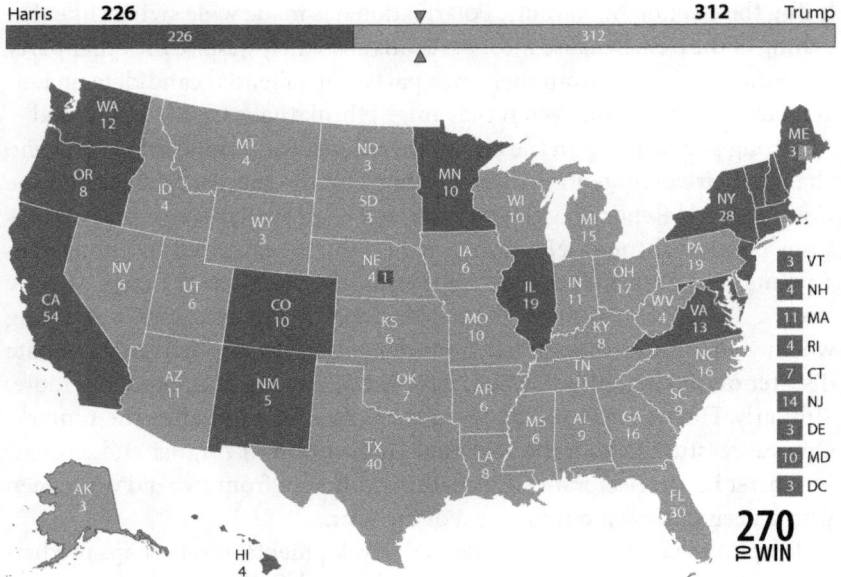

MAP 1. 2024 Electoral College map
Source: "2024 Presidential Election Results," 270ToWin, accessed March 11, 2025, https://www.270towin.com/maps/2024-actual-electoral-map.

TABLE 1. Election outcome by state, 2024 (in percentages)

	Trump	Harris	Trump margin
Alabama	65	34	31
Alaska	55	41	14
Arizona	52	47	5
Arkansas	64	34	30
California	38	58	−20
Colorado	43	54	−11
Connecticut	42	56	−14
Delaware	42	57	−15
District of Columbia	6	90	−84
Florida	56	43	13
Georgia	51	49	2
Hawaii	37	61	−24
Idaho	67	30	37
Illinois	44	55	−11
Indiana	59	40	19
Iowa	56	43	13

(continued)

Table 1 *(continued)*

	Trump	Harris	Trump margin
Kansas	57	41	16
Kentucky	65	34	31
Louisiana	60	38	22
Maine	45	52	−7
Maryland	34	63	−29
Massachusetts	36	61	−25
Michigan	50	48	2
Minnesota	47	51	−4
Mississippi	61	38	23
Missouri	58	40	18
Montana	58	38	20
Nebraska	59	39	20
Nevada	51	47	4
New Hampshire	46	52	−6
New Jersey	46	52	−6
New Mexico	46	52	−6
New York	44	56	−12
North Carolina	51	48	3
North Dakota	67	31	36
Ohio	55	44	11
Oklahoma	66	32	34
Oregon	41	55	−14
Pennsylvania	50	49	1
Rhode Island	42	56	−14
South Carolina	58	40	18
South Dakota	63	34	29
Tennessee	64	34	30
Texas	56	42	14
Utah	59	38	21
Vermont	32	64	−32
Virginia	46	56	−10
Washington	39	57	−18
West Virginia	70	28	42
Wisconsin	50	49	1
Wyoming	72	26	46

Pre–General Election Period

It is impossible to tell the story of the 2024 presidential election without considering the four years preceding it. Many political observers believed that the January 6, 2021, insurrection and invasion of the Capitol Building by Trump's supporters ended his political career. After alleging without evidence for weeks that widespread voter fraud had robbed him of victory in 2020, Trump gave an incendiary outdoor speech in Washington, DC, to an angry crowd that believed his assertions about fraud. After Trump urged them to "fight like hell" for him, the crowd transformed into a violent mob. After marching to the Capitol, it quickly overwhelmed Capitol police and breached the Capitol itself for the first time since the British army did so during the War of 1812. As they marauded through the building, insurrectionists chanted "Kill Mike Pence," in reference to Trump's vice president, who refused his entreaties not to certify the electoral vote count. The National Guard finally restored order several hours later, allowing Congress to perform its role in the certification process in favor of the rightful winner, Joe Biden. For his part in the insurrection, Trump was impeached for the second time by the House of Representatives. Although seven Republican senators voted to remove him, along with all fifty Democrats, the vote fell ten votes short of conviction.

In the months that followed, Trump faced criminal indictments both federal and state, for a range of alleged misdeeds. Although a full account of them is beyond the scope of this chapter, they included unlawfully retaining highly classified documents from his time as president, conspiring to overturn the presidential election through his actions on and before January 6, and falsifying business records to obscure the hush money payments he had made in 2016 to Daniels. As a result, Trump did not seem like a lock to receive the Republican nomination a third time. Even under normal circumstances, it is rare for a party to renominate someone who lost the previous election. Adlai Stevenson, in 1956, was the most recent losing major party candidate to be renominated four years after losing. Grover Cleveland, in 1892, was the only president to have won the White House (1884), lose his next race (1888), and then return to win again.

With Trump seemingly on the ropes, several candidates threw their hats in the ring for the 2024 Republican nomination, but few were considered high quality. One high-quality aspirant was Florida Governor Ron DeSantis. He received significant backing from big-money donors and was perceived as the most viable alternative to Trump. Even so, polls showed that Trump's hold on the party remained strong.[3] With DeSantis not yet officially in the race in January 2023, Trump led him by about 10 percentage points in the polls. By the time DeSantis joined the race in May, he found himself down by 30 points. His candidacy was so unsuccessful that he dropped out before the primary season began in earnest. Another high-quality candidate, Nikki Haley, the former South Carolina governor and UN ambassador under Trump, emerged as the only credible alternative to Trump. But her support among Republican voters in the polls never eclipsed 25 percent. It was abundantly clear by the first months of 2024 that Trump would again be the Republican nominee for president.

The Democratic nomination seemed settled, until it wasn't. Biden enjoyed several important political victories in the first two years of his presidency. The country began to emerge from the pandemic, and his signature legislative achievements, the Bipartisan Infrastructure Law and the Inflation Reduction Act, were enacted. Of course, not all went swimmingly even then. The U.S. withdrawal from Afghanistan in 2021 was chaotic and involved some loss of life. More politically consequential than Afghanistan, inflation rates remained stubbornly high for the first time since the 1970s, in part because of high levels of government spending tied to mitigating the economic slowdown from the pandemic. Most countries experienced similar economic challenges, often worse than those in the United States, but this meant little to American voters.

High inflation is particularly dangerous to incumbent administrations. Unlike high unemployment, which might directly affect 10 percent of the population, inflation affects everyone who shops at the grocery store or buys gas at the service station—basically everyone. Every time people pay for something, they are reminded that prices are higher than they used to be. Even when inflation rates come down, moreover, prices do not. They just increase at a slower rate. As a result, inflation tends to make people feel worse off economically, even if their wages are going up in concert with the rate of inflation.

In 2022, Biden's approval rating remained in the low to mid-40s, not an enviable position with reelection two years away. Usually the first midterm election that the incumbent president's party faces leads to a loss of seats in Congress, especially when the president's approval is low. But Democrats' future electoral fortunes received a shot in the arm from, of all places, the conservative-leaning U.S. Supreme Court. In June 2022, it handed down *Dobbs v. Jackson Women's Health Organization*, which overturned the court's 1973 *Roe v. Wade* decision that ensured abortion rights. *Dobbs* returned regulation of abortion to the states, with many deciding to reduce the number of weeks in which a pregnancy could be terminated by abortion.

A public backlash against the decision ensued. The percentage of Americans calling themselves pro-choice surged, which benefited the Democrats because they are the pro-choice political party.[4] Though it looked like persistent inflation and low Biden approval might lead to big Republican gains in the 2022 midterm election, they failed to materialize. Many credit the unpopularity of the *Dobbs* decision for the Democrats' maintaining control of the U.S. Senate and picking up a couple of seats in the House of Representatives.

It may seem strange to dwell on the 2022 elections in attempting to understand what happened in 2024. The reason I do is that the Democrats' strong showing changed the party's political calculus going forward. When Biden was elected president in 2020, he was seventy-eight years old, and his age, even then, was viewed as a liability. In fact, he implied that, if elected in 2020, he would likely only serve a single term. After the electoral success Democrats enjoyed in 2022, however, Biden felt less pressure to turn things over to the next generation of leaders. Despite persistent media reports that his cognitive acuity might be slipping during the second half of his first term, he sought the party's nomination. No credible candidates challenged him, and he breezed through the primaries, setting the stage for a rematch with former President Trump.

According to the Cook Political Report's polling averages, Biden lagged Trump by a few points as late as May 2024. After Trump's conviction on felony charges in the last days of that month, Biden moved into a polling dead heat with Trump. Democrats were optimistic that Biden would eventually surge past Trump. That did not occur. The first and only debate between Biden and Trump was a disaster for the president. Biden began the night by shuffling across the stage looking diminished physically. His voice throughout the debate was soft and weak. He jumbled words and failed to put thoughts together. His answers to moderators' questions drifted this way and that. In short, he looked like an eighty-two-year-old in decline, not a picture of vibrant presidential leadership, and certainly not one who could serve for another four years. Democratic leaders, such as former House Speaker Nancy Pelosi, and big Democratic donors, including the actor George Clooney, encouraged Biden to exit the race. Soon after the Republican National Convention in mid-July, Biden finally announced his departure.

With barely one hundred days until the election, the only plausible alternative to Biden was Vice President Kamala Harris. She injected enthusiasm into the Democratic faithful. What had looked like a long, impossible slog with postdebate Biden as the candidate transformed into a real possibility of victory overnight. Changing gears so close to the election was a daunting task, but the Harris campaign made a remarkably smooth transition. She chose Tim Walz, the governor of Minnesota, as her running mate. Like Harris, he was in his fifties and possessed a "happy warrior" spirit reminiscent of Hubert Humphrey, a fellow Minnesotan and the

Democrats' presidential nominee in 1968. After a successful convention marked by positive "vibes" and punctuated by celebrity endorsements of the ticket by the likes of Oprah Winfrey, Taylor Swift, and Beyoncé, the Democrats were optimistic they could beat Trump again.

The Fundamentals

Before exploring the dynamics of the campaign for those one hundred or so days, it is critical to establish the terrain on which the battle for president would be fought. Political scientists often refer to this terrain as the fundamentals of the race. Journalists tend to focus on the ups and downs of various campaign events because it gives them something new to write about from day to day, but the fact is that campaigns usually only have a small effect on an election's outcome. Small effects can be decisive when two-party competition is evenly matched, as it has been since 2000, so it's not as if campaigns are unimportant. (I'll return to that topic later.) But they play out within a larger and more important context.

Two contextual factors played an outsize role in shaping the race in 2024. The first was the intense partisanship that grips the country during this polarized era. In decades past, winning presidential candidates could expect to win a bit over 90 percent of their party identifiers' votes, and losing candidates tended to win 80-plus percent of their party identifiers' votes. Party loyalty has jumped dramatically since then. In the 2020 and 2024 presidential elections, about 95 percent of both sets of partisans supported their party's standard-bearer. It didn't matter to Republicans that more than two hundred thousand people had died from COVID-19 and the economy was in freefall in 2020 under their president's stewardship. Nineteen out of twenty of them voted for him in 2024. Similarly, 95 percent of Democrats voted for Harris despite persistent inflation under her administration's stewardship of the economy.

Such high levels of party faithfulness result from what political scientists call affective polarization. It turns out Republicans and Democrats in the electorate do not differ all that much on policy.[5] The average Democrat is somewhat more liberal and the average Republican is somewhat more conservative. But neither side's partisans are especially extreme on policy. When it comes to their feelings about each other, however, they have grown much more negative over time. The best evidence comes from "feeling thermometers," in which survey respondents are asked to evaluate different leaders and groups on a 0–100 scale.[6] If they absolutely dislike the group or person, they are instructed to give a score of 0. If they absolutely love the group or person, they are instructed to give a score of 100. If they feel

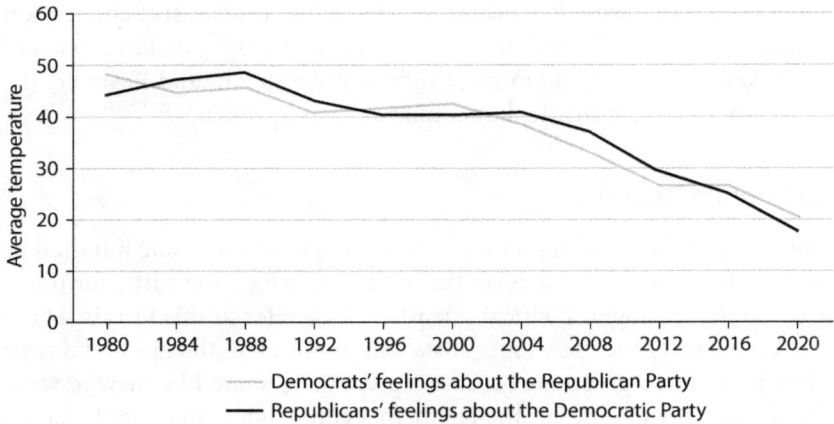

FIG. 1. Opposing party perceptions between Democrats and Republicans from the 1980s to 2020

neutral toward the object, they are instructed to give a score of 50. Respondents can give a score of any number on the scale.

The data in figure 1 trace Republicans' feelings about the Democratic Party and Democrats' feelings about the Republican Party since the 1980s. When the party feeling thermometers debuted in the American National Election Study in 1980, partisans tended to rate the other party near the neutral point of 50. The average score began to decline slowly, then rapidly, over the succeeding decades. By the time of the Trump elections, the average score that both sides gave the other party was below 20. To put that chilliness in some perspective, the average scores that all Americans in the 1970s gave "people who riot in the streets" and "people who smoke marijuana" were also between 10 and 20. It is fair to say that, these days, Republicans detest the Democratic Party and Democrats detest the Republican Party.

That state of affairs has consequences. If you detest, even hate, the other party, you are not going to vote for a candidate who represents it, no matter how poorly your own party might be performing or how mediocre you rate your own party's nominee. That is what explains the lockstep 95 percent support that both Democratic and Republican candidates now get from their own party.

Because most Americans are partisans (even most of those who claim to be independent), high levels of party loyalty mean that the swing vote in an election is much smaller now than it was in decades past. Hence fewer Americans now make voting decisions based on current policies or political conditions, such as the state of the economy, than used to be the case when party ties were weaker. And yet those conditions are still important to a significant, if much smaller, chunk of the electorate. Scholars have demonstrated for decades that economic fundamentals are especially important to who wins and who loses elections.[7] When economic times are good, enough voters reward the incumbent party that it is able to secure reelection. When they are bad, that small group of voters acts with a vengeance, turning the incumbent party out. When party polarization—and the basic equality of support that both parties enjoyed—was less intense, economic fundamentals sometimes led to huge swings in the electorate. During good times, both Ronald Reagan in 1984 and Richard Nixon in 1972 won forty-nine states. During bad times, Jimmy Carter in 1980 managed to win only five states. Now such swings are much smaller, but in a close election they are still decisive.

In 2024, the economic fundamentals suggested a close race. Inflation was higher than voters had become accustomed to, registering between 3 and 4 percent in the summer of 2024. Although rates had come down from a peak of 9 percent in 2022, it was still bad news for the Democrats. Unemployment, in contrast, was at a historic low—good news for the Democrats. Change in gross domestic product was solid, but not spectacular, which was so-so news for Democrats. A Yale economist named Ray Fair has used these three factors and a couple of others to estimate what percentage of the vote the incumbent party can expect to get in the election.[8] His prediction record has been outstanding. The noteworthy thing about Fair's economic voting model is that the economic data he uses are all measured in the middle of the election year, months before the general election campaign even starts. In other words, his economy-based prediction assumes that the candidates' campaigns do not affect the outcome of the race because the two campaigns are conducted equally well and cancel each other out.

In 2024, based on the economic fundamentals, Fair's model predicted that Harris would win 49.29 percent of the two-party vote, which is almost precisely what she won. Several political scientists use slightly different variables to make predictions based on the economic fundamentals.[9] In 2024 they mostly predicted the same thing as Fair: a narrow Trump popular vote victory.

On the surface, the implications of the economic forecasting models must in every other way seem ridiculous when applied to 2024. Harris was the first nonwhite woman candidate for president in history. She only had about one hundred days to campaign. Surely that had to matter. Trump was convicted of thirty-four felonies in New York. Federal indictments hung over him for all of 2024. He was nearly killed by an assassin's bullet. Surely that had to matter, too. One could add a litany of other factors that seemed critical when they emerged in the weeks leading up to the election. Yet the outcome was almost exactly what the economic fundamentals suggested it would be.

Does nothing matter anymore when it comes to election campaigns? Not exactly. There are many ways to assess the effect of the campaign, which I discuss in the following section. Some suggest that Harris's campaign made narrower what could have been a worse defeat. Others suggest that Trump's campaign turned out new voters who ensured his victory.

The General Election Campaign

Even though the forecasting models grounded in economic data gathered before the campaign began predicted the outcome nearly perfectly, that is not to say that the campaigns did not have any influence on the outcome. Indeed, one reason the economic fundamentals were so important was that the Trump campaign made high inflation an important component of its messaging, thereby making economics political. Whether in campaign appearances or in paid advertisements, Trump prompted voters to ask, Are you better off today than you were four years ago? Gallup has been asking that question of Americans around election time for the past forty years. In 1984, 2004, 2012, and 2020, Gallup found more Americans said yes than no, which nearly always was good news for the incumbent party.[10] In each of those elections except 2020, when COVID-19 was ravaging the country, the sitting president won reelection. (Had the pandemic not occurred, many analysts believe Trump would have emerged victorious that year, too.) In 1992, when George H. W. Bush lost reelection to Bill Clinton, only 38 percent said the economy had gotten better during his four years in office. The distribution of opinion about the economy in 2024 was much like it was in 1992. In the mid-September Gallup survey, only 39 percent of Americans said they were better off than they were four years ago. Exit polls, which I analyze later, further demonstrate the negative feelings most Americans had about the economy. These attitudes subjected the Democratic ticket to headwinds that would be challenging to overcome.

Issue Agenda

Campaign success or failure can be understood in many ways. One way is its ability to focus the issue agenda on areas that benefit the candidate. Trump's campaign sought to focus on three issue areas: inflation, of course, but also illegal immigration and what it saw as overreach by Democrats in their support for transgender people.

Illegal immigration has been Trump's go-to issue since he announced his first candidacy for president in 2015. His signature initiative, although never realized during his first four years as president, was to build a wall along the entire U.S.-Mexico border. While in office, his administration turned to increasingly aggressive steps to stem the tide of illegal border crossings, including the controversial decision to separate parents from their preadult children who crossed the border with them. After Biden took office in 2021, he assigned Harris the job others labeled "border czar," which connected the vice president to any successes and failures of the policies the Biden administration employed. Illegal crossings surged from 859,000 in 2019, the year before the pandemic, to 2.2 million in 2022,[11] a development very few Americans were happy about. Although illegal crossings dropped in Biden's last year in office, the immigration issue remained a problem for the Harris campaign.

In addition, Republicans sought to saddle Harris with some of the least popular aspects of activist efforts to extend rights and benefits to transgender people. A *Washington Post*–KFF survey from 2023 provides evidence of the American public's beliefs regarding transgender people.[12] When it comes to laws that would ban discrimination against trans people—whether it relates to military service, getting health insurance, or fair treatment in their jobs and workplaces—large majorities of Americans support them. However, equally large majorities oppose trans women and girls being allowed to participate in any level of organized sports, from the youth level to the professional ranks. The same is true of providing trans children and trans teens with puberty-blocking or hormonal treatments. One of the paid advertisements most used by the Trump campaign focused on Harris's support for using public money to fund gender reassignment surgery for trans people in prison. It closed with the tagline "Kamala Harris is for they/them; Donald Trump is for you," rubbing another sore of political correctness. Another advertisement focused on the unfairness of trans girls being permitted to participate in high school sports.

The Harris campaign hoped to shift the focus elsewhere, highlighting issues more hospitable to Democrats. This was especially true of abortion rights. The new limits on abortion access that were enacted by Republicans in red states after the *Dobbs* decision proved to be broadly unpopular. This was true even in parts of the country that one might expect to be very socially conservative. Several states, including reliably red Kansas, Kentucky, Montana, and Ohio, either voted in referenda for constitutional amendments that would codify abortion rights or voted to reject anti-abortion amendments to their constitutions.[13] Because of the Democrats' successful use of the abortion issue in their 2022 midterm election campaigns, the party hoped that framing the presidential election in terms of abortion rights might prove successful.

The other issues-framing target for the Democrats was Trump himself. His term as president had been in many ways chaotic. He was impeached, but not convicted, twice. He called the media the enemy of the people and his opponents enemies of the state. He threatened to use the power of the government as retribution against his political opponents. According to Glenn Kessler of *The Washington Post*, who kept a count, Trump made over thirty thousand false or misleading statements during his four years in office.[14] One of Trump's former chiefs of staff, John Kelly, a retired Marine Corps general, said that he thought Trump had the characteristics of a fascist. His management of the COVID-19 crisis was often problematic. And, of course, Trump was at the core of the January 6 invasion of the Capitol. Democrats saw Trump as a bad person, and they thought making the race about him would be to their benefit.

Assessing the Effect of the Campaign

One of the difficult things about assessing what effect the campaign had is deciding what constitutes evidence of a campaign effect. This is especially true because campaigns try to influence outcomes in two ways. One is persuasion, coming up with themes and arguments that encourage voters to choose one party over the other. Because of party polarization and the increased strength of party attachments, a smaller sliver of the population is open to persuasive appeals than in decades past. The other path is mobilization. Campaigns know that they have a lot of latent supporters in the electorate who simply don't plan to vote. Campaigns invest significant resources to get these citizens off the couch and to the polls. The data suggest that mobilization efforts have been increasingly bearing fruit. As recently as 1996, fewer than half of Americans eligible to vote turned out. In 2020, however, about two-thirds of eligible voters did. Would the campaigns be able to maintain such high turnout among their supporters in 2024?

Another important consideration is that campaigns do not occur in every place or every state. Rather, presidential campaigns focus their limited resources on the areas where they might have the greatest chance of affecting the outcome. These days, very few states are competitive. Recall from the introduction to this chapter that, over the last seven presidential elections, fully forty states have voted for the same party at least six times. No matter how many resources a campaign invests in most states, they are unlikely to flip them. Instead, the campaigns focus on a small number of so-called battleground states. In 2024, both candidates' campaigns seemed to agree that seven states were up for grabs—Pennsylvania, Michigan, Wisconsin, Nevada, Arizona, Georgia, and North Carolina. The fight was waged in those states, not really in the other forty-three.

That fact is useful when considering how the campaigns influenced the outcome. Trump won all seven battleground states, so it seems obvious that his campaign must have done the better job. After an election, there is a tendency for analysts to conclude that the winning campaign did everything right while the losing campaign did everything wrong. However, it is possible that Trump would have won all those states regardless of the quality of his campaign. Perhaps, instead, the Harris campaign was stronger than the Trump campaign and made the battleground states more competitive than they would have been otherwise.

To start my assessment of the influence of the campaigns, I begin by comparing how electoral outcomes changed between 2020 and 2024 in the seven battleground states where the campaigns took place with the outcomes in the forty-three states where the campaigns really didn't take place. When comparing battleground outcomes with nonbattleground outcomes, Trump improved his standing more in the nonbattleground states (where the campaigns really didn't occur) than in the battleground states (where the campaigns fought intensely). Perhaps not surprisingly given his 6 percentage-point increase in the national popular vote from 2020 to 2024, he received a higher percentage of the popular vote in all fifty states than he had four years earlier. In the seven battleground states, however, the average increase was only 1.84 points. In contrast, his standing improved by an average of 2.33 points in the forty-three nonbattleground states—26 percent higher than in the battleground ones. Trump's increases were particularly pronounced in the four largest nonbattleground states, which are also the four largest states in the country. These are New York (+5.5 points for Trump), Florida (+4.9 for Trump), Texas (+4.1 for Trump), and California (+4.0 for Trump). To the extent that Trump's popular vote improved between 2020 and 2024, then, it was more a function of his strength in states where the campaigns were not actively waged rather than in the states where they were.

Some might be skeptical that the winning campaign was not the superior campaign, so examining vote change by state in different ways is warranted. Another way to consider this question is to look at changing outcomes in neighboring states, one a battleground and the others not. It yields the same pattern. For example, in battleground North Carolina, Trump gained 1 percentage point relative to 2020. In the nonbattleground states that surround North Carolina, he gained 2.1 points in Virginia, 3.1 in South Carolina, and 3.5 in Tennessee. In battleground Pennsylvania, Trump improved by 1.6 points. In the safe states with the longest borders around the Keystone State—New York (+4.1), New Jersey (+4.7), Ohio (+1.9), and Maryland (+2.3)—he improved his showing by more. The same is true with Wisconsin (+0.8) relative to bordering Minnesota (+1.4), Iowa (+2.6), and Illinois (+3.2).

I noted earlier that mobilization of voters is the other way a campaign tries to affect the election. Maybe Trump's efforts relative to Harris's were more successful in the battleground states. It is also useful, then, to examine how voter turnout changed between 2020 and 2024. In 2020, the nation saw the highest turnout rate of the eligible electorate in over one hundred years. The pandemic allowed more voters than ever to vote by mail, a practice that Democrats took much more advantage of than Republicans. That avenue would not be as available in 2024 as it was in 2020. A major wild card of the 2024 election was whether the parties would be able to replicate their voter participation numbers in key areas of the country.

Superimposed on this question was the fact that, in 2024, the two campaigns decided to approach mobilization differently. The Democrats followed the usual playbook. They opened a large number of field offices in battleground states and staffed them with trained organizers and canvassers, who used cutting-edge evidence from social science about how best to encourage people to vote. The Republicans eschewed the traditional approach, viewing it as inefficient and ineffective. Instead they focused their efforts on encouraging "peer-to-peer" mobilization. Rather than sending in people from outside the local communities in which they were trying to turn out the vote, the Trump campaign used social media and podcasts to encourage existing supporters to get the nonvoters among their personal friends and acquaintances out to the polls.[15] The social science behind the idea is also well established. People are more likely to respond favorably to appeals made by those they know than those from strangers.

The turnout numbers provide some evidence that Trump's mobilization efforts were more successful than Harris's. To begin, voter turnout increased substantially in six of the seven battleground states, even above the extraordinary levels achieved in 2020. It was up 5.7 points in Nevada, 5.0 points in Georgia, 3.8 points in Wisconsin, 3.2 points in North Carolina, 2.3 points in Michigan, and 1.4 points in Pennsylvania. Relative to 2020, Trump added a substantial number of votes in all these states, but Harris sometimes got fewer votes than Biden did. It is impossible to know how much of the latter pattern can be explained by Biden voters moving to Trump or Biden voters staying home in 2024. But the pattern of change between 2020 and 2024 across counties in the battleground states seems to suggest more of the second than the first.[16] Consider Pennsylvania, which is where both campaigns spent the most resources. In the five biggest Democratic counties—Allegheny (home to Pittsburgh), Delaware, Lackawanna, Montgomery, and Philadelphia—turnout was lower than in 2020. In contrast, turnout in the more Republican friendly rural parts of the state increased dramatically. Advantage Trump.

The same pattern played out in Detroit and its surrounding suburbs, which is the heart of Democratic support in Michigan. In Wayne County, home to Detroit, Harris lagged Biden's vote numbers by more than sixty thousand. Not only did Trump increase his share of the vote in this Democratic stronghold, turnout in Michigan's red counties went up, not down. In Wisconsin, where voter turnout is always high, Harris got slightly more votes than Biden did in the Democratic counties that include Milwaukee and Madison (home to the University of Wisconsin) and their suburban rings. But, as in the other two Rust Belt prizes of Pennsylvania and Michigan, turnout increases were even more pronounced in more rural counties that vote more Republican. Nevada looked a lot like Wisconsin. In Clark County, a Democratic stronghold that is home to Las Vegas, turnout increased, with Harris getting more votes than Biden did four years earlier. But Trump also got more votes in Clark County than he did in 2020 while also boosting turnout substantially in Republican counties in more rural parts of the state.

The turnout increase among Republicans in 2024 is even more impressive given the change that has occurred in the Republican voting coalition over the last decades. As I will develop more later, those with higher levels of education used to identify with the GOP, while the Democrats did better among voters without college degrees. That relationship has flipped over the last twenty years. Now the GOP is the party that lower-education voters favor. As it relates to turnout, this development is important because there is no demographic characteristic more predictive of whether a person turns out to vote than how much education they have achieved. On average, those with college degrees are much more likely to vote than those without. For Republicans to be successful in the present era, then, they must rely more on voter mobilization efforts than Democrats do because their lower-education base is less likely to vote without a push from the campaign to get to the polls.

The Trump campaign and its affiliated groups seemed to succeed in mobilizing voters in the battleground states. Based on the available data, it is impossible to say they were specifically responsible for getting out more voters for Trump than would have shown up otherwise. It is also possible that more Trump voters than Harris voters were motivated to participate because of the less-than-great economic situation. Regardless, the pattern of change of voter turnout between 2020 and 2024 that I've described is at least consistent with the notion that the Trump campaign had a positive impact in Trump's narrow victory.

Group Bases of Candidate Support

In every election, different groups offer disproportionate support to one candidate or the other. Which groups choose which parties depends a lot on the issue stances that parties take and the issues that are most central to the party system at any particular time. For example, through much of the twentieth century, economic class was the major dividing line between Republicans and Democrats. Lower-income Americans tended to favor the Democratic Party because it offered more programs that redistributed income from the better off to the less well off. Higher-income people, who were less enthusiastic about income redistribution, tended to favor the Republicans, the party that supported less government intervention in the economy. To this day, the stereotype of the "country club Republican" persists. However, the voting patterns in 2024 offer further evidence that the economic class cleavage is no longer a dividing line between the parties.

Table 2 includes a list of group differences in candidate support based on national exit poll data gathered around the time of the election. Accounting for both those who voted early and those who voted on Election Day, the table provides a window on the group bases of support in 2024. For purposes of analysis, we are fortunate to have what is basically a rematch of the 2020 election in 2024, with Harris substituting for Biden. In table 2, I examine key changes in groups' voting behavior between the two elections, which helps account for why Trump went from losing by 4.5 points in 2020 to winning by 1.5 points in 2024.

GROUP-BASED VOTING IN 2024

Let's start the 2024 analysis with voting by income, which is a representation of the class-based voting that used to be so central to American politics. The 2024 exit poll data show that income makes almost no difference at all. Those making under $50,000 favored Trump over Harris by 50–48 percent, while those making over $100,000 favored Harris over Trump by a similarly small margin of 51–47 percent. To the extent that income mattered, higher-income voters were slightly more supportive of the Democratic standard-bearer and lower-income voters were slightly more supportive of the Republican, the opposite of the twentieth-century party divide. When the Democrats were the lower-income, working-class party, union membership was an especially strong bellwether of Democratic support. In 2024, however, only 53 percent of union household voters cast their ballots for Harris, a mere 6 points more than those from nonunion households.

The Harris–Trump matchup had many expecting an especially wide gender gap in voting. Not only is Harris a woman, she campaigned heavily on

TABLE 2. Group voting behavior in 2024 (in percentages)

	Trump	Harris	Difference
Income			
Less than $50K	50	48	+2
$50K–$100K	52	46	+6
More than $100K	47	51	−4
Union household			
Yes	45	53	−8
No	51	47	+4
Gender			
Male	55	43	+12
Female	45	53	−8
Race + gender			
Black men	21	77	−56
Black women	7	92	−85
Latino men	54	44	+10
Latina women	39	58	−19
White men	60	38	+22
White women	53	46	+7
Education (whites)			
College degree	45	53	−8
No college degree	66	32	+34
Religion			
None	27	71	−44
Protestant	63	36	+27
Catholic	59	39	+20
Jewish	22	78	−56
Other religion	34	61	−27

Source: Table is adapted from "Election 2024: Exit Polls," CNN, last updated December 13, 2024, https://www.cnn.com/election/2024/exit-polls/national-results /general/president/0.

Note: A plus sign (+) indicates Trump advantage; a minus sign (−) indicates Harris advantage.

so-called women's issues, especially abortion. Trump, on the other hand, is seen by many critics as having problematic attitudes about gender. Indeed, in 2024, he was found liable in a civil suit for sexual abuse of a woman years before in the changing room of an upscale clothing store, reminding many of the infamous *Access Hollywood* video unearthed in 2016. In that video, he noted one of the perks of celebrity is that women let you "grab them by the pussy." Although a 10-point gender gap emerged in 2024 (Trump won 55 percent of the vote among men but only 45 percent among women), it was not especially large by historical standards. When Trump and Hillary Clinton faced off in 2016, for example, the gender gap was 12 points. And when Biden defeated Trump, the gender gap was 11 points.

Because Harris is of Black and Indian descent, many also expected an especially large racial gap in voting behavior. Racial differences were, in fact, large, with 86 percent of Black exit poll respondents reporting they voted for Harris, compared with 42 percent of white voters. As I'll examine in more detail later, however, this level of support among Black Americans is low compared with support for previous Democratic presidential candidates. In addition, while Harris did win majorities among Hispanic and Asian American voters, her margins were, again, smaller than is typical for Democratic candidates. Breaking down voting by race and gender at the same time reveals important patterns. Among Black women, Harris did as well as Democrats typically do, winning 92 percent of their votes. However, her support among Black men was only 77 percent, well below the historical norm. The exit polls reveal a similar gender divide among Hispanic Americans: 58 percent of Latina women supported Harris, while only 44 percent of Latino men did. White support differed by gender as well, but only by about half as much as among Black and Hispanic voters.

Much has been made of the so-called diploma divide in modern American politics. The 2024 election shows clear evidence of a deep educational divide among white voters. Among white college graduates, 53 percent favored Harris, but only 32 percent of those with no college degree did. Because fewer people go to college than do not go to college in the United States, this gap proved to be an advantage for Trump. It is also worth noting that no diploma divide exists among nonwhites.

Religion provided another split between Trump and Harris voters. Because religious denomination matters less to people's politics now than does extent of church attendance, it is unfortunate that the exit polls did not ask about church attendance specifically. However, when they asked about religious denomination, they did provide a response option of "none." Obviously those who say they do not belong to a religious denomination almost never go to services. Among those who said "none," which was 24 percent of voters, 71 percent said they voted for Harris. In contrast, self-identified Catholics (59 percent) and Protestants (63 percent) voted for Trump. The exit polls reveal especially strong support for Trump among white voters who identify as evangelical or born-again Christian. Among this group, 82 percent voted for Trump.

TABLE 3. Change in group voting behavior between 2020 and 2024 (in percentages)

	2020	2024	Change
Gender			
Women	−15	−8	+7
Men	+8	+12	+4
Race + gender			
Black men	−60	−56	+4
Black women	−81	−85	−4
Latino men	−23	+10	+33
Latina women	−39	−19	+20
White men	+33	+22	−1
White women	+11	+7	−4
Age			
18–29 years old	−24	−11	+13
30–44	−6	−4	+2
45–64	+1	+10	+9
65+	+5	+1	−4
Education + race			
White, college	−3	−8	+5
White, no college	+35	+34	−1
Urbanicity			
Rural	+15	+30	+15
Suburban	−2	+4	+6
Urban	−22	−22	0
First-time voters			
Yes	−32	+11	+43
No	0	0	0

Source: Table is adapted from Zachary B. Wolf et al., "Anatomy of Three Trump Elections: How Americans Shifted in 2024 vs. 2020 and 2016," CNN, last updated December 13, 2024, https://www.cnn.com/interactive/2024/politics/2020-2016-exit -polls-2024-dg/.
Note: A plus sign (+) indicates Trump advantage; a minus sign (−) indicates Democrat advantage.

Turning to political issues, the headwinds that Democrats faced in the 2024 election come into focus. As noted earlier, the condition of the economy generally has an outsize effect on election outcomes. When asked whether the economy was excellent, good, not so good, or poor, only 31 percent said it was either excellent or good. Among those in this group, 92 percent supported Harris, the vice president in the incumbent administration. But fully 68 percent assessed the economy as either not so good or poor, which was terrible news for Harris, as 70 percent of those voters chose Trump. Given such poor economic assessments, it ought not be surprising that only 40 percent said they approved of President Biden, while 59 percent disapproved. Among disapprovers, 82 percent voted for Trump.

To be sure, the Democrats did have some issue advantages. The wisdom of Harris's decision to emphasize abortion rights is well supported in the data. Nearly two-thirds of respondents said they thought abortion ought to be legal in all or most cases. Nearly 70 percent of them cast ballots for Harris. Only 31 percent said they thought abortion ought to be illegal in all or most cases, with 91 percent of them supporting Trump. It is noteworthy that Trump's promise to engage in mass deportation of undocumented immigrants did not reflect the majority opinion of Americans. Only 40 percent of exit poll participants said they thought undocumented people ought to be deported, while 56 percent said they thought they ought to be offered the chance to achieve legal status. Among those in the former group, 87 percent supported Trump, compared with only 22 percent in the latter group.

Changes in Group Support Between 2020 and 2024

The 2024 data provide us a sense of which groups supported the candidates and by how much. But comparing the data from the 2020 and 2024 exit polls can better help us understand how Trump went from losing the national popular vote by 4.5 percentage points to winning by about 1.5 points. Overall he picked up 6 points. That means that almost all groups likely moved in his direction between 2020 and 2024, but some did by more and some did by less. Actually winning a majority of a group's voters is not always the most important thing. Some key groups may have voted more for Harris than for Trump and, therefore, seem like Democratic assets. But if they moved significantly in Trump's direction between the two elections, that is still good news for Trump. That happened for a couple of groups, namely young people and Latinos. Harris won them but by reduced majorities. As Biden proved in 2020 with his improved showing among rural voters relative to Hillary Clinton's, just doing less badly with a group without winning it can still affect a tight election outcome.

Drawing on the national exit poll data from both 2020 and 2024, table 3 presents a range of different social groups (and their intersections) for which change between the elections was noteworthy. By far the biggest change among social groups occurred among Latinos. Latino men went from being +23 for Biden in 2020 to +10 for Trump in 2024, a remarkable 33-point swing. Some analysts have suggested that Harris being a woman explains the move among Latino men, a group known to be more tradition minded. That explanation, however, does not square with the fact that the group provided Hillary Clinton a 31-point edge in 2016 when she ran against Trump. Moreover, Latina women also moved dramatically toward Trump in 2024. They were +39 for Biden in 2020 but only +19 for Harris, a 20-point swing. Although some have noted that Black men also moved toward Trump, the change in this group was relatively small, only 4 points between 2020 and 2024. Both Black and white women moved a bit in the opposite direction, 4 points toward Harris between the two elections.

Voters under the age of thirty also moved dramatically toward Trump. In 2020, the youngest age group favored Biden by 24 percentage points, but that edge fell to 11 points for Harris in 2024, a 13-point swing. While those thirty to forty-four years old voted about the same in both elections, those between forty-five and sixty-four years old tilted toward Trump by an additional 9 points (from +1 in 2020 to +10 in 2024). Harris actually did 4 points better among those over sixty-five, perhaps because they are the only group old enough to have experienced relatively high inflation earlier in their lives; 1984 was the last election year in which inflation was above 4 percent. White voters with college degrees were among the only groups that moved toward the Democrats in 2024 relative to 2020. Biden won the group by 3 points, while Harris won the group by 8. Harris's improvement among college-educated whites, however, was driven entirely by white women. They went from +9 for Biden to +17 for Harris. College-educated white men were +2 for Trump in 2024, which was almost identical to his margin in 2020.

Additionally, the rural-urban divide (re)opened substantially. Among the biggest reasons that Biden defeated Trump in 2020 was that he narrowed the advantage Trump had enjoyed in rural and suburban areas in 2016. When Trump matched up against Hillary Clinton, he won the rural vote by 27 points and the suburban vote by 4. In 2020, Biden also lost rural areas, but only by 15 points, and he managed to eke out a 2-point lead in the suburbs. Biden, a politically moderate, white man in his late seventies, seems to have had an unusual appeal for a Democrat among people living in these geographic areas. With Harris atop the ticket, the suburban vote swung back to Trump by 4 points while rural voters favored Trump by 30 points, a bit more than it favored him over Clinton in 2016.

Finally, Trump's improved fortunes with first-time voters were remarkable and likely speak to the success of his campaign in mobilizing low-propensity, less well-educated voters. In 2020, Biden won first-time voters by 32 points. That makes sense, given how well Democrats generally do with voters under twenty-five. For those between eighteen and twenty-one, any presidential year is, by definition, their first opportunity to vote in a presidential election. With eighteen-to-twenty-nine-year-olds favoring the Democrats in 2024, Trump still managed to best Harris among first-time voters by 11 percentage points. Going from +32 Biden to +11 Trump represents an astonishing 43-point swing. In conjunction with the campaign's effort to mobilize new voters, some argue that Trump's engagement with podcasts in the so-called manosphere made these gains possible. On the suggestion of his college-age son, Barron, he appeared on *The Joe Rogan Experience*, *This Past Weekend* (with Theo Von), *Flagrant* (with Andrew Schulz), the stream of Adin Ross (who is a major social media influencer on Kick), and *Break 50* (with Bryson DeChambeau), just to name a few. It seems plausible to think that some of the first-time voters who supported him were mobilized by these appearances.

Conclusion

Given the changes in the bases of group support between 2020 and 2024, it is fair to wonder whether the United States is entering a period of realignment. Several groups departed sharply from how they usually behave politically. Although it is dangerous to draw conclusions from a single election, it is worth considering the following realignment-related questions. Are Latino voters, a more religious and traditional group than average, becoming a Republican constituency because the group agrees with Republicans on the issues they care about most? Or did Latinos move toward the Republicans in 2024 because group members were especially vulnerable to the negative but temporary economic impact of inflation? Are young people, especially men, likely to continue their movement toward the GOP? Or did their movement between 2020 and 2024 reflect their struggles with high prices and high interest rates (for car loans, for example) rather than concern about Democratic policies? Will the less well-educated and more rural voters who turned out in force for Trump do the same for a Republican leader other than Trump? Vice President J. D. Vance is probably the most likely Republican to succeed him. Will he connect with them in the same visceral way that Trump has?

The evidence right now suggests that 2024 has a lot more similarities than differences with recent presidential elections. In that sense, it once more illustrates the very close divide between the two parties, just with the other side narrowly winning this time relative to the previous election. The Republicans won the popular vote by 1.5 percentage points, but with less than 50 percent overall. A realigning election with the winner securing only 49.8 percent of the national popular vote seems unlikely. Although the GOP will control both houses of Congress, as they did in 2017–18, their majorities will be razor thin. The 220–215 margin they will have in the House is the narrowest to begin a new Congress in the modern era. The Senate moves to 53–47 Republican, but those 53 votes are still too few to overcome any Democratic filibuster, which requires 60 votes to break. Legislative achievement will likely remain difficult even under unified Republican control, just as it has been for almost the entire twenty-first century.

For their part, liberals awaited Trump's second term with a sense of dread. Although Trump said he would not govern like a dictator, he repeatedly promised during the campaign to use the Department of Justice to prosecute his political opponents. His early appointments to high government positions were based on personal loyalty to him rather than their expertise in their subjects, hoping to challenge what many Republicans refer to as a "deep state" of liberal bureaucrats who thwart what the GOP sees as needed change. Trump's apparently close relationship with Soviet President Vladimir Putin signaled declining U.S. support for Ukraine in its war with Russia. And the United States' usual multilateral approach to alliances and trade agreements, which has been the norm since the end of World War II, seems to be under threat from Trump. Many of his former advisers have noted that he has little appreciation for the value of these connections.

To some, democracy would seem to be on the run around the world, not just from Trump's sometimes autocratic-seeming impulses. Antiestablishment and antidemocracy parties have become increasingly strong. This has been true for years in relatively new democracies in eastern Europe, such as Hungary and Poland. Emerging world powers, including India and Brazil, have also chosen right-wing populist leaders who do not express much concern for democratic governance. Similar parties are increasingly popular in more developed western European democracies like France and Germany as well. Such developments are discomfiting to those who are satisfied with the inherent messiness of democratic processes, but they are a model to those who would rather invest power in a single strong leader who is not bound by those processes.

It might be the case that high inflation was more responsible for Trump's election than was his personal style and policy appeal. Regardless, many parts of Trump's personal style, which have been touched on throughout this essay, seem grotesque to those who voted against him in the election. Beyond his lies and half truths, his role in the January 6 insurrection, and his alleged treatment of women and racial minorities over the decades, a Trump mega-rally held in late October 2024 at Madison Square Garden in New York City embodied Trumpism to his detractors. Speakers at the event referred to Puerto Rico as a "floating island of garbage" and called Harris "the Antichrist" and "the devil," claiming that "her pimp handlers will ruin the country" and connecting Black people to watermelons. That a plurality of voters voted for Trump despite the range of racist and misogynist tropes that were brought to bear on his behalf that day and at other times throughout the campaign leaves liberals wondering about the future of diversity and equality in the United States. That he seemed to receive no penalty for these especially problematic statements on Election Day leaves many wondering whether Trump was right in 2016 when he said, "I could stand in the middle of Fifth Avenue and shoot somebody, and I wouldn't lose any voters, OK?"

Notes

1. Trump was the first *major party* candidate, but Teddy Roosevelt, while running as a Bull Moose in 1912, was also the target of an assassin's bullet. He was wounded at a rally in Milwaukee, Wisconsin, the month before the election.
2. For links to Trump-versus-Biden and Trump-versus-Harris data over the course of 2024, see "CPR 2024 National Polling Average," Cook Political Report, accessed February 13, 2025, https://www.cookpolitical.com/survey -research/cpr-national-polling-average/2024.
3. I use the averages from FiveThirtyEight here. See "Latest Polls," FiveThirtyEight, accessed February 13, 2025, https://projects.fivethirtyeight.com /polls/president-primary-r/2024/national/.
4. As evidence, see, for example, Lydia Saad, "Broader Support for Abortion Rights Continues Post-Dobbs," Gallup, June 14, 2023, https://news.gallup .com/poll/506759/broader-support-abortion-rights-continues-post -dobbs.aspx.
5. Morris P. Fiorina, *Culture War? The Myth of a Polarized America*, 3rd ed. (Longman, 2010).
6. For a full discussion on affective versus ideological polarization, see Marc J. Hetherington and Thomas Rudolph, *Why Washington Won't Work* (University of Chicago Press, 2015).
7. Gregory B. Markus, "The Impact of Personal and National Economic Conditions on the Presidential Vote: A Pooled Cross-Sectional Analysis," *American Journal of Political Science* 32, no. 1 (1988): 137–154.

8. For the details of his model and his predictions, see "President and House 2024," Fair Model, Yale University, accessed February 13, 2025, https://fairmodel.econ.yale.edu/vote2020/indeane2.htm.

9. For the issue of *PS: Political Science and Politics* that cataloged these forecasts, see "Now Online | Special Issue on Forecasting the 2024 US Elections: PS: Political Science and Politics," Political Science Now, October 18, 2024, https://politicalsciencenow.com/now-online-special-issue -on-forecasting-the-2024-us-elections-ps-political-science-politics/.

10. For an article detailing Gallup's economic evaluations question since 1984, see Mary Claire Evans, "Majority of Americans Feel Worse Off Than Four Years Ago," Gallup, October 18, 2024, https://news.gallup.com/poll/652250 /majority-americans-feel-worse-off-four-years-ago.aspx.

11. For over-time fluctuations in illegal border crossings into the United States, see "Apprehensions and Expulsions Registered by the United States Border Patrol from the 1990 Fiscal Year to the 2023 Fiscal Year," Statista, July 5, 2024, https://www.statista.com/statistics/329256/alien-apprehen sions-registered-by-the-us-border-patrol/.

12. Details about the survey and more findings can be found in Laura Meckler and Scott Clement, "Most Americans Support Anti-Trans Policies Favored by GOP, Poll Shows," *Washington Post*, May 6, 2023, https://www.washing tonpost.com/education/2023/05/05/trans-poll-gop-politics-laws/.

13. For a full account of these state constitutional amendments, see "Ballot Tracker: Outcome of Abortion-Related State Constitutional Amendment Measures in the 2024 Election," KFF, last updated November 6, 2024, https://www.kff.org/womens-health-policy/dashboard/ballot-tracker -status-of-abortion-related-state-constitutional-amendment-measures/.

14. Kessler's final count as Trump left office in January 2021 can be found in Glenn Kessler et al., "Trump's False or Misleading Claims Total 30,573 over 4 Years," *Washington Post*, January 24, 2021, https://www.washingtonpost .com/politics/2021/01/24/trumps-false-or-misleading-claims-total-30573 -over-four-years/.

15. See Tim Alberta's excellent article in *The Atlantic* detailing the contrasts: Tim Alberta, " Trump Is Planning for a Landslide Win," *Atlantic*, July 10, 2024, https://www.theatlantic.com/politics/archive/2024/07 /trump-campain-election-2024-susie-wiles-chris-lacivita/678806/.

16. See Michael C. Bender, "Why Was There a Broad Drop-Off in Democratic Turnout in 2024?," *New York Times*, November 11, 2024, https://www .nytimes.com/2024/11/11/us/politics/democrats-trump-harris-turnout .html, which details many of the findings I report in this discussion.

Campaign Finance

TRENDS AND DEVELOPMENTS IN 2024

CHARLES R. HUNT

THE 2024 ELECTION was a historic and unexpected one in the world of campaign finance. One party's candidate dropped out three months before Election Day; his replacement, if successful, would have been the first woman to hold the office; and the other party's candidate survived two assassination attempts and a felony criminal conviction. These catalyzing events drove record daily fundraising and spending totals for the campaigns and their affiliates. And yet in other ways, it was business as usual concerning many of the trends political scientists and analysts have observed during the past several cycles. Vast quantities of campaign cash clearly continued to shape elections of all sorts at the federal level. But ensuring the actual effectiveness of these funds in changing voters' minds, as well as directing these funds to the right places and races, remains a significant challenge for parties and their allies, whether campaigns broke new ground or not.

Political scientists have long demonstrated the difficulty of accurately measuring the actual effects of fundraising and spending on election outcomes.[1] This chapter will make no such attempt—there is still much to learn about the voters, the nonvoters, the candidates' decisions, and the national political environment that coincided with the 2024 election. Indeed, the voters appear to be just as polarized, partisan, and "calcified" as ever,[2] no matter how many fundraising emails or candidate advertisements are thrown their way. The overwhelming majority of Americans who voted in 2020 voted for the same party for president in 2024; for the fourth presidential election in a row, the outcome was closely contested and significantly uncertain going into Election Day; and control of both chambers of Congress was decided on razor-thin margins yet again. This continuation of a competitive status quo raises serious questions about the efficacy of the massive outlays made by candidates and their allies to persuade undecided voters or to turn out their supporters.

TABLE 1. Total cost of elections (in billions, 2024 dollars)

	Total cost	Congressional	Presidential
1998	$3.1	$3.1	n/a
2000	$5.6	$3.0	$2.6
2002	$3.8	$3.8	n/a
2004	$6.9	$3.7	$3.2
2006	$4.4	$4.4	n/a
2008	$7.6	$3.6	$4.0
2010	$5.2	$5.2	n/a
2012	$8.6	$5.0	$3.6
2014	$5.1	$5.1	n/a
2016	$8.5	$5.4	$3.1
2018	$7.1	$7.1	n/a
2020	$18.3	$10.6	$7.7
2022	$9.5	$9.5	n/a
2024[a]	$15.9	$10.3	$5.5

Source: "Total Cost of Election (1990–2024)," OpenSecrets, accessed March 11, 2025, https://www.opensecrets.org/elections-overview/cost-of-election.

[a]Through December 9, 2024.

Nevertheless, candidates, parties, and outside groups continued to raise and spend money in mind-boggling amounts. As table 1 indicates, 2024 does not appear to have been the most expensive election in American history; that title stays with 2020, which, adjusting for inflation, appears to have cost a couple billion more than 2024. However, this discrepancy can be chalked up in large part to the significantly more competitive presidential primary elections that took place in 2020 on the Democratic side. In 2020, the Democrats raised nearly $4.2 billion (in 2024 dollars) selecting their nominee, including about $2.5 billion in self-funding from Michael Bloomberg and Tom Steyer, compared with 2024 Republicans, who spent less than $1 billion in a very uncompetitive set of primaries. Meanwhile, the combined cost of congressional races was also comparable with 2020, and outstripped both 2018 and 2022.

The cost of American election campaigns for both Congress and the presidency has clearly continued to grow. But this continuation in aggregate trends masks a variety of crucial differences between the candidates, the parties, and the ways they funded their efforts to win Congress and the White House. Elections have become more expensive, but they have also diversified in the variety of ways in which money finds its way into the campaign. This chapter will chart both of these trends and place them in the context of modern political science research. In doing so, we can better understand the catalyzing, headline-grabbing events throughout the campaign that drove another cycle of explosive presidential fundraising; the differing legal routes the two major presidential candidates took to funding their campaigns; and how modern political science can help to explain the often bewildering spending landscape in congressional races.

Money's Role in Choosing (and Rechoosing) a Nominee

To say that the 2024 presidential election provided a few surprises is to understate to the extreme. Donald Trump was already an unconventional candidate in his previous two elections; but this time, he was a defeated former president running as a semi-incumbent in a crowded Republican primary field. With full knowledge that he was the front-runner, Trump refused to debate the other candidates, who themselves seemed very reluctant to criticize Trump. These nuances were major contributors to the shape and size of the "money chase" in the Republican primary, which did not end up being very competitive.

But these developments, and the amounts of campaign cash associated with them, paled in comparison to the shock waves sent in the summer of 2024 following a dismal, and itself unprecedented, June debate between Trump and the incumbent, President Joe Biden.

The Republicans

After the 2022 midterm elections, commentators from across the ideological spectrum were increasingly skeptical that Trump was necessarily the favorite for the 2024 Republican presidential nomination. A number of Trump's handpicked congressional candidates went down in flames in 2022, losing very winnable seats and turning the anticipated "red wave" into little more than a trickle. Trump's electoral positioning, along with a slew of criminal indictments and a growing number of viable Republican primary challengers, made his renomination far from certain. By early 2023, a number of polls showed Trump neck and neck with Florida Governor Ron DeSantis, who won a resounding reelection in 2022.[3]

Trump's position was unusual in a number of ways, and nearly unprecedented. His criminal indictments (one of which resulted in a felony conviction) were a first for a serious modern presidential candidate. But Trump was also a semi-incumbent, having been elected in 2016 and defeated for

TABLE 2. Republican primary candidate fundraising summary through April 31, 2024

Candidate	Total fundraising	% outside groups	% self-funded	% small donors
Donald Trump	$243,952,385	51	0	15
Ron DeSantis	$197,224,968	84	0	3
Nikki Haley	$147,600,142	62	0	10
Vivek Ramaswamy	$50,700,570	17	61	10
Tim Scott	$45,851,209	73	0	8
Doug Burgum	$41,221,945	59	34	2
Chris Christie	$21,054,342	66	25	0
Mike Pence	$11,491,680	47	0	20
Asa Hutchinson	$4,432,258	64	1	12

Sources: Individual Contributions and Independent Spending Bulk Data Files, Federal Election Commission (2024). https://www.fec.gov/data/browse-data/?tab=bulk-data.

reelection in 2020. As such, Trump maintained a fundraising advantage throughout the primary campaign, but it was a narrow one. Even after his public struggles in 2021 and 2022, Trump maintained a strong base of supporters. As table 2 indicates, Trump led the rest of the eventual Republican field by far in total monetary support from small donors, relying on them more than any of his rivals but former Vice President Mike Pence (though Pence only raised a little over $11 million throughout his short primary campaign).

Some of Trump's other rivals for the nomination borrowed alternative routes to financial viability used by Democrats in 2020. Some relied heavily on self-funding, most notably South Dakota Governor Doug Burgum, a wealthy former tech and real estate investor; and venture capitalist Vivek Ramaswamy. Both men failed to win significant voter support in the primaries but secured key posts in Trump's second administration. Meanwhile, Trump's more viable "mainstream" Republican opponents secured significant support from outside groups, including dedicated candidate super PACs, to boost their profiles. These included DeSantis, former South Carolina Governor and UN Ambassador Nikki Haley, and Senator Tim Scott of South Carolina. DeSantis was the most notable beneficiary of super PAC money, securing over $50 million in combined support from groups like Never Back Down and Fight Right.

Regardless of where their funding came from, the modern campaign finance environment enabled a number of candidates to compete with former President Trump on the money front. But in the end, big fundraising and spending in support of DeSantis—as well as of Haley, who ended up being Trump's chief rival once the primaries began in earnest—seemed to make little dent in the Republican primary electorate's views about who their nominee should be. Trump won all but two of the primary contests. Haley won only Vermont and Washington, DC, and DeSantis dropped out following a second-place finish in the Iowa caucuses.

THE DEMOCRATS

Although many Democrats were not entirely supportive of President Joe Biden's reelection run, 2022 and 2023 came and went without another viable candidate jumping in to oppose him, and Biden insisted on running again despite persistently lackluster job approval ratings. What this produced was a primary election process that was both uneventful and typical for an incumbent president: high levels of support from Democratic primary voters, low turnout, and a clear reluctance among other potential Democratic presidential candidates to challenge him. Biden coasted to victory in every Democratic primary, and it quickly became clear that America was headed for a 2020 rematch.

Into the summer, Biden maintained a slight fundraising edge over Trump, leaving much of his campaign war chest unspent in an easy primary election victory. But the Democrats' campaign finance landscape—and the entire 2024 presidential race—was upended by an unorthodoxly timed June debate between Trump and Biden, in which Biden all but confirmed the chief fear of many Democrats: that his advanced age (Biden was eighty-one at the time) had diminished his faculties and ability to wage a full-scale campaign. Biden stumbled in his answers, failed to articulate a second-term agenda, and came across poorly to the national audience.[4]

Although Democratic leaders did not immediately call on Biden to step aside, the broader conversation about his future—and the pressure on him to drop out and endorse a different candidate—grew steadily over the next several weeks. Eventually, on July 21, 2024, Biden formally dropped out of the presidential race and immediately endorsed Vice President Kamala Harris to run in his place.[5]

The "open primary" some called for featuring not just Harris but other potential Democratic nominees like Michigan Governor Gretchen Whitmer, California Governor Gavin Newsom, and Pennsylvania Governor Josh Shapiro did not materialize. Harris made hours of phone calls securing support from Democratic members of Congress, other party dignitaries, and some of those potential rivals for the nomination.

Perhaps the most decisive factor tipping the scales in Harris's favor, however, was the unprecedented campaign finance situation that Biden's decision to step aside left in its wake. Biden had been fundraising for his reelection bid throughout 2023 and 2024, and accumulated a little under $100 million by the time he decided to bow out.[6] Had a new Democratic nominee started from scratch financially, they would have been at a significant disadvantage against Trump, who was sitting on over $125 million.

Harris's big advantage—besides being a qualified candidate and the symbolic "next in line" as Biden's vice president—was that she could legally take over Biden's entire campaign operation, including the fundraising war chest he had accumulated. As campaign finance experts, from those at Harvard University[7] to ones at the Brennan Center for Justice,[8] agreed, because Harris's name was present on Biden's campaign as part of the official ticket, she was entitled to the money raised by the "Biden–Harris" campaign. This did not stop the Trump campaign from filing an official Federal Election Commission complaint protesting the transfer.[9] But the complaint went nowhere.

Had another candidate emerged as the Democrats' standard-bearer, the money wouldn't have been completely wasted; Biden could have legally transferred the funds to Democratic Party committees or other allied groups to spend independently on behalf of any Democratic nominee. But no campaign but Harris's could receive the money directly and immediately. As a result, she began her campaign in late July with $95 million in the bank.

A History-Making General Election

The Democrats' candidate switch was largely seen as a positive development on the left, reflected in a new slew of polling showing Harris far outpacing Biden in the matchup with Trump. The Democrats' chances to win had been revived, but with a widely recognized but not well-known vice president now topping the ticket, much work remained to be done in the next one hundred days to educate the public about Harris, her biography, and her positions.

Trump's task was oddly similar. By 2024, most Americans already had strong opinions about the former president. As a result, the Trump campaign's main effort was also to define Harris, only negatively. The two campaigns took very different approaches to funding their advertisements and other efforts to define themselves and their opponent. These efforts were shaped by catalyzing events that either drove or diminished voter enthusiasm.

Democratic Enthusiasm and Catalyzing Fundraising Events

The two presidential campaigns were at times diametrically opposed in terms of their campaign strategies. They also took starkly different approaches to funding their efforts to reach voters and turn them out to vote.

Harris faced an uphill battle as a new and relatively untested candidate suddenly thrust into the national spotlight. Luckily for Harris, renewed Democratic enthusiasm fueled an unprecedented small-dollar fundraising bonanza that continued to Election Day. In the few days leading up to Biden's announcement that he would drop out, his campaign was raising between $500,000 and $2 million per day. On the day Biden dropped out and endorsed Harris, the campaign (which soon belonged to Harris) raised $23 million. In the next two days, during which it became clear that Harris would be the Democrats' choice, she raised $41 million. This trend continued past the immediate aftermath of Biden's decision, and reflected a lasting and fundamental surge in Democratic enthusiasm. In contrast to Biden, who raised only $63 million during the month before he dropped out, Harris raised $270 million during the month after he dropped out, as well as many millions more during the Democratic National Convention in Chicago.

This unprecedented surge in fundraising for Harris was driven largely by a sea change in enthusiasm among small donors and Democratic activists. Gallup's polling at the time found that in March 2024, only about 55 percent of Democrat-identifying voters reported feeling "more enthusiastic than usual" about voting. By August, 78 percent did, compared with only 64 percent of Republicans.[10]

For Democrats, this enthusiasm gap mirrored a similar gap between the two major presidential candidates in terms of funding from small donors—that is, individual contributions of less than $200. These donations made up around 21 percent of fundraising for all presidential and congressional races in 2024, a similar proportion to 2020. The Center for Responsive Politics and other organizations have attributed these higher-than-usual percentages to digital outreach efforts on behalf of both parties through ActBlue (Democrats) and WinRed (Republicans) that make it easier than ever to donate small amounts.[11]

As table 3 indicates, the gap between Harris and Trump among small donors was significant and marked a major reversal from the last two elections in which Trump was also a candidate. The 2024 election was the third in a row in which Trump was outraised and outspent by his opponent. But for the first time, it was Trump's opponent, not him, whose supporters generated the most small donations. Harris ended up getting 42 percent of her

TABLE 3. Fundraising summary, 2024 presidential general election (millions)

	Harris (D)	Trump (R)
Campaign committee	$1,003	$382
Outside groups / affiliated super PACs	$843	$976
Combined total	$1,846	$1,358
% small donors	42	29

Source: Individual Contributions and Independent Spending Bulk Data Files, Federal Election Commission (2024), https://www.fec.gov/data/browse-data/?tab=bulk-data.

Note: Does not include Democratic National Committee or Republican National Committee.

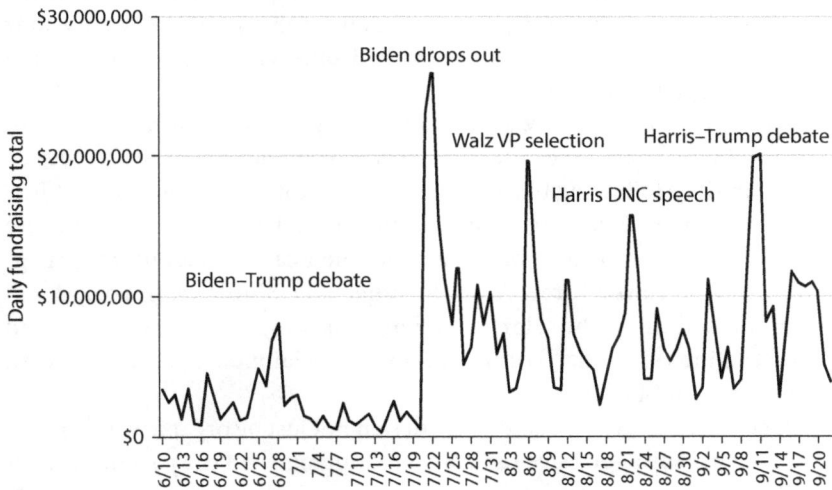

FIG. 1. Biden/Harris daily fundraising totals, June–November 2024
Source: Individual Contributions Bulk Data File, Federal Election Commission, 2024, https://www.fec.gov/data/browse-data/?tab=bulk-data.

campaign funds from small donations, compared with Trump's 29 percent. Compare that with 2020, when Trump received close to half (49 percent) of his financial support from small donors, with Biden clocking in at 39 percent.

The Harris campaign's reliance on small-dollar fundraising, sparked by the jolt of grassroots support the campaign enjoyed upon Biden's decision to leave the race, is even more apparent in light of the major spikes in fundraising observed in figure 1. This figure charts the Biden (and then Harris) campaign's daily average fundraising totals between early June and late September 2024.

Several striking patterns in this figure offer a window into the political roller coaster the Democratic Party rode throughout the summer of 2024. The first is the obvious relief and excitement caused by Biden's decision to drop out on July 21. A second is that the Harris campaign's daily fundraising remained high. From the day she took over the campaign until Election Day, Harris's daily fundraising totals never fell below Biden's daily average leading up to withdrawal.

Instead, Harris regularly peaked with daily totals of $10 million or more. These days were clearly aligned with key catalyzing moments in the campaign that successfully channeled natural voter enthusiasm into both small and large donations. Massive single-day totals were reached when Harris announced Tim Walz as her vice-presidential running mate ($20 million on August 6); when she delivered her acceptance speech at the Democratic National Convention ($16 million on August 20); and in the twenty-four hours during and following Harris's only debate with Trump ($20 million apiece on September 10 and 11).

This phenomenon of reactive fundraising is not new in American politics. Take, for example, the flood of campaign donations to Democrats and their allies following the September 2020 death of Supreme Court Justice Ruth Bader Ginsburg.[12] In this instance, Democratic voters were reacting not positively to good news about their candidates but rather negatively to a perceived threat from the other side. Similarly, in 2024 donations flooded into the Harris coffers following a highly publicized August 12 interview that Trump did on the social media platform X with its owner, Elon Musk.[13]

Of course, spikes in donations are driven not just by organic voter enthusiasm but also by aggressive fundraising campaigns on the part of the candidates. These appeals for contributions have becoming increasingly numerous and creative with each passing year. Political scientist Adam Bonica tracked all Democratic Party–affiliated fundraising emails in 2024. They totaled over three thousand emails, but as the election grew closer, the appeals grew in both volume and aggressiveness, peaking at forty-eight in a single day. The emails also increasingly employed tactics like shaming, faking personal messages, and out-and-out begging on the part of "the candidate" for just a few more dollars.[14]

These aggressive tactics may work. Without a doubt, Harris was a prolific fundraiser, and her ascendance to the top of the ticket did wonders for Democrats' ability to run a robust, well-funded campaign. But many have wondered whether these approaches turn off more voters than they turn out.[15] For Democrats, the small-dollar discomfort didn't end when, after

Harris lost the election, fundraising emails continued well into November and early December in order to pay down the debs the campaign had accrued. As Democrats continue their search for answers as to why they lost or how to reconnect with voters, their fundraising tactics may be a good place to start.

Donald Trump and Campaign Outsourcing

The Trump campaign also enjoyed a great deal of enthusiasm, but from a very different group of political actors. Trump's fundraising numbers among small donors in 2024 were in stark contrast to his much more robust numbers in 2020 and even 2016. This time around, Trump's biggest financial boosters were not small donors but the largest ones imaginable. As noted in table 3, Harris's campaign committees far outraised Trump's. However, Trump's support from a broad constellation of outside groups—and outside individuals—far surpassed Harris's. This result was not accidental; rather, it was part of a coordinated strategy by the Trump campaign to outsource much of its financial and campaign activities to super PACs and other outside groups funded largely by billionaires.

Although wealthy individuals like Timothy Mellon and Miriam Adelson each spent or donated over $100 million to support Trump's election effort, perhaps no individual has ever been as personally invested in an American election as Elon Musk, the richest man in the world. Musk made his fortune with groundbreaking companies like Tesla and SpaceX. His direct involvement in politics has been a recent development, coinciding with his 2022 decision to buy the social media platform Twitter, which he renamed X. As the 2024 campaign unfolded, Musk became steadily and more publicly supportive of Trump's election bid, eventually spearheading a number of unorthodox ventures.

Many of Musk's efforts were unconventional; for example, a scheme in which he gave away $1 million per day to purportedly random voters in Pennsylvania. The sweepstakes was challenged by Philadelphia District Attorney Larry Krasner as a violation of state campaign finance law, but it was allowed to continue after Musk's attorneys argued in court that the voters weren't chosen by chance but instead were "paid spokespeople" for America PAC, the super PAC Musk created and funded to help elect Trump.[16] Musk also created another group, RBG PAC, which spent tens of millions on ads strongly implying that the late Justice Ruth Bader Ginsburg agreed with Trump on the issue of abortion.

Despite his strange tactics and campaign appearances with Trump, Musk leveraged a wide-open federal campaign finance system to achieve his ends and influence the election. When all was said and done, Musk had spent, donated, or given away more than a quarter of a billion dollars to help Trump win. The vast majority of that sum (about $238 billion) was donated directly to America PAC.[17] Musk made other large donations to the Senate Leadership Fund, which supports Republican Senate candidates, and the MAHA Alliance PAC, a group affiliated with eventual Trump Health and Human Service Secretary Robert F. Kennedy Jr.[18]

DARK MONEY AND SUPER PACS IN 2024

Musk's PACs were not the only outside spenders investing in the 2024 election. On the whole, outside groups accounted for about $4.5 billion of the total spending in the 2024 presidential and congressional contests, far outstripping these groups' previous totals of $2.9 billion in 2020 and $1.4 billion in 2016.[19] In recent years, spending on the part of super PACs— organizations that can raise and spend unlimited amounts of money donated by individuals and groups, but which must disclose their donors— has skyrocketed, while the ostensible amount of money spent by "dark money" organizations has appeared to decline. Dark money is raised by 501(c)(4) nonprofit organizations in unlimited amounts and spent without needing to disclose the names of their donors. Dark money groups often spend their money on so-called issue ads whose purpose may be obvious even though they cannot expressly advocate voting for or against a particular candidate. From its high-water mark of $313 million in 2012, a little over $100 million of dark money was spent using this untraceable cash in 2020.[20]

In 2024, however, spending by dark money organizations bounced back to about $175 million in reported dollars spent. But in addition to increased spending compared with 2020, dark money groups in 2024 had multiple other ways to wield financial influence over the election. Many critics argue that dark money groups simply invested elsewhere—or at another time. This is because dark money groups must only report to the Federal Election Commission the money they spend on issue ads and other political activities within sixty days of an election. Dark money spent (or donated to affiliated super PACs) in 2024 before September 5 isn't on the Federal Election Commission's books, making that money what the Brennan Center's Ciara Torres-Spelliscy calls "black hole money."[21] Considering how difficult it is to trace such money to its sources, it is likely impossible to know how much early dark money spending occurred. It may be that super PACs held off their own spending until their affiliated dark money

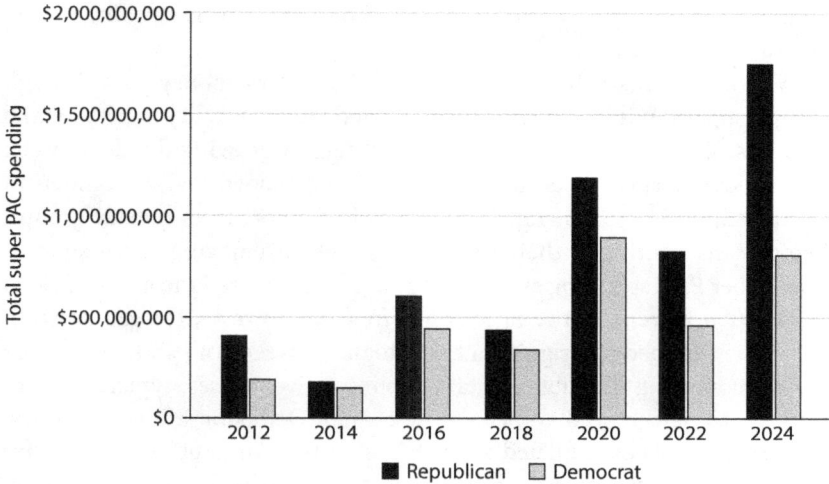

FIG. 2. Total super PAC spending in support of each major party, 2012–2024
Source: "2024 Outside Spending, by Super PAC," OpenSecrets, https://www.opensecrets
.org/outside-spending/super_pacs/.

groups finished spending with impunity before the sixty-day "general election season."

Super PACs did indeed spend a record total of $2.6 billion in 2024, besting the $2 billion spent in 2020 and more than doubling the amount of spending they did in 2016 (figure 2).[22] And although super PACs are required to disclose their donors, a record number of these donors came from dark money sources like 501(c)(4) groups or even shell companies, acting as a kind of pass-through to anonymize these donations. In 2024, these groups were the source for nearly a quarter (about $1 billion) of the total dollars flowing into super PACs, reflecting a tidal shift in the strategy dark money groups are taking to influence federal elections. In 2012, dark money was spent directly rather than donated to other groups like super PACs at a six-to-one ratio. In 2024, the ratio was twenty-six-to-one in the other direction. This strategy was apparent on both sides in the presidential campaign: For example, Trump's largest super PAC (MAGA, Inc.) raised nearly $80 million in the final weeks of the election, but over $50 million of that came from another Trump-affiliated dark money group called Securing American Greatness. Harris, meanwhile, relied largely on the Future Forward super PAC, which raised over $160 million in the last fundraising period before the election; but nearly 80 percent of these donations came from Future Forward's dark money nonprofit, Future Forward USA Action.

Whether from small donors, billionaires, or dark money pass-through groups, super PACs in 2024 further cemented their centrality in presidential elections. They also highlighted a preexisting but growing divide between the parties in terms of their use of and reliance on super PACs to compete in elections. Just as Trump edged out Harris in support from outside groups, Republicans continued their unbroken streak of enjoying more support from super PAC spending ever since these groups entered the national campaign finance arena in the early 2010s. In 2024, however, the gap between the parties jumped to a significant new high. Between 2014 and 2020, super PACs supporting Republicans and conservative causes typically spent between 20 percent and 40 percent more than Democrat-affiliated groups; in 2024, Republican-affiliated super PACs more than doubled the amount their Democrat-leaning counterparts spent. The gap has been steadily growing since the 2018 midterm elections; and with high-flying billionaires like Musk and Mellon willing to invest millions in these PACs each cycle, it seems unlikely this advantage will diminish anytime soon.

Continuing Trends in Congressional Elections

In congressional elections, a number of factors—including the nationalization of House and Senate elections and the increased focus on winning and retaining party majorities in Congress—ensured not only that these races would not fly under the radar in 2024 but also that they would be some of the year's most expensive elections. In this section, I analyze the effects of partisan fundamentals, incumbency, and negative partisanship on campaign finance in these crucial elections, as well as what these patterns tell us about the state of congressional politics in a polarized era. I also investigate increasing divides not just between the parties but between the incentives for financial involvement of individual donors and independently spending outside groups.

The 2022 midterm elections were a reminder to both parties that every seat counts in Congress. Republicans took back the U.S. House with a margin of fewer than a dozen seats, and Democrats managed to maintain control of the Senate by tying fifty-fifty, with Vice President Harris casting the tiebreaking vote on many major pieces of legislation and judicial and executive branch nominations. In the following two years, both parties looked to 2024 with trepidation. Democrats were dogged by high inflation and consistently low approval ratings for President Biden, as well as a very difficult

U.S. Senate map. Democrats were defending seats not just in swing states Pennsylvania, Wisconsin, Michigan, and Arizona but also in the increasingly red states Montana, Ohio, and West Virginia.

Even so, Republicans were in dire straits of their own after two years of chaotic rule over the House of Representatives, during which they deposed Speaker Kevin McCarthy of California and eventually replaced him with Mike Johnson of Louisiana. Meanwhile, resignations and special election losses shrank the small GOP's majority even more.

Basic political fundamentals—a closely divided Congress, a polarized electorate, and a dwindling number of competitive seats—were decisive factors in the race for the majority in both the House and the Senate. In the end, Republicans were successful on both fronts, but only just. When the 119th Congress was gaveled into session in January 2025, Republicans enjoyed only a five-seat majority in the House and a six-seat majority in the Senate. In the face of such close divisions, massive sums of money make a difference.

As in 2020, much of the Democrats' and Republicans' spending in the battle for control of Congress in 2024 came not from the candidates but from a record expansion of independent expenditures by outside groups. More than $1.3 billion in independent expenditures was spent in the twelve most expensive Senate races. The highest-spending groups focused with laser-like intensity on the races most likely to decide whether Republicans would win a majority in the Senate.

This ongoing, single-minded focus on securing and retaining majorities in the two chambers of Congress has been put into historical context by many scholars, including Frances Lee in her 2016 book *Insecure Majorities: Congress and the Perpetual Campaign*. Lee cites the increasing volatility of majority control in Congress as a key determinant of congressional gridlock and polarization.[23] Other authors have connected the parties' majoritarian "insecurity" with independent spending in elections of all sorts. For example, my own work with coauthors found that at the state level, partisan competition—including the likelihood of shifts in state legislative majorities—has a much more consistent and substantial effect on the size and manner of independent spending than the types of campaign finance laws in those states.[24] The independent spending groups are partisan in nature if not in name and have a high stake in which party has a governing majority, even if that means supporting some candidates who differ with the group on certain issues.

As a result, even ostensibly narrowly focused issue groups are spending more money exclusively on one party or the other, and are directing those

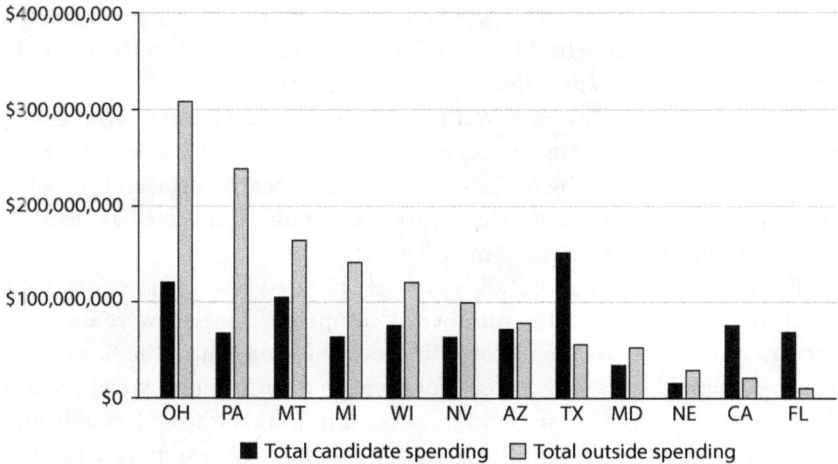

FIG. 3. Total candidate fundraising and non-candidate spending in select U.S. Senate races, 2024
Source: Individual Contributions and Independent Spending Bulk Data Files, Federal Election Commission, 2024, https://www.fec.gov/data/browse-data/?tab=bulk-data.

dollars to the most competitive races—races that more often than not feature ideologically middling candidates rather than progressive or conservative champions.[25] A significant number of high-profile groups displayed these motivations in 2024, continuing the trend from throughout the Trump years. Groups like Vote Save America, an outside group associated with the left-wing Crooked Media podcast empire, raised and spent millions on the key races at the federal, state, and local levels that were most competitive and thus would benefit the most from the extra cash.[26]

These patterns demonstrate a key difference between most outside spenders and those who donate directly to candidates. Independent expenditures from outside groups tend to correlate strongly with how competitive a race is. Donors to candidates, especially small donors, usually do so as an act of political expression.[27]

With these bedrock motivations in mind, the two countervailing trends in figure 3 are perhaps not surprising. This figure displays aggregated spending totals by U.S. Senate candidates' official campaigns and by outside groups (including parties). The trend for outside spenders is relatively clear: Parties and independent expenditure groups are spending in ways that correlate with a combination of how close a Senate race is perceived to be and how pivotal the race likely will be for securing a majority in the Senate for one party or the other. Although Senate races in

Texas and Florida appeared to be close in 2024, they did not turn out to be close in reality. More importantly, they were races that, if won by Democratic candidates, almost assuredly would have meant that Democrats nationally were having a good year and had already won their Senate majority in other, better-polling states like Pennsylvania, Ohio, and even Montana. This made these races a comparatively low return on investment for outside spenders.

Spending on the part of the candidates' campaigns, however, followed a very different pattern. Although nearly all of their races saw sizable candidate spending of $50 million or more, the biggest spenders were in races not likely to be particularly close, and certainly not ones that were likely to decide control of the Senate. The three races that stand out in total candidate spending were in Texas, California, and Florida. Texas and California in particular featured among the most despised members of Congress on both the Democratic and Republican sides: Senator Ted Cruz (R) of Texas, who was up for reelection against Democratic House member Collin Allred; and Rep. Adam Schiff (D) of California, who was the leading Democrat running to replace the late Senator Dianne Feinstein. Florida's incumbent Republican Rick Scott had also drawn significant ire from Democrats in recent years as one of Trump's most stalwart defenders in the Senate, and a potential future member of the chamber's Republican leadership.

In Cruz's and Schiff's races, the story was especially clear: Mostly Democratic donors from around the country, polarized on a partisan basis, acted based on their anti-GOP "negative partisanship" and donated hundreds of millions of dollars to a (mostly hopeless) effort by a Democratic challenger to unseat Cruz. These donors took a similar approach to well-known Trump antagonist Schiff, despite his almost certain victory in deep-blue California. Allred and Schiff were among the highest-earning candidates in terms of out-of-state donations, despite running in two of the largest and richest states in the country. They (and Cruz) were among the top five highest-earning Senate candidates of the election.

In short, it appears that the Democratic Party and other independent expenditure groups were laser-focused on the races most crucial to winning a majority in the Senate, even as many of their rank-and-file donating supporters were motivated by their hostility to well-known candidates like Cruz and Schiff. Of course, it is impossible to know whether the excess funds they sent to places like Texas and California would have made the difference in much closer Democratic losses like Pennsylvania and Ohio. But surely the parties—particularly the Democrats—will continue to think through how to redirect candidates' campaign cash in more efficient ways

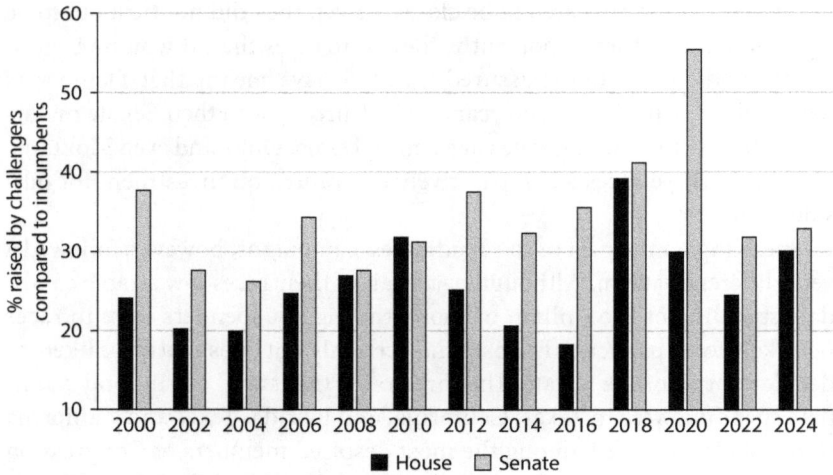

FIG. 4. Challenger fundraising as percentage of incumbent fundraising in U.S. House and Senate elections, 2000–2024
Source: Individual Contributions Bulk Data File, Federal Election Commission, 2024, https://www.fec.gov/data/browse-data/?tab=bulk-data.

in the future, particularly if they focus on securing a majority in congressional chambers.

A number of other tendencies were apparent in spending by the candidates themselves. In the century's first ten congressional elections, incumbents consistently outspent challengers in the aggregate. The incumbency advantage—be it in the traditional form of name recognition and constituency service or the trend toward increasingly safe partisan seats—appeared to reign supreme. As figure 4 illustrates, challengers flipped the script in 2020, outspending incumbents in Senate races, the only time this has happened in modern congressional elections. However, these totals were something of a mirage. Although high-flying but ill-fated red-state Democratic challengers like Jamie Harrison (SC) and Amy McGrath (KY) accounted for more than $250 million in 2020, the average incumbent still outspent the average challenger by a five-to-one ratio. Since then, it has become clear that 2020 was an outlier. The 2022 and 2024 congressional contests brought challengers down to earth. In 2024, challengers accounted for about 30 percent of the fundraising in incumbent-held seats in both the House and the Senate.

It appears, then, that at least in the realm of fundraising, the incumbency advantage remains firmly in place. The appetite for funding incumbents appears healthier than ever, and at least in Congress, incumbents reaped the rewards. The House saw the highest incumbent reelection rate (97 percent) since 2004, and only three incumbent senators lost their seats. These senators included Jon Tester of Montana and Sherrod Brown of Ohio, both of whom massively outraised their opponents; but in Republican-trending states, their status as Democrats was too much to overcome. Other incumbents, such as Tammy Baldwin (WI), Jacky Rosen (NV), and Rick Scott (FL), raised comparatively less than Tester or Brown but secured victories anyway.

Money clearly was not decisive in many congressional races. Democrats outraised Republicans in all but two of the key Senate races featured in figure 3—Texas and Florida—and both were won by Republicans. But Democrats also lost races where they outspent Republicans by huge margins. Drawing conclusions about the best and most efficient ways to spend money in congressional elections is a hotly debated topic. This chapter cannot and will not solve this particular conundrum. But it does offer another piece of evidence that, in many cases, no amount of money is enough to overcome unfavorable partisan fundamentals.

Conclusion

The 2024 campaign revealed a collection of both continuing trends and new questions about the role of money in federal elections. Many of the campaign-finance–related headlines marking this contentious election feel like history repeating itself: More money was spent than in just about any other election in history, and this money was geared almost exclusively toward competitive states and districts across the country. At the same time, new trends began to emerge that could offer hints about the future of campaign fundraising and spending. For example, new financiers entered the political arena and found novel ways to leverage the campaign finance legal system in order to spend these record amounts.

Clearly an important set of differences between the Democratic and Republican Parties has emerged on a number of important fronts that will be crucial to monitor in elections to come. Both parties have an array of both small donors and supportive millionaires and billionaires willing to shell out a great deal to support their causes. But the tactical divide between the parties on the campaign finance front is becoming more apparent: Small-dollar donations from Democrats are flooding in directly to candidates and the party organization. These donations, at both the presidential and congressional levels, appear to be fueled in large part by emotion, enthusiasm, and negative partisan feelings about Republican "villains."

These drivers, along with reactive donating in response to catalyzing media and campaign events, are leading to a cavalcade of dollars flowing directly into candidate committees, in which campaigns have more control over the money, as well as the tactics and strategies they fund. However, many of these donations went either to candidates who didn't need them or to ones who were unlikely to win.

Republicans, meanwhile, are reaping the benefits of having wealthy benefactors and their own campaign finance vehicles of choice: super PACs and other noncandidate, nonparty organizations. Their approach, too, has its benefits and drawbacks. These noncandidate organizations can raise and spend virtually unlimited amounts of money, often received from undisclosed sources that might raise scrutiny from the press or the opposition if they were revealed. But in relying so heavily on benefactors like Elon Musk, Donald Trump and the Republicans ceded not just explicit control over how the money was spent but autonomy over the campaign operations that money was used to fund. Even so, new research has examined the many ways in which outside groups and the official campaigns find ways to coordinate, even when such coordination is technically against the law.[28]

Much of the debate about the role of money in American elections revolves around the proposition that money affects outcomes. The outsize influence of big donors, or super PACs, or independent-spending billionaires may not be nearly so concerning if the billions spent are being wasted or grievously misspent on vanity projects. The actual electoral consequences of these dollars, or these divergent party strategies, remain difficult to know for certain. However, political scientists and journalists alike should continue to question and evaluate the efficacy of these massive sums of money being injected into the process. As the amount of money and cost of campaigns continue to grow unabated, politics—and vote choices—appear more than ever to be nearly set in stone.

Notes

1. Gary Jacobson, "Campaign Spending Effects in U.S. Senate Elections: Evidence from the National Annenberg Election Survey," *Electoral Studies* 25, no. 2 (2006): 195–226.
2. John Sides et al., *The Bitter End: The 2020 Presidential Campaign and the Challenge to American Democracy* (Princeton University Press, 2022).
3. "2024 Republican Presidential Nomination," RealClear Polling, accessed February 13, 2025, https://www.realclearpolling.com/polls/president/republican-primary/2024/national.

4. William A. Galston, "Biden's Debate Performance Threatens His Ability to Win," Brookings, July 5, 2024, https://www.brookings.edu/articles /bidens-debate-performance-threatens-his-ability-to-win/.

5. Zeke Miller et al., "Biden Drops Out of 2024 Race After Disastrous Debate Inflamed Age Concerns. VP Harris Gets His Nod," Associated Press, July 21, 2024.

6. Jessica Piper and Hailey Fuchs, "Kamala Harris Takes Over War Chest as Biden Campaign Becomes Harris for President," *Politico*, July 21, 2024, https://www.politico.com/news/2024/07/21/kamala-harris-biden -campaign-funds-00170136.

7. Scott Young, "Can Kamala Harris Access Biden Campaign Funds?," *Harvard Law Today*, July 24, 2024, https://hls.harvard.edu/today/can-kamala -harris-access-biden-campaign-funds/.

8. Daniel I. Weiner, "Can Harris Use Biden's Campaign Money?," Brennan Center for Justice, July 29, 2024, https://www.brennancenter.org/our-work /analysis-opinion/can-harris-use-bidens-campaign-money.

9. Kristen Holmes et al., "Trump Campaign Files FEC Complaint Trying to Block Biden Funds Transferring to Harris," CNN, July 23, 2024, https:// www.cnn.com/2024/07/23/politics/trump-campaign-fec-complaint -block-biden-harris-funds/index.html.

10. Jeffrey M. Jones, "Democrats Drive Surge in Election Enthusiasm," Gallup, August 29, 2024, https://news.gallup.com/poll/649397/democrats -drive-surge-election-enthusiasm.aspx.

11. Ollie Gratzinger, "Small Donors Give Big Money in 2020 Election Cycle," OpenSecrets, October 30, 2020, https://www.opensecrets.org/news/2020 /10/small-donors-give-big-2020-thanks-to-technology/.

12. Daniel Politi, "Donations to Democratic Groups Soar After Ruth Bader Ginsburg's Death," *Slate*, September 19, 2020.

13. Shannon Bond et al., "Light on News, Heavy on Personality in Elon Musk and Donald Trump X Interview," NPR, August 12, 2024, https://www.npr .org/2024/08/12/g-s1-16698/trump-musk-x-interview.

14. Adam Bonica, "1/ A thread on the madness of Dem fundraising and why it needs to change Look at this chart of political fundraising emails I received in 2024:—3,212 fundraising emails in total.—48 in a single day! Badgering your supporters is disrespectful," Bluesky, December 3, 2024, https://bsky.app/profile/adambonica.bsky.social /post/3lcg3vjt2cs26.

15. Nicole Narea, "Why Are Political Campaigns Always Guilt-Tripping Us to Donate?" *Vox*, October 9, 2024.

16. Maryclaire Dale, "Elon Musk's $1 Million-a-Day Voter Sweepstakes Can Proceed, a Pennsylvania Judge Says," Associated Press, November 4, 2024.

17. Clarissa-Jan Lim, "Here's How Much Money Elon Musk Spent to Help Trump Win the Election," MSNBC, December 6, 2024, https://www

.msnbc.com/top-stories/latest/elon-musk-trump-donations-2024
-election-rcna183231.

18. Julia Ingram and Steve Reilly, "Elon Musk Spends $277 Million to Back
Trump and Republican Candidates," CBS News, December 6, 2024,
https://www.cbsnews.com/news/elon-musk-277-million-trump-repub
lican-candidates-donations/.

19. "Introduction," OpenSecrets, accessed February 13, 2025, https://www
.opensecrets.org/outsidespending/.

20. "Dark Money," OpenSecrets, accessed February 13, 2025, https://www
.opensecrets.org/dark-money/basics.

21. Ciara Torres-Spelliscy, "Dark Money in the 2020 Election," Brennan Center for Justice, November 20, 2020, https://www.brennancenter.org/our
-work/analysis-opinion/dark-money-2020-election.

22. "Outside Spending, by Super PAC," OpenSecrets, accessed February 13,
2025, https://www.opensecrets.org/outside-spending/super_pacs.

23. Frances E. Lee, *Insecure Majorities: Congress and the Perpetual Campaign*
(University of Chicago Press, 2016).

24. Charles R. Hunt et al., "Assessing Group Incentives, Independent Spending, and Campaign Finance Law by Comparing the States," *Election Law
Journal* 19, no. 3 (2020): 374–391.

25. Hunt et al., "Assessing Group Incentives."

26. "Vote Save America PAC Contributions to Federal Candidates," Open-
Secrets, accessed February 13, 2025, https://www.opensecrets.org/political
-action-committees-pacs/vote-save-america/C00835587/candidate
-recipients/2024.

27. Leonie Huddy et al., "Expressive Partisanship: Campaign Involvement,
Political Emotion, and Partisan Identity," *American Political Science
Review* 109, no. 1 (2015): 1–17.

28. Gabriel Foy-Sutherland and Saurav Ghosh, "Coordination in Plain Sight:
The Breadth and Uses of 'Redboxing' in Congressional Elections," *Election Law Journal* 23, no. 2 (2024): 149–172.

The Media

HOW MEDIA NORMS HELPED DONALD TRUMP WIN

Marjorie Randon Hershey

Chicago Tribune journalist Jon Margolis explained his decision to stop covering political news and move to the sports beat this way: He had never seen a sports story that read, "The Chicago Cubs defeated the St. Louis Cardinals today by a score of 3–2. The Cardinals denied it."[1]

Spin is not rare in politics, and its consequences can be profound.[2] But one particular interpretation of the 2024 election, like those in 2020 and 2016, stood out. The Republican presidential candidate, Donald Trump, announced before each election that he would not commit to accepting the election results if he lost.[3] He was, in short, refusing the "loser's consent"—the norm in a democracy that election results, presuming that the election was fair, must be accepted by the losing candidates.[4]

Trump's statements were unprecedented for an American presidential candidate. They implied that he planned (or hoped to provoke) a coup if he lost, preventing the peaceful transfer of power fundamental to any democratic system. In fact, after losing in 2020, Trump prompted a march on the Capitol Building ending in violence, to stop Congress from performing its constitutional duty to count the electoral votes showing that Democrat Joe Biden had won.

This chapter suggests that covering Trump and his efforts to undermine the legitimacy of U.S. elections is one of the biggest challenges American media have faced in decades. The story of Trump's coverage, especially given his narrow victory in 2024, underscores the critical role of journalists in protecting a democracy. How should media outlets deal with a presidential campaign in which the acceptance of core democratic principles hangs in the balance? If journalists uncritically report candidates' denials of the vote totals, then they risk recirculating false charges of voter fraud and normalizing antidemocratic behavior. If they avoid this trap by focusing mainly on campaign strategy and the actual vote totals, they trivialize a genuine threat. And if they call out the false statements, their media outlets will be accused of partisan bias.

Journalists had identified those challenges by 2024 but failed to deal effectively with them. One reason is that some candidates use the institutional norms of American journalism—standards that define "news" and direct media attention toward certain types of stories and not others—to control their coverage to a degree that other candidates can't replicate. This raises questions about the adequacy of those media norms in fulfilling journalists' essential constitutional role.

Media Coverage of the 2024 Election

When it began, the 2024 presidential campaign looked like a yawner. Columnist Philip Bump pointed out, "Americans under the age of 11 have never experienced a Republican presidential nominee who wasn't Donald Trump."[5] The presumptive Democratic nominee was the incumbent president, Biden. The campaign was shaping up to be a rerun of 2020.

Then everything changed. After a dull primary season, a painfully poor performance by Biden in the first presidential debate in June produced intense and ultimately successful pressure on him to withdraw from the campaign. In a rare display of array, Democratic Party leaders and convention delegates agreed within hours to name Vice President Kamala Harris as their new presidential nominee.

Until Biden withdrew, coverage of his administration was largely negative.[6] Many economic indicators were improving,[7] yet most media reports reflected the naysayers.[8] Researchers found Biden's press coverage to be as negative as, and often more negative than, Trump's during his fourth year in office[9]—that is, when Biden got media coverage at all.

As the incumbent president in 2024, Biden would have been expected to dominate media reports. But he couldn't compete with the media phenomenon that was Donald Trump. In 2016, Trump received more coverage than all sixteen of his opponents for the Republican nomination combined.[10] That prevented these candidates from attracting public notice.[11] The pattern repeated in 2020.[12] Even during the early months of the new Biden administration in 2021, almost half of the stories about his presidency mentioned Trump, though the latter was now a private citizen.[13] Again in 2024, Trump received a disproportionate amount of coverage on every media platform.[14] The *Columbia Journalism Review* called out the media "obsession with Trump" that led to "his ability to act as the press's assignment editor."[15] The media attention allowed Trump to control the national political debate, even when out of office, to a degree that few other public figures have achieved.

Copious amounts of coverage do not always help a candidate. If the coverage is mainly negative, as Trump's often was, it might weaken the candidate's public support. However, Trump dealt effectively with this threat by inoculating his supporters against unflattering coverage, telling his audience frequently that mainstream media were untrustworthy. He claimed that any media criticism of him was "fake news," that journalists were "scum" and even "enemies of the American people" out to destroy him, and therefore that none of their reporting should be believed. Trump said so in virtually every campaign speech and most of his social media posts in 2024, as he had in 2020 and 2016.[16] As a result, he was uniquely able to benefit from the avalanche of press attention he received without suffering from its critical tone, at least in the eyes of his supporters.

In fact, when Trump won the 2024 election with 49.8 percent of the popular vote, reporters didn't stress the narrowness of his win. Instead, they echoed Trump's own claim that he had "an unprecedented and powerful mandate"[17] by calling it a "sweeping victory"[18] (*USA Today*) and a "decisive victory"[19] (Associated Press). The evidence said otherwise. In fact, three candidates have won the presidency since 2000 with less than a majority of the popular vote, and Trump has been two of those candidates.

Journalists as well as their critics knew they were giving Trump an unfair advantage, at least in the amount of coverage.[20] After the 2016 election, many journalists were concerned enough about having given Trump such an edge that they asked publicly how to avoid repeating it.[21] They failed. In both 2019–20 and early 2023, the same questions reappeared. Columnists' headlines warned, "If Trump Runs Again, Do Not Cover Him the Same Way"[22] and advised, "How the Media Can Cover Trump Better This Time."[23] Trump's advantage in coverage did ebb for a time when Harris replaced Biden as the Democrats' candidate, because that event was so novel, but Trump's dominance of the news soon returned.[24]

Media Coverage Has Systemic Biases

If journalists acknowledged this imbalance and criticized themselves for it, why did they not correct it? How could one candidate so markedly dominate media coverage in three successive presidential races? One possible explanation is that Trump often tried to intimidate journalists—as, for instance, when he told an ABC reporter questioning him about previous racist statements, "I don't think I've ever been asked a question in such a horrible manner. . . . And for you to start off a question and answer period . . . in such a hostile manner, I think it's a disgrace."[25] A more likely possibility is that systemic biases in media norms, very different from the type of bias often alleged,[26] led journalists to focus obsessively on Trump. That thwarted their ability to hold Trump accountable for his conduct throughout this period.

Expectations about media coverage of politics have changed over time, but definitions of "news" have remained largely constant, to the point of becoming media norms.[27] Many of these norms as to what is newsworthy derive from the first need of any medium: to hold an audience. Thus, what constitutes news involves content that attracts viewers and readers: current events that involve drama, conflict, outrage, rule-breaking, novelty, timeliness, and, of course, accessibility to the reporter.[28] Events with these qualities can better attract an audience big enough to pay the bills and lend prestige to a media outlet than covering the millions of more mundane events that fill our days. Another, more recent set of media norms refers to objectivity, balance, and fairness.[29] In practical terms, *balance* is usually interpreted to mean presenting "both sides," even if there are more than two sides, and even if one of the sides is not true.[30] For many news media, and especially for the writers of the First Amendment, holding government accountable is another important component of a media outlet's role.[31]

All three of Trump's presidential campaigns have been remarkably skilled at providing news media with a constant flow of content meeting these criteria. As Trump explained in 2016, when speaking to rallies, he often looked not at the audience but at the TV cameras, "checking to see if the red lights on the cameras were ablaze, indicating that his words were going out live on cable. [If the lights went off,] 'I would say something new to keep the red light on,' Trump said—and if that happened to diverge from what he had said even weeks before, that was secondary to keeping the red light on."[32] The result, as media analyst Thomas Patterson noted, is that "Trump is to reporters as honey is to bears. Journalists prize conflict, and Trump delivers it in abundance."[33]

Because Trump has such a finely honed ability to deliver audiences to media outlets, covering him boosts news organizations' bottom line. Because stories about Trump draw big audiences, media outlets' revenues have been pumped up by the increased viewership and readership. CBS chair Les Moonves admitted that Trump's candidacy "may not be good for America, but it's damn good for CBS."[34] Beginning with the first Trump campaign, audiences for cable news shows and traditional news outlets such as *The New York Times* and *The Washington Post* doubled or tripled, and new media outlets established niches.[35] One month after Trump left the presidency in 2021, CNN lost 45 percent of its prime-time viewers. When he declared he was running again, cable news audiences began to rise once more.[36] As poll aggregator Nate Silver noted, "It was just a truism in 2016 and 2020 that if you wanted to drive traffic on the Internet, you framed the story around Donald Trump."[37]

The Norm That "News" Is What's Dramatic, Conflict-Filled, and Unusual

As a real estate developer and reality TV star, Trump had decades of practice in feeding journalists the steady stream of clickbait that kept reporters' bylines in the news and their media outlets attracting audiences. That served his need for public attention.[38] He salted his public statements with enough shock value to increase their newsworthiness. News audiences had not been accustomed to a presidential candidate so willing to deviate from traditional presidential behavior: for example, regularly calling anyone who challenged him "human scum that is working so hard to destroy our Once Great Country," "suckers," "evil people," "thugs and monsters," and "wackos."[39] Shortly before the 2024 election, Trump continued to mispronounce Harris's first name in rallies, repeated that she was "retarded," called her a "shit vice president," and questioned the manhood of her vice-presidential running mate, Governor Tim Walz.[40] Trump claimed (as he had with Biden in 2020) that Harris intended to ban cows, abolish suburbs and the Fourth of July, eliminate windows from new buildings, abolish the oil and natural gas industries, require all Americans to learn to speak Chinese, and start World War III.[41] The constant repetition of these norm-breaking charges kept him in the news, as well as normalizing such aberrant language in viewers' minds.[42]

Trump's behavior also made him an irresistible draw for media organizations. He was the only president in history to be impeached twice by the House of Representatives and to be charged with unlawful conduct in trying to steal a national election. Journalists were riveted when Trump became the first president to be indicted by a grand jury, on thirty-four counts of falsifying business records. As one reported, "Hour after hour on Tuesday, the story occupied the full attention of broadcast and cable news networks. They waited for glimpses of Trump's face to interpret his expression, followed his motorcade's movements from the air, speculated on how it must feel to be arrested. The coverage recalled better days for now-struggling cable news outlets, through two presidential campaigns and two impeachment trials, when Trump occupied hours of airtime."[43]

During his trial, Trump attacked the judge as "totally compromised" and "corrupt"[44]—unusual behavior for a criminal defendant. Even Trump's absence from an event became big news. When he skipped a 2023 Republican debate in Iowa, an Associated Press story devoted its lead and most of the rest of the story not to the points made by the candidates who were present but to how many of them mentioned the absent Trump in their remarks.[45]

News values clearly affected President Biden's decision to exit the campaign. Biden's performance in the first presidential debate, held in June, was unexpectedly poor;[46] his delivery was halting, and he seemed weak. Trump, too, demonstrated an obvious weakness in the debate; he was found to have made at least nineteen false statements in ninety minutes.[47] That's one lie every 4.7 minutes. Journalists had to decide whether their lead story should be Trump's consistent lying or Biden's apparent ineffectiveness. Both were serious issues. But it was Biden's lapses that dominated media reports. As journalist Jennifer Schulze reported, *The New York Times* carried 142 news stories and 50 opinion pieces about Biden's weak performance during the week following the debate, far outweighing its coverage of Trump's falsehoods.[48] Soon after, several major legacy outlets called for Biden to step aside as the Democratic nominee, but not for Trump to leave the race. Both Biden's verbal stumbles and Trump's lies were old news at that point. But the drama of Biden's weakness, in a race that had been static for months, played to Trump's advantage in news coverage.

The novelty of such a late change in a party's presidential nominee, as well as Harris's becoming the first Black woman and Indian American to gain a major party's presidential nomination, temporarily disrupted Trump's command of the news cycle. Starting two days after Harris became the presumptive nominee, mentions of her on cable news shows and Google searches for her eclipsed those of Trump for a time. But just a few weeks later, Trump regained the spotlight with new insults. He held a photo op in a no-politics portion of Arlington National Cemetery, after which his aides intimidated a cemetery staffer who tried to stop them. Then, after Harris was seen as besting Trump in their only presidential debate, Trump again commanded headlines with a lie about Haitian immigrants in Ohio eating residents' pets.

In both news coverage and Google searches (figure 1), then, Trump has far eclipsed his opponents ever since his first appearance as a presidential candidate. As the figure shows, this was true not only of Trump's initial campaign, when he was a relative novelty, but throughout every year of Biden's term as president—a remarkable finding.

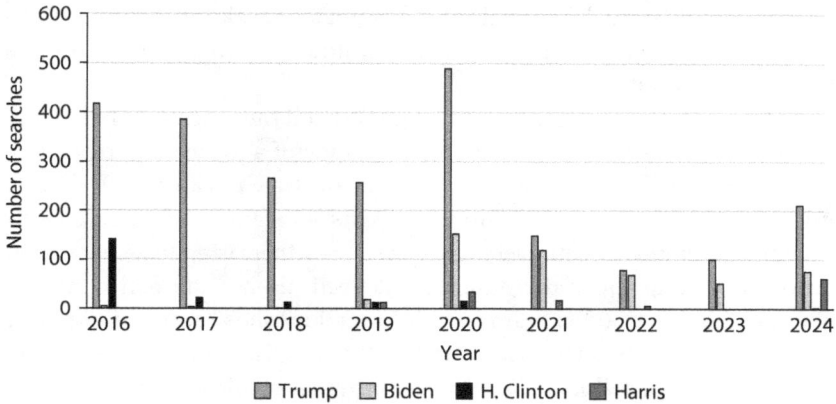

Fig. 1. The Trump advantage: Google searches for Trump, Biden, Harris, and Hillary Clinton, 2016–2024
Source: Calculated from Nate Silver, "This Was Trump's Election to Lose. And He Just Might," *Silver Bulletin*, September 13, 2024, https://www.natesilver.net/p/this-was -trumps-election-to-lose.

Effects of the Norm of News "Objectivity" and "Balance"

Another norm of modern media coverage, at least in the "mainstream" media, is that coverage should be objective—that news organizations should present both sides as deserving of consideration and should defer to public officials by reporting their major statements. Although the First Amendment was enacted at a time of universal partisanship in the press, a century later the notion that journalism should be factual, impartial, and independent of partisan sources became accepted because the emerging new media of broadcasting and mass-circulation newspapers required a large audience to make profits.[49] Since the canceling of the fairness doctrine in the 1980s[50] and the rise of Fox News, MSNBC, and other partisan cable networks and internet sites, partisan media have resurged. With the rise of conservative media, mainstream outlets have often been accused of liberal bias. That has caused mainstream journalists to work even harder to show that they are not partisan or biased.

The challenge of the objectivity norm is that it lends itself too easily to the pitfall of false equivalence. When journalists report negative behavior by one side in an election, they often feel the need to report a negative act by the other side in the same story, even if the two behaviors are not comparable.[51] Similarly, journalists may feel pressure to report lies told by a candidate without identifying them as lies because of the notion that media people should let public officials and candidates speak for themselves. To call a candidate's false statement a "lie" would seem to put the reporter's objectivity in doubt.

But reporters then face the conundrum, What if the statement is a lie? Not saying so would call into question the accuracy of a journalist's reporting. During Trump's first term, fact-checkers demonstrated that he made false or misleading claims 30,573 times over four years—an average of 20 falsehoods in public pronouncements every day of his term, increasing to 39 per day in 2020.[52] A Trump spokesperson even redefined lies as "alternative facts."[53] Trump's falsehoods often referred to information whose accuracy could be easily checked, such as his false claim that the crowd at his first inauguration was the largest in history.[54] Yet most mainstream media outlets were reluctant to use the word *lie*. "To lie, editors reasoned, means to intend to be untruthful. Since journalists couldn't be inside politicians' heads, how were we supposed to know if—by this definition—they were really lying?"[55] Instead, reporters used euphemisms such as "alleged" and "inaccurate claim," which sounded like gentler violations of the norm of objectivity.

Trump's tactics included throwing so many lies at his audience in a speech that journalists were unable to keep up. This tactic—known as the Gish Gallop, after the originator of the strategy[56]—dominated Trump's approach in the first presidential debate. The volume of Trump's misstatements was enormous, from arguing that infanticide is legal in Democrat-run states to claiming that no terrorist attacks had occurred during his term of office.[57] The sheer volume of falsehoods left journalists stymied in their effort to correct the record. Perhaps as a result, debate coverage, rather than detailing this barrage of lies, focused instead on Biden's weakness.[58]

The most consequential of Trump's false statements was his repeated claim of widespread fraud in the 2020 election. Even after all fifty states certified their results, Trump continued to say he had won a "landslide" victory. According to the Pew Research Center, the lie gained widespread currency among his voters: In a January 2021 survey, three-quarters of Trump supporters incorrectly said he was "definitely or probably the rightful winner of the election."[59]

Covering the "Big Lie"

As early as June 2020, Trump began laying the groundwork for an outlandish story: that although he was behind in the polls at the time, and his approval ratings in most respected polls during his presidency had never topped 50 percent, the only way he could lose in 2020 was if the vote count was fraudulent. After a poorly attended rally, he tweeted, for instance, "RIGGED 2020 ELECTION; MILLIONS OF MAIL-IN BALLOTS WILL BE PRINTED BY FOREIGN COUNTRIES, AND OTHERS. IT WILL BE THE SCANDAL OF OUR TIMES!" (June 22, 2020). It was a brazen attempt to convince his supporters that the only legitimate elections were those that Trump won. This stance, combined with the polarization of American politics and the fact that Trump supporters tended to talk mainly with other Trump supporters, gave it widespread credibility among Republicans.

On election night in 2020, when a large portion of votes had not yet been tallied, Trump announced that he had won and that any subsequent vote counting (for example, of the large numbers of mailed-in ballots) would be evidence of voter fraud. His supporters mounted more than sixty court challenges to election results. Although virtually all those lawsuits were rejected under the most intense scrutiny given any U.S. presidential election,[60] Trump doggedly insisted that he was still the lawful president and called media outlets that reported the actual vote totals "fake news." Other Republican candidates soon took up the lie. In the 2022 midterms, twenty-three Republican candidates for secretary of state in nineteen states—the office that oversees vote counting in state elections—claimed that the 2020 vote count was false and Trump had won.[61]

Trump used the same playbook in 2024. His repeated claims that massive election fraud was underway continued right up to Election Day,[62] including that Democrats were importing undocumented immigrants to vote unlawfully for Harris.[63] Because of these massive "frauds," he urged his supporters, "you have to fight for the right of the country."[64] Trump's claims of widespread voter fraud stopped immediately when he was called the winner in 2024, and posts on X's "Election Integrity" page dropped precipitously.[65]

In short, Trump was advantaged by the media norm of objectivity. It enabled him to flood the zone with lies but largely avoid being held accountable for them by inoculating audiences with charges that the media were biased against him. Similarly, the need to appear objective required journalists to repeat Trump's frequent use of dehumanizing language when referring to immigrants, calling them "animals," "not human," "violent criminals," and "poisoning the blood of our country"[66] without characterizing them as racist tropes. Stories about the "horse race"—who's ahead in the polls?—fit more easily into the norm of objectivity, even though they focus media attention on a matter much less important than protecting democracy. And ironically, journalists' efforts to follow that norm of objectivity did not protect them from frequent charges by conservatives that the mainstream media had a liberal bias.[67]

How Did Trump's Dominance of Media Coverage
Affect the Election?

Trump's overwhelming advantage in the volume of media coverage—the result of his exploitation of these media norms—affected the political environment in several ways. It led to widespread dissemination of false information, because reporters could be criticized for violating the norm of objective journalism if they did not convey both candidates' charges, even if one candidate lied profusely. It even put journalists in the position of having to publicize frequent and intense criticisms of themselves, as they tried to show their objectivity by repeating Trump's claims.[68]

Trump's frequent references to "fake news" were accompanied by an increase in Republicans' distrust of media, excepting Fox News and other conservative outlets. In 2016, early in Trump's campaign, fully 70 percent of Republican identifiers reported at least "some trust" in national news organizations. By late 2019 that had dropped to 49 percent, and again to 35 percent in 2021.[69] In a 2024 Gallup poll asking how much trust people had in ten civic institutions, respondents ranked the news media dead last. Fewer than a third of respondents said they trusted the media to report the news fully, accurately, and fairly, compared with 36 percent who expressed no trust at all.[70] This was especially true among Republicans (figure 2). In a 2021 YouGov poll, a remarkable 92 percent of Trump voters strongly or somewhat agreed that "the mainstream media today is just part of the Democratic Party."[71] Republicans who strongly approved of Trump were much more likely than others to say that journalists have "very low ethical standards."[72]

Republican distrust of the media didn't start with Trump; Republicans have expressed less trust in the media's fairness and accuracy since President Richard Nixon's attacks on the press in the 1960s and early 1970s. But figure 2 shows clearly that in 2016, during Trump's first campaign, trust levels among Republicans dropped to the level usually reached only by used-car dealers and people selling home repairs door-to-door. Distrust in the national media has now become a salient part of the Republican identity.[73]

Similarly, Trump's false claim that the 2020 election results had been rigged affected his supporters' feelings about democracy in general. Polls in October 2024 showed that almost 60 percent of all respondents were concerned or very concerned about voter fraud in the 2024 election, including 86 percent of Republicans[74]—higher than was the case in 2020.[75] So was the number of Republican candidates who claimed on social media that the 2024 elections would be rigged, including almost half of

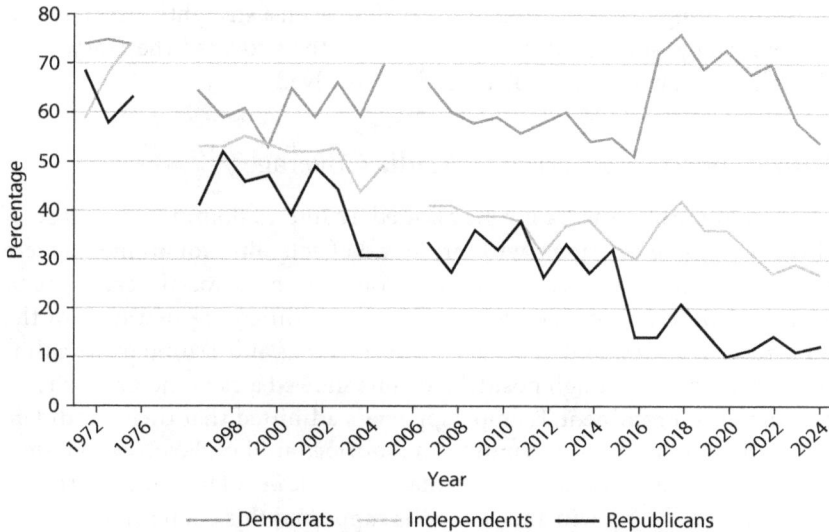

FIG. 2. How much do Republicans and Democrats trust mass media?
Note: Percentages are those responding "a great deal" or "a fair amount" to the question, "In general, how much trust and confidence do you have in the mass media—such
as newspapers, TV and radio—when it comes to reporting the news fully, accurately
and fairly—a great deal, a fair amount, not very much or none at all?"
Source: Gallup data cited in Megan Brenan, "Americans' Trust in Media Remains at
Trend Low," Gallup, October 14, 2024, https://news.gallup.com/poll/651977/americans
-trust-media-remains-trend-low.aspx.

Republican candidates for Congress or top state offices.[76] Some of the negative feeling may have been performative—a desire to express solidarity
with the Trump movement—but it raises serious questions about Republicans' willingness to defend democratic institutions against attacks from
the inside.

Finally, mainstream and conservative media failed to uncover the depth
and breadth of Trump's efforts to overturn his 2020 election loss until long
after the evidence had become overwhelming. Although investigators published a memo from a Trump lawyer listing methods to invalidate the
election result and return Trump to the White House, "there was no on-air
news coverage [of this compelling memo]—literally zero on the three
major broadcast networks: ABC, NBC, and CBS. Not on the evening
newscasts watched by more than 20 million Americans. . . . Not on the
morning shows the next day. . . . (Some late-night hosts did manage to play
it for laughs.)"[77] Perhaps journalists had become so inured to Trump's

norm-breaking that they gave short shrift to even a straightforward threat to democracy—or feared charges of bias if they covered the story, even though later court cases verified the facts involved.

What Constrained Trump's Media Coverage?

In sum, important media norms allowed Trump to dominate coverage of three successive elections, with profound effects. But not all media were equally susceptible to Trump's brand of domination. As was the case in 2020 and 2016, different media outlets offered very different portrayals of the 2024 race. The presidential debate between Harris and Trump offers a dramatic example. Although postdebate polls showed a clear victory for Harris, and even prominent Trump supporters admitted that their candidate had done a poor job, between nine and fourteen million Fox News viewers saw a completely different commentary. Fox viewers learned that Trump had just scored a big win and that polls supported this contention.[78]

Similarly, consider media coverage of Trump's efforts right after the 2020 election to get Georgia election officials to "find 11,000 votes"—in short, to falsify the popular vote count so Trump could overturn Biden's victory in the state. Fox News reported the story much less frequently than did the two other most popular cable news channels, CNN and MSNBC (figure 3). How much viewers learned about Trump's election interference, then, depended in part on which channel they watched.[79]

Of course, people do not randomly choose which media outlets to watch or read. Partisan sorting in the media audience, with conservatives tending toward outlets such as Fox News and liberals preferring MSNBC, means that a significant portion of the politically involved population hears only consistently conservative or consistently liberal media content.[80] In swing states, individuals' choice of media outlets such as Fox News, conservative talk radio and podcasts, X, and friends and family was linked with support for Trump.[81]

Media portrayals on Fox News and other right-wing outlets stating that Trump's crimes were not disqualifying and that even if they were, Biden was no less crooked, encouraged the belief among some Trump supporters that any effort to overturn the election result was justified.[82] Trump's ability to shape his media coverage varied according to the partisan leanings of the media outlet involved.

Trump's ability to spread misinformation was further amplified when he created his own social medium, Truth Social, in 2022, after Twitter and Facebook banned him for inciting violence on January 6, 2021. Trump

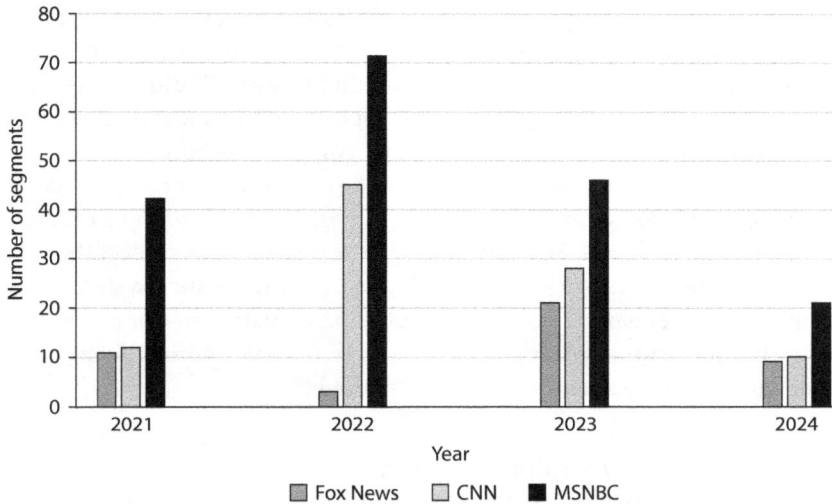

FIG. 3. Cable outlets differ in reporting Trump's attempt to "find votes," 2021–2024
Note: Data points are fifteen-second segments in which the words "find 11,000 votes" appear.
Source: Calculated from the GDELT Project.

reached "only" eight million followers on Truth Social—about a tenth of the number he had formerly reached on Twitter. Yet Truth Social gave him an unmediated outlet, which he used extensively, in an increasingly inflammatory tone.[83] And when Trump supporter Elon Musk bought Twitter, claiming that it had censored right-wing posts, it, too, became a pro-Trump echo chamber.[84]

Trump used Truth Social to pre-interpret his 2024 felony trial in New York for supporters. Before and during the trial, he labeled the judge in the case "corrupt," "a whacked out nut job," and a "devil" who "literally crucified" defense witnesses,[85] and stated that the jurors ("supposedly American"), the prosecution, and its witnesses would all be part of a criminal conspiracy not to be trusted. Right after the jury returned a guilty verdict, he posted, "It's all RIGGED, the whole system is RIGGED" (May 30, 2024). In another criminal trial, he "truthed" about the prosecutor, "HAPPY EASTER TO ALL, INCLUDING CROOKED AND CORRUPT PROSECUTORS AND JUDGES THAT ARE DOING EVERYTHING POSSIBLE TO INTERFERE WITH THE PRESIDENTIAL ELECTION OF 2024, AND PUT ME IN PRISON, INCLUDING THOSE MANY PEOPLE THAT I COMPLETELY & TOTALLY DESPISE BECAUSE THEY WANT TO DESTROY AMERICA, A NOW FAILING NATION" (March 31, 2024).

Other Trump allies quickly followed his lead, calling the New York trial and its guilty verdict "a sham show trial," a "kangaroo court," "total witch-hunt," and "worthy of a banana republic" and terming Trump "a political prisoner."[86] He extended his effort to delegitimize the upcoming election by claiming that the U.S. Postal Service is "going to lose hundreds of thousands of ballots. Maybe purpose-ly. Or maybe just through incompetence."[87] Posts such as these gave voters reason to question the election result even before ballots were cast. His messages urged readers to also suspect the U.S. Department of Justice, President Biden, and even the justice system more generally. His extensive use of his Truth Social platform—an average of twenty-nine "truths" a day—enabled him to hammer home the message that democratic institutions cannot be trusted.[88]

How Media Norms Kept Journalists from Holding Trump Accountable

Important norms of media coverage, as interpreted by the mainstream media, have been a vital part of Trump's success in dominating U.S. politics for almost a decade. These norms—the older one defining "news" as that which is dramatic and conflict-filled and the more recent one urging mainstream journalists to be "objective" and present both sides—have allowed Trump to exercise disproportionate influence in elections and political discourse. The result is that major media outlets have become unintentionally complicit in efforts to undermine central aspects of American democracy, including the integrity of elections and the pivotal democratic role of the media themselves.

The media's need for audiences and the advertising dollars audiences attract, joined with Trump's ability to provide them, may indicate that journalists simply aren't able to hold someone like him accountable. The media were not alone; traditional Republican leaders were also unable to prevent their candidates and officeholders from making false claims about voter fraud.[89] Other core democratic institutions have been better able to defend themselves. For instance, courts in several cases penalized media coverage that enabled Trump's behavior. Fox News was required to pay almost $800 million to the election technology company Dominion Voting Systems, after a court ruled not only that Fox programs claimed falsely that Dominion rigged the 2020 election in favor of Biden but that Fox executives were aware the claims were false.[90] Yet the canons of "objective journalism" proved inadequate to the needs of a democratic polity during this highly contentious time.

Trump's resulting dominance of media coverage imposed a substantial opportunity cost on viewers and readers. Because any media outlet's capacity to cover stories is finite, the outsize coverage of Trump necessarily came at the cost of covering other major stories. As the *Columbia Journalism Review* pointed out, "Not only has the Trump obsession often drowned out bigger stories—crises like climate change, racism, immigration, anti-trans discrimination, inadequate healthcare, poverty, and gun violence, all of which predated Trump and will outlast him—it has forced us to see them, when we see them at all, through the distorting, flattening lens of the man himself."[91] It has long been clear that some of the most important forces affecting Americans' lives—from increasing economic inequality to the effects of tariffs, taxes, and interest rates on household budgets—are much less likely to meet the media definition of "news" than are the daily utterings of norm breakers and the drama of conflicts.[92] When media outlets decide what to cover based on what will generate the largest audiences for advertisers or virality for social media influencers, the public will pay a price in terms of the volume and types of information readily available to them.

Similarly, fear of violating the norm of objectivity can keep journalists from portraying reality accurately. As Trump's coherence in rallies and interviews came to be questioned during the fall of 2024,[93] many mainstream news outlets reported bizarre or incoherent Trump remarks as though they made sense, presumably to avoid being criticized for favoring the Harris campaign. Consider the coverage of a Las Vegas Trump rally in which the candidate rambled for some time about sharks, transportation, and electric currents and opined that he'd rather be electrocuted than killed by a shark. *The New York Times* headlined, "Election Updates: Trump Rallies in Las Vegas," and CNN led with "Trump Proposes Eliminating Taxes on Tips at Las Vegas Campaign Rally."[94] Some criticized this as "sanewashing" Trump's comments and failing to raise important questions about an elderly candidate's cognitive capability, even though media figures had raised similar questions about Biden's capabilities. One columnist remarked, "Political media bent on not offending the GOP or its voters wind up covering an election that bears little resemblance to the real one."[95]

Most significantly, the media fixation on Trump permitted him to undermine public trust in central democratic institutions for the purpose of increasing his own vote totals. Some candidates in the past may have tried to fool their constituents into believing that voter fraud was a reason to overrule verified election results. But without the megaphone that modern media attention gave Trump, such a distortion of democratic practices could not be as effective. As the editor of the Cleveland *Plain Dealer* wrote during the 2024 primaries, "The truth is that Donald Trump undermined faith in our elections in his false bid to retain the presidency. . . . There aren't two sides to facts."[96]

What Can Be Done to Help Journalists Protect Democracy?

If some journalistic norms conflict with the needs of voters in a democracy, it makes sense to reconsider those norms. First, editors and journalists need to reconsider their definition of what makes news. Social scientists have written for decades that reporting about new polls, conflicts within a campaign, and candidate stumbles is a kind of fast-food version of journalism: familiar, attractive on the surface, and easy to digest.[97] But although such journalism is often assumed to be more palatable to large audiences, it does not necessarily engage more citizens—especially those with low political interest—or provide them with useful information. It also is not responsible at a time when democratic principles are under attack.[98] Of course media need to attract big audiences. But it is possible for journalists to direct voters' attention to significant issues, even complicated ones, with good writing and engaging approaches.

Dealing with the norm of objectivity is harder. There will always be debate about what constitutes "objectivity" in media coverage. Reporters can't make audiences sample a wide range of viewpoints; selective exposure and selective perception are standard features of voters' political information gathering.[99] Besides, misinformation often comes in more enticing packages than objective facts; conspiracy theories attract attention by offering drama, conflict, and suspense, just as popular entertainment shows do. Some researchers find that misinformation spreads faster and farther than real news, especially on social media.[100]

One possible remedy is increased investigative reporting, to put facts in context. It isn't sufficient for news outlets to report partisan claims of election fraud without at least some investigation of their factual basis, the claimants' records of accuracy, and the implications of the claims for the functioning of government. Similarly, it is not responsible to cover every mention of "vote fraud" in the most carefully watched election in U.S. history without presenting verifiable data on the extent to which such fraud has actually been proved.

Such changes won't be easy. They will generate charges of partisan bias from those who benefit from a failure to investigate false claims. Providing context requires effort, time, and space, which are costly and may seem less appealing to readers and viewers than clickbait is. Change will generate fears about drops in audiences and thus in revenue; most news outlets will struggle to resist the ratings boost that covering Trump has provided during the past decade.

They will do so at a time when boosting ratings has become vital. Newspaper employment has fallen by more than half during the past two decades, especially in printed newspapers,[101] as internet advertising drains newspaper publishers' revenue, and concentration of ownership encourages the owners of news outlets to maximize their profits.[102] The result is that in a large portion of the nation, a single reporter must cover issues ranging from hunger and homelessness to city elections to gardening tips. In more than two hundred daily newspapers between 1999 and 2017, news coverage of local government and elected officials dropped by half, and the trend is continuing.[103] About a quarter of all local print newspapers stopped printing between 2005 and 2020.[104] That means we know less and less about the institutions of governance that affect us the most.[105]

Simply adding fact-checking features to existing media coverage is not enough; it, too, has fallen victim to charges of partisan bias. The media moderators of the September 2024 presidential debate were harshly criticized for correcting four of Trump's false statements in real time, including the lies that it was legal in some states to execute babies after they were born and that Haitian immigrants in Ohio were stealing and eating Americans' pets. As Jonathan V. Last pointed out, "The first duty of a journalistic institution is not to be 'fair' to the politicians it covers. It is to make certain that its audience is presented an accurate view of reality."[106] Besides, labeling Trump's statements "baseless" or "lacking evidence" may be literally accurate, but it may also reduce audiences' trust in reporting, with so many convinced that the mainstream media are "out to get" Trump.[107]

False equivalence—presenting negative information about one side to balance criticism of the other side—is not the same as objectivity. If the evidence is unbalanced, then a "balanced" news report portrays reality inaccurately. Evidence shows increasingly that the current party system is asymmetric: Since the late 2000s, the leadership and primary electorate of the Republican Party has moved further to the right than the Democratic Party has moved to the left.[108] Yet the norm of objectivity presses journalists to pretend that the two parties are mirror images of each other and that a candidate who refuses to give the "loser's consent" in an election is simply taking a routine position in a democratic campaign.

After the 2020 election, some media outlets responded to election denialism by creating "democracy beats" to address the challenges posed by disinformation. In the words of one such organization, "The democracy beat is distinct from the broader politics or government beat. These reporters will focus exclusively on the modern threats to our democracy. . . . They'll cover something that is, at its heart, a local story. It will unfold far from the spotlights of Washington. And it will do the most basic and vital things that journalism is supposed to do: Safeguard democracy. Tell the truth."[109] Initial research found that local journalists primed to consider the need to protect democracy were more likely to take election denial seriously in their coverage.[110]

To be capable of holding government and candidates accountable, media organizations must survive. The growth of "news deserts" is especially common in lower-income and rural communities, which have fewer sources of advertising revenue.[111] People in these areas are then forced to rely on the vagaries of social media or online news sources, which are generally more focused on national news than on local and state governments and politics.[112] That leaves local and state officials freer to act with little scrutiny and removes an important stimulus to local political engagement.

Nonprofits have begun to fill the void.[113] These include organizations whose coverage, at all levels of government, does not depend on meeting the profit levels typically required by traditional media. Such outlets not only can help make up for the sharp declines in reporting of state and local issues but can also be less driven by the financial need to focus on the dramatic, the bizarre, and the norm breakers. If they are sufficiently well funded by donors committed to the protection of a democracy, rather than to the promotion of a candidate or a party—a big "if"—then they would be less vulnerable to the predicament faced by reporters in shorthanded newsrooms: covering candidates or issues they are unfamiliar with. Such unfamiliarity can result in journalists falling back on transcribing what their sources tell them rather than serving as informed investigators. Newsletters and blogs can also offer informed investigations.[114]

Media organizations also need to defend themselves more actively against forces trying to undermine them. When a presidential candidate tells supporters at a rally that he "wouldn't mind" if they shoot at the journalists at that rally,[115] it's not enough just to report his words. Reasonable people do not take a neutral stand on threats to kill them. Current media, and schools training journalists, need to find ways to make accurate portrayals of important topics more enticing and personal. Journalists must prevent the norms of their profession from enabling a weakening of democracy in the United States.

But that doesn't leave the rest of us off the hook. More and more, Americans are moving away from news consumption and toward the infotainment offered by social media, bloggers, podcasters, and other nontraditional sources whose only norms involve attracting audiences.[116] One writer recalled the 1974 removal of President Richard Nixon from office through impeachment: "Nixon was brought down by the work of aggressive journalists, along with a federal judge, a unanimous Supreme Court, and a bipartisan Congress—by strong democratic institutions. But they worked only because Americans still believed in them—because two-thirds of the public, which had just given Nixon a landslide victory, could not abide a criminal in office. That was a different public."[117] When audiences tolerate undemocratic behavior in our search for entertainment, we deserve what we get.

Notes

1. Quoted in Ronald D. Elving, "Campaign Data Can Be Calculated Nonsense," *CQ Weekly*, August 19, 1995, 2602.
2. See, for example, Marjorie Randon Hershey, "Do Constructed Explanations Persist?," *Congress and the Presidency* 38, no. 2 (2011): 131–151.
3. For example, see Yvonne Wingett Sanchez et al., "Republicans Say They Will Trust the Election Results as Long as Trump Wins," *Washington Post*, July 19, 2024.
4. See Geoffrey Layman et al., "Political Parties and Loser's Consent in American Politics," *Annals of the American Academy of Political and Social Science* 708, no. 1 (2024): 164–183.
5. Philip Bump, "Like 2020, Voters View 2024 Through the Lens of Trump," *Washington Post*, June 10, 2024.
6. Roge' Karma, "Is Economic Pessimism the Media's Fault?," *Atlantic*, January 12, 2024.
7. "How Is the US Economy Doing After COVID-19?," World Economic Forum, February 2, 2023, https://www.weforum.org/agenda/2023/02/us-economy-covid19-inflation/.
8. Quoted in Jeff Stein and Ashley Parker, "Inflation Pinch Challenges Biden Agenda, but President Says Worst Will Soon Pass," *Boston Globe*, December 10, 2021.
9. Dana Milbank, "The Media Treats Biden as Badly as—or Worse Than—Trump. Here's Proof," *Washington Post*, December 3, 2021.
10. Marjorie Randon Hershey, "The Media: Covering Donald Trump," in *The Elections of 2016*, ed. Michael Nelson (CQ Press, 2018), 117–118.
11. On 2016, see John Sides et al., *Identity Crisis* (Princeton University Press, 2019).

12. Gary C. Jacobson, "The Presidential and Congressional Elections of 2020: A National Referendum on the Trump Presidency," *Political Science Quarterly* 136, no. 1 (2021): 11–45.

13. Kirsten Worden and Amy Mitchell, "Trump Mentioned in About Half of Biden Stories During Early Weeks in Office," Pew Research Center, May 24, 2021, https://www.pewresearch.org/short-reads/2021/05/24/trump-mentioned-in-about-half-of-biden-stories-during-early-weeks-in-office-but-less-so-over-time/.

14. Luba Kassova and Richard Addy, "How the Democrat-Leaning News Media Is Unwittingly Aiding Trump," *Fortune*, October 25, 2024.

15. Jon Allsop and Pete Vernon, "How the Press Covered the Last Four Years of Trump," *Columbia Journalism Review*, October 23, 2020, https://www.cjr.org/special_report/coverage-trump-presidency-2020-election.php.

16. See, for example, Marjorie Randon Hershey, "Media and the 2020 Presidential Campaign," in *The Elections of 2020*, ed. Michael Nelson (University of Virginia Press, 2021), 138–160.

17. Fred Lucas, "Trump Heralds 'Unprecedented and Powerful Mandate' in Victory Speech," Daily Signal, November 6, 2024, https://www.dailysignal.com/2024/11/06/trump-heralds-unprecedented-and-powerful-mandate-in-victory-speech/.

18. See, for example, Zac Anderson, "Trump Campaign Threats in Spotlight," *Herald Times*, November 8, 2024.

19. Steve Peoples and Bill Barrow, "Election Takeaways: Trump's Decisive Victory in a Deeply Divided Nation," Associated Press, November 6, 2024, https://apnews.com/article/trump-harris-presidential-election-takeaways-d0e4677f4cd53b4d2d8d18d674be5bf4.

20. See David Umberti, "Trump's Media Domination by the Numbers," *Columbia Journalism Review*, September 16, 2015, https://www.cjr.org/analysis/trumps_media_domination_by_the_numbers.php.

21. See, for example, Margaret Sullivan, "Five Ways the Media Can Avoid 2016 Errors," *Washington Post*, July 27, 2020.

22. Margaret Sullivan, "If Trump Runs Again, Do Not Cover Him the Same Way," *Washington Post*, October 12, 2022.

23. Perry Bacon Jr., "How the Media Can Cover Trump Better This Time," *Washington Post*, May 9, 2023.

24. Data from the GDELT Project.

25. Quoted in Tina Sfondeles et al., "Trump Lies About Kamala Harris' Race, Bashes Moderator at Black Journalists Convention in Chicago," *Chicago Sun-Times*, July 31, 2024.

26. James Rainey, "In Study, Evidence of Liberal-Bias Bias," *Los Angeles Times*, July 27, 2008.

27. See W. Lance Bennett, *News: The Politics of Illusion*, 10th ed. (University of Chicago Press, 2016).

28. Hershey, "2020 Presidential Campaign," 140.
29. "Objectivity" has become an American media norm only relatively recently. For the first century of its existence, almost all media outlets were partisan. See Marcus Prior, *Post-Broadcast Democracy* (Cambridge University Press, 2007).
30. See, for example, Maxwell T. Boykoff and Jules M. Boykoff, "Balance as Bias: Global Warming and the US Prestige Press," *Global Environmental Change* 14, no. 2 (2004): 125–136.
31. For example, Ayala Panievsky, "Covering Populist Media Criticism," *International Journal of Communication* 15 (2021): 2136–2155.
32. Philip Rucker and Marc Fisher, "Welcome to Washington's New Normal," *Washington Post*, November 23, 2016.
33. Thomas E. Patterson, "How the News Media—Long in Thrall to Trump—Can Cover His New Run for President Responsibly," *Conversation*, November 15, 2022, https://theconversation.com/how-the-news-media -long-in-thrall-to-trump-can-cover-his-new-run-for-president-respon sibly-194122.
34. Patterson, "How the News Media."
35. Dan Kennedy, "For Five Years, Trump Outrage Has Fueled Media Profits," WGBH, January 27, 2021, https://www.wgbh.org/news/commentary /2021-01-27/for-five-years-trump-outrage-has-fueled-media-profits-so -now-what.
36. George Packer, "Is Journalism Ready?," *Atlantic*, January/February 2024.
37. Nate Silver, "This Was Trump's Election to Lose. And He Just Might," *Silver Bulletin*, September 13, 2024, https://www.natesilver.net/p/this-was -trumps-election-to-lose.
38. Conor Friedersdorf, "When Donald Trump Became a Celebrity," *Atlantic*, January 6, 2016.
39. For instance, see his Memorial Day 2024 "truth" at Bradley Cortwright, "Trump Wishes a 'Happy Memorial Day' to the 'Human Scum' Working 'So Hard to Destroy Our Once Great Country,'" *Independent Journal Review*, May 27, 2024, https://ijr.com/trump-happy-memorial-day-human -scum-working-destroy-great-country/.
40. Marianne LeVine and Isaac Arnsdorf, "Trump Delivers Profanity, Below-the-Belt Digs at Catholic Charity Banquet," *Washington Post*, October 18, 2024.
41. For some examples, see Aaron Blake, "Trump's Laundry List of Increasingly Bizarre Claims," *Washington Post*, August 12, 2024.
42. Timothy L. O'Brien, "Don't Normalize Trump's Threats of Violence," *Bloomberg*, April 1, 2024, https://www.bloomberg.com/opinion/articles /2024-04-01/don-t-normalize-trump-s-threats-of-violence.
43. David Bauder, "Trump's Arrest a Throwback for TV News," *Herald Times*, April 6, 2023.

44. Jesse McKinley et al., "Gag Order Against Trump Is Expanded to Bar Attacks on Judge's Family," *New York Times*, May 31, 2024.

45. Thomas Beaumont, "GOP Field Hardly Mentions Trump," *Herald Times*, August 8, 2023.

46. Nate Silver, "Blaming the Media Is What Got Democrats into This Mess," *Silver Bulletin*, July 8, 2024, https://www.natesilver.net/p/blaming-the -media-is-what-got-democrats.

47. Robert Farley et al., "Fact-Checking the Biden-Trump Debate," FactCheck .org, June 28, 2024, https://www.factcheck.org/2024/06/factchecking-the -biden-trump-debate/.

48. Jacob L. Nelson, "Why Are Journalists Obsessed with Biden's Age?," *Conversation*, July 10, 2024, https://theconversation.com/why-are-journalists -obsessed-with-bidens-age-its-because-theyve-finally-found-an-inter esting-election-story-234141?.

49. See Stephen J. A. Ward, "Inventing Objectivity," in *Journalism Ethics*, ed. Christopher Meyers (Oxford University Press, 2010), 137–139.

50. Marjorie Randon Hershey, "Resolved: Congress Should Enact a New Fairness Doctrine for the 21st Century," in *Debating Reform*, 4th ed., ed. Michael Nelson and Richard Ellis (CQ Press, 2020), chap. 5.

51. For example, see Declan Fahy, "Objectivity, False Balance, and Advocacy in News Coverage of Climate Change," *Oxford Research Encyclopedia of Climate Science*, March 29, 2017, https://oxfordre.com/climatescience /display/10.1093/acrefore/9780190228620.001.0001/acrefore -9780190228620-e-345.

52. Glenn Kessler et al., "Trump's False or Misleading Claims Total 30,573 over 4 Years," *Washington Post*, January 24, 2021.

53. Allison Graves and Linda Qiu, "Kellyanne Conway's Back and Forth with Chuck Todd on 'Alternative Facts,' Annotated," PolitiFact, January 23, 2017, https://www.politifact.com/article/2017/jan/23/kellyanne-conways -back-and-forth-chuck-todd-alter/.

54. Kessler et al., "Trump's False or Misleading Claims."

55. Sullivan, "If Trump Runs Again."

56. See Heather Cox Richardson, *Letters from an American*, Substack post, June 27, 2024, https://heathercoxrichardson.substack.com/p/june-27-2024.

57. "Here's a Look at Some of the False Claims Made During Biden and Trump's First Debate," Associated Press, June 28, 2024, https://apnews .com/article/fact-check-misinformation-election-debate-trump-biden -577507522762aa10f6ee5be3a0ced2bb.

58. For example, see Shane Goldmacher and Jonathan Swan, "Biden Failed to Ease Worries About His Age. Trump Forcefully Made His Case," *New York Times*, June 27, 2024.

59. Michael Dimock and John Gramlich, "How America Changed During Donald Trump's Presidency," Pew Research Center, January 29, 2021,

https://www.pewresearch.org/politics/2021/01/29/how-america-changed
-during-donald-trumps-presidency/.

60. Madeline Heim, "Yes, Department of Homeland Security Declared Nov. 3
Election Most Secure in American History," PolitiFact, November 17,
2020, https://www.politifact.com/factchecks/2020/nov/17/tammy-baldwin
/yes-department-homeland-security-declared-nov-3-el/.

61. Adam Edelman, "These Candidates Say Trump Won in 2020," *NBC News*,
May 1, 2022, https://www.nbcnews.com/politics/2022-election/candidates
-say-trump-won-2020now-running-oversee-future-elections-rcna26241.

62. Marianne LeVine et al., "Trump Escalates False Claims of Fraud, Setting
Stage to Cry Foul If He Loses," *Washington Post*, November 4, 2024.

63. Julia Ingram and Madeleine May, "The X Factor," *CBS News*, October 21,
2024, https://www.cbsnews.com/news/elon-musk-trump-social-media
-election-2024/.

64. Colby Itkowitz and Hannah Allam, "With False 'Coup' Claims, Trump
Primes Supporters to Challenge a Harris Win," *Washington Post*,
August 19, 2024.

65. Julia Ingram, "When Trump's Victory Became Clear, Online Claims of
Election Fraud Quieted," *CBS News*, November 8, 2024, https://www
.cbsnews.com/news/trump-victory-online-claims-election-fraud-quieted/.

66. Nathan Layne et al., "Trump Calls Migrants 'Animals,' Intensifying Focus
on Illegal Immigration," Reuters, April 3, 2024, https://www.reuters.com
/world/us/trump-expected-highlight-murder-michigan-woman
-immigration-speech-2024-04-02/.

67. My thanks to Andrew Trexler for this point.

68. For example, see Jill Colvin and Jonathan J. Cooper, "Trump Talks About
Reporters Being Shot and Says He Shouldn't Have Left White House After
2020 Loss," *ABC News*, November 3, 2024, https://abcnews.go.com/US
/wireStory/harris-church-trump-muses-reporters-shot-115447144.

69. Pew data quoted in Jeffrey Gottfried and Jacob Liedke, "Partisan Divides
in Media Trust Widen, Driven by a Decline Among Republicans," Pew
Research Center, August 30, 2021, https://www.pewresearch.org/fact-tank
/2021/08/30/partisan-divides-in-.

70. Megan Brenan, "Americans' Trust in Media Remains at Trend Low," Gallup, October 14, 2024, https://news.gallup.com/poll/651977/americans
-trust-media-remains-trend-low.aspx.

71. Meredith Conroy, "Why Being 'Anti-Media' Is Now Part of the GOP Identity," FiveThirtyEight, April 5, 2021, https://fivethirtyeight.com/features
/why-being-anti-media-is-now-part-of-the-gop-identity/.

72. Dimock and Gramlich, "How America Changed."

73. Conroy, "Why Being 'Anti-Media.'"

74. NPR / PBS News / Marist poll results in Miles Parks, "Driven by Republicans, Most Americans Are Concerned About Fraud in the 2024 Election,"

All Things Considered, NPR, October 3, 2024, https://www.npr.org/2024/10/03/nx-s1-5130284/election-concerns-voter-fraud-trump-harris-poll.

75. Aaron Blake, "Trump Backers Are More Primed to Doubt the Election Than They Were in 2020," *Washington Post*, October 16, 2024.

76. Clara Ence Morse et al., "Over 230 Republican Candidates Have Cast Doubt on the 2024 Election," *Washington Post*, October 23, 2024.

77. Margaret Sullivan, "A Trump Lawyer Wrote an Instruction Manual for a Coup," *Washington Post*, September 30, 2021.

78. Dana Milbank, "Fox News Cleans Up Another Trump Mess," *Washington Post*, September 13, 2024.

79. The data, from GDELT, are explained in Philip Bump, "No Amount of Evidence Will Convince Republicans of Trump's 2020 Guilt," *Washington Post*, October 3, 2024.

80. See Matthew Tyler et al., "Partisan Enclaves and Information Bazaars," *Journal of Politics* 84, no. 2 (2022): 1057–1073.

81. Philip Bump, "The Era of Speaking Power to Truth," *Washington Post*, November 7, 2024.

82. Philip Bump, "A Fifth of Trump Supporters Think He Committed a Serious Crime," *Washington Post*, March 4, 2024.

83. Neil Bedi et al., "Inside Trump's Truth Social Conspiracy Theory Machine," *New York Times*, October 29, 2024.

84. Madison Czopek, "How Elon Musk Ditched Twitter's Safeguards and Primed X to Spread Misinformation," PolitiFact, October 23, 2023, https://www.politifact.com/article/2023/oct/23/how-elon-musk-ditched-twitters-safeguards-and-prim/.

85. See one such transcript at "Donald Trump Speaks After Hush Money Conviction," Rev, June 3, 2024, https://www.rev.com/transcripts/donald-trump-speaks-after-hush-money-conviction.

86. David Smith, "Lawless and Disorderly," *Guardian*, June 1, 2024.

87. Wayne Allen Root, right-wing radio personality, interview, reported in Gustav Kilander, "Trump Is Already Threatening to Sue Post Office Because They'll 'Maybe Purpose-ly' Lose Mail-in Ballots," *The Independent*, September 18, 2024, https://www.independent.co.uk/news/world/americas/us-politics/donald-trump-mail-in-ballots-b2614603.html.

88. Derek Hawkins et al., "How Trump Has Become Angrier and More Isolated on Truth Social," *Washington Post*, April 22, 2024.

89. See Marjorie Randon Hershey and Barry C. Burden, *Party Politics in America*, 19th ed. (Routledge, 2025), chaps. 1 and 16.

90. See Jeremy W. Peters and Katie Robertson, "Fox News Settles Defamation Suit for $787.5 Million, Dominion Says," *New York Times*, April 18, 2023.

91. Jon Allsop and Pete Vernon, "How the Press Covered the Last Four Years of Trump," *Columbia Journalism Review*, October 23, 2020, https://www.cjr.org/special_report/coverage-trump-presidency-2020-election.php.

92. See, for example, Thomas E. Patterson, *The Mass Media Election* (Praeger, 1980).

93. Amna Nawaz, "Trump's Rambling Speeches Raise Questions About Mental Decline," PBS, October 24, 2024, https://www.pbs.org/newshour/show/trumps-rambling-speeches-raise-questions-about-mental-decline.

94. "Election Updates: Trump Rallies in Las Vegas," *New York Times*, June 9, 2024, https://www.nytimes.com/live/2024/06/09/us/biden-trump-election-sunday-shows; Alayna Treene et al., "Trump Proposes Eliminating Taxes on Tips at Las Vegas Campaign Rally," CNN, June 9, 2024, https://edition.cnn.com/2024/06/09/politics/donald-trump-nevada-rally/.

95. Jennifer Rubin, "How to Cover an Abnormal Presidential Race," *Washington Post*, June 7, 2024. Note that although it was these bizarre comments that led to Trump's disproportionate media coverage, once his norm-breaking became normalized, the need to demonstrate objectivity came more into play.

96. Chris Quinn, "Letter from the Editor," *Plain Dealer* (Cleveland), April 6, 2024.

97. C. Anthony Broh, "Horse-Race Journalism: Reporting the Polls in the 1976 Presidential Election," *Public Opinion Quarterly* 44, no. 4 (1980): 514–529.

98. Andrew Trexler, "The Unequal Challenge of Learning from Under-Informative News," working paper, OSF Preprints, June 28, 2024, https://osf.io/preprints/osf/s7nv4.

99. Natalie Jomini Stroud, "Polarization and Partisan Selective Exposure," *Journal of Communication* 60, no. 3 (2010): 556–576.

100. Peter Dizikes, "Study: On Twitter, False News Travels Faster Than True Stories," Massachusetts Institute of Technology, March 8, 2018, https://news.mit.edu/2018/study-twitter-false-news-travels-faster-true-stories-0308.

101. See, for example, Steve Waldman, "Our Local-News Situation Is Even Worse Than We Think," *Columbia Journalism Review*, February 25, 2022, https://www.cjr.org/local_news/local_reporters_decline_coverage_density.php.

102. See, for example, Liam Reilly, "Los Angeles Times Editor Resigns After Newspaper Owner Blocked Plans to Endorse Harris," CNN, October 23, 2024, https://www.cnn.com/2024/10/23/media/los-angeles-times-endorsement-harris-resign/index.html.

103. See Danny Hayes and Jennifer L. Lawless, *News Hole* (Cambridge University Press, 2021).

104. Margaret Sullivan, "What Happens to Democracy When Local Journalism Dries Up?," *Washington Post*, November 30, 2021.

105. Erik Peterson, "Paper Cuts," *American Journal of Political Science* 65, no. 2 (2021): 443–459.

106. Jonathan V. Last, "What More Do You People Want from Kamala Harris?," *Bulwark*, September 11, 2024, https://www.thebulwark.com/p/what-more-do-you-people-want-from.

107. Matt Bai, "I Say, Without Evidence, That the Media's Trump Qualifiers Are Backfiring," *Washington Post*, September 18, 2024.

108. See Matt Grossman and David Hopkins, "Ideological Republicans and Group Interest Democrats," *Perspectives on Politics* 13, no. 1 (2015): 119–139; and Jacob S. Hacker and Paul Pierson, "Confronting Asymmetric Polarization," in *Solutions to Political Polarization in America*, ed. Nathaniel Persily (Cambridge University Press, 2015).

109. Andrew Donohue, "The Rise of the Democracy Beat," NiemanLab, accessed October 18, 2024, https://www.niemanlab.org/2020/12/the-rise-of-the-democracy-beat/.

110. Erik Peterson et al., "Election Denial as a News Coverage Dilemma," working paper, OSF Preprints, April 27, 2024, https://osf.io/preprints/socarxiv/sw2q8.

111. "The State of Local News 2023," Local News Initiative, Northwestern University, November 16, 2023, https://localnewsinitiative.northwestern.edu/projects/state-of-local-news/2023/.

112. Danny Hayes and Jennifer L. Lawless, "The Decline of Local News and Its Effects," *Journal of Politics* 80, no. 1 (2018): 332–338.

113. Naomi Forman-Katz et al., "Nonprofit News Outlets Are Playing a Growing Role in Statehouse Coverage," Pew Research Center, April 29, 2022, https://www.pewresearch.org/fact-tank/2022/04/29/nonprofit-news-outlets-are-playing-a-growing-role-in-statehouse-coverage/.

114. An example is Heather Cox Richardson's *Letters from an American*.

115. See, for example, Hannah Knowles and Meryl Kornfield, "Trump Says He Doesn't Mind Someone Shooting at Journalists at Rally," *Washington Post*, November 3, 2024.

116. See A. B. Stoddard, "Dems Need New Mediums—and a New Message," *Bulwark*, November 21, 2024, https://www.thebulwark.com/p/dems-need-new-mediumsand-a-new-message.

117. George Packer, "Is Journalism Ready?," *Atlantic*, January/February 2024.

The Presidency

TRUMP'S SECOND TERM AND AMERICAN DEMOCRACY

PAUL J. QUIRK

ONE CONCLUSION FROM THE CAMPAIGN and outcome of the 2024 presidential election is in little doubt: that the U.S. political system is in trouble. There is, of course, fundamental disagreement about the nature of that trouble. Democrats, many commentators, editorial writers for major newspapers, and a sizable group of prominent Republicans had declared not only that Donald Trump was profoundly unfit for the presidency but also that his election would put American democracy in serious danger. Democracy, they said, was on the ballot.[1] A majority of the voters dismissed the warnings and awarded Trump a second term as president.

There are two possibilities: One is that something has gone wrong with a broad segment of the political-opinion elite. Trump's most severe critics may have exaggerated legitimate concerns about him or promoted false or misleading criticisms of him, intentionally or not. The other possibility is that the dire warnings about Trump have been mostly or entirely justified. If that is the case, then two serious problems become apparent. First, voters have failed to understand or take seriously critical advice from some of the country's most informed and reliable observers. Second, the president is indeed profoundly unfit for office and a danger to democracy. Either scenario represents an unprecedented kind of trouble for the United States.

This chapter will seek to clarify these issues. My account takes cognizance of conflicting views—those of both Trump's supporters and his opponents. However, it does not simply give automatic equal weight to contending claims.[2] In the end, it finds that the serious concerns about the effects of Trump's second term are indeed warranted and considers the prospects for American democracy.

The Opinion-Leadership Disconnect
on Trump as President

Among opinion-leading elites, aside from predictable partisan voices, there was a massive imbalance in endorsements favoring the Democratic nominee, Kamala Harris, over Trump.[3] Elite criticism of Trump and his candidacy was often far more severe, and included far more numerous and prominent voices from his own party or ideological direction, than has ever occurred in a presidential election.[4] Nevertheless, a majority of the public ignored or discounted the warnings and voted for Trump in the election.

This opinion elite–mass public disconnect represents a breakdown in the processes of opinion leadership that have existed for most of the modern era.[5] As political scientists have shown, there has been a relationship of mutual influence between ordinary citizens and various categories of more heavily involved and influential actors, which we refer to under the broad label *political elites*.[6] Elites include elected and appointed public officials, representatives of interest groups and nongovernmental organizations, business leaders, political commentators and public intellectuals, news reporters, experts on various subjects, and others. In the historically typical relationship, such elites take guidance from the values and concerns of ordinary citizens. But they also obtain and consider more extensive, up-to-date, and refined information about contested issues and provide a stream of informed opinions and judgments, mostly through the mass media, to the public. Finally, the public generally takes guidance on particular issues and choices, including choices of candidates, from that stream of messages. Of course, elite opinion is often divided along partisan or ideological lines. In general, public opinion reflects the state of elite opinion. So when elites display substantial agreement on a major issue, with a readily apparent majority in one direction, public opinion tends to follow.[7]

A pivotal role in these processes is performed by a fairly large, diverse subset of such elites whose views, to varying degrees, are free of partisan, ideological, or other precommitments.[8] They include, for example, news commentators who are ideological centrists or moderates; advocates for various interests or causes that are not highly partisan or ideological; elected officials and other party members who sometimes deviate from their party's line (most often, those with competitive electoral constituencies); news reporters for general-audience outlets; and other experts (including academics) who strive to minimize partisan or ideological bias in their professional work. With respect to bias, they range from those elected politicians who sometimes decline to follow a party line to specialized experts who strive to avoid any partisan leaning. In partisan or ideological controversies, these *centrist-independent elites*, as I will call them, assess and respond to facts and arguments without strong partisan or ideological biases. To the extent they agree on an issue, they will swing the overall majority of elite opinion in the agreed direction. And the majority of public opinion will generally follow. This influence of centrist-independent elites makes public opinion better informed.

With increasingly polarized politics, the influence of centrist-independent elite opinion has been in decline in recent decades. But even in that context, the 2024 election witnessed an extraordinarily sharp disconnect between such opinion—uniformly and urgently opposed to Trump—and the decisions of a majority of voters.

News Organization and Academic Views

No polls measure the views of centrist-independent elites, a sprawling, loosely defined category. But two indicators, reflecting selected members of this category, make it clear that a broad consensus rejected Trump. A recent poll of academic experts on the presidency, collecting their rankings of all the presidents, ranked Trump dead last—that is, as the worst president in American history.[9] We can assume a significant Democratic bias in any recent poll of academics, even in an aspirationally nonpartisan exercise.[10] But these presidency experts gave high rankings to many of the Republican presidents, including Ronald Reagan. And they rated Trump the worst Republican.

A more pertinent indicator, more clearly free of strong partisan bias, is available in newspaper endorsements. Major newspapers (broadly defined) that made endorsements favored Harris over Trump by a margin of fifty to three.[11] The identity of the three Trump-endorsing newspapers is instructive: the *New York Post*, a low-brow conservative tabloid owned by Rupert Murdoch (who also owns Fox News); *The Washington Times*, a conservative outlet owned by the Unification Church; and the *Las Vegas Review-Journal*, which is owned by the estate of a major Trump donor, billionaire Sheldon Adelson. Unlike the poll of academics, this imbalance in endorsements does not represent merely a Democratic lean. In the 2012 presidential election, major newspaper endorsements were nearly evenly divided between Democrat Barack Obama and Republican Mitt Romney.[12]

The *New York Times* editorial endorsing Harris provided a representative assessment of Trump's candidacy.[13] The editorial characterized his policies as ideologically extreme and his decision-making as often reckless and uninformed. It cited Trump's persistent denial of the seriousness of the COVID-19 pandemic as catastrophically harmful. The editors described Trump as lazy, uninterested in reliable information or qualified advice, and prone to making decisions based on personal gain. It pointed to his highly suspect friendliness toward Russia and charged him with weakening Western alliances, undermining the rule of law, disregarding constitutional limits, and attempting to overthrow a legitimate election. In the *Times'* words, Trump "systematically undermined public confidence in the result of the 2020 election and then attempted to overturn it—an effort that culminated in an insurrection at the Capitol to obstruct the peaceful transfer of power. . . . He has promised to be . . . unrestrained by checks on power built into the American political system." His election, the *Times* concluded, would be "dangerous for American democracy." The *Times*, although broadly nonpartisan, has endorsed the Democratic candidate in all recent presidential elections. But it never before made a declaration like its opening sentence in this instance: "It is hard to imagine a candidate more unworthy to serve as president of the United States than Donald Trump."

Republican Opposition to Trump

Beyond academic specialists and newspaper editorial boards, many prominent Republicans, particularly former officeholders, severely criticized Trump and endorsed Harris. Such views extended beyond the familiar voices of anti-Trump Republicans like Liz Cheney, Adam Kinzinger, Mitt Romney, and the "Never Trumpers"—notable conservatives who had opposed Trump as early as the 2016 campaign. Republicans for Harris, a group representing about two hundred prominent Republicans, issued a public letter explaining their opposition to Trump.[14] George W. Bush's Attorney General Alberto Gonzales wrote an op-ed making the case that Trump would undermine the rule of law.[15]

Most remarkably, individuals who had been close to Trump and played prominent roles in his first administration offered some of the harshest judgments: Trump's Vice President Mike Pence said, "I believe that anyone who puts themselves over the Constitution should never be president of the United States." His former White House Chief of Staff John Kelly described Trump as "the most flawed person I have ever met," adding, "If he's re-elected, God help us." Trump's national security adviser John Bolton and Attorney General William Barr—individuals with hardcore Republican and conservative credentials—issued severe condemnations. Bolton said, "He's fundamentally ignorant and he really doesn't care about the facts." Bolton judged that Trump "cares almost exclusively about his own interests." Barr, whose service as attorney general had been widely criticized as improperly devoted to Trump's personal interests, said that a second Trump term would be "a horror show."[16] Trump received by far the most widespread and severe criticism of a presidential candidate by members of their own party in modern American history.[17] In sum, Trump's critics among newspaper editors, prominent Republicans, and other centrist-independent opinion leaders warned that a second Trump presidency would bring several distinct kinds of potentially disastrous performance: conservative or right-wing-populist ideology taken to extremes, reckless freelancing and disregard of informed opinion, exploitation of the office for personal financial gain, deference toward Russia and defection from the Western alliance, pursuit of personal revenge, undermining of constitutional limits on presidential power, and efforts to impose authoritarian control beyond the duration of the term.

Most of these critics did not comment on the psychological sources of Trump's conduct. Indeed, most psychiatrists and psychologists refrained from publicly offering opinions about Trump's mental health, in the absence of an in-person examination. But some, claiming a professional duty to warn the public, declared Trump psychologically unfit for the presidency. They pointed to publicly observable traits that, in their view, made him dangerous—impulsivity, extreme egotism, an exaggerated sense of his capabilities and achievements, lack of empathy, and disregard for norms and rules. They sometimes noted that those traits, among others that Trump displayed, were consistent with certain recognized psychological disorders: namely, narcissistic personality, antisocial personality, and malignant narcissism. Many of them also claimed that Trump was suffering significant cognitive decline.[18]

Pro-Trump Elites

Along with Trump's campaign team, various political allies and right-wing media outlets supported his reelection. Their central appeal was policy oriented in a conventional way—promising that Trump's return would bring constructive conservative policy change on taxes, immigration, and other issues, along with another round of conservative judicial appointments. Regarding the various charges of criminality and other misconduct, his fully committed allies simply repeated his claims that the 2020 election was stolen and that he was the innocent victim of multiple "witch hunts." In contrast, supporters who wanted to maintain credibility with a general audience—for example, the editorial writers for the *New York Post* and *Las Vegas Review-Journal*—dealt with these matters by not mentioning them.[19] Neither paper's editorial commented at all on Trump's 2020 election denial or any of his criminal charges. In explaining his vote for Trump in a *Los Angeles Times* op-ed, Scott Jennings, a regular Republican panelist on CNN, just barely mentioned them. He wrote, "I was none too pleased with Trump after January 6, 2021"—and went on to say nothing more about that episode, nor about any other matter of Trump's prolific alleged misconduct.[20]

The Electorate's Response

Voter opinion diverged sharply from the centrist-independent elite consensus. Despite the categorical condemnation of Trump by such elites and even many of his presumptive allies, a majority of voters supported him. At earlier stages of the campaign, about two-thirds of the public considered each of the four federal criminal indictments of Trump as serious. About one-third of Republican voters said they would not vote for Trump if he were convicted of a felony. By the time of the election, however, nearly all Republicans voted for Trump and only about one-third of the electorate identified the state of democracy as the most important issue affecting their vote.[21] In a postelection interview, Trump remarked with some accuracy, "I won on the border and I won on groceries."[22]

The next three sections will examine Trump's first term as president; the multiple criminal, civil, and investigative proceedings against him; and the events of his 2024 presidential campaign to assess the grounds that existed, by the latter stages of the campaign, for the conflicting expectations for a second term. We will then proceed to consider the postelection transition and the first six weeks of the term, as the early evidence on the actual results.

Trump's First Term

The record of Trump's first term is presumably an important guide to the character and outcomes of his second term. Although new issues and circumstances will arise, much about his decision-making and priorities will repeat. In addition, some of his second-term approach will reflect lessons he learned in the first term, for good or ill.

Management, Decision-Making, and Leadership

In his first term, Trump's methods of decision-making and leadership departed, in wide-ranging and fundamental ways, from those that are generally associated with effective presidential performance and have been used, though not always consistently, by all other recent presidents.[23] These departures stemmed from Trump's prior experience managing a moderately sized family business, his lack of experience in government, and his inflated perceptions of his own knowledge and abilities.[24]

Trump's first-term appointments to high-level positions revealed an unconventional and often casual approach. He was slow to fill major roles, leaving many positions vacant for extended periods or even permanently, asserting that many high-level positions were unnecessary. Among his appointees, some had reasonably strong credentials. For instance, Secretary of State Rex Tillerson brought extensive experience as the former CEO of ExxonMobil, where he managed a vast multinational corporation and had significant dealings with foreign governments. Secretary of Defense James Mattis was a retired four-star Marine Corps general with more than four decades of military service, including leadership roles in major combat operations. Some other high-profile appointees faced accusations of conflicts of interest or had records of hostility toward the missions of their agencies. Scott Pruitt, appointed to lead the Environmental Protection Agency, had repeatedly sued the agency in his previous role as Oklahoma attorney general and was known for his close ties to the fossil fuel industry.

A notable feature of Trump's first term was his reliance on family members for significant roles. Most importantly, Trump's son-in-law Jared Kushner was tasked with an extraordinarily broad portfolio, ranging from guiding Middle East peace negotiations and criminal justice reform to overseeing pandemic response strategies and managing U.S.-China trade relations. This breadth of responsibility, unprecedented for any presidential aide, drew widespread criticism, especially because Kushner had no experience in any of those areas.[25]

Trump's decision-making processes were consistently haphazard, and often chaotic. In a marked deviation from modern presidential practice, there was no structured advisory system, even on paper. According to Speaker of the House Paul Ryan, Trump made major decisions based on his most recent conversation on the subject and changed his mind just as casually. He had little interest in obtaining expert advice. He often skipped the daily intelligence briefings that all other presidents had received in the post–World War II era. Intelligence officials struggled to develop special briefing practices that accommodated his limited attention span. Trump frequently dismissed established expertise, asserting his superior understanding with statements such as, "I know more than the generals." He baldly contradicted elementary economics—declaring, "Trade wars are good, and easy to win."[26]

Trump's methods led to frequent conflicts with senior officials and an exceptionally high rate of turnover in high-level administration positions.[27] The administration experienced the highest turnover rate for senior appointees, during its first three years, of any modern presidency—with more than sixty-five departures of cabinet members, agency heads, and other senior officials. Trump had four chiefs of staff during his four-year term. As we will see later, Trump took a lesson from his conflicts with appointees—namely, that he needed to ensure, above all else, that future appointees and subordinates would be completely loyal and obedient to him, regardless of any conflicting obligations.

Some defenders of Trump's methods argued that his reliance on instincts enabled swift decision-making and disrupted entrenched ways of doing things. In an article titled "Donald Trump: A Great Decision Maker?," James Jay Carafano of the Heritage Foundation argued that Trump's approach facilitated the inclusion of diverse perspectives, bypassed bureaucratic delays, and enabled swift responses to emerging challenges.[28] However, Carafano did not point to any particular decisions as evidence for the effectiveness of this casual, seat-of-the-pants approach. In fact, Trump was widely criticized for numerous decisions that he made with little or no deliberation, often in conflict with informed opinion on the matters.[29] Such decisions included imposing tariffs on China, withdrawing troops from Syria, meeting with North Korean dictator Kim Jong-Un without prior conditions, withdrawing from the Iran nuclear deal, and downplaying the severity of the COVID-19 pandemic.

DEALING WITH CONGRESS

During his first two years, with Republican majorities in both chambers, Trump maintained generally good relations with Senate Majority Leader Mitch McConnell and Speaker Ryan.[30] In fact, he often delegated major policy initiatives, such as tax reform and health care, to congressional leaders—although he sometimes complicated their work by making unexpected demands or withdrawing support for a particular measure at later stages of bill development. On the 2017 tax cuts, Trump provided only broad goals such as cutting corporate taxes and simplifying the tax code. Intentionally or not, his deference to Republican congressional leaders on specific provisions accommodated the limitations of advisory processes and decision-making capability in the White House.

Trump's abrupt reversals on policy issues created political problems for Republicans. During their 2017 effort to repeal and replace the Affordable Care Act (or Obamacare), Trump initially championed a bill developed by House Republican leaders, pressuring rank-and-file Republican lawmakers to approve it, despite expected costs to them in constituency support. Yet after its passage in the House, Trump publicly criticized the bill as "mean" and demanded major changes, leaving Republicans who had agreed to his demands feeling betrayed.[31] Trump's failure to provide steady guidance likely contributed to the ultimate failure of the health care repeal effort.

In another departure from recommended practice, Trump on several occasions declared ambitious plans for policy development, only to postpone action repeatedly or abandon the project altogether. He promised a comprehensive infrastructure bill numerous times but it never materialized, and the several cancellations of White House–declared "infrastructure week" became a running joke in the media. Trump's persistently repeated promise to build a wall along the U.S.-Mexico border was mostly unfulfilled. Congress balked at the huge expense and dubious effectiveness of the project, and although Trump managed to redirect about $15 billion in military funds to its construction, only a small fraction of the promised two-thousand-mile wall was completed.

In a dramatic and consequential departure from past practice, Trump exerted exceptionally forceful and even coercive presidential influence over members of his party in Congress. Far more than any prior president, he publicly attacked fellow partisans whom he considered recalcitrant and called for their constituencies to defeat them in primary elections. Trump was able to exert this influence not only because his base supporters eagerly punished the members he targeted but also because he was willing to risk losing their seats to Democrats. While this strategy enhanced his control over Republicans in Congress, it came at a cost. In a few cases, Republican members lost their seats to Democrats in the 2018 midterm elections. Importantly, Trump's control over other Republicans extended beyond legislative matters to the members' positions on the various investigations, impeachment proceedings, and prosecutions that Trump battled during and after his first term.

PUBLIC COMMUNICATION

During his first term, Trump's methods and style in communicating with the public were distinctive in two respects. First, he continued to hold frequent, campaign-style rallies, the presentation format that had catapulted him to electoral victory in 2016. Using simple, informal language and bombastic statements, he entertained crowds with exaggerated claims about his achievements, extreme denunciations of opponents, and often-crude insults to various individuals and groups. His supporters viewed the performances as authentic and relatable.

Second, and utterly singular, Trump's public statements were riddled with falsehoods. Fact-checking organizations documented a constant stream of false or misleading claims during his presidency, far surpassing those of any previous U.S. political figure. According to *The Washington Post*, which kept a daily record, Trump made over thirty thousand false or misleading claims during his four years in office. His repeated lies often conflicted with definitive photographic, video, or documentary evidence, and he often persisted with falsehoods even after they were publicly exposed. At the same time, Trump labeled any critical reporting, and the news outlets that carried it, "fake news," claiming that reports were simply false. Undoubtedly, some major news organizations were prone to cover news stories that were unfavorable for Trump more extensively than those that were favorable.[32] In contrast with the voluminous documentation of Trump's lies, however, neither Trump nor any pro-Trump commentator or media outlet has ever presented evidence of any systematic or intentional falsehood nor even frequent or persistent error, adverse to Trump, on the part of mainstream news organizations.[33]

A majority of the public recognized that many of Trump's claims were unreliable or simply false. Polls consistently showed that only a minority of Americans—in a 2020 Gallup poll, just 34 percent—regarded him as trustworthy. But Trump's core supporters and large majorities of Republicans apparently accepted many or most of his false claims. When Trump claimed that the 2020 election had been stolen—a claim that had been consistently rejected in findings of the Justice Department, the Department of Homeland Security, two consulting firms that the White House hired to investigate the election, and more than fifty court rulings—surveys showed that about three-quarters of Republicans endorsed the claim.[34]

POLICY RESULTS

Many of Trump's supporters, including the three conservative major newspapers that endorsed him in 2024, have framed their support as grounded in strong approval of his policies. Trump did have a number of policy successes from the perspectives of conservatives and business groups. However, if one defines policy success somewhat more strictly, as requiring that a policy meet any one or more of several criteria—popular acceptance, broad endorsement by relevant experts, political durability, or apparent production of desired results—then Trump's policy successes were quite limited.

By far Trump's most significant and enduring accomplishment from a conservative standpoint—one that shaped other policies indirectly—was his appointment of conservative judges to the federal courts, especially the Supreme Court. He successfully nominated three relatively young justices—Neil Gorsuch, Brett Kavanaugh, and Amy Coney Barrett—reshaping the court's ideological balance for decades to come. In addition, Trump appointed 231 judges to the lower federal courts, at the time the most by any president in a single term since the 1970s. These appointments were not a difficult feat in the circumstances: A conservative legal group, the Federalist Society, essentially selected the nominees; and with the filibuster recently abolished for judicial nominations, the disciplined Senate Republican majority confirmed them, all but automatically.

The Supreme Court appointments, in particular, had dramatic and enduring policy consequences, mainly after Trump's presidential term had ended. Most importantly, in the 2022 *Dobbs v. Jackson Women's Health Organization* decision, the court overturned the historic (and, to many conservatives, infamous) *Roe v. Wade* decision and thus ended federal constitutional protection for abortion rights. In other major decisions, the court sharply reduced judicial deference to regulatory agencies in interpreting their legal authority and gave former presidents broad immunity from criminal prosecution.

Aside from his judicial appointments, Trump's first-term accomplishments most cited by conservatives were the Tax Cuts and Jobs Act of 2017 and the wide-ranging deregulatory actions taken by federal regulatory agencies during his presidency. The tax measure reduced personal income taxes and both cut and simplified corporate income taxes, with projected revenue reductions estimated at more than $1.5 trillion over a ten-year period. Liberals complained, with debatable justification, that the tax cuts were designed mostly to benefit corporations and the wealthy. In fact, the reductions in tax rates were similar for all tax brackets. But that naturally gave larger cuts in absolute terms to those who pay higher taxes. Wealthier people also received more of the benefits of the corporate cuts.

A more serious complaint about Trump's tax cuts, not tied to liberal policy preferences, was that they were not balanced by spending reductions, resulting in a roughly $500 billion first-year increase in the federal budget deficit and making them fiscally unsustainable in the long term. Mostly for that reason, the Trump tax cuts received little support from academic economists. Informed approval came mainly from hardcore antitax conservatives, who ignored long-term fiscal consequences, and from business, which received a large share of the tax cuts.[35]

On deregulation, agencies such as the Environmental Protection Agency, the Occupational Safety and Health Administration, the Food and Drug Administration, and about two dozen others aggressively rolled back regulations across various sectors.[36] They cut back or eliminated regulations on coal-burning power plants, methane emissions standards, net neutrality, overtime pay, and obligations of financial advisers, among many other matters. In doing so, the agencies made little effort to assess the costs and benefits of the targeted rules and often failed to give stakeholders the opportunity to comment required by law.[37] Such actions resulted in numerous legal challenges, and many of the decisions were reversed by the Biden administration.

Most political- or opinion-elite supporters of Trump overlook the tariff issues, trade disputes, and retaliatory actions by trading partners that were prominent features of his economic management. Nearly all economists, along with most conservatives and business leaders, oppose trade barriers as a general matter.[38] Although the effects of a sweeping change in trade policy are difficult to assess, it is not likely that Trump's trade restrictions benefited the economy.[39]

Trump's immigration and border policies, including a ban on entry from several Muslim countries and the separation of asylum-seeking families at the U.S.-Mexico border, were among the most contentious of his presidency. These policies followed through on some of the main themes of his election campaign and appealed to his political base. Overall, however, Trump was not able to reduce illegal border crossings, which were largely driven by developments in the immigrants' home countries.[40]

Trump's handling of the COVID-19 pandemic has been widely criticized as a calamitous failure. A full assessment is in fact somewhat complicated. On one hand, the administration's Operation Warp Speed helped in developing effective vaccines in record time. But Trump's persistent effort to deny or minimize the severity of the virus, promotion of a medically unsupported treatment (hydroxychloroquine), and sometimes bizarre suggestions (internal use of bleach or of ultraviolet light) complicated public health messaging on the pandemic. His rhetoric contributed to vaccine hesitancy, particularly among Republicans; a study checking voter registration rolls for names found in death records showed that Republican voters died in disproportionate numbers during the pandemic.[41] In later, taped interviews with journalist Bob Woodward, Trump claimed that he had known that the COVID-19 pandemic was extremely serious even as he publicly denied it.[42] In the end, if the United States had matched the average experience of the other wealthy G7 countries, it would have had about 188,000, or 40 percent, fewer deaths from the COVID-19 virus.[43]

In foreign policy, Trump's approach to NATO exemplified his administration's contradictory policies.[44] On one hand, he pressured allies to increase defense spending, achieving some success in this regard. On the other hand, his repeated criticism of NATO, conflicting remarks about the U.S. commitment to collective defense, and promotion of Russian interests in various matters (including resistance to providing military aid to Ukraine) weakened trust in the United States among its allies and undermined the alliance's cohesion. Trump's isolationist and pro-Russian tendencies contradicted a broad bipartisan consensus in support of U.S. leadership of the Western alliance.

Finally, as discussed earlier, two of Trump's often-stated domestic priorities—infrastructure renewal and repeal of the Affordable Care Act— came to nothing. In the case of infrastructure, Trump failed to offer a proposal on a subject that had obvious potential for bipartisan agreement.[45] In attempting to repeal Obamacare, Trump signed on to a project that Republicans had been obsessed with since the program's creation in 2010, but that had become dubious politically as the program gradually became quite popular.[46]

In summing up his claimed accomplishments, Trump regularly declared that "we had the strongest economy in the history of our nation." In fact, the performance of the economy during Trump's first term was unremarkable.[47] While gross domestic product growth and unemployment rates improved in the first three years, these results only continued trends that began during the later years of the Obama presidency. The COVID-19 pandemic caused a sharp economic downturn during Trump's final year, but it had similar effects in all the other developed countries. His overall economic results do not support any verdict, positive or negative, about the substantive merits or actual effects of his policies.

DEMOCRATIC PROCESSES

The direst warnings about a second Trump term concerned potential threats to democracy and the constitutional system. Even before his attempt to overturn the 2020 election, Trump's conduct in office provided clear grounds for such concern.

On many accounts, Trump was exceptionally aggressive in taking action on policy matters through executive orders that exceeded even generous interpretations of the president's legal authority.[48] His Muslim travel ban, use of military funds to build a portion of the wall on the Mexican border, and unilateral decisions to impose tariffs—all undertaken with questionable statutory authority—were heavily criticized as executive overreach. That said, ambitious expansion of the president's power has been a regular feature of the history of the presidency.[49] One can view Trump's unilateralism on policy matters as nothing more than a continuation of that history.

Far more problematic with respect to democratic norms, Trump refused to respect Congress's right to information about executive branch conduct—a long- and firmly established constitutional principle central to the system of checks and balances.[50] On numerous occasions during congressional investigations that threatened him, including impeachment proceedings, he barred requested testimony from executive branch officials and ordered them to withhold requested documents—even ordering subordinates to defy valid congressional subpoenas.

Moreover, as an extensive *New York Times* investigative report revealed in 2024, Trump, during his first term, ordered the Justice Department and other agencies to investigate numerous individuals who had opposed him.[51] He pressured the department to investigate figures such as Hillary Clinton and FBI Director James Comey, among many others. In some cases, the agencies resisted or deflected his demands; in others, they conducted the highly improper investigations.

Trump exhibited several other authoritarian tendencies. He threatened news organizations with legal action, advocated changes in libel law to make it easier to sue them, and constantly disparaged unfavorable coverage as "fake news"—conduct that at least threatened to inhibit freedom of the press. In several instances, Trump signaled an inclination to use the military, contrary to existing law, to deal with domestic disturbances. And he repeatedly expressed admiration for foreign dictators, sometimes with overt suggestions that the United States would benefit from similar arrangements.[52] In 2016 he remarked that Russian President Vladimir Putin "has very strong control over a country. . . . He's been a leader. Far more than our president has been a leader." He said that North Korean dictator Kim Jong-Un "speaks and his people sit up at attention. I want my people to do the same." After China eliminated term limits for the office of president, Trump said that Xi Jinping "[is] now president for life. . . . I think it's great. Maybe we'll have to give that a shot." No prior president, in public, has expressed such overtly authoritarian musings.

After his defeat in the 2020 election, Trump, unwilling to cooperate in an orderly transfer of power, embarked on a sustained, multifaceted, and determined effort to overturn the election result. I will discuss this effort further in the next section. For now, I simply note that the effort, in the last months of his presidency, left no doubt that Trump was, at least in that period, an enemy of democracy.

Trump on Trial: Lawsuits, Impeachments, and Prosecutions

Trump has faced an extraordinary number of lawsuits, prosecutions, impeachment proceedings, and other investigations involving allegations of criminal or other offenses. Although in many cases the merits of the allegations have not been formally determined, several major cases have already been decided against him or his organizations, including a criminal conviction of Trump himself in the New York hush money–campaign finance case.[53] Trump's opponents have viewed this record as conclusive grounds for declaring him profoundly unfit for office, while his supporters have treated it as irrelevant.

Trump's legal entanglements have been extraordinary in their number and variety.[54] Over the years, the several Trump organizations have faced numerous lawsuits, including multiple allegations of business fraud. Suits against Trump University and the Trump Foundation resulted in major settlements and penalties, including a mandated dissolution of the latter as a bogus charity.

Trump faced extensive investigations regarding his 2016 presidential campaign and its possible involvement with Russian interference in the election. Robert Mueller's investigation, while not finding direct collusion with Russia, did find numerous suspicious and at least ethically improper interactions, and it documented multiple instances of Trump apparently obstructing justice.[55] Mueller did not present a formal finding of criminal obstruction only because Justice Department policy did not allow an incumbent president to be prosecuted.[56]

Trump's presidency was further marked by two impeachments.[57] The first, in December 2019, centered on two charges: abuse of power and obstruction of Congress. Trump was accused of leveraging military aid to pressure Ukrainian President Volodymyr Zelenskyy to announce an investigation into Joe Biden and his son Hunter Biden. The second article of impeachment charged Trump with obstructing Congress by directing officials to defy subpoenas during its inquiry. The second impeachment, in January 2021, focused on "incitement of insurrection" related to the January 6 Capitol riot. Trump was accused of encouraging his supporters to disrupt the certification of the Electoral College results. Although he was acquitted in the Senate in both impeachments, he was the first president to receive votes for his impeachment and removal by members of his own party.

Following his presidency, Trump has faced criminal indictments related to the mishandling of classified documents at Mar-a-Lago; his efforts to overturn the 2020 election (with federal charges and a separate case in Georgia, along with being named as an unindicted coconspirator in a similar case in Arizona); and falsification of business records in the hush money–campaign finance case. He also faced civil lawsuits seeking damages for the January 6 insurrection. The Trump Company in separate trials was found guilty criminally, and liable for damages, on charges that involved wide-ranging, multimillion-dollar tax and loan fraud. Trump has been accused of sexual assault multiple times and was found liable for sexual assault and defamation in the cases brought by E. Jean Carroll. While Trump did not win verdicts in any of these cases, all pending criminal charges were dropped after his reelection, leaving several charges unresolved. All of these legal troubles add up to accusations of truly prolific misconduct, both criminal and civil, of multiple kinds, spanning many years and continuing to nearly the present day.

Trump's supporters usually discount the relevance of his alleged offenses, if they mention them at all, on the basis of sweeping, unsubstantiated claims that the proceedings against him were politically motivated, which is what Trump says about them.[58] But those claims lack credible evidence. As critics have pointed out, Manhattan district attorney Alvin Bragg, the prosecutor in the hush money–campaign finance case, promised to prosecute Trump as part of his own election campaign—on its face an indication of political motivation. But the circumstances made this campaign promise almost obligatory. The preceding district attorney, Cyrus Vance Jr., had conducted a highly visible criminal investigation into Trump's business fraud issues. A great deal of incriminating evidence was public knowledge, largely from a major *New York Times* investigation.[59] And two prominent prosecutors, hired by Vance for the case, had resigned in protest of his declining to bring charges. Bragg's campaign had to deal with an obvious question of whether he would shrink from the political risks of prosecuting the former president.

As for the federal cases, Justice Department rules wall off its prosecutorial deliberations from presidential interference, and in any case Trump's cases were handed off to special counsel Jack Smith, under rules designed to prevent even the appearance of political control, before any charging decisions were made. Despite Trump's allegations, there has been no evidence that President Biden gave any instructions to Attorney General Merrick Garland or to Smith about how to deal with Trump. In fact, Garland—noted for his cautious, strictly nonpartisan, institutionalist approach—dragged his feet on prosecuting Trump for two years, until revelations by the House January 6 committee virtually forced him to act. One can suspect, as a general matter, that any special counsel, appointed to investigate possible offenses by an extremely high-profile defendant, is likely to bring charges. But Trump's allegations of unusual or improper political influence were without foundation.

Speculation about prosecutors' motives aside, the main grounds for charging Trump, and much of the evidence, have been publicly available in all these cases. The hush money–campaign finance case was certainly the least serious. It concerned fraudulent reporting, as a Trump Company legal expense, of a $130,000 payment to a porn actress, days before the 2016 election, for silence about her relationship with Trump.[60] In portraying the seriousness of the crime, Bragg argued that Trump had hidden the payoff in order to prevent the voters from learning about his affair and thus had perpetrated a fraud on the electorate. Nevertheless, there was disagreement among legal commentators about whether the offense was serious enough—and the legal theory of the case solid enough—to warrant a felony indictment. Comparing the case to the prosecution of mobster Al Capone for tax evasion in the 1930s, some suggested that Bragg's charging decision was a response to Trump's plausible-deniability escape from fraud charges on which the Trump Company and its chief accountant, Allen Weisselberg, had already been criminally convicted.[61]

By contrast, very few centrist-independent commentators have doubted the seriousness of the charges or the credibility of the evidence in the two federal cases or the Georgia case.[62] Among the many items of powerful incriminating evidence, Trump, in a recorded phone call, pressured the governor of Georgia to "find" just enough votes for him to win the state's electoral votes in the 2020 election, and broadly threatened him with criminal prosecution if he did not comply. Until the Mar-a-Lago documents case was assigned to an evidently biased Trump-appointed judge, it was generally expected to yield the easiest conviction of all. Trump's former attorney general William Barr predicted a guilty verdict and former White House lawyer Ty Cobb called the case "a slam-dunk." Along with a vast amount of other evidence, prosecutors had obtained an audio recording of Trump, in a meeting with two visitors in his Bedminster, New Jersey, office, casually showing them a highly confidential military document and mentioning, in passing, that the document had not been declassified.

In all three of the pending criminal cases, prosecutors laid out the grounds for their charges in detailed indictments, including what most observers considered strong evidence of serious crimes.

Trump's legal troubles are relevant to expectations for his second term, and beyond, in three important ways. First, Trump has demonstrated a pattern of viewing prosecutors, judges, and other participants in his cases as personal enemies, and may seek to use the powers of the presidency for retribution. Such actions would pose a serious threat to the integrity of the legal system, potentially deterring officials and jurors from performing their duties. Second, Trump's apparent history of flouting the law suggests that he may continue to engage in unlawful behavior during a second term; that danger has been magnified by the Supreme Court's 2024 decision granting former presidents broad immunity from criminal prosecution. Finally, the election of a president with a well-documented record of serious misconduct poses a profound challenge to public confidence in the rule of law. Trump's persistent attacks on the legitimacy of investigations and prosecutions, combined with his efforts to delay legal proceedings, undermine the notion of accountability. Such an erosion of trust could have far-reaching implications, from weakening democratic institutions to emboldening future leaders to disregard legal constraints.

The Campaign

Trump's 2024 campaign provides further, more recent evidence for assessing his intentions and capabilities as president and anticipating the character and consequences of his second term. For the most part, his conduct of the campaign reinforced the policy directions established in his first term and confirmed the implications of his legal troubles.

By the standards of a typical presidential campaign, the Trump 2024 campaign focused slight attention on matters of policy.[63] At the campaign's instruction, the Republican convention produced a minimalist, sixteen-page party platform. (The Democratic platform came in at a more typical ninety-two pages.) More significant, the campaign itself produced no substantial policy papers. Along with offering a link to the party platform, the campaign website provided a list titled "President Trump's 20 Core Promises to Make America Great Again," each item of which was stated in a single sentence. It promised tax cuts (emphasizing benefits for workers), reduction of inflation, control of the border, and energy-production and manufacturing preeminence, among other goals. It also included more contentious promises to "carry out the largest deportation operation in

American history" and to "protect innocent children from the radical left's gender insanity."[64]

To an unknown degree, the campaign apparently relied on the work of an affiliated group, called the 2025 Project, to do the substantive policy and management planning for a second Trump administration.[65] But the project's role and significance were controversial. Developed by a group convened by the conservative Heritage Foundation, the project outlined sweeping plans for governance, including consolidating executive power, eliminating the independence of the Department of Justice and federal law enforcement, and implementing broad conservative reforms. Trump initially appeared to embrace the project, but as criticism mounted over the plan's ideological extremity, he disavowed and (falsely) denied any connection with it. As a result, the role that the project will have in setting Trump's second-term agenda is uncertain.

Trump himself demonstrated little apparent interest in policy. His rallies and personal appearances were characterized by a widely noticed shortage of substantive policy discussions. He made some very general points on policy. He attacked the Biden administration's performance, especially on inflation and border control. He ridiculed progressive ideology, particularly on transgender issues. For the most part, he made sweeping promises to solve major problems without offering any concrete policy proposals. Among other examples, Trump claimed he would end inflation, make food prices affordable, achieve energy independence, end the wars in Ukraine and Gaza, and eradicate crime—always without explaining how he would do so.

Two of his major policy proposals—broadly increasing tariffs and rapidly deporting all undocumented immigrants—were widely criticized as catastrophically unworkable.[66] Economists warned that sweeping tariffs would harm U.S. consumers and businesses. Business leaders and immigration experts pointed out that mass deportation would be logistically impossible and economically disastrous. Forced to address state-level no-exception bans on abortion, Trump vacillated about his own views and insisted, consistent with the Supreme Court's *Dobbs* ruling, that abortion policy should be decided by the states.

Observers of Trump's campaign rallies found them markedly rambling and incoherent—with increasingly mainstream suggestions that he was demonstrating significant cognitive decline.[67] Some commentaries had pointed out as early as 2017, based on comparisons with his public appearances in the 1990s, that there were telltale changes in Trump's speech patterns—smaller vocabulary, shorter sentences, simpler thoughts, more repetition, and the like. The 2024 campaign exposed apparent evidence of further decline. These included moments of apparent confusion about his opponent (Kamala Harris, not Joe Biden or Barack Obama), repetitive and bizarre anecdotes ("the late, great Hannibal Lecter"), and lapses in judgment, such as disparaging the city of Detroit at the Detroit Economic Club and challenging Harris's Black identity during an appearance before an association of Black journalists. Trump's inability to stay focused on substantive messages—veering into scurrilous personal attacks, such as repeatedly calling Harris "stupid"—reinforced concerns about his attention span, judgment, and self-discipline.

Trump obviously was troubled by the issue of cognitive decline. He brought it up often, making grandiose statements about his intellectual abilities and claiming (inaccurately) to have "aced" a difficult cognitive test.[68] He dismissed criticism of his rambling speeches, saying that he was constructing "the weave"—that is, discussing "like, nine different things [that] all come back brilliantly together."[69] Trump's performance in his debate with Biden temporarily quelled doubts, as he was far more articulate than his stumbling, obviously diminished opponent. Campaign insiders noted that Trump's stronger performances occurred when he was well rested, with noticeable lapses during evening rallies.

With the campaign punctuated by court appearances, procedural disputes, and jury rulings, Trump's rallies had a recurring theme: "For those who have been wronged and betrayed, I am your retribution." Audiences at his rallies cheered the declarations. Going further, Trump identified many of the targets. He labeled leading Democrats Nancy Pelosi and Adam Schiff, along with "the radical left," as "the enemy from within," suggesting that they posed threats to the nation. He called for indictment of former Representative Liz Cheney for her role on the January 6 committee. He suggested that General Mark Milley, Trump's chairman of the Joint Chiefs of Staff, should be executed for treason. He also targeted Vice President Harris, claiming she should be impeached and prosecuted for enabling illegal immigration. Altogether, Trump made more than one hundred threats to prosecute or punish perceived enemies.[70] While many of these threats may have been mere bluster, they represented a clear and direct signal of Trump's intention to use the power of government to punish critics and opponents—a hallmark of authoritarian rule.

The Transition

The postelection transition period began to reveal what the president-elect, no longer constrained by the requirements of campaign rhetoric, actually intended to do, how he intended to do it, and the support he would have in Congress. Some of Trump's actions were consistent with a conventional conservative agenda, the priorities of his first term, and the general policy directions of his campaign. The more notable features of the transition, however, pointed to even more extreme and wide-ranging departures from normal presidential policymaking than many of his critics had expected. In particular, the authoritarian tendencies evident in his first term and campaign were even more pronounced during the transition.

Support in Congress

The results of the congressional elections gave Republicans razor-thin majorities in both the Senate and, especially, the House of Representatives. In the House, the Republican majority stood at 220–215; in the Senate, 53–47. These slim margins mean that Trump's legislative success will sometimes require near-unanimous support from Republican lawmakers. Trump's relationships with Republican leaders appear somewhat mixed. In the Senate, Majority Leader John Thune, a pragmatic mainstream Republican, firmly rejected Trump's election denialism in 2020 and came around to endorsing his 2024 candidacy only after his preferred candidate exited the Republican primaries. But Thune soon cultivated a collaborative relationship with Trump, declaring that Trump's agenda is the Republican agenda. Nevertheless, he was unlikely to serve Trump as a loyal foot soldier. In the House, Mike Johnson was reelected as Speaker with exactly the bare minimum of required votes (218), and only after Trump intervened to secure votes from two of the three initially opposed members. With the party's bare majority of seats, Johnson's ability to maintain control of the House was highly uncertain amid the sometimes bitter factional conflicts within the Republican caucus.

The potential limitations of Trump's congressional support are significant. The Senate filibuster will constrain congressional action on divisive partisan or ideological measures. On ordinary (nonbudget) legislation, overcoming that barrier will require support from sixty senators—including seven Democrats—to invoke cloture and proceed to a roll-call vote. For that reason, reconciliation bills will be the primary tool for advancing Trump's agenda, as they were for Biden's. Much of Trump's legislative agenda, therefore, will have to be packaged in massive, multipart omnibus bills, containing only budget-relevant provisions. Such bills are challenging to negotiate and are enacted only once per year. His initiatives may face resistance from moderate Republicans such as Senators Susan Collins and

Lisa Murkowski, from fiscal conservatives concerned about the federal debt, or perhaps from an emergence of constitutional conservatives concerned about the separation of powers and other constitutional values. Trump's continuing ability to coerce congressional Republicans may be put to repeated tests.

Looking ahead, the slim Republican majorities are likely to be at severe risk in the 2026 midterm elections. For one thing, the Republicans will have twenty Senate seats to defend, compared with the Democrats' thirteen. More important, the president's party almost always loses seats in the midterm elections.[71] The capture of the House by Democrats during Trump's first term in 2018 led to an adversarial relationship with him for the remainder of his term, a result that will likely repeat if Democrats gain control of either chamber after 2026.

Appointments

By comparison to any previous presidency, including his own first term, Trump's initial second-term personnel selections and appointments produced an extraordinary amount of criticism and controversy. His top priority in making these selections was personal loyalty, with all other traditional qualifications clearly secondary—and in some cases, effectively ignored. Indeed, he briefly attempted to prevent the standard FBI background checks for some of his controversial nominees.

Some of his selections did have substantial credentials for their positions. Trump selected Susie Wiles, the cochair of his presidential campaign, to be his White House chief of staff, the first woman to hold that position. Although her senior experience was exclusively in campaigns, she was widely considered a brilliant strategist. Marco Rubio, the chair of the Senate Foreign Relations Committee and a somewhat guarded advocate for Trump, was nominated as secretary of state. With his mainstream Republican views and extensive, high-level experience in foreign policy, Rubio was the least controversial choice among Trump's key appointees. Nominees for the Departments of the Treasury, Energy, and the Interior—wealthy businessmen—lacked government experience but were qualified by long-term business interests in their departments' programs. Stephen Miller, appointed deputy chief of staff for policy and homeland security adviser, and Tom Homan, appointed border czar, had played major roles in the hardline immigration policies of Trump's first term.

Several of Trump's announced appointees, however, lacked credible qualifications, faced ethical objections, or both. In a choice that stunned

Washington, Trump initially named Representative Matt Gaetz, possibly his most hardcore, election-denying, and aggressive ally in Congress, as his nominee for attorney general. Gaetz had minimal legal experience, had been under extensive criminal investigation himself, and was currently under investigation by the House Ethics Committee. Amid widespread criticism of his selection and doubts that he would be confirmed, Gaetz withdrew from the nomination. Shortly after his withdrawal, the Ethics Committee published its report, finding substantial evidence that Gaetz had committed multiple crimes, including use of illegal drugs, procurement of prostitution, and statutory rape.[72]

Trump replaced Gaetz as attorney general nominee with Pam Bondi, a former Florida attorney general and one of the principal attorneys on the Trump legal team that brought numerous lawsuits attempting to overturn the 2020 election result. He added Kash Patel, a former aide to Trump ally and Republican congressman Devin Nunes, as FBI director. Patel had extensive experience in intelligence, national security, and law enforcement; but he had gained prominence primarily through long-running efforts to discredit investigations into Trump's alleged misconduct. Trump's selections of Gaetz, and then Bondi, to head the Justice Department and Patel to head the FBI signaled a firm and unconcealed intention to assert direct presidential control over law enforcement, presumably in service to his personal and political interests. His selection of the monumentally unfit Gaetz, in particular, signaled an apparent belief that he could appoint whomever he wished to any position and the Republican Senate would confirm them.

Other selections also raised serious concerns. Pete Hegseth, nominated as secretary of defense, initially encountered resistance owing to his inflammatory statements as a Fox News contributor and his lack of any senior experience in defense management, national security, or government. His most relevant experience, as merely an officer in the Army National Guard, was not remotely comparable to that of any defense secretary since the department's creation in 1947. There were also multiple allegations—denied by Hegseth but not thoroughly investigated—of spousal abuse, sexual assault, alcohol abuse, and financial mismanagement in a veterans' organization. In confirmation hearings, Hegseth repeatedly avoided making a commitment to resign as secretary if he drank on the job. Trump's choice for secretary of health and human services, Robert F. Kennedy Jr., had only tangentially relevant experience and had opposed vaccination against polio and other diseases as well as other generally accepted public health policies. His rejection of mainstream medical science would almost certainly have disqualified him for the position, responsible for most health programs and medical research, in any previous administration.

Tulsi Gabbard's nomination as director of national intelligence also drew criticism. Gabbard, a former Democratic congresswoman who had become an outspoken supporter of Trump, lacked high-level intelligence or national security experience, had shown sympathy for Vladimir Putin's foreign policy and been criticized as promoting Russian disinformation, and had ties to the murderous Syrian dictator Bashar al-Assad, before his overthrow in December 2024.

In a major departure from normal staffing and organization, Trump announced plans to create an informal presidential advisory commission—a so-called Department of Government Efficiency (DOGE)—that would identify inefficiencies and recommend cuts in budgets and personnel. It was to be led by Elon Musk, the tech industry magnate who had donated nearly $300 million to Trump's campaign, and Vivek Ramaswamy, a biotech entrepreneur, former presidential candidate, and political commentator. As critics pointed out, neither Musk nor Ramaswamy had prior government experience, and DOGE would lack normal governmental oversight and accountability.

While some Republican senators praised Trump's appointees for their alignment with conservative values and loyalty to Trump, the group as a whole included an extraordinary and unprecedented number of individuals without credible qualifications for their positions or with other, readily apparent grounds for serious objection. William Webster, a widely respected former head of both the FBI and the CIA—appointed to those positions by a Democratic and a Republican president, respectively—expressed grave concerns about Bondi, Patel, and Gabbard. Webster stated, "These nominees lack the essential experience and integrity required for their roles and pose a direct threat to the security and independence of the nation's law enforcement and intelligence institutions."[73]

Policy

If a populist-leaning, conservative president (like Trump) who was also pragmatic and evidence based (unlike Trump) had assumed office in 2025, he or she would have had a full plate of substantively constructive, politically feasible policy initiatives to consider. Some of them would have involved reversing or scaling back certain costly and ambitious liberal policies that were adopted during the Biden administration. Such a president would have sought to reduce the federal budget deficit or at least made sure not to increase it. Cost-cutting reform of entitlements programs, especially Medicare and Social Security, and a balanced reform of immigration policy would have been priorities. Donald Trump was uninterested in doing any of these things.

To a degree unmatched in any presidency in the modern era, Trump's major policy announcements during the transition were ideologically extreme, devoid of evidence-based policy analysis, and regarded by informed critics as dangerous or even destructive. In his unconventional advisory role, Musk proposed slashing the federal budget by 30 percent and federal employment by 25 percent. Trump touted the plan as "a revolutionary step to make government leaner and more accountable, saving taxpayers billions." However, no systematic or deliberative process undergirded the proposed cuts—suggesting that they either would be reckless and harmful or would never occur.

Trump's tax cut plans—including eliminating taxes on overtime pay, tips, and Social Security benefits—were estimated to cost $6–$10 trillion over ten years, equivalent to roughly 8–10 percent of the federal budget at a time when the budget deficit, by informed consensus, was already a grave problem. Former Federal Reserve Chair Janet Yellen warned, "The trajectory of U.S. debt is unsustainable and poses significant risks to long-term economic growth and fiscal stability."[74] A responsible, evidence-based administration would have wanted to know what very large budget cuts would be made before entertaining further tax cuts. Significantly, as president-elect, Trump pushed unsuccessfully for Congress to suspend the debt ceiling for the first several months of his administration.

Trump's proposed tariffs, including threats of dramatic hikes, also lacked economic justification. While praising tariffs as a general matter, he made wildly varying statements about their size and the targeted countries. At times he promised tariffs as high as 100 percent on imported goods and threatened sweeping penalties against countries like China to deal with trade imbalances.[75] On other occasions, he suggested smaller, targeted increases. In any case, there has been little or no support for major increases in tariffs among economists, who emphasize the benefits of low trade barriers and robust international trade for domestic economic growth. In his public remarks, Trump demonstrated an elementary misunderstanding of how tariffs work, asserting that the foreign nations pay the tariffs. In reality, the American importer pays them (literally, by writing a check to the government) and passes on the costs to domestic businesses and consumers. Economists warned that major tariff increases would have severe repercussions for the American economy.[76]

Trump's similarly inconsistent stances on mass deportations of undocumented immigrants raised both humanitarian and economic concerns. His occasional, most extravagant promise on the subject—to deport all illegal residents within two years—catered to his MAGA base but was obviously unworkable. Such a policy would remove an estimated 4–5 percent of the U.S. labor force, disproportionately harming industries like agriculture, construction, and hospitality—industries that quite openly and for many decades have relied heavily on undocumented workers. At other moments, Trump suggested focusing deportations, very narrowly, on those with criminal records. The uncertainty produced by these dramatically inconsistent positions is in itself costly, putting more than ten million long-term undocumented residents at risk and unable to plan for their future.

Some of Trump's policy declarations were so extreme and ungrounded that it was unclear whether they were serious, were just intended to troll his critics, or represented a fantasy of absolute power. After a tense meeting about trade, Trump posted a reference to Canadian Prime Minister Justin Trudeau as "governor" of "the Great State of Canada." At a rally, he elaborated, "We should annex Canada; they've been riding on our coattails for too long," and made similar statements multiple times thereafter.[77] In a similar vein, Trump demanded that Panama return control of the Panama Canal to the United States. "The Canal is ours; it was a mistake to give it away," referring to the 1977 treaty that ceded control to Panama. Finally, Trump floated the idea of purchasing Greenland from Denmark, calling it "a strategic opportunity for America," and described the transaction as the "real estate deal of the century."[78] All of these statements were dismissed, all but universally, as divorced from reality.

Retribution and Authoritarian Threat

Trump's good feelings following his election victory did not moderate his desire for retribution or his inclinations toward authoritarian methods. If anything, having the election settled in his favor seemed to free him from perceived political constraints. He renewed his pledge to pardon January 6 insurrectionists, a move harshly criticized by Judge Beryl Howell, who presided over some of their trials, for undermining accountability. He also pressed the Republican members of a House subcommittee to issue a report recommending an FBI investigation into Liz Cheney for her work on the January 6 committee.[79] The Republicans produced the report, leveling charges of witness tampering that were dismissed by legal commentators as lacking evidence. Trump continued to call for prosecution of Adam Schiff.

He also extended his efforts to intimidate and punish news organizations that reported adversely about him. He sued and obtained a $15 million settlement from ABC News over a debatable error in a commentary by George Stephanopoulos about the finding of Trump's liability in the E. Jean Carroll case.[80] More remarkably, he threatened to sue *The Des Moines Register* and its highly-respected polling company for a poll in the week before the election that indicated, incorrectly, that Harris would win in Iowa. Trump won the state by 13 points. But his accusation that the highly respected polling company had published a deliberately misleading poll had no basis in evidence and may have been intended primarily to deter news organizations from publishing any critical information about him.

Trump in Office

After the inauguration, any expectation that Trump would settle into something like a normal conservative presidency quickly vanished. His early decisions produced some likely policy accomplishments, at least from a conservative perspective, and a few preliminary successes in foreign policy. But his inclination toward extreme action, reckless and uninformed decision-making, disdain for norms and institutions, and aspirations to authoritarian rule reemerged immediately in exaggerated form. In some instances, there were grounds to suspect impaired judgment. Within a month, developments pointed toward multiple potential policy calamities and a constitutional crisis.

In the first days after his swearing in, Trump and his administration ordered or announced a sweeping array of major, often radical policy changes. Within two weeks, Trump issued at least twenty-five major executive orders. Seeking media coverage of the speedy action, he often signed the orders in front of television cameras, with stacks of leather-bound documents piled on his desk. His appointees in various agencies took numerous additional major actions, presumably with Trump's approval. The administration—often led by the semiofficial operative Elon Musk—put a hold on delivery of funds for all existing federal grants; stopped the processing of grant applications for federal funding of scientific, medical, and other research; ordered the denial of all applications for birthright citizenship; canceled all diversity, equity, and inclusion programs in federal agencies; conducted high-profile immigration raids in several major cities, commenced mass deportation of undocumented immigrants, and deployed military personnel to the Mexican border; instituted a pause on all delivery of foreign aid; ordered the closure of the U.S. Agency for

International Development and the Consumer Financial Protection Bureau; and fired tens of thousands of government employees in various other agencies, among numerous other important actions.[81] Trump also made proposals, demands, or threats on major foreign-policy issues, including tariffs and foreign trade, the war in Ukraine, the Israel–Hamas war, and several other matters.

A number of major actions tracked Trump's campaign promises and Republican priorities in more or less expected ways. Thus Trump committed to extending tax cuts; began rolling back climate-related and other environmental regulations; ended federal diversity, equity, and inclusion programs; reversed the Biden administration's progressive gender policies; and pushed for negotiated settlements of the wars in Ukraine and Gaza.

On a variety of significant matters, however, Trump's actions were unexpectedly extreme, apparently reckless or uninformed, or simply disconnected from reality. The administration launched a number of aggressive initiatives aimed at identifying and deporting illegal immigrants—including raids of workplaces in several major cities, with mass arrests of individuals lacking proof of legal residence.[82] Trump himself made contradictory statements about whether he intended to deport all illegal residents—an estimated eleven million. Any sweeping deportation program would disrupt the lives of millions of individuals who had entered the United States illegally, many years earlier, and then worked, paid taxes, raised families, and committed no other crimes while the government openly tolerated their presence.[83] Humanitarian considerations aside, illegal immigrants represent about 5 percent of the workforce and about half of it in the agriculture, hotel, and restaurant industries. Deporting any large fraction of these workers in a short time would have disastrous effects on those industries, with significant harm to the economy. The administration's early raids and arrests alone provoked widespread fear of further raids, resulting in employee absences and loss of production in those industries.[84]

Cutting federal spending is a perennial policy goal for conservatives, and non-partisan experts generally agree that certain categories of that spending—especially in the Social Security and Medicare programs—are unsustainable. But the Trump team's wide-ranging spending cuts and employee firings—orchestrated by Musk and DOGE—were imposed without apparent planning or deliberation, or specific publicly stated rationales.[85] The administration ordered mass firings at agencies that included the Centers for Disease Control; the National Institutes of Health; the Federal Aviation Administration; the Veterans' Administration; the Social Security Administration; the Department of Defense (ordered to make an 8 percent budget cut); the Internal Revenue Service; the Department of Homeland Security, including 150 employees of the Cybersecurity and Infrastructure Security Agency; the Central Intelligence Agency; and the National Nuclear Security Administration—all agencies with broadly accepted missions, targeted for cuts without public explanation. When critics pointed out that the National Nuclear Security Administration was responsible for safekeeping of the nation's nuclear weapons stockpile, the administration immediately moved to rehire the terminated employees.

The administration also ordered a hold on all expenditures under numerous federal grant programs—without taking time to consider the multitude of purposes the grants served or the effects of the sudden loss of funding on grant recipients and their clients.[86] The National Institutes of Health, for example, was required to immediately stop processing all grants for medical research. The action blocked about $1 billion in spending on medical research in the first two months of 2025. Among other effects, it was expected to force shutdowns or interruptions of many ongoing studies, resulting in waste of their prior funding, research effort, and treatment of patients. Musk and Trump repeatedly claimed that DOGE was finding and eliminating large amounts of "waste, fraud, and abuse," but did not provide evidence of it.[87]

While the budget and personnel cuts were reckless, Trump ordered or announced plans to order major increases in import tariffs that had essentially no support among independent economists. In a confusing sequence of announcements, Trump threatened, declared, postponed, reinstated, and redefined major tariff increases—up to 25 percent tariffs on all products and services from Canada, Mexico, China, and the European Union. In general, according to theory and evidence that is not controversial in economics, tariffs, under most conditions, reduce economic welfare in both the exporting and the importing countries. When one country's tariffs result in retaliatory tariffs by a targeted country, the effect is compounded. In an editorial, *The Wall Street Journal* denounced Trump's tariff plans as heading toward "the dumbest trade war in history."[88]

For at least several weeks, Trump was deterred from going forward with most of the tariffs as financial markets reacted negatively to the expected economic harm and all of the threatened countries demonstrated firm intentions to retaliate. Whether he would eventually impose broad tariffs or not, Trump had given all of the country's major trading partners reason to distrust their trading relationships with the United States and seek more reliable relationships with other countries, a long-term, invisible loss for the American economy.

Trump's most unexpected positions—indeed, incomprehensible to most observers—were a series of demands and declarations that called for major expansions of American territory. Within days of the inauguration, Trump demanded that the United States annex Canada, making it the fifty-first state; that Denmark sell Greenland to the United States, making it an American territory; that the United States retake control of the Panama Canal; and that it take full ownership of Gaza, after moving the Palestinian residents to other locations.[89] Each of the countries targeted by these demands expressed absolute determination to reject them. European leaders pointed out that the North Atlantic Treaty Organization (NATO) would defend Denmark militarily, if necessary. Apart from Trump's subordinates and loyal supporters, virtually no one took his expansionist notions seriously, except to voice concern about the disruption that would result if he took action to pursue them. Moreover, Trump persisted in pressing all of these notions, even after their resounding rejection by the relevant governments and other leaders. He threatened to use tariffs to destroy the Canadian economy, if it did not agree to annexation. In what can only be described as a juvenile taunt, he repeatedly referred to the prime minister of Canada as "Governor Trudeau." Regarding Gaza, he claimed that all of the parties, including the relevant regional powers, supported his plan when, in fact, the relevant regional powers—Egypt, Saudi Arabia, and Jordan— categorically rejected it.

The Economist magazine titled an article about Trump's territorial ambitions "The 1897 Project," recalling the long-abandoned and out-of-favor imperialism of the William McKinley presidency.[90] Many noted that Trump's expansionist demands, however disconnected from reality, did serious damage to American interests—provoking hostility and distrust toward the United States among important allies and around the world.

The central issues of American foreign- and national-security policy in this era concern the high-stakes strategic rivalry between the United States and its allies, on the one hand, and Russia and China, on the other. In the first weeks of the new term, the administration put American intentions with respect to that rivalry in doubt. Trump appeared interested in strengthening NATO, the transatlantic military alliance that has been at the center of American national-security strategy for eighty years. He chastised member countries for not meeting agreed targets for military spending and thus, in his view, relying too heavily on the United States for the defense of Europe.[91] European leaders worried that Trump was heading toward withdrawing U.S. troops from Europe, leaving NATO's ability to deter Russian aggression in a precarious state. In an interview with *Politico*, Trump's first-term national-security adviser John Bolton remarked, "I was there when he almost withdrew [from NATO]. . . . [His] goal here is not to strengthen NATO, it's to lay the groundwork to get out."[92]

In addition, the administration abruptly turned away from NATO's and the Biden administration's firm support for Ukraine in its defense against Russian invasion.[93] Trump quickly convened a meeting with Russia to begin peace negotiations, excluding Ukraine and NATO from participation. He demanded that Ukraine give the United States a 50 percent stake in revenues from its rich deposits of rare earth minerals in exchange for continuing military support. The United States then voted against a UN resolution that called on Russia to withdraw its military forces. And, in an acrimonious confrontation in the Oval Office, Trump belittled Ukrainian President Volodymyr Zelenskyy and criticized Ukraine's rejection of Russian demands. Regarding potential Chinese aggression, the administration, through a series of inconsistent actions and statements, created uncertainty about its commitment to helping Taiwan deter a threatened military attack by China and maintain Taiwanese independence.[94]

Trump's motivation in compromising American support for NATO and Ukraine has been murky and indeed suspect. No significant school of foreign-policy thought, liberal or conservative, has called for American actions that would weaken NATO or abandon leadership of the Western alliance. In fact, before Trump's takeover of the party, Republicans were strong and consistent supporters of both.[95] The administration's early posture on the Russia–Ukraine war may have reflected honest judgments about the limits of a possible agreement with Russia and the risk of nuclear escalation. Trump's history with Ukraine, Russia, and Russian President Vladimir Putin, however, points more strongly to an actual preference for the Russian side. In any case, American withdrawal from leadership of the Western alliance would have dire consequences for the rules-based world order and the security of liberal democracies. In response to the situation, the European Union's foreign-policy chief declared that "the Free World needs a new leader" and that Europe would assume the role.[96]

In the first weeks after the inauguration, Trump made the threat that his second term poses for American democracy unmistakable. He largely abandoned any pretenses that he would respect legal or constitutional limits on his authority, tolerate legitimate political opposition, or seek to preserve or protect the constitutional system or democracy. Trump, Musk, and other administration officials took actions that aimed both at asserting unilateral power on current issues and at suppressing criticism and political competition in future debates and elections.

Trump used a range of methods to seize unilateral power to impose his policies. Certainly, many of his executive orders, including some highly controversial ones, were presumably consistent with existing law and within the scope of his authority as president. Many of them merely reversed orders that had been issued in the same way by prior presidents, especially Barack Obama and Joe Biden. But Trump, Musk, and others took numerous actions that apparently exceeded the president's authority.[97] They blocked expenditures that had been appropriated by Congress; fired, without cause, thousands of federal employees who had permanent status; closed programs and entire agencies that had been established by law; and ordered removal of the heads of independent agencies who had statutory fixed terms. In one of his first acts, Trump summarily fired seventeen inspectors general, ignoring direct statutory language requiring thirty days' prior notification of Congress. In another, Trump ordered an end to birthright citizenship, despite the plain words of the Fourteenth Amendment—"All persons born or naturalized in the United States, and subject to the jurisdiction thereof, are citizens of the United States and of the State wherein they reside."[98]

Many presidents have stretched their legal authority on a few issues. But Trump issued orders that flew in the face of existing law on dozens of matters. When numerous Trump orders and administration decisions were being delayed or overturned by federal courts, Trump, J. D. Vance, and other officials questioned the legitimacy of judicial review and made veiled threats about refusing to comply with court decisions.[99] The administration also used a tactic of delaying or minimizing compliance, leading judges to impose more detailed orders and threaten to find the administration in contempt. In a social media post, Trump declared, "He who saves his country does not violate any law," an explicit rejection of constitutional limits on presidential power.[100]

Some of the administration's actions directly targeted officials responsible for identifying and exposing executive branch wrongdoing. Inspectors general are supposed to operate independently of the president and his political appointees in order to monitor agencies' compliance with law. The first independent agency whose head Trump attempted to remove, the Office of Special Counsel, monitors personnel practices for compliance with the merit system, enforces the prohibition of partisan political activity by government employees, and protects federal whistleblowers from retaliation. Trump's early targeting of these particular officials was virtually an announcement that he expected his administration to violate laws.

Beyond claiming and attempting to exercise unilateral power on current issues, Trump took numerous steps that were evidently aimed at hampering or interfering with regular democratic processes in order to maintain political power, for himself or other Republicans, in the future. On obviously bogus grounds, he pushed the House Republicans to seek a criminal investigation of former Representative Liz Cheney, who had chaired the House committee on the January 6 insurrection. After verbally attacking his former Chairman of the Joint Chiefs of Staff Mark Milley and his former National Security Advisor John Bolton for their criticism of him, Trump canceled their Secret Service protection, exposing them to possible violence or assassination.[101] These actions were retaliation against past enemies; but they also served as threats against future opponents.

Reinforcing those threats, Trump ordered the firing of all the prosecutors in the Justice Department who had worked on either of the federal prosecutions of him. Breaking with past practice, he removed several top officials of the FBI and replaced them with trusted, yet far less qualified, loyalists. Violating their statutory fixed terms, Trump also demanded resignations by Democratic members of the Privacy and Civil Liberties Oversight Board, which monitors surveillance activities of the FBI, CIA, and National Security Agency. Neutralizing the board would facilitate illicit surveillance of political opponents. All these unprecedented actions signaled that federal law enforcement will be used to punish or harass Trump's preferred targets.

Trump and other administration officials used a variety of means—violating law or established norms—to block or punish critical coverage by independent media. Trump prohibited executive branch officials from speaking to the press, normally a major source of public information. To punish them for news coverage that Trump objected to, the White House barred the two leading news agencies—the Associated Press (AP) and Reuters—from attending White House news conferences, and the AP from covering events in the Oval Office.[102] With Trump threatening to revoke the broadcast licenses of major news networks, his new chairman of the Federal Communications Commission began investigations of alleged political bias on the part of several news outlets, including ones owned by NBC and CBS. While attacking independent news media, Trump defended his policy decisions and other actions with a stream of falsehoods.[103] Often, the falsehoods were blatantly obvious to any informed person—suggesting that Trump did not mind people noticing that he lies, that he was unable to distinguish his lies from reality, or that he had forgotten information that conflicted with his narratives.[104]

Finally, Trump and various appointees took multiple actions that, at least potentially, prepared for direct interference with, or overturning of, an election. In one of his first acts as president, he pardoned everyone who had been convicted or accused of crimes in the January 6 insurrection, including those who had brought weapons to the Capitol, planned to invade the building, or committed violent acts against police officers. In effect, he declared the insurrection to prevent the peaceful transfer of power to have been legitimate. He announced plans to dissolve the independent commission that manages the U.S. Postal Service and bring it under the control of the Commerce Department. Although the plan had a credible rationale based on the U.S. Postal Service's financial difficulties, critics worried that a postal service responsive to Trump's demands would fail to provide timely and nonpartisan delivery of mail-in ballots.[105] Moreover, and with more transparent motivation, Trump included the Federal Election Commission in an executive order that, if sustained by the courts, would give the president control over independent agencies.[106] If upheld with respect to the Federal Election Commission, the order would enable Trump to choose his preferred interpretations of campaign finance law and control the resulting investigations and enforcement activities.

The administration took extraordinary steps to seize control of the Department of Defense, including dismissals of the chairman of the Joint Chiefs of Staff, the navy chief, the air force deputy chief, and the top lawyers of the army, navy, and air force.[107] The dismissals were criticized as politicizing the department and endangering national security by five former defense secretaries, including Trump's first-term appointee James Mattis.[108] In taking such dramatic steps, the administration apparently intended primarily to reshape Defense Department management on diversity, equity, and inclusion issues; military culture; and strategic focus. But there were also apparent implications for Trump's authoritarian threat. In the weeks after his 2020 election defeat, Trump briefly considered ordering the military to seize voting equipment to enable his campaign team to inspect them. In addition, of course, the military is often the final arbiter in conflict over an authoritarian coup.

We do not know which elections or terms of office Trump is actually concerned about enough to attempt interference or manipulation. Certainly, he has a huge stake in the 2026 midterm elections, which could thoroughly transform the character of his term. Under the Constitution's two-term limit for the presidency, he would not be eligible for reelection in 2028. Most likely, he would want to ensure the election of a Republican successor as president and Republican majorities in the House and Senate. But we cannot dismiss the possibility that he would attempt to overturn the two-term limit. He has occasionally teased the notion of doing so. At the 2025 Conservative Political Action Conference, his former White House strategist Steve Bannon declared, "The future of MAGA is Donald Trump! We want Trump in '28."[109] Trump has even associated himself, ostensibly playfully, with the title of "king" and the accoutrements of monarchy—symbolism that American political leaders other than Trump have rigorously avoided. In view of the hints, we cannot dismiss the possibility that Trump might seek to remain in power after 2028.

Conclusions and Prospects

A central feature of the 2024 election was an unprecedented, profound disconnect between centrist-independent opinion leaders and ordinary voters in their assessments of a candidate for the presidency. A clear preponderance of centrist-independent opinion elites—including nearly all major newspapers that made endorsements, and even his vice president and numerous top appointees from his first term—opposed Trump as fundamentally unfit for office and a danger to democracy. A majority of voters ignored the advice.

The sources of that disconnect are fairly clear. The broad, categorical rejection of Trump by those opinion elites was not driven by some perverse personal interest or hidden ideological agenda. In fact, by expressing their opposition to Trump, many prominent Republicans and conservatives knowingly made major sacrifices in their careers. Rather, anti-Trump elite opinion was, if anything, the response that one would have expected to Trump's first term; his multiple impeachments, civil lawsuits, and criminal charges (and the abundant publicly available evidence about them); and his 2024 campaign. Trump's record, before the election, provided ample grounds to explain the critics' urgent warnings—including the judgment that his second term would pose serious threats to the American constitutional system and democracy.

The voters' side of the disconnect is more complicated. The crucial starting point was Trump's development of a cultlike following among a sizable fraction of Republican voters.[110] These followers were devoted to Trump, credulous about his claims, dismissive of criticism or negative information about him, and oblivious to contrary messages, even from other Republican leaders. Trump himself already sensed his supporters' cultlike commitment during the 2016 campaign, when he presciently remarked, "I could stand in the middle of Fifth Avenue and shoot somebody, and I wouldn't lose any voters."[111]

This hardcore base, the MAGA cult, created the conditions for the broader disconnect between voters and elites. Trump was able to use his influence with that base to intimidate and control other Republican office-holders. As a result, they were generally unified in supporting him during the 2024 campaign. That unity was undoubtedly crucial in enabling him to maintain support from nearly all Republican voters, even though many of them had reservations.[112] Right-wing news media, most importantly Fox News, facilitated Trump's capture of the Republican Party, promoting even his demonstrably false claims to their audiences. With most Republican elected officials on board with Trump's messages, the mainstream media, in most day-to-day coverage, treated his candidacy as normal. As a result, a majority of the electorate treated Trump's efforts to overturn the 2020 election and his threat to democracy as if they were normal issues of policy or performance. "Trump tried to overturn an election? But Biden allowed rising grocery prices!"

In the first six weeks of his second term, Trump and his administration encountered many of the consequences that one would expect from their various extreme and often reckless actions, uninformed policies, abandonment of allies, and authoritarian methods. There were more than one hundred legal challenges against various executive actions, and courts had already issued at least ten nationwide injunctions blocking them. (By comparison, the Obama administration received twelve such injunctions in eight years; and the George W. Bush administration only six in eight years.) The Supreme Court had already upheld two major preliminary injunctions.

On the international front, Canada, Mexico, the European Union, the United Kingdom, and China imposed or threatened retaliatory tariffs. NATO (in regard to Greenland and Denmark) and China declared their willingness, if necessary, to confront the United States in military conflict. Dozens of foreign leaders condemned Trump's abandonment of Ukraine. European leaders recognized and lamented the end of American leadership of the free world.

On the domestic front, numerous groups that have not normally opposed Republicans protested the administration's budget and personnel cuts—including biomedical researchers, agricultural interests, hotel and restaurant industry groups, auto industry leaders, government employees' unions, residents of rural areas, and ordinary consumers. As disproportionate recipients of federal funds, Republican states experienced disproportionate pain. Republican Congress members encountered angry constituents at normally friendly town halls, prompting party leaders to advise against holding them.

Meanwhile, economic trends were generally unfavorable, partly because of Trump's policies. The stock market reacted negatively to the prospect of broad increases in import tariffs and other countries' retaliation. Grocery prices continued to increase. Consumer confidence was down. With the combination of government budget cuts and employee layoffs, disruption of immigrant-dependent labor markets, expected tariff-induced price increases on imported goods, and losses of export income, economists warned of a period of rising inflation and declining income and growth—so-called stagflation. In his March 4 speech to a joint session of Congress, Trump made a rare sort of admission: "We may face some hard economic times in the short term."[113] (Economists would not agree that the adverse effects of his policies were only short term.)

The effects of all these developments on Trump's political support, however, were broadly consistent with past patterns. Trump's approval rating of 44 percent in early March was lower than that of any other polling-era president at the same stage. But it was about the same as his own rating at the same point in his first term. While a majority of Americans disapproved of his performance, most Republicans approved, and many of them—Trump's base—retained their cultlike devotion. With occasional exceptions, Republican Congress members, in public remarks or roll-call votes, remained abjectly obedient to him. When *The Atlantic* magazine asked each of the 271 Republican members of Congress two questions whose obvious correct answers would offend Trump—whether Russia invaded Ukraine, and whether Putin is a dictator—only nineteen were willing to answer.[114] Several Republican House members threatened to impeach judges who defended the prerogatives of Congress by blocking Trump's executive orders.

Evidently, many Republican Congress members expressed different views in private. Conservative columnist Peggy Noonan reported shortly after the inauguration, "Republican lawmakers, including those most supportive of the president, are beside themselves with anxiety. When you speak to them—off the record, between friendly acquaintances—and ask how it's going, they shift, look off, shrug: You know how it's going. A GOP senator who supports the president had a blanched look. 'He doesn't do anything to make it easy.'"[115] In the weeks following those conversations, Trump gave such Republicans far more grounds for anxiety.

The prospects for Trump's second term are extraordinarily uncertain. The first six weeks pointed toward historic levels of conflict and disorder, both domestic and international. For the future of American democracy, the central uncertainty concerns how far Trump will go in furtherance of his authoritarian aspirations, and how much support he will receive in doing so. The future of American democracy may depend on whether, amid the likely tumultuous events of his second term, Trump loses some of his cultish following among many Republican voters and thus his unprecedented control of nearly all Republican officeholders.

Notes

1. Tom Nichols, "The Moment of Truth," *Atlantic*, November 2024.
2. James Fallows, "False Equivalence," *Atlantic*, accessed February 14, 2025, https://www.theatlantic.com/author/james-fallows/false-equivalence/.
3. Political-opinion elites are defined here as individuals who attend to politics and government as a full-time occupation and, either regularly or on occasion, present opinions or analysis on political issues that reach a relatively large audience. The category differs from that of political elites by excluding some people who have political influence but rarely express opinions publicly, such as high civil servants and most lobbyists, and by including some who may not have influence but do provide analysis or express opinions publicly, such as journalists and academics.
4. In a handful of cases in the modern era before Trump, significant groups within one of the parties have severely criticized their party's presidential nominee—moderate Republicans opposed to Barry Goldwater in 1964, anti–Vietnam War Democrats opposed to Hubert Humphrey in 1968, and moderate Democrats opposed to George McGovern in 1972. In all cases, the main grounds for criticism were serious or even profound differences on policy; and there were few, if any, prominent advocates of voting for the other party's nominee. As we will see, Republican criticism of Trump, especially in 2024, has been more broadly based and far more urgent and severe.
5. Martin Gilens and Naomi Murakawa, "Elite Cues and Political Decision Making," in *Political Decision-Making, Deliberation and Participation*, ed. Michael X. Delli Carpini et al. (Emerald, 2002).
6. Nothing in the analysis in this chapter depends on a precise definition of elites. Our rough definition includes individuals and groups who, as at least an important part of their "day jobs," participate somehow in politics or government, or in providing information and opinions to ordinary citizens. The concept in itself makes no assumption about how many individuals meet the definition. A key point is that elites have incentives to pay close attention to the issues and relevant information within their purview. On their relation with ordinary citizens, see Robert Lerner et al., "Elite vs. Mass Opinion: Another Look at a Classic Relationship," *International Journal of Public Opinion Research* 3, no. 1 (1991): 1–25; and

Alexandra Guisinger and Elizabeth N. Saunders, "Mapping the Boundaries of Elite Cues: How Elites Shape Mass Opinion Across International Issues," *International Studies Quarterly* 61, no. 2 (2017): 425–441.

7. John Zaller, *The Nature and Origins of Mass Opinion* (Cambridge University Press, 1992).

8. Jonathan Rauch, *The Constitution of Knowledge: A Defense of Truth* (Brookings Institution Press, 2021).

9. Amelia Neath, "Trump Ranks as Worst President in US History in New Academics Poll," *Independent*, February 20, 2024, https://www.independent.co.uk/news/world/americas/us-politics/trump-worst-president-poll-b2498963.html.

10. Mitchell Langbert and Sean Stevens, "Partisan Registration and Contributions of Faculty in Flagship Colleges," National Association of Scholars, January 17, 2020, https://www.nas.org/blogs/article/partisan-registration-and-contributions-of-faculty-in-flagship-colleges.

11. "News Media Endorsements in the 2024 United States Presidential Election," Wikipedia, last modified January 12, 2025, https://en.wikipedia.org/wiki/News_media_endorsements_in_the_2024_United_States_presidential_election. See also Andrew Howard, "NYT Endorses Harris as 'the Only Choice for President,'" *Politico*, September 30, 2024, https://www.politico.com/news/2024/09/30/new-york-times-kamala-harris-endorsement-00181639.

12. Seth Cline, "Nation's Biggest Newspapers Favor Obama, but Many Disillusioned," *U.S. News and World Report*, November 6, 2012.

13. "The Only Patriotic Choice for President," *New York Times*, September 30, 2024.

14. Alex Gangitano, "Harris Team Launches GOP Group with Endorsements from Ex-Trump Officials, Key Republican Voices," *Hill*, October 4, 2024, https://thehill.com/homenews/campaign/4809725-kamala-harris-campaign-gop-initiative-prominent-republican-voices/.

15. Alberto R. Gonzales, "Former Attorney General Alberto Gonzales Will Support Kamala Harris," *Politico*, September 12, 2024, https://www.politico.com/news/magazine/2024/09/12/alberto-gonzales-kamala-harris-endorsement-00178746.

16. Sarah Smith and Max Matza, "Mike Pence Tears into Donald Trump at 2024 Campaign Launch," *BBC News*, June 7, 2023, https://www.bbc.com/news/world-us-canada-65839793; Louise Hall, "Ex-Chief of Staff John Kelly Told Friends That Trump's Dishonesty Is 'Astounding' and 'Pathetic,' Report Claims," *Independent*, October 17, 2020, https://www.independent.co.uk/news/world/americas/us-politics/trump-john-kelly-chief-of-staff-white-house-dishonesty-b1084832.html; Phillip Nieto, "Former Trump Senior Aide Tells Morning Joe Trump Is 'Fundamentally Ignorant' on Foreign Policy: 'He Doesn't Care About the Facts!,'" *Mediaite*, February 1, 2024,

https://www.mediaite.com/tv/former-trump-senior-aide-tells-morning -joe-trump-is-fundamentally-ignorant-on-foreign-policy-he-doesnt-care -about-the-facts; Julia Shapero, "Barr: Trump Will Deliver 'Chaos' and 'Horror Show,'" *Hill*, May 5, 2023, https://thehill.com/homenews/campaign /3990804-barr-trump-will-deliver-chaos-and-horror-show/.

17. Franklin D. Roosevelt's vice president in his first two terms, John Nance Garner, fell out with FDR on policy matters and ran against him for the Democratic nomination in 1941.

18. Bandy X. Lee, ed., *The Dangerous Case of Donald Trump: 27 Psychiatrists and Mental Health Experts Assess a President* (Thomas Dunne Books, 2017); Jessica Glenza, "More Than 200 Health Professionals Say Trump Has 'Malignant Narcissism' in Open Letter," *Guardian*, October 24, 2024, https://www.theguardian.com/us-news/2024/oct/24/trump-nyt-ad -george-conway-pac.

19. "The Post Endorses Donald Trump for President—the Clear Choice for a Better Future," *New York Post*, October 25, 2024; "Las Vegas Review-Journal Endorses Donald Trump for President," *Las Vegas Review-Journal*, October 13, 2024.

20. Scott Jennings, "Why I Voted for Trump," *Los Angeles Times*, November 6, 2024.

21. "Americans See Federal Criminal Charges Against Trump as Serious, 51% Say He Should Be Prosecuted, 62% Say Politics Is Motivating DOJ's Case, Quinnipiac University National Poll Finds; Supreme Court Job Approval Hits All-Time Low," Quinnipiac University, June 22, 2023, https://poll.qu .edu/poll-release?releaseid=3874; Russell Payne, "Poll Suggests That Majority of Republicans Would Vote for Trump Even If He Is Convicted of Felonies," *New York Sun*, December 15, 2023, https://www.nysun.com /article/poll-suggests-that-majority-of-republicans-would-vote-for -trump-even-if-he-is-convicted-of-felonies.

22. Donald Trump, interview by *Time*, December 12, 2024, https://time.com /7201565/person-of-the-year-2024-donald-trump-transcript/.

23. On Trump's methods, see Paul J. Quirk, "Presidential Competence," in *The Presidency and the Political System*, 11th ed., ed. Michael Nelson (CQ Press, 2019); James P. Pfiffner, "Organizing the Trump Presidency," *Presidential Studies Quarterly* 49, no. 1 (2019): 118–140, https://pfiffner.gmu.edu /wp-content/uploads/2018/11/Organizing-the-Trump-Presidency -Pfiffner.pdf; James P. Pfiffner, "Donald Trump and the Norms of the Presidency," *Presidential Studies Quarterly* 51, no. 2 (2021): 322–343, https:// pfiffner.gmu.edu/wp-content/uploads/2022/05/Donald-Trump-and-the -Norms-of-the-Presidency-Jim-Pfiffner.pdf; and Michael Nelson, *Trump: The First Two Years* (University of Virginia Press, 2019).

24. On the size of the Trump business: It reports having roughly twenty thousand employees, which apparently includes employment by the

company's franchisees and contractors. By comparison, another hotel company, Marriott International, has roughly twenty times that number, more than four hundred thousand. See "The Trump Organization," Wikipedia, accessed January 2025, https://en.wikipedia.org/wiki/The_Trump _Organization; and "Marriott International Number of Employees 2010– 2023," Macrotrends, accessed January 2025, https://www.macrotrends.net /stocks/charts/MAR/marriott/number-of-employees.

25. Brian Bennett, "Inside Jared Kushner's Unusual White House Role," *Time*, January 16, 2020.

26. Mark Mazzetti, "The Poisoned Relationship Between Trump and the Keepers of U.S. Secrets," *New York Times*, August 11, 2022.

27. Kathryn Dunn Tenpas, "Tracking Turnover in the Trump Administration," Brookings Institution, January 19, 2021, https://www.brookings.edu /articles/tracking-turnover-in-the-trump-administration/.

28. James Jay Carafano, "Donald Trump: A Great Decision Maker?," *National Interest*, February 23, 2020.

29. Caitlin Oprysko, "Trump Defends Surprise Syria Withdrawal Despite Withering GOP Criticism," *Politico*, December 20, 2018, https://www .politico.com/story/2018/12/20/trump-defends-syria-withdrawal -1070943; Bill McCarthy and Miriam Valverde, "Fact-Checking Donald Trump's Claims About Syria and US Troop Withdrawal," PolitiFact, October 8, 2019, https://www.politifact.com/article/2019/oct/08/fact -checking-donald-trumps-claims-about-syria-and/.

30. "President Trump's Relationship with Congress in the First Year," American University School of Public Affairs, October 24, 2017, https://www .american.edu/spa/news/trump-first-year.cfm.

31. Peter Sullivan, "Trump Calls House Healthcare Bill 'Mean,'" *Hill*, June 13, 2017, https://thehill.com/policy/healthcare/337651-trump-calls-house -healthcare-bill-mean/.

32. There is a vast and, in recent years, extremely sophisticated literature on partisan and ideological bias in news media. The findings, overall, are quite mixed. See, for example, Ceren Budak et al., "Fair and Balanced? Quantifying Media Bias Through Crowdsourced Content Analysis," *Public Opinion Quarterly* 80, no. S1 (2016): 250–271.

33. The most prominent effort to support Trump's claims is Mark R. Levin, *Unfreedom of the Press* (Threshold Editions, 2019). It does not present any such evidence. A reviewer in a liberal outlet described the evidence of media bias as "approaching parody." See Annalisa Quinn, "'Unfreedom of the Press' Is Full of Bombast and Bile," NPR, May 21, 2019, https://www.npr .org/2019/05/21/724983201/unfreedom-of-the-press-is-full-of-bombast-and -bile. A reviewer in the conservative *Washington Times* is highly complimentary but only cites Levin's quotes of harsh opinions about Trump that were reported in mainstream media and does not mention any claimed

pattern of falsehood. See John R. Coyne, "Book Review: *Unfreedom of the Press* by Mark R. Levin," *Washington Times*, May 26, 2019.

34. "Nearly 8 in 10 Republicans Believe There Was Widespread Voter Fraud in Presidential Election, Quinnipiac University National Poll Finds; Nearly Half of All Voters Say Trump Should Be Prosecuted," Quinnipiac University, December 10, 2020, https://poll.qu.edu/Poll-Release?releaseid=3734.

35. For businesses, as for individuals, the act provided similar benefits in proportionate terms for most businesses. It set the corporate income tax at a flat rate of 21 percent, regardless of the level of taxable income. For firms with income over $10,000,000 the prior rate was 35 percent, so the cut was 14 percent. The benefits were almost the same—with the prior rate only 1 percent lower—for firms with more than $75,000 in taxable income.

36. Philip A. Wallach and Kelly Kennedy, "Examining Some of Trump's Deregulation Efforts: Lessons from the Brookings Regulatory Tracker," Brookings Institution, March 8, 2022, https://www.brookings.edu/articles /examining-some-of-trumps-deregulation-efforts-lessons-from-the -brookings-regulatory-tracker/.

37. Cary Coglianese et al., "Deregulatory Deceiving," *Regulatory Review*, November 2, 2020, https://www.theregreview.org/2020/11/02/coglianese -sarin-shapiro-deregulatory-deceiving/; Philip A. Wallach, "Examining Some of Trump's Deregulation Efforts: Lessons from the Brookings Regulatory Tracker," Brookings Institution, October 1, 2020, https://www .brookings.edu/articles/examining-some-of-trumps-deregulation -efforts-lessons-from-the-brookings-regulatory-tracker/.

38. Raymond J. Keating, "Strong Support for Free Trade Among Economists . . . and the American Public," Small Business and Entrepreneurship Council, August 27, 2019, https://sbecouncil.org/2019/08/27/strong-support -for-free-trade-among-economists-and-the-american-public/; Steven Greenhouse, "Unions Deny Stand over Trade Policy Is Protectionism," Institute for Agriculture and Trade Policy, April 24, 2000, https://www .iatp.org/news/unions-deny-stand-over-trade-policy-is-protectionism.

39. The difficulty in assessing the effects of sweeping trade restrictions occurs because many other changes in policy and economic conditions occur in the same period.

40. Eugene Kiely et al., "Trump's Final Numbers," FactCheck.org, October 8, 2021, updated July 26, 2024, https://www.factcheck.org/2021/10/trumps -final-numbers/; Mark Hoekstra and Sandra Orozco-Aleman, "Illegal Immigration: The Trump Effect," NBER Working Paper No. 28909 (National Bureau of Economic Research, June 2021), https://www.nber.org /system/files/working_papers/w28909/w28909.pdf.

41. Jacob Wallace et al., "Excess Death Rates for Republican and Democratic Registered Voters in Florida and Ohio During the COVID-19 Pandemic," *JAMA Internal Medicine* 183, no. 7 (2023): 758–767.

42. Quint Forgey, "'This Is Deadly Stuff': Tapes Show Trump Acknowledging Virus Threat in February," *Politico*, September 9, 2020, https://www .politico.com/news/2020/09/09/trump-coronavirus-deadly-downplayed -risk-410796. Trump explained to Woodward that he had minimized the COVID-19 threat because he wanted to avoid public panic. It is of course possible that, instead, he had deluded himself into believing the threat was minimal but did not want to admit that to Woodward. In the first year of the pandemic, Trump seemed to regard dire warnings about it as harmful to his public support.

43. Janice Hopkins Tanne, "Report Highlights 'Devastating Impacts' of Trump on Every Aspect of US Health," *BMJ* 372 (2021): n439.

44. See Paul K. Macdonald, "America First? Explaining Continuity and Change in Trump's Foreign Policy," *Political Science Quarterly* 133, no. 3 (2018): 401–434.

45. Mallory Shellbourne, "Trump's Infrastructure Plan Hits a Dead End," *Hill*, May 17, 2018, https://thehill.com/policy/transportation/388071 -trumps-infrastructure-plan-hits-a-dead-end/.

46. Dylan Scott and Sarah Kliff, "Why Obamacare Repeal Failed," *Vox*, July 31, 2017, https://www.vox.com/policy-and-politics/2017/7/31/16055960 /why-obamacare-repeal-failed.

47. Don Beyer, "The Trump Presidency: A Final Economic Scorecard," February 12, 2021, https://www.jec.senate.gov/public/_cache/files/7d9aa96b -429a-494c-907f-3ccc5bb31a14/the-trump-presidency---a-final-economic -scorecard.pdf.

48. David M. Konisky and Neal D. Woods, "Environmental Federalism and the Trump Presidency: A Preliminary Assessment," *Publius: The Journal of Federalism* 48, no. 3 (2018): 345–371.

49. Sidney M. Milkis and Michael Nelson, *The American Presidency: Origins and Development, 1776–2021*, 9th ed. (CQ Press, 2022).

50. *Congressional Oversight and Investigations* (Congressional Research Service, updated May December 3, 2024), https://crsreports.congress.gov /product/pdf/IF/IF10015.

51. Michael Schmidt, "As President, Trump Demanded Investigations of Foes. He Got Some Results," *New York Times*, September 21, 2024.

52. Chris Cillizza and Brenna Williams, "15 Times Donald Trump Praised Authoritarian Rulers," CNN, July 2, 2019, https://amp.cnn.com/cnn/2019 /07/02/politics/donald-trump-dictators-kim-jong-un-vladimir-putin /index.html.

53. The payment of hush money is entirely legal. The legally complex charges in this case were actually about falsification of Trump Company business records and violation of federal campaign finance reporting requirements.

54. David A. Graham, "The Cases Against Trump: A Guide," *Atlantic*, January 6, 2025.

55. Robert S. Mueller III, *Report on the Investigation into Russian Interference in the 2016 Presidential Election*, vol. 1 (U.S. Department of Justice, March 2019), https://www.justice.gov/storage/report.pdf.

56. Department guidelines barred criminal indictment of a sitting president. Mueller, interpreting that constraint broadly, decided it would be improper to present a finding of criminal offenses because, without an indictment and trial, Trump would not have the opportunity to defend himself against the charges and obtain a verdict in court.

57. Neal Katyal, *Impeach: The Case Against Donald Trump* (Hachette Books, 2020).

58. Ali Swenson, "Republicans Who See Trump Conviction as Politically Motivated Vow to 'Indict the Left,'" Associated Press, June 4, 2024, https://apnews.com/article/1c35203e6fd5a62d490969bea1eb9174.

59. David Barstow et al., "Trump Engaged in Suspect Tax Schemes as He Reaped Riches from His Father," *New York Times*, October 2, 2018.

60. Roger Parloff, "Was D.A. Bragg Right to Bring the New York Charges Against Trump?," *Lawfare*, May 28, 2024, https://www.lawfaremedia.org/article/was-d.a.-bragg-right-to-bring-the-new-york-charges-against-trump.

61. Although Trump was often described as a hands-on manager and few outside Trump's defense team credited the notion that Weisselberg and others at the company would commit crimes, for the company's benefit, on their own accord, Trump gave few instructions in writing and, crucially, Weisselberg (out of loyalty or fear) served time rather than testify against him. On legal analysts' views of the hush money–campaign finance case, see Michael R. Sisak et al., "Trump Conviction in Hush Money Case Raises Legal and Political Questions," Associated Press, May 31, 2024.

62. For details and commentary, see Melissa Murray and Andrew Weissmann, *The Trump Indictments: The Historic Charging Documents with Commentary* (W. W. Norton, 2024).

63. Molly Jong-Fast, "Donald Trump's 'Shock and Awe' Campaign," *Vanity Fair*, January 6, 2025.

64. "President Trump's 20 Core Promises to Make America Great Again," Donald J. Trump for President, accessed March 7, 2025, https://www.donaldjtrump.com/platform.

65. "What Is Project 2025? A 5-Minute Overview of the Conservative Playbook," *Newsweek*, August 28, 2024; Paul Dans and Steven Groves, eds., *Mandate for Leadership: The Conservative Promise* (Heritage Foundation, 2023), https://static.project2025.org/2025_MandateForLeadership_FULL.pdf.

66. Michelle Hackman and Tarini Parti, "The Five Biggest Roadblocks to Trump's Immigration Agenda," *Wall Street Journal*, January 1, 2025; Valentina Romei et al., "Donald Trump's 'Maganomics' Will Damage Growth, Economists Tell FT Polls," *Financial Times*, January 1, 2025.

67. Dhruv Khullar, "Trump's Health, and Ours," *New Yorker*, October 24, 2024; Margaret Hartmann, "The 8 Most Bizarre and Baffling Trump Rally Rants," *New York Magazine*, October 4, 2024; Hafiz Rashid, "Cognitive Decline? Experts Find Evidence Trump's Mind Is Slowing," *New Republic*, August 8, 2024.

68. Ashley Parker and Dan Diamond, "A 'Whale' of a Tale: Trump Continues to Distort Cognitive Test He Took," *Washington Post*, January 19, 2024.

69. Margaret Hartmann, "Trump Tries to Rebrand Incoherent Rambling as 'the Weave,'" *New York Magazine*, September 4, 2024.

70. "Trump Makes More Than 100 Threats to Prosecute or Punish Perceived Enemies," *Morning Edition*, NPR, October 22, 2024, https://www.npr.org /2024/10/22/nx-s1-5155032/trump-makes-more-than-100-threats-to -prosecute-or-punish-perceived-enemies.

71. Robert S. Erikson, "The Puzzle of Midterm Loss," *Journal of Politics* 50, no. 4 (1988): 1011–1029; George Pandya, "An Investigation into the Correlation Between a President's Approval Rating and the Performance of His Party in the Midterm Elections," arXiv preprint, March 2015, https:// arxiv.org/abs/1503.07545.

72. The report found evidence that Gaetz had frequently used illegal drugs, paid women for sex on multiple occasions, and had paid for sex with an underage girl. "What We Learned from the House Ethics Report on Matt Gaetz," *New York Magazine*, December 23, 2024.

73. William H. Webster, letter to U.S. senators, December 26, 2024, quoted in Julian Borger, "Ex-FBI and CIA Head Urges Senate to Reject Trump Picks Patel and Gabbard," *Guardian*, December 27, 2024.

74. Janet Yellen, "Congress, Raise the Debt Limit," *Wall Street Journal*, September 19, 2021.

75. Focusing on trade balances with particular trading partners is clearly, and very simply, incorrect: The United States could have a favorable overall balance of trade by only buying goods from one country and only selling other goods to another country. There are no grounds for expecting equal purchases from and sales to any country.

76. Romei et al., "Donald Trump's 'Maganomics.'"

77. Michael Crowley, "Trump's Talk of Annexing Canada Alarms Allies," *New York Times*, February 15, 2025.

78. David E. Sanger and Lisa Friedman, "Trump's Wish to Control Greenland and Panama Canal: Not a Joke This Time," *New York Times*, December 23, 2024.

79. "Chairman Loudermilk Releases Second January 6, 2021 Report," Committee on House Administration, December 17, 2024, https://cha.house.gov /2024/12/chairman-loudermilk-releases-second-january-6-2021-report. See also Sonam Sheth, "Liz Cheney Denies Allegations in New Report Accusing Her of Witness Tampering," *Newsweek*, December 18, 2024.

80. Stephanopoulos said that Trump had been found liable for rape. In fact, the finding by the New York jury had been liability for sexual abuse. But the factual basis for the finding—forced digital penetration—is defined as rape in many other states.

81. Charlie Savage, "Trump Brazenly Defies Laws in Escalating Executive Power Grab," *New York Times*, February 5, 2025.

82. Michelle Hackman, "Trump to Begin Large-Scale Deportations Tuesday," *Wall Street Journal*, January 17, 2025.

83. For example, the Internal Revenue Service collected taxes from noncitizens with no questions asked about their immigration status. Businesses generally known to hire large numbers of illegal immigrants rarely encountered enforcement efforts. Children of such immigrants, whether birthright citizens or themselves illegal, encountered no barriers to attending public schools. Contrary to Trump's rhetoric, illegal immigrants have a lower crime rate than citizens. See Michael T. Light et al., "Comparing Crime Rates Between Undocumented Immigrants, Legal Immigrants, and Native-Born US Citizens in Texas," *Proceedings of the National Academy of Sciences* 117, no. 51 (December 2020): 32340–32347.

84. Jeffrey S. Passel and D'Vera Cohn, "A Portrait of Unauthorized Immigrants in the United States," Pew Research Center, April 14, 2009, https://www.pewresearch.org/hispanic/2009/04/14/a-portrait-of-unauthorized-immigrants-in-the-united-states/.

85. Jonathan Lemire, "Is DOGE Losing Steam?," *Atlantic*, March 6, 2025.

86. Jeff Stein et al., "White House Pauses All Federal Grants, Sparking Confusion," *Washington Post*, January 28, 2025.

87. Maggie Haberman et al., "At Oval Office, Musk Makes Broad Claims of Federal Fraud Without Proof," *New York Times*, February 11, 2025.

88. "The Dumbest Trade War in History," *Wall Street Journal*, January 31, 2025.

89. Sanger and Friedman, "Trump's Wish"; Kathryn Watson, "Trump Trolls Justin Trudeau as 'Governor' of the 'Great State' of Canada," *CBS News*, December 10, 2024, https://www.cbsnews.com/news/trump-trolls-justin-trudeau-as-governor-of-the-great-state-of-canada/; Daniel Estrin and Kat Lonsdorf, "Trump Says the U.S. Will 'Take Over' Gaza and Relocate Its People. What Does It Mean?," *All Things Considered*, NPR, February 5, 2025, https://www.npr.org/2025/02/05/nx-s1-5287576/trump-gaza-takeover.

90. "The 1897 Project," *Economist*, February 14, 2025.

91. Jonathan Lemire and Lorne Cook, "Trump Questions NATO's Commitment to U.S. amid Defense Spending Disputes," Associated Press, March 6, 2025.

92. Kelly Garrity, "Why John Bolton Is Certain Trump Really Wants to Blow Up NATO," *Politico*, February 13, 2024, https://www.politico.com/news/magazine/2024/02/13/bolton-trump-2024-nato-00141160.

93. Hegseth declared Ukraine's goals of regaining lost territory and joining NATO unrealistic, a virtual endorsement of Russia's demands. Trump praised Russian President Vladimir Putin, made scurrilous accusations against Ukrainian President Volodymyr Zelenskyy, and initiated preliminary peace talks with Russia, excluding Ukraine and Europe from participation. In blatant contradiction of the actual history, he declared that Ukraine should not have started the war.

94. Kathrin Hille, "Taiwan Pushes for Closer US Ties as China Threat Looms," *Financial Times*, March 4, 2025.

95. For instance, the 2016 law that sanctioned Russia for its 2014 invasion of the Crimea—the Global Magnitsky Human Rights Accountability Act—passed the Senate, 95–1, and the House, 402–3.

96. Nadeem Badshah, "'Free World Needs a New Leader,' Says EU Foreign Chief After Trump-Zelenskyy Row," *Guardian*, February 28, 2025.

97. "Where Do the Legal Cases Against Trump's Executive Orders Stand?," Reuters, January 30, 2025.

98. There are strong policy grounds for imposing limitations on birthright citizenship. But to do so would require either a constitutional amendment or a sharp reversal of long-standing judicial precedent.

99. Nate Raymond, "Trump, Allies Ramp Up Attacks on Judges as Musk Calls for Impeachments," Reuters, February 13, 2025.

100. Maggie Haberman et al., "Trump Suggests No Laws Are Broken If He's 'Saving His Country,'" *New York Times*, February 15, 2025. The rhetorical trick here is hiding the implication that a president, or perhaps anyone, is free to break laws if they merely believe or claim that they are doing so to save the country.

101. Trump's verbal attacks—including a remark that Milley should be executed—posed risks to both former officials from Trump's violence-prone supporters. In addition, Bolton had already been the target of an assassination plot by Iranian operatives, in retaliation for a 2020 U.S. drone attack that killed an Iranian military commander.

102. The AP had declined to recognize Trump's comically inappropriate and ineffective attempt to change the name of Gulf of Mexico, by his mere order, to "Gulf of America."

103. Peter Baker, "Trump's Alternative Reality: How Falsehoods Drive His Political Agenda," *New York Times*, February 23, 2025.

104. In an Oval Office conversation with French President Emmanuel Macron, Trump stated, entirely falsely, that European assistance to Ukraine had been in the form of loans and would be repaid. In front of cameras and reporters, Macron corrected him, pointing out that none of the European aid had been loans. Days later, Trump repeated the lie and was publicly corrected again, in an on-camera conversation with U.K. Prime Minister Keir Starmer. Finally, he repeated it and was

corrected, yet again, in a meeting with the recipient of the aid, President Zelenskyy.

105. Dominic Rushe, "US Postal Service Faces Murky Future as Trump Mulls Dismantling Institution," *Guardian*, March 2, 2025. Trump attacked the legitimacy of mail-in ballots, and attempted to limit their collection and counting, in the 2020 and 2024 elections.

106. Affected agencies include, among others, the Securities and Exchange Commission, the Federal Communications Commission, and the Federal Reserve Board. Such agencies are designated as independent in the statutes establishing them. By statute, the members are required to be bipartisan and serve fixed terms, and they are not subject to removal by the president, except for cause. If the executive order is upheld by the courts, the ruling would overturn more than a century of consistent precedent.

107. "Will Donald Trump and Elon Musk Wreck or Reform the Pentagon?," *Economist*, February 13, 2025.

108. Lolita C. Baldor, "Former Defense Chiefs Call for Congressional Hearings on Trump's Firing of Senior Military Leaders," Associated Press, February 28, 2025.

109. Steve Bannon, "Full Speech at CPAC 2025," C-SPAN, February 20, 2025, https://www.c-span.org/program/public-affairs-event/steve-bannon -speaks-at-cpac/656141.

110. Benjamin E. Goldsmith and Lars J. K. Moen, "The Personality of a Personality Cult? Personality Characteristics of Donald Trump's Most Loyal Supporters," *Political Psychology* 46, no. 1 (2025): 225–243.

111. Maggie Haberman, "Donald Trump Says He Could 'Shoot Somebody' and Not Lose Voters," *New York Times*, January 23, 2016.

112. On Republicans' reservations about Trump during the campaign, see Meredith McGraw et al., "Haley's Endorsement of Trump Doesn't Mean Her Supporters Will Follow Her," *Politico*, September 30, 2024, https://www .politico.com/news/2024/09/30/nikki-haley-trump-supporters-00181772.

113. "Speech: Donald Trump Addresses a Joint Session of Congress at the U.S. Capitol—March 4, 2025," Roll Call, March 4, 2025, https://rollcall.com /factbase/trump/transcript/donald-trump-speech-joint-session -congress-2025-march-4-2025.

114. Elaine Godfrey, "Did Russia Invade Ukraine? Is Putin a Dictator? We Asked Every Republican Member of Congress," *Atlantic*, February 26, 2025.

115. Peggy Noonan, "Trump and the Collapse of the Old Order," *Wall Street Journal*, February 8, 2025.

Congress

CHOOSING A (PRECARIOUSLY) UNIFIED GOVERNMENT

Gary C. Jacobson

Led by Donald Trump's remarkable comeback, the Republican Party won control of the White House, Senate, and House of Representatives in 2024. Insofar as Trump delivers on his campaign promises, the election results portend radical changes in national policy on immigration, the environment, trade, regulation, health care, civil rights, and foreign affairs as well as in government organization and staffing, most notably for the armed services and agencies within the Justice and Health and Human Services Departments. Trump's manifest contempt for institutions and norms that might limit his power to achieve "wins" in these domains, and his thirst for revenge against anyone who has sought to hold him accountable for his misdeeds, threatens equally radical assaults on the rule of law. The Republican House and Senate delegations, deferential to Trump even before his reelection and depleted of members prepared to resist him on principle, will not be disposed to stand in his way on most matters. Democrats, the mainstream news media, and other public and private institutions targeted by Trump can be expected to oppose him vigorously, portending at least several years of fierce political conflict over Trump's reactionary agenda and authoritarian aspirations.

Elections have consequences, and a narrow majority of voters clearly rejected the status quo in 2024. But the national Republican "wave" that opened the door to radical changes in American politics and policy was small by historical standards, and voting patterns in both the presidential and congressional elections displayed much more continuity than discontinuity with the recent past. Trump's share of the popular vote rose from 46.8 percent in 2020 to 49.8 percent in 2024, an increase derived more from a decline in votes for the Democrat (Kamala Harris won 6.3 million fewer votes than Joe Biden) than from an increase in support for Trump

TABLE 1. Nationalization and continuity in presidential elections lost by the incumbent party, 1952–2024

Year	Swing to winning party (state average)	Standard deviation of the swing	Correlation with previous election (state vote)
1952	11.5	6.2	.78
1960	5.2	10.7	.43
1968	10.9	11.8	.27
1976	13.9	9.0	.23
1980	7.0	4.4	.83
1992	6.9	3.8	.78
2000	5.8	3.3	.93
2008	5.1	3.8	.93
2016	2.1	3.6	.94
2020	1.8	1.4	.99
2024	2.2	1.2	.99

Source: Compiled by author.

(up 3.1 million votes over 2020). On average, Trump's gain across all states was 2.3 percentage points; in the six states that switched from Biden in 2020 to Trump in 2024, giving him his Electoral College victory, his average gain was 1.9 points.

In historical context, these were modest swings to the candidate taking the White House from the other party. Before 2016, elections in which the incumbent president's party lost produced notably larger partisan shifts in the winner's favor, always more than 5 percentage points and sometimes much more (table 1). In the last three elections, average vote swings across states have been much smaller. They have also become much more uniform, with the very small standard deviations revealing just how thoroughly nationalized these contests have become (the smaller the standard deviation, the more uniform the swing across states and thus the more nationalized the election). The correlation between current and previous outcomes across all the states, which reached .99 in the two most recent elections, underlines the extraordinary continuity in aggregate voting patterns across elections during the Trump era. Although, as other chapters in this volume attest, multiple factors contributed to Trump's victory, these aggregate results are consistent with the idea that its main source was a broad national unhappiness with the direction of the country, driven by worries about the economy and illegal immigration—a negative referendum on the Biden–Harris administration that outweighed concerns about Trump's fitness for office

TABLE 2. Membership changes in the House and Senate during the Trump era

	Republicans	Democrats	Independents
House of Representatives			
Elected in 2016	241	194	
Elected in 2018	199	235	
Elected in 2020	213	222	
Elected in 2022	222	213	
Before the 2024 election	221	214	
Elected in 2024	220	215	
Incumbents reelected	187	181	
Incumbents defeated	7	4	
Open seats retained	25	25	
Open seats lost	2	4	
Senate			
After the 2016 election	52	46	2[a]
After the 2018 election	53	45	2[a]
After the 2020 election	50	48	2[a]
After the 2022 election	49	49	2[a]
Before the 2024 election	49	47	4[a]
Elected in 2024	53	47	2[a]
Incumbents reelected	9	12	
Incumbents defeated	0	3	
Open seats retained	2	6	
Open seats lost	0	1	

Source: Compiled by author.
[a]The two independents, Bernie Sanders (VT) and Angus King (ME), caucus with the Democrats; Joe Manchin (WV) and Kyrsten Sinema (AZ) switched to independent after being elected as Democrats in 2022; neither ran for reelection in 2024.

among the minority of voters who held ambivalent opinions about the candidates and parties.[1] As such, it was much more a vote against the status quo than for Trump's promises.

The 2024 congressional results, summarized in table 2, registered even smaller shifts in voter preferences. Republicans lost one seat net in the House, shrinking their already precarious margin over the Democrats to five. Had it not been for a successful 2023 partisan gerrymander in North Carolina designed to give Republicans three additional seats, Democrats would have won a 218–217 majority.[2] Republicans took the Senate by defeating three Democratic incumbents and taking one open seat, with all but one of their gains occurring in deeply red states won easily by Trump. As analyses presented later will document, partisan loyalty and straight-ticket voting matched the historical highs reached in 2020, and the link between presidential and down-ballot results was again extraordinarily tight. Trump's victory, though narrow, thus helped his party take the Senate and retain control of the House, enabling him to initiate radical changes in national policy despite the absence of anything resembling a popular mandate for them.

A "Calcified" Electorate

The small, uniform interelection swings characterizing the three elections with Trump on the ballot, and the stability of recent congressional election results, reflect the rigidity in voting behavior, termed "calcification" by John Sides, Chris Tausanovitch, and Lynn Vavreck in their landmark account of the 2020 election,[3] produced by extreme levels of partisan polarization. As voters' political and social identities, ideological leanings, and issue preferences have moved into closer alignment over the last several decades, partisans' political attitudes have become more consistent internally and more distinct and distant from their counterparts in the rival party, and their opinions of the other party have become much more negative.[4] Consequently, Americans exhibit "less willingness to defect from their party, such as breaking with their party's president or even voting for the opposing party. There is thus less chance for new and even dramatic events to change people's choices at the ballot box."[5]

Pre-Election Trends in Voters' Preferences

The 2024 elections did not lack dramatic events. What early in the year looked to be a static, uninspiring rerun of the 2020 contest between two aging and unpopular candidates, Joe Biden and Donald Trump, was thoroughly upended during the summer. Biden's disastrous performance in a debate with Trump on June 27 and the attempted assassination of Trump on July 13 were followed by a unified and enthusiastic Republican convention, giving Republican prospects a major lift. So much so that on July 21, under growing pressure from Democratic leaders and donors who feared a November down-ballot wipeout, Biden withdrew and endorsed Harris as his replacement. Democrats—leaders, activists, and ordinary voters alike—quickly and with little dissent rallied to her cause.[6] The surge in Democratic enthusiasm that shifted momentum toward the Democrats' side was

TABLE 3. Shifts in presidential and house preferences during the campaign

	Presidential vote		Generic House vote	
	Change	Trump's share (%)	Change	Republicans' share (%)
Before Biden–Trump debate		50.3		49.6
After Biden–Trump debate	1.1	51.4	0.1	49.7
Harris replaces Biden	−2.4	49.0	−0.6	49.1
After Harris–Trump debate	−1.0	48.0	−0.2	48.8
After vice-presidential debate	1.2	49.2	1.1	49.7
Final result		50.8		50.3
Number of surveys	338		108	

Notes: All the presidential vote coefficients are $p < .001$. None of the House coefficients are statistically significant. Equations were estimated with survey sponsor fixed effects.

furthered, at least temporarily, by Harris's superior performance in the September 10 debate with Trump. Another attempt to assassinate Trump was foiled on September 15. The final formal event was the vice-presidential debate on October 2.

Voters, in aggregate, responded to these events systematically, with modest but statistically significant shifts in presidential preferences that were echoed, albeit very faintly, in shifts in House vote intentions. The evidence is in table 3, which reports the results of regressing voters' prospective choices between the major party candidates in surveys taken after the beginning of 2024 on the succession of notable shocks, measured as categorical variables taking values of 0 before and 1 after each event.[7] The first column in each pair displays the coefficients estimating the effect of each event; the second, the estimated share of reported preferences for Trump or the Republican House candidate following the event. The coefficients indicate that Biden's debate performance and its aftermath reduced his support by about 1 percentage point, putting him behind Trump by 2.8 points. Harris's replacement of Biden diminished Trump's share by 2.3 points, and her superior performance in their debate cost him another point, giving her an estimated 52.0–48.0 lead. Harris's lead faded by 1.2 points after the beginning of October, ending at 50.8 to 49.2 in these surveys. Although survey data suggest that J. D. Vance performed a bit better than Tim Walz in the vice-presidential debate, the shift that followed is probably best interpreted as an ebbing of the surge toward Harris occasioned by her debate with Trump.

After all of these shocks, Trump's aggregate preference share at the end of the campaign was only 1.1 points different from what it had been before any of these events. Estimated effects of other events during the campaign were even smaller than those shown here. Trump's two attempted assassinations had a small positive effect on his projected vote share, but in neither instance did the coefficient approach statistical significance. The same, perhaps surprisingly, is true of his conviction in the hush money case on May 30. These variables are therefore not included in the equation, and their insignificant impact underlines how difficult it is for even dramatic events to move aggregate opinion in a calcified electorate. The final pre-election surveys underestimated Trump's actual vote share by 1.4 percentage points; the polls again evidently fell short in sampling Trump supporters, but not by so much as in 2016 and 2020.[8]

The House Elections

Events in the presidential campaign had much smaller effects on the prospective House vote, although the signs on the coefficients match those for presidential preferences. On the whole, aggregate House vote intentions remained remarkably stable amid the turmoil in the presidential race, further evidence of a "calcified" partisan electorate. Still, Democratic elites understandably worried about Biden heading their ticket. He was unpopular, with only about 40 percent of voters approving of his job performance, and no president has ever won reelection with such dismal numbers. Pre-election survey data indicated that the Democrats' down-ballot prospects would be strongly linked to his fate. On average, in polls asking the generic House vote question taken in 2024 before Biden's withdrawal, more than 97 percent of prospective voters for both Trump and Biden who expressed a House preference intended to vote a straight ticket.[9] These numbers did not change appreciably after Harris replaced Biden, remaining at about 97 percent for both Trump and Harris supporters. Party loyalty—respondents choosing the candidate of the party with which they say they identify—also averaged 97 percent in these polls. Pre-election surveys thus projected congressional elections to be at least as partisan, polarized, and president centered as they were in 2020, when all-time highs had been reached on these dimensions.[10]

These projections were realized in the final vote (table 4). The connection between the presidential preferences and congressional results at the district level was extremely tight, as it had been in 2020. The correlation between the 2024 House and presidential votes matched the all-time high

TABLE 4. The district-level presidential vote and House results, 2000–2024

House election year	Presidential vote year	House/ president vote correlation	Districts with split results	% winners correctly predicted	Value of incumbency	Standard deviation of vote swing
2000	2000	.803	87	80.4	8.6	6.4
2002	2000	.805	63	86.2	8.5	
2004	2004	.839	60	86.4	6.8	5.5
2006	2004	.839	69	83.5	6.5	6.0
2008	2008	.851	83	80.7	7.1	6.0
2010	2008	.917	73	91.3	4.8	6.3
2012	2012	.952	26	94.0	2.5	
2014	2012	.942	31	94.3	3.7	4.3
2016	2016	.950	35	94.7	2.9	4.6
2018	2016	.974	34	96.1	1	4.3
2020	2020	.987	16	95.9	1.5	3.0
2022	2020	.983	23	94.7	1.5	
2024	2024	.987	16	96.1	1.2	2.3

Source: Compiled by author.

of .987 set in 2020. Only 16 of the 435 districts were won by the party whose presidential candidate had lost the district in 2024—13 won by Democrats and 3 by Republicans—equaling the previous low reached in 2020. A simple logit model estimating the impact of the district presidential vote on a party's probability of winning the seat predicted the actual winner with 96 percent accuracy. The House elections also set a new record for nationalization, with the smallest standard deviation of the interelection swing (the vote change across stable districts with major party competition in both elections) ever observed.[11] The district-level swing itself averaged only 0.4 percentage points in the Republicans' favor. The party's national victory in 2024 helped them retain the majority they had won 2022 with a net pickup of nine seats but failed to augment it.

As the vote for House candidates has become so dominated by partisanship, the value of incumbency, measured in vote shares, has dropped to levels last seen in the 1950s.[12] The estimated House incumbency advantage for 2024 is a mere 1.2 percentage points, dramatically smaller than it was at the beginning of the century. For the same reasons, the effect of candidate quality as measured by previous experience in elected office was also very small; its estimated value was only 0.6 percentage points, the low for the postwar period.[13] The personal House vote—a choice based on candidates as individuals, detached from their party label—has grown increasingly rare. The local- and candidate-focused electoral order prevailing in the final decades of the twentieth century has now been almost entirely superseded by a fully nationalized president- and party-centered electoral regime. Incumbents still win reelection at very high rates, not because of advantages derived from office holding but rather because the great majority serve districts that favor their party in an era when very few voters are willing to cross party lines.

House members seeking reelection in 2024 were very successful. Only four, two from each party, lost to primary election challengers.[14] Republican incumbents won 96 percent of their general election contests; Democratic incumbents, 98 percent of theirs. Ten of the eleven incumbents who did lose in 2024 were defending districts that favored the rival party's presidential candidate in 2024. Six of them were freshmen serving their first terms. The only apparent remnant of an incumbency advantage appears in the victories of the thirteen members (ten Democrats and three Republicans) who won reelection in politically uncongenial districts; but the frequency of such wins (3.4 percent) was no higher than in the fifty-six open seats (those lacking an incumbent), two of which (3.6 percent) went to the party of the presidential loser. Overall, of the seventeen districts that changed party hands in 2024, sixteen went to the party of the presidential winner. In five of these cases, the losses were the consequence of new districts drawn after the 2022 election rather than any change in voters' party preferences.[15]

Like Trump, Republican House candidates generally benefited more from a falloff in votes for Democrats than from an increase in votes for them. Compared with 2020, the Democratic House vote was down by 6.6 million; the Republican vote was up by 2.1 million. Republican gains in vote shares as well as House seats were thus achieved mainly in the 2022 midterm, not in 2024 (table 5). The midterm swing against the president's party, modest as it was,[16] produced the Republican House majority; Trump's coattails merely kept them from losing it.

Data from the national exit poll also suggest that depressed Democratic turnout helped keep the House in Republican hands. Reported party loyalty was extremely high in this survey, with 96 percent of both Republicans and Democrats voting for their party's House candidate, even higher than in the 2020 exit poll, in which 95 percent of Democrats and 94 percent of Republicans remained loyal to their party.[17] But the proportion of Democrats in the 2024 exit poll was down 5 points, 32 percent compared with 37 percent in 2020, while the proportion of Republicans remained about the same

TABLE 5. National turnout and voting in U.S. House elections, 2014–2024

	Turnout (%)	Democrats		Republicans	
		Votes (millions)	Share (%)	Votes (millions)	Share (%)
2014	36.7	35.6	45.5	40.1	51.2
2016	60.1	61.8	48.0	63.1	49.1
2018	50.0	60.5	53.4	50.8	44.8
2020	66.7	77.5	50.8	72.9	47.7
2022	46.2	51.3	47.3	54.2	50.0
2024	63.7	70.8	47.4	74.8	50.2

Source: Compiled by author.

(35 percent compared with 36 percent). A more detailed picture of individual voting behavior in the 2024 House elections awaits the posting of the major academic surveys, but it would be very surprising if they did not find similarly high levels of party loyalty that, along with very high levels of straight-ticket voting, would make depressed turnout among Democrats a critical contributor to the election of a unified Republican government.

Money in the House Elections

The electoral standoff that resulted in only a handful of party switches in the 2024 House elections emerged from a furious battle for majority control that inspired huge investments in candidates' campaigns and in independent efforts on their behalf funded by national party and political action committees. Total spending by and for House candidates in the general election exceeded $2.5 billion.[18] Most of these expenditures were, as always, concentrated in the small subset of the competitive races. The evidence is in figure 1, which displays the distribution of funds across districts according to party prospects as classified by the authoritative *Cook Political Report*.[19] The average candidate in a toss-up district spent more than $6.6 million and was helped by an additional $10.5 million spent by outside groups, with total spending exceeding $17.1 million. Both parties' candidates in these contests were more than amply funded; every one of the forty-four were backed by more than $9 million, and twelve, by more than $20 million. These are very large sums by historical standards. No candidate could blame the loss of a potentially competitive race on a lack of resources; in the twelve districts that changed party hands without the help of redistricting, the winner averaged $18.3 million in support; the loser, $19.3 million. Similarly, among the

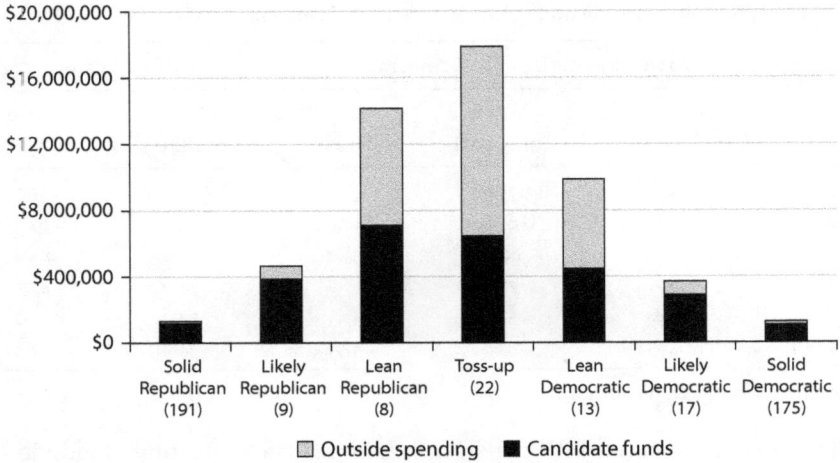

FIG. 1. Average campaign funding for House candidates, by district competitiveness (final Cook estimate)
Note: The number of districts is in parentheses.

twelve candidates who managed to hold on to districts that had gone to the other party's presidential candidate in 2020, the winners were supported by an average of $12.6 million; the losers, by $9.3 million. The contest in California's Forty-Fifth District, in which Democratic challenger Derek Tran edged out Republican incumbent Michelle Steel by 653 of the more than 315,000 votes cast, set the record, with $22.5 million spent for Tran and $27.5 million spent for Steele. More than 67 percent of the total was outside spending.

Campaign money was abundant in 2024 but hardly decisive. In half of the toss-up districts, the loser had more financial support than the winner; both had more than enough for a full-scale professional campaign. The content rather than the volume of messages is what mattered. Across all House races, the candidate supported by more money won 85 percent of the time, while the candidate whose presidential candidate had prevailed in 2020 won 96 percent of the time. Candidates, parties, and their allied interest groups are caught up in a relentless arms race in the small subset of battleground districts that now decide control of House. Campaign spending is subject to diminishing returns, putting the value of extreme spending levels in doubt, but no campaign wants to do the experiment it would take to find out when enough is enough. The supply of money keeps growing because both sides are desperate to win control of the highly polarized and closely divided House, and the demand seems limitless, so saturation campaigning in any race that is potentially competitive seems here to stay. The outside groups that play such a large financial role in these races are national in scope and focus, contributing importantly to the nationalization of elections in which they participate. Campaign finance practices also encourage party conformity in Congress because leaders direct the flow of contributions and outside party spending to favored candidates. The two parties' House and Senate party campaign committees spent more than $1.6 billion trying to elect their candidates in 2024, and the winners are expected to express their gratitude by loyalty to the team.

The Senate

Going into the 2024 election, Democrats controlled the Senate by a thread. Republicans held forty-nine seats, Democrats only forty-seven, but they had the support of three of the four independents, Bernie Sanders (Vermont), Angus King (Maine), and Joe Manchin (West Virginia). The fourth, Krysten Sinema (Arizona), had recently left the Democratic Party but declined to caucus with the Republicans, leaving Democrats with a bare fifty–forty-nine majority. The configuration of states with Senate elections in 2024 gave them little chance of keeping it. Democrats held twenty-three of the thirty-four seats in play, three in states won handily by Trump in 2020 (Ohio, Montana, and West Virginia). None of the eleven seats defended by Republicans were in states won by Biden. To retain control, the Democrats would have had to win in at least three states won by Trump in 2020 and 2024 while holding on to seats in the five states narrowly won by Biden in 2020 that switched to Trump in 2024: Arizona, Michigan, Nevada, Pennsylvania, and Wisconsin.

Not surprisingly, they fell short, although not from lack of effort. Table 6 summarizes the results for these states. West Virginia, Trump's second-best state (after Wyoming) in all three of his elections, was a sure Republican win once Joe Manchin retired. Republican challengers also defeated the Democratic incumbents in Montana, Ohio, and Pennsylvania. All three Democrats had previously had the good fortune to run in years favorable to their party (2006, 2012, and 2018); this time their luck ran out. In Montana, Jon Tester had won in 2012 by outpolling Barack Obama by 6.9 percentage points, 48.6 percent to 41.7 percent, with the help of the 6.6 points drained off by a Libertarian Party candidate. In 2024, Tester again ran well ahead of the top of the ticket but not by nearly enough to overcome Harris's poor showing. Ohio's Sherrod Brown had run slightly ahead of Obama, who won the state narrowly in 2012. By 2024 Ohio had turned reliably red; Brown ran 3.8 points

TABLE 6. Results in states held by Democrats and won by Trump in 2024

	Presidential winner		Major party vote share (%)		
	2020	2024	Democrat	Harris	Difference
Glenn Elliott, WV	Trump	Trump	28.8	28.7	0.1
Jon Tester, MT	Trump	Trump	46.4	39.7	6.7
Sherrod Brown, OH	Trump	Trump	48.1	44.3	3.8
Bob Casey, PA	Biden	Trump	49.9	49.1	0.8
Elissa Slotkin, MI	Biden	Trump	50.2	49.3	0.9
Tammy Baldwin, WI	Biden	Trump	50.4	49.6	0.8
Jacky Rosen, NV	Biden	Trump	50.9	48.4	2.5
Ruben Gallego, AZ	Biden	Trump	51.2	47.2	4.0

Source: Compiled by author.

ahead of Harris, insufficient when Harris was winning only 44.3 percent of the vote.

The only state in this category where the Democrat's loss was not fore-ordained was Pennsylvania, where Bob Casey, running less than 1 point ahead of Harris, came up short with 49.9 percent of the vote. The four other Democrat incumbents in the same situation—competitive states won by Biden but lost by Harris—were successful. Elizabeth Slotkin (Michigan), Tammy Baldwin (Wisconsin), and Jacky Rosen (Nevada) all pulled out narrow victories in states Harris lost narrowly. Ruben Gallego outpolled Harris by the widest margin of any in this group, essential to his victory in light of Harris's weak performance in Arizona. He was helped by drawing as his opponent Kari Lake, most noted for refusing to concede her loss in the race for governor in 2022 and persisting in the delusory claim that she and Trump were fellow victims of electoral theft.

In the two previous presidential elections when Trump headed the Republican ticket, 2016 and 2020, only one of sixty-nine Senate contests did not go to the party of the winning presidential candidate (Republican Susan Collins of Maine in 2020). The 2024 Senate elections showed that split verdicts were not entirely a thing of the past, but it was a close thing. As figure 2 shows, the four states that delivered split results in 2024 were clustered very close to the 50–50 point on both axes. The correlation between the presidential and Senate vote remained very high—in fact, at .957, higher than in any previous postwar election (table 7). The tally of senators representing states won by their own party in the most recent presidential election fell to eighty-nine of one hundred, still second highest on record. Only

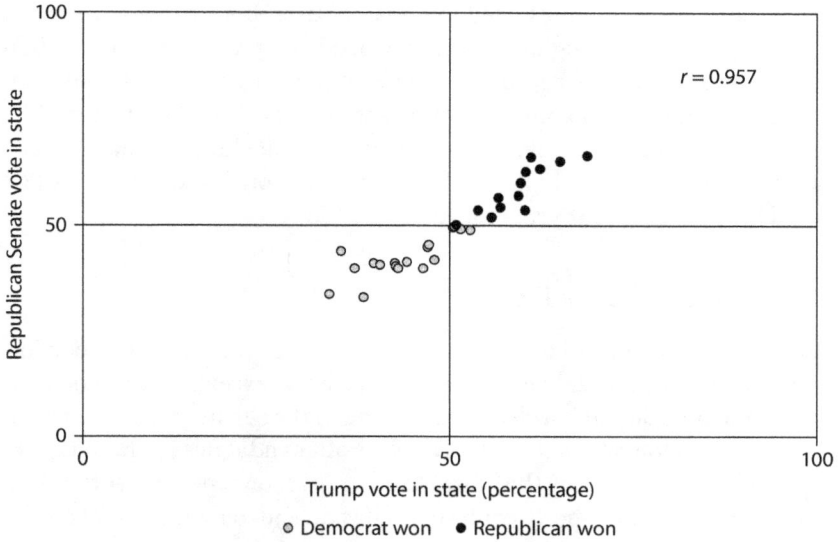

FIG. 2. Statewide vote for Trump and the Republican Senate candiate, 2024

TABLE 7. The nationalization of Senate elections, 1980–2024

Year	Same party victory (%)	Senate/president vote correlation	Senators from party of presidential winner	Split Senate state delegations
1980	61.8	.528	54	25
1984	48.4	.379	51	23
1988	48.4	.174	47	21
1992	70.5	.253	67	21
1996	70.5	.625	63	19
2000	70.5	.453	71	14
2004	79.4	.578	75	17
2008	80.0	.730	76	15
2012	81.8	.798	79	18
2016	100.0	.935	86	14
2020	97.1	.950	94	6
2024	88.2	.957	89	3

Source: Compiled by author.

three states are now represented by senators from both parties. The 2024 Senate elections were slightly less nationalized and president centered than in 2016 and 2020 only because Republican Senate candidates could not match Trump's vote share in four of the states that shifted to his side. The best single predictor of a Senate win in 2024 was actually the state's presidential vote in 2020; only Pennsylvania did not vote for senator as it had voted for president four years earlier.

Money in the Senate Elections

Competition for control of the Senate has inspired stunning levels of campaign spending in recent years,[20] and 2024 was no exception. Data on candidate and outside general election spending in the Senate races, listed from the highest to lowest combined totals for both candidates in the state, are reported in table 8. Led by the more than $410 million reported for the Ohio Senate race, the seven hotly contested states defended by Democrats listed in table 6 top the list. In Montana, donors and outside groups invested more than $274 million in the Senate candidate's campaigns in a state with only 880,000 eligible voters, the total amounting to more than $306 per potential voter, far more than any other state in any previous election; the prior record, also held by Montana, was $124 per eligible voter in 2020. Jon Tester did not lose for want of financial support; neither did Brown or Casey. All of the Democrats who won in states taken by Trump had spending advantages, but with the possible exception of Lake in Arizona, their opponents were also more than competitively funded.

The financial data reveal several other aspects of the 2024 campaign. In Texas and Maryland, the disadvantaged party's candidate showed enough promise to attract serious money. Ted Cruz had won reelection narrowly in Texas in 2018, and Democratic funders hoped he would be similarly vulnerable in 2024 to Colin Allred, a Democratic congressman and former professional football player. The Republican candidate in Maryland, Larry Hogan, had been a popular governor with proven crossover appeal to Democrats. Both challengers enjoyed generous financial support but could not overcome the adverse partisan leanings of their state's electorates. The same is true of Lucas Kunce, challenger to Republican senator Josh Hawley in Missouri; his well-funded campaign helped him run a couple of points better than Harris, but he had no chance in a state Trump won by 18 points. Deb Fisher, the Republican incumbent in the very red state of Nebraska, survived a well-funded challenge by an independent candidate, Dan Osborn, who emphasized his blue-collar roots and insisted he would not

TABLE 8. 2024 Senate election results and campaign spending (in thousands of dollars)

	Candidate	% vote	Candidate spending	Outside spending	Total spending	$ per voter	% outside
Ohio	Sherrod Brown (D)	46.5	101,356	181,473	202,015	22.58	22.6
	Bernie Moreno (R)	50.1	26,142	97,241	207,615	23.20	87.4
Pennsylvania	Bob Casey (D)	48.6	63,170	141,333	160,411	16.20	16.2
	Dave McCormick (R)	48.8	35,373	82,779	176,706	17.84	80.0
Montana	Jon Tester (D)	45.5	95,786	77,809	173,595	193.32	44.8
	Tim Sheey (R)	52.6	27,380	73,579	100,959	112.43	72.9
Texas	Colin Allred (D)	44.6	92,436	14,401	106,837	5.30	13.5
	Ted Cruz (R)	53.1	103,929	40,589	144,517	7.17	28.1
Michigan	Elissa Slotkin (D)	48.6	50,885	60,921	111,806	14.62	54.5
	Mike Rogers (R)	48.3	12,795	73,150	85,945	11.24	85.1
Wisconsin	Tammy Baldwin (D)	48.6	58,633	50,247	108,880	24.28	46.1
	Eric Hovde (R)	48.3	31,514	49,911	81,425	18.16	61.3
Nevada	Jacky Rosen (D)	47.9	49,271	54,858	104,129	46.05	52.7
	Sam Brown (R)	46.2	23,231	41,028	64,259	28.42	63.8
Arizona	Ruben Gallego (D)	50.1	64,843	49,452	114,295	21.21	43.3
	Kari Lake (R)	47.7	25,890	20,353	46,243	8.58	44.0
Florida	Debbie. Mucarsel-Powell (D)	42.8	36,216	1,017	37,233	2.26	2.7
	Rick Scott (R)	55.6	47,001	9,138	56,139	3.40	16.3
Maryland	Angela Alsobrooks (D)	54.6	30,332	19,742	50,074	11.33	39.4
	Larry Hogan (R)	42.8	12,042	29,238	41,280	9.34	70.8
California	Adam Schiff (D)	58.8	61,952	176	62,128	2.39	0.3
	Steve Garvey (R)	41.3	19,670	357	20,027	0.77	1.8
Nebraska	Dan Osborn (I)	46.5	14,916	28,388	43,304	30.49	65.6
	Deb Fischer (R)	53.2	8,906	1,033	9,939	7.00	10.4
Missouri	Lucas Kunce (D)	41.8	22,237	4,051	22,616	4.85	6.56
	Josh Hawley (R)	55.6	27,388	3,429	30,818	6.61	11.1
Vermont	Bernie Sanders (I)	61.5	33,294	0	33,294	63.29	0.0
	Gerald Malloy (R)	31.3	613	0	613	1.17	0.0
Massachusetts	Elizabeth Warren (D)	58.1	28,279	0	28,279	5.48	0.0
	John Deaton (R)	38.9	2,163	2,111	4,274	0.83	49.4
Virginia	Tim Kaine (D)	54.4	21,004	106	21,066	3.30	0.29
	Hung Cao (R)	45.4	9,139	106	9,245	1.45	1.1

(continued)

TABLE 8 *(continued)*

	Candidate	% vote	Candidate spending	Outside spending	Total spending	$ per voter	% outside
New York	*Kirsten Gillibrand* (D)	56.2	24,457	0	24,621	1.78	0.66
	Mike Sapraicone (R)	38.7	1,301	0	1,301	0.09	0.0
Minnesota	*Amy Klobuchar* (D)	56.2	23,639	79	23,719	5.53	0.3
	Royce White (R)	40.5	1,422	0	1,422	0.33	0.0
New Mexico	*Martin Heinrich* (D)	55.1	13,306	1,614	14,920	9.57	10.8
	Nella Domenici (R)	44.9	6,714	717	7,431	4.77	9.6
Tennessee	Gloria Johnson (D)	34.2	7,348	4	7,352	1.38	0.1
	Marsha Blackburn (R)	63.8	14,127	392	14,519	2.72	2.7
New Jersey	Andy Kim (D)	53.6	11,712	1,278	12,989	2.02	9.8
	Curtis Bashaw (R)	44	4,157	650	4,807	0.75	13.5
Connecticut	*Chris Murphy* (D)	58.6	14,348	0	14,348	5.38	0.0
	Matt Corey (R)	39.7	206	55	261	0.10	21.1
Utah	Caroline Gleich (D)	31.6	1,181	103	1,284	0.54	8.1
	John Curtis (R)	62.1	5,231	7,793	13,024	5.48	59.8
Washington	*Maria Cantwell* (D)	59.1	12,683	2	12,685	2.25	0.0
	Raul Garcia (R)	40.6	712	0	712	0.13	0.0
Delaware	Lisa Blunt Rochester (D)	56.6	9,745	14	9,759	12.62	0.1
	Eric Hansen (R)	39.5	390	0	390	0.50	0.0
Mississippi	Ty Pinkins (D)	37.2	1,038	0	1,038	0.48	0.0
	Roger Wicker (R)	62.8	8,619	51	8,670	3.98	0.6
Wyoming	Scott Morrow (D)	23.5	45	0	45	0.10	0.0
	John Barrasso (R)	73.2	6,816	1	7,799	17.63	12.60
North Dakota	Katrina Christiansen (D)	33.4	2,953	0	2,953	5.01	0.0
	Kevin Cramer (R)	66.3	4,232	101	4,334	7.35	2.3
Rhode Island	*Sheldon Whitehouse* (D)	59.9	6,218	0	6,218	7.52	0.0
	Patricia Morgan (R)	39.9	296	349	645	0.78	54.0
Maine	*Angus King* (I)	50.7	5,760	0	5,760	5.08	0.0
	Demi Kouzounas (R)	33.8	1,015	0	1,015	0.89	0.0

(continued)

TABLE 8 *(continued)*

	Candidate	% vote	Candidate spending	Outside spending	Total spending	$ per voter	% outside
Indiana	Valerie McCray (D)	38.8	127	0	127	0.02	0.0
	Jim Banks (R)	58.7	5,873	405	6,279	1.24	6.5
Nebraska	Preston Love (D)	37.4	237	35	272	0.19	12.9
	Pete Ricketts (R)	62.6	5,339	9	5,348	3.77	0.2
West Virginia	Glenn Elliott (D)	27.8	844	0	844	0.61	0.0
	Jim Justice (R)	68.8	3,866	4	3,871	2.79	0.1
Hawaii	*Mazie Hirono* (D)	62.1	4,429	4	4,433	4.27	0.1
	Bob McDermott (R)	30.7	24	0	24	0.02	0.0

Source: Compiled by author.

Note: Incumbents are in italics.

caucus with the Democrats; Fisher ran about 6 points behind Trump but still won by more than 6 points.

In short, lavishly funded campaigns could not overcome inherent partisan advantages in states that were solidly red or blue. Anticipating this reality, donors and outside groups did not bother to try in all but a few states. The Senate races in states lower on the list thus featured lopsided resource balances and lopsided outcomes favoring the dominant party. The result was, as in the House contests, the concentration of campaign resources in a few selected races. The seven competitive states listed in table 6, comprising 21 percent of the contests, accounted for 65 percent of total expenditures and 88 percent of outside expenditures. And again as in the House races, money was far less important than the state's partisan complexion in determining the victor.

Congressional Demographics After 2024

The long upward trend toward greater demographic diversity in congressional representation stalled in the House in 2024 but continued, marginally, in the Senate. The proportion of Black, Hispanic, Asian or Native American in the House remained at 28 percent. The number of women elected to the House fell from 128 in 2022 to 125; among the 11 losing incumbents, 5 were women, 4 of them losing to men, and 6 were nonwhite, 3 losing to white candidates. These outcomes were not the consequences of the incumbent's gender or ethnicity, however; controlling for district partisanship, incumbency status, and campaign spending, neither gender nor ethnicity had any significant effect on challengers' vote shares or election victories in 2024. The tally of women senators remained unchanged at 25 after the election, but two Black women, Democrats Lisa Blunt Rochester in Delaware and Angela Alsobrooks in Maryland, won open Senate seats, and two Latinos, Democrat Ruben Gallego in Arizona and Republican Bernie Moreno in Ohio, also joined the Senate, raising the minority count in that chamber from 12 to 16. On some dimensions, however, Congress has grown less diverse and less representative of the population; for example, currently all but one senator and more than 94 percent of U.S. representatives are college graduates, compared with 40 percent of the adult population.

The Democratic congressional delegations remain far more diverse than the Republican delegations. Ninety-four of the women elected to the House are Democrats; 31, Republicans. Of the nonwhite members, 95 are Democrats, 18 are Republicans. Women form 44 percent of the Democratic House delegation; ethnic minorities, 44 percent. Five percent of Democrats are from the LGBTQ community (including the first transgender person elected to Congress, Sarah McBride of Delaware); only 29 percent are straight white men. In contrast, only 14 percent of House Republicans are women, 8 percent are nonwhite, and none identify as LGBTQ; 80 percent are straight white men—numbers unlikely to trouble a party that currently, like its leader, vehemently condemns all deliberate efforts to increase diversity, equity, and inclusion in public and private institutions. The Democratic Senate delegation also includes more women (16) and nonwhite people (11) than the Republican delegation (9 and 5, respectively). White men still hold sway in the Senate, representing 53 percent of Democrats and 74 percent of Republicans, but their share is down from 84 percent at the beginning of the century.

Prospects for the 119th Congress

The 118th Congress (2023–25), with Democrats controlling the Senate and Republicans the House, earned a reputation for dysfunction and unproductive gridlock. The Republican House majority elected in 2022 took an unprecedented four days and fifteen ballots to elect Kevin McCarthy Speaker. Ten months later, eight members of a far-right faction devoted to performative obstruction engineered his removal for the sin of relying on bipartisan votes to avoid a debt ceiling crisis and government shutdown. Republicans then took three chaotic weeks to agree on Mike Johnson of Louisiana as his replacement. Internal Republican conflicts, as well as deep disagreements with the Democratic Senate, resulted in the smallest legislative output for any modern Congress. The ideological gap between the parties continued to widen in both chambers, extending the six-decade trend toward greater partisan polarization into new record territory in the 118th Congress.[21]

None of the contributors to dysfunction and polarization were punished by voters in 2024. Only one of the Republican rebels who helped depose McCarthy lost—Bob Good (Virginia's Fifth District), defeated in a primary by a fellow far-right election denier who won Trump's support after Good endorsed Ron DeSantis in the presidential primary. More generally, ideological extremism cost Republican incumbents some votes but no seats because virtually all of the more extreme members represent very safe districts.[22] No member located to the right of the most moderate quintile in the distribution of Republican DW-NOMINATE scores—standard measures of a member's location on the ideological spectrum calculated from roll-call votes—lost;[23] all seven losers were from the most moderate 20 percent. The four losing Democratic incumbents were also more moderate than the Democratic average, but not significantly so. Three of the four departing Democratic senators were more moderate than their party's median, and the Senate lost its second most moderate Republican, Mitt Romney of Utah. One postelection analysis determined that 70 percent of members leaving Congress in 2024 were from the half of the membership that was more willing to engage in cross-party collaboration.[24]

Voters as a whole have reacted indifferently to congressional actions that might be seen as weakening American political institutions. For example, voting against certification of Biden's 2020 election, against Trump's second impeachment, or against establishing a commission to investigate the 2021 Capitol invasion reduced neither vote shares nor the probability of winning in the 2022 election.[25] A vote against certification was again unrelated to a Republican incumbent's electoral fate in 2024. None of this is surprising considering that a majority of voters in these districts opted for a presidential candidate who had openly schemed to overturn the results of the fair and free election that he had clearly lost.

Nothing in the results of the 2024 elections offers hope for a lessening of polarized conflict in the new 119th Congress, even setting aside President Trump's provocative agenda. The Republican House margin is down to five seats, giving recalcitrant factions even greater leverage within the party and therefore more opportunity to make trouble for party leaders than they had in the 118th Congress. Then, that leverage was exercised by a hard-right clique associated with the Freedom Caucus. They may be less inclined to bedevil the leadership in the new Congress, at least for a while and until the thirst for attention from the right-wing media sphere becomes too powerful to resist. Almost all are strong Trump supporters and will presumably follow his wishes, cooperating with Speaker Johnson and other party leaders insofar as they are acting at his behest. But it will take only three defectors (assuming Democrats are united) to defeat Republican proposals, and considerably more than three House Republicans represent constituents who are not Trump fans and who will find it politically dangerous to support his more disruptive and reactionary proposals. Much will depend on how the handful of relatively moderate Republicans respond to Trump's specious claim of a sweeping popular mandate.

Senate Republicans faced a test of loyalty to Trump even before they considered his legislative agenda. They were asked to consent to an assortment of executive branch nominees, sharing only an aptitude for flattering Trump, that includes some individuals of questionable character, qualifications, and notions about reality. They did so with very little dissent. Trump's unorthodox choices for important senior positions underline his vast ambitions to demolish and then rebuild the federal agencies into instruments responsive to his will. How far Senate and House Republicans are willing to accommodate him will have a profound effect on the future shape of the American political system.

Whatever radical changes in policy and government structure the Republican congressional majorities decide to pursue will almost certainly have to be accomplished in the first two years of Trump's presidency. Based on the historical record, Republican prospects for holding on to the House after the 2026 midterm are not good. Their margin is very small. In only one postwar midterm (1998) did the president's party not lose seats; the average loss is twenty-six seats. The less popular the president, the more seats lost, so the Republican House majority's fate will depend in good part on public reaction to Trump's decisions and their consequences. There are plenty of scenarios—inflation or recession induced by tariffs, administrative chaos from decimated federal agencies, economic and social dislocation from a drive to expel undocumented workers and their families—that would damage Trump's public standing and thus Republican midterm fortunes. The calcification of the electorate now limits the downside for the president's party at the midterm, but only if the first two years of Trump's administration turn out to be a ringing popular success are Republicans likely to retain their House majority.

Republicans have a much better chance of keeping the Senate. They hold twenty of the thirty-three states to be contested in 2026; only one, served by the Senate's most moderate Republican, Susan Collins of Maine, did not favor Trump in 2024. Collins has always won reelection handily and has announced she will run for a sixth term in 2026. The only other state the Democrats might have a shot at is North Carolina, which elected Democrats as governor and lieutenant governor in 2024 while Trump was winning the state, 50.1 percent to 47.6 percent. Two of the states Democrats will defend, Georgia and Michigan, switched to Trump in 2024. The other states in play for 2026 have voted consistently red or blue in the last three elections, so another election with competition concentrated in a small subset of states is the most likely consequence. The Republicans planning to run for reelection in 2026 will worry more about managing their dealings with Trump than about challenges from Democrats; the greater threat is the primary opponent backed by Trump (and multibillionaire Elon Musk) they might face if they go too far in resisting his demands. More generally, Trump's polarizing presence has loomed over congressional elections every two years since 2016 and is almost certain to have even more of an impact in 2026.

Appendix: Survey Sources

Survey data used in this chapter were acquired from survey reports and data accessed through the FiveThirtyEight website, the Roper Center, news reports, and the survey sponsors' websites.

ABC News / Ipsos	Harvard Harris
ABC News / *Washington Post*	*Huffington Post* / YouGov
American Perspectives Survey	IDB/Tipp
ANES 2024 Pilot Study	Ipsos/Reuters
AP-NORC	Marquette University
Axios/Momentive	Monmouth University
Bright Line Watch	Morning Consult
CBS News and CBS News /	Navigator Research
YouGov	NBC News / *Wall Street Journal*
Civiqs	*New York Times* / Sienna
CNN	NPR/Marist
Data for Progress	Pew Research Center
Echelon Insights	PRRI (Public Religion Research
Economist/YouGov	Institute)
Fox News	Public Policy Polling
Gallup	Quinnipiac University

Suffolk University
Survey Monkey
University of Massachusetts /
   YouGov

Wall Street Journal / GBAO
Washington Post / University of
   Maryland
Yahoo News / YouGov

Notes

1. Ron Brownstein, "Many Women Were Unsure About Trump's Style and Agenda. Why Did They Vote for Him Anyway?," CNN, November 19, 2024, https://www.cnn.com/2024/11/19/politics/women-voters-trump-analysis/index.html.
2. The gerrymander turned an even seven-seven party balance into a ten-four Republican majority in a state where the parties are closely balanced (Trump won the state in 2024 by 3 points, but Democrats won the other statewide offices, governor and lieutenant governor, by 15 and 2 points, respectively). The North Carolina Supreme Court had rejected an earlier Republican gerrymander, but after the 2022 election turned a four-three Democratic court majority to a five-two Republican majority, the new majority decided it had no authority over redistricting, enabling the Republican legislative majority to do as it pleased. See Sarah Michels, "Why Have NC Congressional Districts Changed for 2024?," *Carolina Public Press*, November 1, 2024, https://carolinapublicpress.org/66873/why-have-nc-congressional-districts-changed-for-2024/.
3. John Sides et al., *The Bitter End: The 2020 Presidential Election and the Challenge to American Democracy* (Princeton University Press, 2021).
4. Alan I. Abramowitz and Steven W. Webster, "Negative Partisanship: Why Americans Dislike Parties but Behave Like Rabid Partisans," *Political Psychology* 39, no. S1 (2018): 119–135; Shanto Iyengar and Masha Krupenkin, "Partisanship as Social Identity; Implications for the Study of Party Polarization," *Forum* 16, no. 1 (2018): 23–45.
5. Sides et al., *Bitter End*, 6.
6. Lauren Egan et al., "Democrats Rally Around Harris to Replace Biden," *Politico*, July 21, 2024, https://www.politico.com/news/2024/07/21/democrats-rally-harris-00170085.
7. Data sources for these and other surveys used in this chapter are listed in the appendix.
8. Gary C. Jacobson, "Explaining the Shortfall of Trump Voters in the 2020 Pre- and Post-Election Surveys," paper presented at the Annual Meeting of the Midwest Political Science Association, Chicago, April 3–6, 2022.
9. The generic House vote question asks respondents which party's candidate they would vote for if the election were held that day. On average, about 93 percent express a major party choice in both contests; the analysis includes forty-four surveys before Biden's withdrawal, forty-one afterward.

10. Gary C. Jacobson, "The Presidential and Congressional Elections of 2020: A National Referendum on the Trump Administration," *Political Science Quarterly* 136, no. 1 (2021): 11–45.

11. Again, the smaller the standard deviation, the more uniform the swing across districts, and thus the more nationalized the election. All previous postwar election swings have larger standard deviations. The figure cannot be computed for years ending in 2 because redistricting destroys comparability.

12. The value of incumbency is estimated here by a modified version of the Gelman–King index that substitutes the district-level presidential vote in the current or, for midterms, most recent presidential election for the lagged vote, allowing years ending in 2 and districts redrawn between apportionment decades to be included. For details, see Gary C. Jacobson, "It's Nothing Personal: The Decline of the Incumbency Advantage in U.S. House Elections," *Journal of Politics* 77, no. 3 (2015): 861–873.

13. For comparison, see Jamie Carson and Gary C. Jacobson, *The Politics of Congressional Elections*, 11th ed. (Rowman and Littlefield, 2024), 42, 63.

14. Republican Jerry Carl lost to fellow Republican incumbent Barry Moore in Alabama's reconfigured Second District; Republican Bob Good, who had made the mistake of supporting Ron DeSantis in the presidential primary, lost Virginia's Fifth District to John McGuire, an election denier strongly supported by Trump. Two Democrats, Jamaal Bowman (New York's Sixteenth District) and Cori Bush (Missouri's First District), lost to challengers supported by more than $10 million in spending by pro-Israel super PACs who objected to their pro-Palestinian leanings. The incumbent party held on to all four seats in the general election.

15. In addition to the North Carolina gerrymander noted earlier, courts had ordered the creation of new districts in Alabama and Louisiana designed to allow Black voters a chance to elect candidates of their choice, producing two solidly Democratic districts in the process.

16. Gary C. Jacobson, "The 2022 Elections: A Test of Democracy's Resilience and the Referendum Theory of Midterms," *Political Science Quarterly* 138, no. 1 (2023): 1–22.

17. "Election 2024: Exit Polls," CNN, November 24, 2024, https://www.cnn.com/election/2024/exit-polls/national-results/general/president/0; "Exit Polls," CNN, November 10, 2020, https://www.cnn.com/election/2020/exit-polls/house/national-results.

18. The data are from the Federal Election Commission and reported in "Congressional Races," Open Secrets, accessed February 18, 2025, https://www.opensecrets.org/races/.

19. "The CPR House Race Ratings," *Cook Political Report*, November 1, 2024, https://www.cookpolitical.com/ratings/house-race-ratings. *The Cook Political Report*'s classifications were very accurate: All but one of

the 413 races classified as favoring a party were won by that party; the toss-ups divided exactly in half, 11 won by Republican, 11, by Democrats.

20. Gary C. Jacobson, "The 2022 Election: A Test of Democracy's Resilience and the Referendum Theory of Midterms," prepared for delivery at the Annual Meeting of the Midwest Political Science Association, Chicago, April 13–16, 2023, 20–23; Gary C. Jacobson, "Congress: Ever More Partisan, Polarized, and National," in *The Elections of 2020*, ed. Michael Nelson (University of Virginia Press, 2021), 200–205.

21. Jeff Lewis, "Polarization in Congress," Voteview, October 23, 2023, https://voteview.com/articles/party_polarization.

22. Regressing their Democratic challenger's vote share on the district presidential vote in 2020 and the Republican's DW-NOMINATE score, a standard measure of ideological location, controlling for campaign spending, produced a large and statistically significant ($p < .001$) coefficient, suggesting that the vote share of the most conservative Republican would be 3.3 points lower than for the most moderate Republican.

23. The data on DW-NOMINATE scores are from Jeffrey B. Lewis et al., Voteview: Congressional Roll-Call Votes Database, 2024, https://voteview.com/.

24. Joanne Hunter, "Analysis Shows Disproportionate Departure of 'Bridgers' in Congress," *Hill*, October 24, 2024, https://thehill.com/homenews/house/4922180-capitol-hill-collaborative-lawmakers-leaving/

25. Larry Bartels and Nicholas, "House Republicans Were Rewarded for Supporting Donald Trump's 'Stop the Steal' Efforts," *PNAS* 120, no. 34 (2023): e2309072120.

The Supreme Court

NAVIGATING THE 2024 ELECTIONS

John Anthony Maltese

Leading up to the 2024 presidential election, it appeared that the U.S. Supreme Court might have more opportunities to influence the election's outcome than at any time since its infamous decision in *Bush v. Gore*, the case that resolved a dispute over the recount of votes in Florida and effectively determined who won the 2000 presidential election.[1] Although Donald J. Trump's decisive victory in 2024 precluded the wave of litigation that a disputed election would surely have produced, the high court had already issued rulings that helped to shape the electoral playing field.

Most directly, it decided a case dealing with whether or not states could use a long-forgotten clause in the Fourteenth Amendment of the Constitution to keep Trump off the ballot. It also agreed to hear a case involving presidential immunity. Though not directly related to the election, the court's decision to hear the immunity case effectively ended any chance that Trump could be tried on federal charges before the election.

Convictions in either the election interference case (involving Trump's role in trying to overturn the results of the 2020 election) or the classified documents case (involving national security documents that Trump improperly took from the White House after leaving office, and which he refused to return when the government tried to retrieve them) might have influenced the outcome of the election.

Initially, many assumed that convictions in those cases would hurt Trump. However, his conviction on 34 felony counts of falsifying business records related to hush money paid to adult film star Stormy Daniels in a New York state case actually bolstered his standing by galvanizing his base. Republican lawmakers rallied around Trump;[2] his campaign reported its best fundraising day ever ($52.8 million dollars in donations in the hours after the guilty verdict);[3] and a June 2024 *New York Times* / Siena College poll showed that the guilty verdicts made no difference to more than two-thirds of those polled, with Trump leading President Joe Biden among both registered voters and likely voters.[4] Senator Mitt Romney (R-UT), no supporter of Trump, chided President Biden for not pardoning Trump to avert what he described as a "win-win" for Trump.[5]

The Supreme Court braced for election-related cases amid larger concerns about the court's legitimacy. Throughout the 2024 election season, Gallup approval ratings of the court remained near historic lows. Only 44 percent approved of the Supreme Court's job performance in a Gallup poll conducted September 3–15, 2024.[6] That was up slightly from the record low of 40 percent in September 2021, after the Supreme Court denied an emergency request to block a controversial Texas law that imposed a near-total ban on abortions.[7] Nine months later, the Supreme Court overturned the abortion rights decision *Roe v. Wade* in *Dobbs v. Jackson Women's Health Organization*.[8]

In contrast, 62 percent had approved of the Supreme Court's performance in a September 2000 Gallup poll. From 2000 to 2010, the court enjoyed majority-level approval in all but two of these polls. Since 2010, the court has received majority approval in only three of the fourteen years through 2024. Likewise, trust in the federal judiciary as a whole fell from 80 percent in 1999 to a low of 47 percent in 2022, with a slight rebound to 49 percent in 2023. "Before 2022," Gallup noted, "trust in the judicial branch averaged 68%."[9] A broader poll released in December 2024, asking whether respondents have confidence in the U.S. judicial system and courts in general, showed that confidence plummeting to a new low of 34 percent. Gallup noted, "The decline in confidence in the U.S. judicial system not only means the U.S ranks below other rich nations; it is also among the steepest declines Gallup has measured globally on this metric."[10]

Several factors, aside from controversial rulings like *Dobbs*, may help to account for this loss of credibility. One was the further politicization of the Supreme Court confirmation process. When Justice Antonin Scalia, a conservative stalwart appointed by Ronald Reagan, died on February 13, 2016, the Republican-controlled Senate refused even to consider a nominee from President Barack Obama, a Democrat, even though there were more than ten months left in Obama's term. Despite a long tradition of presidents nominating and the Senate considering Supreme Court nominees in election years, Senate Majority Leader Mitch McConnell (R-KY) said, "The American people should have a voice in the selection of their next Supreme Court justice. Therefore, this vacancy should not be filled until we have a new president."[11]

President Obama put forward a nominee anyway, the centrist chief judge of the District of Columbia Circuit Court of Appeals, Merrick Garland, but the Republican-dominated Senate followed through on its promise not even to hold hearings on his nomination. This allowed President Trump to nominate Scalia's successor: U.S. Court of Appeals Judge Neil Gorsuch. Democrats, who felt that a seat on the Supreme Court had been stolen from them, and who considered Gorsuch to be too ideologically extreme a nominee, mounted a filibuster. Lacking the sixty votes needed to overcome the filibuster, the Republican-controlled Senate proceeded to change the rules, abolishing filibusters of Supreme Court nominees, just as Democrats had earlier abolished filibusters of lower federal court nominees.[12] By requiring sixty votes to confirm, filibusters had arguably helped to promote consensus nominations. Doing away with them paved the way for more partisan, ideologically extreme nominees from both ends of the political spectrum. With the filibuster no longer an obstacle, the Senate proceeded to confirm Gorsuch by a vote of fifty-four to forty-five on April 7, 2017. By then, fourteen months had passed since Scalia died.

President Trump also had the opportunity to replace another Reagan appointee, Justice Anthony Kennedy, who retired in 2018, with Brett Kavanaugh, a court of appeals judge on the District of Columbia Circuit. The Senate ultimately confirmed Kavanaugh by an even closer vote than for Gorsuch (fifty to forty-eight) after dramatic confirmation hearings that included testimony from a woman who alleged that Kavanaugh had sexually assaulted her when they were both in high school. Then, on September 18, 2020—less than two months before the 2020 presidential election—Justice Ruth Bader Ginsburg died. Appointed by Bill Clinton, Ginsburg had helped to anchor the liberal wing of the court. This time, in an audacious turnaround from his stance when Justice Scalia died, McConnell announced, "President Trump's nominee [to fill Ginsburg's vacancy] will receive a vote on the floor of the United States Senate." President Trump nominated Court of Appeals Judge Amy Coney Barrett on September 26, and the Senate confirmed her on October 26, by a vote of fifty-two to forty-eight. A week later, Joe Biden defeated President Trump and Democrats regained control of the Senate, but only after Barrett's confirmation solidified a six-to-three conservative majority that led to the controversial decision to overturn *Roe v. Wade*.

Ideological divides on the Supreme Court have long been common. It is only recently, however, that ideology and presidential partisanship have aligned. Even the stark divide between the conservative "Four Horsemen" on the court, who struck down New Deal policies put forward by President Franklin D. Roosevelt in the 1930s, and the liberal "Three Musketeers," who upheld those policies, was ideological, not partisan. In 2018, Lee Epstein and

Eric Posner studied five-to-four and five-to-three decisions by the Supreme Court since 1953. They noted that through the 1950s and 1960s, "the ideological biases of Republican appointees and Democratic appointees were relatively modest." Votes by Republican appointees were sometimes more liberal than those by Democratic appointees. Not until the 1970s did the ideological gap between Democrats and Republicans widen.[13]

Epstein and Posner pointed out that even as late as the early 1990s, ideology did not necessarily predict the party of the president who appointed a justice. Byron White, the only remaining Democratic appointee then on the court, voted "more conservatively than all but two of the Republican appointees, Antonin Scalia and William Rehnquist," while several Republican appointees "frequently cast liberal votes." These included Harry Blackmun, appointed by Richard Nixon; John Paul Stevens, appointed by Gerald Ford; Sandra Day O'Connor, appointed by Ronald Reagan; and David Souter, appointed by George H. W. Bush.

No more. From 2007 to 2017, only Anthony Kennedy voted against the ideology of the president who appointed him with any regularity. In 1953, Epstein and Posner categorized 50 percent of votes by Republican appointees in five-to-four and five-to-three decisions as liberal, as opposed to 47 percent of votes by Democratic appointees. By 2017, they categorized 88 percent of votes by Democratic appointees as liberal, opposed to only 14 percent of Republican appointees. "For the first time in living memory," they concluded, "the court will be seen by the public as a party-dominated institution, one whose votes on controversial issues are essentially determined by the party affiliation of recent presidents."[14]

In a later study, Epstein extended the analysis to all nonunanimous, orally argued decisions. She found that during the Warren Court era (1953–69), the partisan gap in those cases averaged 8 percentage points, with 53 percent of Republican appointees casting liberal decisions versus 61 percent of Democratic appointees. In contrast, the partisan gap increased nearly five times to 37 percentage points during the first seventeen years of the Roberts Court era (2005–22).[15] This widening gap, which coincided with the increased political polarization of voters and elected officials, threatened to undermine the legitimacy of the court. Once the court comes to be perceived as a party-dominated institution, it is harder to accept that its decisions are just and equitable. Or, as Justice Sonia Sotomayor asked rhetorically during oral arguments in the *Dobbs* case, "Will this institution survive the stench" created by "the public perception that the Constitution and its reading are just political acts?" Answering her own question, she said, "I don't see how it is possible."[16]

Exacerbating the "stench" were reports of possible ethical breaches by various Supreme Court justices at both ends of the political spectrum, including Sotomayor. A series of news stories beginning in 2023 revealed that Clarence Thomas had failed to disclose, as required by federal law, real estate sales to, as well as gifts from and luxury travel provided by, the Republican billionaire Harlan Crowe.[17] Reports also emerged that Sotomayor had used government resources to promote her books.[18] Meanwhile, the political activism of Justice Thomas's wife, Ginni, attracted scrutiny,[19] as did two flags flown at the homes of Justice Samuel Alito by his wife, Martha-Ann, both of which were associated with the views of rioters who breached the U.S. Capitol Building on January 6, 2021.[20]

Amid all of this, former President Trump, embroiled in a series of criminal and civil cases brought against him, continued his long-standing public attacks on courts and judges. As early as the 2016 presidential campaign, Trump complained about an Indiana-born U.S. District Court judge presiding over a class-action suit against Trump University for fraud and breach of contract, questioning whether he could be impartial because of his Mexican heritage. When the judge, Gonzalo Curiel, ordered the release of documents outlining Trump University's predatory marketing practices, Trump complained, using racially tinged language. "I have a Mexican judge," he said dismissively at one of his campaign rallies—"a hater," eliciting a chorus of boos from the crowd. "They ought to look into Judge Curiel," he added, "because what Judge Curiel is doing is a total disgrace."[21]

As president, Trump has had ample opportunity to complain about court rulings. In just the first two years of his first term in office, federal judges ruled against his policies at least sixty-three times.[22] President Trump routinely dismissed such rulings, from judges appointed by Republican and Democratic presidents alike, as "totally biased," "terrible," "ridiculous," "very dangerous and unwise," "so political," a "disgrace," a "joke," a "laughingstock," "horrible, dangerous, and wrong," and even "not law."[23] When, in November 2018, he disparaged a ruling because it was decided by an "Obama judge," Chief Justice John Roberts, a George W. Bush appointee, issued a highly unusual rebuke: "We do not have Obama judges or Trump judges, Bush judges or Clinton judges. What we have is an extraordinary group of dedicated judges doing their level best to do equal right to those appearing before them. That independent judiciary is something we should all be thankful for."[24] Trump, in turn, immediately rejected Roberts's claim that the judiciary was independent.[25]

Critics charged that such attacks, particularly coming from the president of the United States, threatened the rule of law. The left-leaning Brennan

Center for Justice accused Trump of undermining "our entire system of government" because courts, as bulwarks of the law and Constitution, "depend on the public to respect their judgments and on officials to obey and enforce their decisions." "Separation of powers," it added—which allows courts to enforce the rule of law—"is not a threat to democracy; it is the essence of democracy."[26]

After Trump left office in 2021, the criminal and civil cases brought against him unleashed an ongoing litany of attacks by him against the judges presiding over those cases. "These are animals," he said at a January 2024 campaign rally. "These are bad people. These are radical left lunatics that want to hurt me."[27] He called U.S. District Court Judge Tanya Chutkan, who presided over his election interference case, "the most evil person."[28] His dismissed New York Judge Lewis Kaplan, who presided over his defamation civil trial, as a "bully" and a "Radical Left Democrat judge" who "denied me due process" in a "sham" trial,[29] while calling Judge Arthur F. Engoron, who found Trump liable for fraud, "deranged."[30] Trump described Juan Merchan, the New York judge who presided over his hush money trial, as "totally compromised" and attacked his daughter as "a rabid Trump hater."[31] He accused Merchan on his social media platform Truth Social of presiding over a "kangaroo court." Such criticisms of judges on Truth Social and other pro-Trump social media sites prompted some of those commenting on the posts to call for violence. For example, one comment in response to his "kangaroo court" post about Judge Merchan read, "I hope Trump has that judge hanged for Treason." Another read, "Judge needs a hatchet to the face"— to which another replied, "And his whore daughter."[32] A real fear as Trump reentered office in 2025 was that, having spent years delegitimizing courts, he might now overtly defy them.

President Biden also criticized individual Supreme Court rulings, sometimes in harsh terms. Although he was hesitant to criticize specific justices or the court itself, that distinction may have been lost on some.[33] Over time, however, Biden's criticisms became more full-throated. After the Supreme Court's 2023 decision in *Students for Fair Admissions v. Harvard* ending affirmative action in higher education, President Biden declared, "This is not a normal court."[34] A year later, when he proposed an enforceable ethics code on Supreme Court justices "to restore trust and accountability," he criticized the court for issuing "extreme opinions" that had "undermined law and established civil rights principles and protections."[35]

Given all of this, it is perhaps not surprising that trust in the Supreme Court and the federal judiciary as a whole has waned. And given that lack of trust, a contested presidential election in which the Supreme Court had to weigh in through rulings that might determine the victor could have been disastrous for the court's legitimacy. Luckily, that did not happen. Nonetheless, the Supreme Court had already issued controversial rulings in the two cases mentioned above.

Most notably, *Trump v. Anderson* dealt with whether states could remove Trump from the ballot.[36] At issue was section 3 of the Fourteenth Amendment to the U.S. Constitution. The enduring importance of the Fourteenth Amendment, ratified in the aftermath of the Civil War, rests squarely on section 1, which contains the due process, equal protection, and privileges or immunities clauses—all of which protect individual rights from governmental abuse. Over time, sections 2, 3, and 4 fell into obscurity.

Section 2, a compromise designed to protect the right to vote for African Americans without directly saying so, gave Congress the power to punish states by reducing the number of representatives apportioned to Congress from those that denied the vote to males twenty-one years of age or older. Although many states proceeded to deny African American males the right to vote anyway, Congress never once exercised its section 2 authority, leading one scholar to write that the clause "has the unfortunate privilege of being dead as long as it has been alive."[37]

Section 4, the so-called public debt clause, was crafted to protect financial obligations made by the U.S. government in pursuit of the Civil War (notably pensions owed to U.S. soldiers), and to prohibit both the federal government and the states from paying any debts in aid of insurrection or rebellion against the United States by the Confederacy, or for any claim of loss or emancipation of any slave. This section, too, had come to be viewed as a historical relic, although the clause briefly emerged from obscurity in 2023 as a possible course for President Biden to invoke if Congress failed to raise the federal debt ceiling.[38]

Until recently, section 3 (the one at issue in *Trump v. Anderson*) appeared to be yet another Civil War relic. It reads, in full,

> No person shall be a Senator or Representative in Congress, or elector of President and Vice-President, or hold any office, civil or military, under the United States, or under any State, who, having previously taken an oath, as a member of Congress, or as an officer of the United States, or as a member of any State legislature, or as an executive or judicial officer of

any State, to support the Constitution of the United States, shall have engaged in insurrection or rebellion against the same, or given aid or comfort to the enemies thereof. But Congress may by a vote of two-thirds of each House, remove such disability.

Designed to disqualify officeholders who had engaged in insurrection or rebellion during the Civil War, this so-called disqualification clause also gave Congress the authority to "remove such disability." Like the public debt clause, the language of section 3 did not appear to be time-bound to the insurrection or rebellion related to the Civil War. And, like the public debt clause, it reemerged from obscurity during the Biden administration when President Trump refused to accept the outcome of the 2020 presidential election.

Although Biden won the 2020 national popular vote by a seven-million-vote margin, as well as a decisive Electoral College victory of 306 to 232, Trump—based on misinformation and disinformation—claimed widespread voter fraud. He and his allies filed challenges in state and federal courts in places where the results were closest—sixty-four cases in all.[39] At least eighty-six judges across the ideological spectrum, including ones appointed by Trump, rejected every claim of voter fraud.[40] The only challenge that Trump and his supporters won, related not to voter fraud but to a procedural irregularity in Pennsylvania, affected only a small number of votes.[41]

Undeterred, Trump mounted a Stop the Steal campaign to block Congress's certification of the Electoral College results that would declare Biden the winner. On December 14, 2020, the Electoral College officially confirmed the results of the election: 306 electoral votes for Biden, 232 for Trump. By then, Trump had allegedly used knowingly false claims of voter fraud to pressure state legislators and election officials to change electoral votes from Biden to Trump, organized fraudulent slates of electors in seven targeted states, and pressured his Justice Department to conduct sham election crime investigations and claim false concerns—even though Justice Department officials repeatedly told him that such claims were false, and repeated knowingly false claims to supporters. When all that failed, he urged his vice president, Mike Pence, to reject electoral votes from states that Biden had narrowly won but where Trump baselessly claimed fraud.[42]

As president of the Senate, Pence would preside over the joint session of Congress convened to certify the results on January 6, 2021. Although Pence's role was strictly ceremonial, Trump called on him to use that opportunity to reject the votes. Pence instead rejected that call, publicly issuing a letter that said, "It is my considered judgment that my oath to support and defend the Constitution constrains me from claiming unilateral authority to determine which electoral votes should be counted and which should not."[43]

On the day Congress was set to meet, Trump organized a massive March to Save America rally in Washington, DC. Speaking to the crowd shortly before the joint session of Congress convened, he repeated his false claims of election fraud and declared, "If Mike Pence does the right thing, we win the election." Responding to Pence's letter, in which the vice president claimed the Constitution did not allow him to do what the president wanted him to do, Trump said, "You're not going to have a Republican Party if you don't get tougher." Then, apparently mocking Pence, he said, "They want to play it so straight. . . . 'The Constitution doesn't allow me to send them back to the States.' Well, I say, yes it does. . . . When you catch somebody in a fraud, you're allowed to go by very different rules." Describing the certification of Biden's victory as an "egregious assault on our democracy," Trump then urged the crowd to go to the Capitol to protest the certification:

> Because you never take back our country with weakness. You have to show strength and you have to be strong. We have come to demand that Congress do the right thing and only count the electors who have been lawfully slated. . . . We will not be intimidated into accepting the hoaxes and the lies that we've been forced to believe. Over the past several weeks, we've amassed overwhelming evidence about a fake election. . . . Mike Pence has to agree to send it back. *(Audience chants: "Send it back.")* . . . And if you don't fight like hell, you're not going to have a country anymore.[44]

Soon thereafter, a group of people who had listened to the speech followed the president's directive and marched to the Capitol. There, over one thousand rioters broke through police barriers and stormed the Capitol Building in order to disrupt the certification of the election. Along the way they broke windows, vandalized offices, smeared human excrement on the walls, erected gallows (chanting "Hang Mike Pence"), and forced the vice president and members of Congress to seek safety in secure locations. More than one hundred police officers were injured. According to a court filing by special counsel Jack Smith, Trump responded to news that Pence might be in danger by saying, "So what?"[45] The attack led to almost 1,500 people being charged with criminal offenses. Approximately 894 of them had pleaded guilty by August 2024 (288 to felonies and 606 to misdemeanors); 186 more were convicted at contested trials. Charges ranged from entering a restricted federal building to assault with a deadly weapon, with at least 562 of those convicted receiving jail sentences.[46]

The events of January 6 also led the U.S. House of Representatives to adopt, just one week before Trump's term expired, an article of impeachment against the president for "incitement of insurrection." Although Senate Majority Leader McConnell said that he was open to voting to convict Trump, he delayed the Senate trial until after Trump left office. That made it easier for Republicans, including ultimately McConnell, to vote for acquittal because Trump no longer held office. Trump's own lawyers at the time argued that, in fact, the Senate could not convict him because he had already left office. They pointed instead to the criminal justice system as the appropriate avenue to seek accountability (a view, as we shall see, that a different set of Trump lawyers later reversed). In the end, fifty-seven senators (every Democrat plus seven Republicans) voted to find Trump guilty, and forty-three voted not guilty. While this was the first time since 1868 that a majority of the Senate had voted to convict a president (and the first time ever that a bipartisan majority had voted to do so), the vote fell short of the two-thirds majority of sixty-seven votes needed to convict. Had he been convicted, Trump would have been ineligible to hold public office on a separate vote.

Talk about using section 3 of the Fourteenth Amendment to remove Trump from office emerged immediately after the January 6 attack. Did Trump engage in "insurrection or rebellion" when he sought to overturn the election and encouraged his followers to march to the Capitol? If so, section 3 suggested he could be disqualified from holding public office unless a two-thirds vote of each house of Congress waived the disability. Could this be an avenue—apart from (and perhaps easier than) impeachment—to remove Trump from office?

After Trump left office and the Senate failed to convict him in its impeachment trial, the question turned to whether section 3 could be used to disqualify Trump from holding office in the future. After Trump announced that he planned to run for president in 2024, voters and advocacy groups in at least thirty-four states filed challenges in state and federal court in an effort to use section 3 to keep Trump off the ballot. Three states, Colorado, Illinois, and Maine, had already disqualified Trump, and challenges were pending in eleven other states, when the U.S. Supreme Court agreed to hear Trump's appeal of the Colorado decision to keep him off the ballot.[47]

In *Anderson v. Griswold*, a group of Colorado voters had sought to prevent Trump from appearing on the state's primary ballot, arguing that section 3 disqualified him from holding office because he had engaged in insurrection.[48] The trial court concluded that the voters had a justiciable claim, and that there was clear and convincing evidence that President Trump had engaged in insurrection as that term is used in section 3. However, it also concluded that section 3 did not apply to the president because that office is not explicitly mentioned in the first sentence of section 3, while U.S. senators, representatives, and presidential electors are. Although section 3 does say that no person who engaged in insurrection or rebellion shall "hold any office, civil or military, under the United States," the trial court agreed with Trump's lawyers that the president is not an "officer of the United States" within the meaning of section 3.[49]

By a four-to-three vote, the Colorado Supreme Court, on December 19, 2023, reversed the lower court's conclusion that the president is not an officer of the United States. It pointed to dictionary usage from the time of the Fourteenth Amendment's ratification that defined *office* as "a 'particular duty, charge or trust conferred by public authority, and for a public purpose,' that is 'undertaken by . . . authority from government or those who administer it.'" (Quoting a contemporaneous edition of *Webster's Dictionary*.) It also quoted Samuel Johnson's *Dictionary of the English Language*, "defining 'office' as 'a publick charge or employment; magistracy'" and an 1823 federal court decision that defined an "office" as "a public charge or employment" to conclude, "The Presidency falls comfortably within these definitions."[50] The decision continued, "We do not place the same weight the district court did on the fact that the Presidency is not specifically mentioned in Section Three. It seems most likely that the Presidency is not specifically included because it is so evidently an 'office.' In fact, no specific office is listed in Section Three; instead, the Section refers to 'any office, civil or military.' . . . True, senators, representatives, and presidential electors are listed, but none of these positions is considered an 'office' in the Constitution. Instead, senators and representatives are referred to as 'members' of their respective bodies."[51]

The Colorado Supreme Court also responded to the lower court's claim that even if the presidency is an office, it is not an office "under the United States" because "the President and elected members of Congress are the government of the United States, and cannot, therefore be serving 'under the United States.'" The Colorado Supreme Court said, "We cannot accept this interpretation." It continued, "A conclusion that the Presidency is something other than an office 'under' the United States is fundamentally at odds with the idea that all government officials, including the President, serve 'we the people.' . . . A more plausible reading of the phrase 'under the

United States' is that the drafters meant simply to distinguish those holding federal office from those held 'under any State.'"[52] The Colorado Supreme
Court thus concluded that "because President Trump is disqualified from
holding the office of President under Section Three, it would be a wrongful
act under the Election Code for the Secretary to list President Trump as a
candidate on the presidential primary ballot."[53]

President Trump immediately appealed the ruling to the U.S. Supreme
Court, which heard oral arguments on February 8, 2024. It considered one
question: "Did the Colorado Supreme Court err in ordering President
Trump excluded from the 2024 presidential primary ballot?"[54] Almost a
month later, on March 4, 2024, the court issued an unsigned per curiam
opinion concluding that the Colorado Supreme Court had, indeed,
erred. All nine justices agreed that "States have no power under the Constitution to enforce Section 3 with respect to federal offices, especially the
Presidency." They explained, "As an initial matter, not even the respondents
contend that the Constitution authorizes States to somehow remove *sitting*
federal officeholders who may be violating Section 3. Such a power would
flout the principle that 'the Constitution guarantees "the entire independence of the General Government from any control by the respective
States."' . . . The respondents nonetheless maintain that States may enforce
Section 3 against *candidates* for federal office. But the text of the Fourteenth
Amendment, on its face, does not affirmatively delegate such a power to
the States."[55] Indeed, the justices ruled, allowing individual states to
enforce section 3 could lead to a situation such as the one that was emerging with Trump: "A single candidate would be declared ineligible in some
States, but not others, based on the same conduct (and perhaps even the
same factual record)." The resulting "patchwork" could "dramatically
change the behavior of voters, parties, and States across the country, in
different ways and at different times." The justices continued, "The disruption would be all the more acute—and could nullify the votes of millions and change the election result—if Section 3 enforcement were
attempted after the Nation has voted. Nothing in the Constitution requires
that we endure such chaos—arriving at any time or different times, up to
and perhaps beyond the Inauguration."[56]

Four of the justices (Amy Coney Barrett, Ketanji Brown Jackson, Elena
Kagan, and Sonia Sotomayor) would have left the court's decision at that,
but the five-member majority (Chief Justice John Roberts, Samuel Alito,
Neil Gorsuch, Brent Kavanaugh, and Clarence Thomas) went on to delineate more specifically how federal enforcement should proceed. They
pointed to section 5 of the Fourteenth Amendment, an enabling clause

similar to such clauses in many post–Civil War amendments ("The Congress shall have power to enforce, by appropriate legislation, the provisions of this article"), and concluded that Congress alone could enforce section 3. They also prescribed how and when Congress should proceed when using that enforcement power.

In a concurring opinion joined by Justices Kagan and Jackson, Justice Sotomayor urged restraint. "'If it is not necessary to decide more to dispose of a case, then it is necessary *not* to decide more,'" she wrote, pointedly quoting the words of Chief Justice Roberts. "Today, the Court departs from this vital principle, deciding not just this case, but challenges that might arise in the future." She continued, "Although only an individual State's action is at issue here, the majority opines on which federal actors can enforce Section 3, and how they must do so. The majority announces that a disqualification for insurrection can occur only when Congress enacts a particular kind of legislation pursuant to Section 5 of the Fourteenth Amendment. In doing so, the majority shuts the door on other potential means of federal enforcement. We cannot join an opinion that decides momentous and difficult issues unnecessarily, and we therefore concur only in the judgment."[57]

Justice Barrett's separate concurrence seemed to chide both the majority and the other three concurring justices. Like Justice Sotomayor, she agreed that the court should do no more than rule that "States lack the power to enforce Section 3 against Presidential candidates. That principle is sufficient to resolve this case, and I would decide no more than that. It does not require us to address the complicated question whether federal legislation is the exclusive vehicle through which Section 3 can be enforced." But she also seemed to fear that Sotomayor's concurrence amplified disagreement among the justices: "The majority's choice of a different path leaves the remaining Justices with a choice of how to respond. In my judgment, this is not the time to amplify disagreement with stridency. The Court has settled a politically charged issue in the volatile season of a Presidential election. Particularly in this circumstance, writings on the Court should turn the national temperature down, not up. For present purposes, our differences are far less important than our unanimity: All nine Justices agree on the outcome of this case. That is the message Americans should take home."[58]

Trump v. Anderson was not the only case heard during the volatile 2024 election season that had the potential to influence the election outcome. During the previous year, Trump had faced multiple criminal and civil cases against him. Before the primary season began, he had already been held liable by a federal jury for sexual abuse and defamation in *Carroll v. Trump.*[59] Meanwhile, a New York State judge in another civil suit, *New York v. Trump*, issued a summary judgment that Trump and others associated with the Trump Organization had committed fraud by inflating the value of its assets.[60] After an ensuing trial, the judge held, on February 16, 2024— just one week before the New Hampshire primary—that Trump and his companies were liable for $354.8 million in damages.[61] Meanwhile, Trump faced charges in a New York hush money case (in which a jury ultimately found him guilty of thirty-four felony counts of falsifying business records), as well as federal criminal charges in two other cases brought by special counsel Jack Smith. The first involved charges of interfering in the outcome of the 2020 election. The second focused on Trump's misuse of classified documents. He also faced state criminal charges in Georgia, stemming from his alleged efforts to overturn his electoral defeat in that state.[62]

On December 23, 2023, Trump's lawyers filed an appeal in the election interference case filed by Smith. They argued that Trump had been act- ing in his official capacity to ensure election integrity and that presidents have immunity from prosecution for official conduct. In stark contrast to what a different set of Trump's own lawyers had suggested during his second impeachment trial, they also argued that the indictment against Trump should be dismissed, citing the impeachment judgment clause in Article 1, section 3, clause 7: "The Party *convicted* shall nevertheless be lia- ble and subject to Indictment, Trial, Judgment and Punishment, according to Law." On this basis they claimed that impeachment and Senate convic- tion must precede a president's criminal prosecution.[63] In truth, during his second impeachment trial, Trump's lawyers had assured senators that acquittal would not leave Trump "in any way above the law" because once he was out of office he could still face criminal prosecution. Now they claimed that the Senate's acquittal of Trump established an absolute bar to criminal prosecution.[64]

Initially, some observers viewed Trump's appeal primarily as an attempt to delay his trial in hope of winning reelection before it could proceed. Trump had already tried to delay the trial until 2026.[65] Now, awaiting the results of the appeal from a three-judge panel of the Court of Appeals for the District of Columbia Circuit, Judge Chutkin was forced to postpone the start of the trial, which originally was set for March 4, 2024—smack in the middle of the presidential primaries.[66] The three-judge panel included two judges appointed by Democrats and one appointed by a Republican. The panel's unanimous rejection of Trump's immunity claim in a carefully crafted fifty-seven-page ruling on February 6, 2024, seemed to give the

Supreme Court "an easy off ramp" to avoid involvement in the case.[67] Had the Supreme Court denied Trump's appeal from the District of Columbia Circuit, that court's ruling would have stood and the trial could have proceeded. Instead, on February 28, 2024, the Supreme Court agreed to hear Trump's appeal and set oral arguments for the week of April 22.[68] Trump clinched the Republican nomination for president on March 12, 2024, and the Supreme Court did not issue its ruling in *Trump v. United States* until July 1, 2024, with the Republican National Convention set to convene on July 15. The timing made it all but impossible to hold a trial before the election, no matter how the court ruled.

In a bitterly divided six-to-three ruling that split along partisan lines, the Supreme Court recognized, for the first time ever, that former presidents have immunity from at least some criminal prosecutions. It held that presidents have absolute immunity for official acts within their exclusive sphere of constitutional authority—that is, in areas where the Constitution gives the president the sole authority to act. It further held that presidents have at least presumptive immunity when exercising official acts outside that "conclusive and preclusive" authority in what the majority called the president's "outer perimeter" of official responsibility. Without such immunity, the majority explained, a president's fear of criminal prosecution would threaten to "distort Presidential decisionmaking." Forced to make decisions under "the pall of potential prosecution," presidents might hesitate, thereby significantly undermining "the independence of the Executive" and violating separation of powers. It concluded, however, that separation of powers does not bar prosecution for "unofficial acts" a president might commit.[69]

The majority did not precisely delineate the line between "official" and "unofficial," and warned that in distinguishing between the two, "courts may not inquire into the President's motives. Such an inquiry would risk exposing even the most obvious instances of official conduct to judicial examination on the mere allegation of improper purpose."[70] Admitting that the distinction between official and unofficial acts "can be difficult" to ascertain, it remanded the case to the district court to make the initial determinations.

The majority did, however, conclude that discussions by President Trump with his attorney general and other Justice Department officials fell within the absolute immunity covered by the president's "conclusive and presumptive" power. "Investigative and prosecutorial decisionmaking," Justice Roberts explained, "is 'the special province of the Executive Branch,'" and the president's "'management of the Executive Branch' requires him to have 'unrestricted power to remove the most important of his subordinates'— such as the Attorney General—'in their most important duties.'" He added,

"Trump is therefore absolutely immune from prosecution for the alleged conduct involving his discussions with Justice Department officials."[71] The special counsel's indictment had charged Trump with directing the Justice Department "to conduct sham election crime investigations and to send a letter to the targeted states that falsely claimed that the Justice Department had identified significant concerns that may have impacted the election outcome."[72] Absolute immunity shielded the president from prosecution for engaging in these conversations, and for threatening to fire officials who would not carry out his scheme.

On the other hand, the court noted that President Trump's attempts to convince Vice President Pence to use his ceremonial role in the certification process to reject slates of electors did not fall within the "conclusive and presumptive" powers that trigger absolute immunity. They were, however, presumptively privileged because conversations between a president and vice president fall within the "outer perimeter" of official conduct. It would be "the Government's burden to rebut the presumptive immunity" on remand.[73]

Beyond a president's enjoying absolute immunity for official acts conducted under their "conclusive and presumptive" powers, and at least presumptive immunity for official acts conducted within the "outer perimeter" of official conduct, five members of the majority (Roberts, Thomas, Alito, Gorsuch, and Kavanaugh) held that a jury could not even consider evidence regarding a president's official conduct. For example, the indictment alleged that Justice Department officials repeatedly told the president that his election fraud claims were false, but that the president proceeded to peddle the claims nonetheless.[74] This five-person majority held that, in addition to the president's being absolutely immune from criminal prosecution for conversations with the Justice Department, the content of those conversations could not be used in a criminal trial to show a broader conspiracy that might allow the president to be prosecuted on other charges.

The main dissenters, Justice Sotomayor joined by Justices Kagan and Jackson, reacted with fury. In unusually forceful language, Justice Sotomayor wrote that the majority opinion was "deeply wrong," "unnecessary and misguided," and would have "disastrous consequences for the Presidency and for our democracy." She also dismissed the majority's "illogical evidentiary holdings," claimed that they had "no firm grounding in constitutional text, history or precedent," and wrote, "No matter how you look at it, the majority's official-acts immunity is utterly indefensible."[75] She concluded, "In sum, the majority today endorses an expansive vision of Presidential immunity that was never recognized by the Founders, any sitting

President, the Executive Branch, or even President Trump's lawyers, until now. Settled understandings of the Constitution are of little use to the majority in this case, and so it ignores them."[76] In response to the fear that the threat of criminal prosecution would stifle presidential decision-making and violate separation of powers, Justice Sotomayor wrote, "It is a far greater danger if the President feels empowered to violate federal criminal law, buoyed by the knowledge of future immunity."[77]

Justice Sotomayor agreed that some criminal statutes may be unconstitutional as applied to presidents. In such cases, the president "can move to dismiss the charges on that ground."[78] But the majority's immunity claim, she argued, went much further. It "replaced a presumption of equality before the law with a presumption that the President is above the law for all of his official acts." Moreover, she argued that the sweep of the majority opinion left little room for prosecution. "Under the majority's test, if it can be called a test, the category of Presidential action that can be deemed 'unofficial' is destined to be vanishingly small."[79]

Sotomayor then unleashed an uninhibited volley against the majority:

> Looking beyond the fate of this particular prosecution, the long-term consequences of today's decision are stark. The Court effectively creates a law-free zone around the President, upsetting the status quo that has existed since the Founding. This new official-acts immunity now "lies about like a loaded weapon" for any President that wishes to place his own interests, his own political survival, or his own financial gain above the interests of the nation. The President of the United States is the most powerful person in the country, and possibly the world. When he uses his official powers in any way, under the majority's reasoning, he will now be insulated from criminal prosecution. Orders the Navy's Seal Team 6 to assassinate a political rival? Immune. Organizes a military coup to hold onto power? Immune. Takes a bribe in exchange for a pardon? Immune. Immune, immune, immune.[80]

The majority responded vigorously, accusing the dissent of striking "a tone of chilling doom that is wholly disproportionate to what the Court actually does today" and of using "cherry-picked sources" to justify its conclusions.

> Like everyone else, the President is subject to prosecution in his unofficial capacity. But unlike anyone else, the President is a branch of government, and the Constitution vests in him sweeping powers and duties.

Accounting for that reality—and ensuring that the President may exercise those powers forcefully, as the Framers anticipated he would—does not place him above the law; it preserves the basic structure of the Constitution from which that law derives.

The dissents' positions in the end boil down to ignoring the Constitution's separation of powers and the Court's precedent and instead fear mongering on the basis of extreme hypotheticals about a future where the President "feels empowered to violate federal criminal law." The dissents overlook the more likely prospect of an Executive Branch that cannibalizes itself, with each successive President free to prosecute his predecessors, yet unable to boldly and fearlessly carry out his duties for fear that he may be next.[81]

As in *Trump v. Anderson*, Justice Barrett concurred with the majority opinion. But she declined to join part III-C of the opinion, which said that a jury could not even consider evidence concerning a president's official conduct. And while she joined the rest of the majority opinion, she made a point of saying that she "would have framed the underlying legal issues differently." The majority, she noted, described "the President's constitution protection from certain prosecutions as an 'immunity.'" While she embraced the principle that she believes the majority meant by the term, she indicated that she would have avoided the term *immunity* in favor of a two-step analysis of criminal statutes.

As I see it, that term [*immunity*] is short-hand for two propositions: The President can challenge the constitutionality of a criminal statute as applied to official acts alleged in the indictment, and he can obtain interlocutory review of the court's ruling. . . . Properly conceived, the President's constitutional protection is narrow. . . . Congress has concurrent authority over many Government functions, and it may sometimes use that authority to regulate the President's official conduct, including by criminal statute. . . .

I would thus assess the validity of criminal charges predicated on most official acts—i.e. those falling outside of the President's core official power—in two steps. The first question is whether the relevant criminal statute reaches the President's official conduct. Not every broadly worded statute does. . . . If the statute covers the alleged official conduct, the prosecution may proceed only if applying it in the circumstances poses no "dange[r] of intrusion on the authority and functions of the Executive Branch." . . . This two-step analysis—considering first whether the statute applies and then whether its application to the particular facts is constitutional—is similar to the approach that the Special Counsel presses in this Court.[82]

Justice Ketanji Brown Jackson argued something similar in her dissenting opinion. After noting that she agreed with "every word" of Justice Sotomayor's "powerful dissent," Jackson emphasized that presidents do have a defense against certain criminal statutes being applied to them. They may "raise, and attempt to prove, affirmative defenses that 'excuse conduct that would otherwise be punishable.'" Nonetheless, she emphasized that "a defense is *not* an immunity." Under the majority's formulation, she complained, immunity can protect even "unquestionably and intentionally egregious criminal behavior."[83]

Everyone on the court rejected Trump's claim that former presidents could only be prosecuted if the Senate had convicted them in an impeachment trial, but the vitriolic exchanges between the majority and the dissenters about the rest of the opinion largely obscured that point of agreement. As noted earlier, the court's ruling and its timing had an indirect bearing on the election: Trump's criminal prosecutions would not proceed before the election. Then, when Trump won, special counsel dropped both the election subversion and mishandling of classified documents cases.

Just days before the election, the justices again split along partisan lines over whether to grant Virginia's emergency request to stay a lower federal court order that had temporarily blocked, pending appeal, Governor Glenn Youngkin's executive order to cancel the voter registration of more than sixteen hundred voters who were suspected of being noncitizens unless they could prove their citizenship within fourteen days.

The Biden administration and other challengers claimed that Youngkin's order violated the National Voter Registration Act, which prohibits the systematic removal of ineligible voters within ninety days of an election. Virginia argued that the act did not apply to noncitizens because they had never been eligible to vote, even though the purge mistakenly targeted some citizens who clearly were eligible to vote. In a one-paragraph unsigned order that Justices Sotomayor, Kagan, and Jackson did not join, the court sided with Virginia, stayed the lower court order, and allowed Youngkin's order to stand, pending appeal.[84]

Had the court faced ongoing litigation to resolve issues associated with a contested election, partisan divisions among the justices—especially if accompanied by the strident rhetoric used in *Trump v. United States*—would likely have undermined the legitimacy of its rulings and potentially led to further instability. Trump's decisive victory prevented that from happening, but damage to the legitimacy of courts had already been done. Perhaps Mitt Romney was correct to assert that President Biden should have pardoned Trump when he first took office.

Aside from possibly helping to unite the nation and heal the divisiveness that Trump himself had fostered, a pardon might have helped to turn the page on Trump. The irony of the many criminal cases brought against him is that they put Trump precisely where he wanted to be: in the spotlight. It also allowed Trump to wrap himself in the mantle of victimhood. "If they can do this to me, they can do this to anyone," he intoned after his conviction for falsifying business records.[85] Moreover, a pardon might have protected the legitimacy of courts and the rule of law by insulating President Biden from charges of weaponizing the federal judiciary and by shielding courts and judges from the destabilizing attacks that Trump unleashed throughout the proceedings against him. And, with a pardon, there never would have been a federal prosecution for Trump to appeal, and thus no opportunity for the Supreme Court to rule on the issue of presidential immunity.

Would Trump have run for reelection had he been pardoned? Probably. But, banned as he was from Twitter and other social media platforms, it might have been harder for him to regain the national stage. A pardon would also have eliminated the need for Trump to return to office in order to shield himself from prosecution and its consequences.

Having won the 2024 election, Trump has a chance to shape the future direction of the Supreme Court. It is unlikely that any members of the court's liberal wing will choose to retire in the next four years. Indeed, Sotomayor, then seventy years old, ignored suggestions that she step down in time for President Biden to nominate a replacement while Democrats still controlled the Senate.[86] However, Republican control of the White House and Senate under Trump may encourage older members of the conservative wing to retire. Clarence Thomas was seventy-six years old when Trump returned to power, while Samuel Alito was seventy-four and John Roberts turned seventy days after Trump was inaugurated. Filling any or all of those seats with young replacements could insure a conservative majority on the court for decades.

Regardless of what happens on the Supreme Court, President Trump—with a Republican-controlled Senate in place at least initially—will be able to fulfill the opportunity, started in his first term, to reshape the lower federal judiciary in his image. Like Supreme Court justices, lower federal court judges are nominated by the president and subject to the advice and consent of the Senate. Once confirmed, they have life tenure. Since the Supreme Court only hears about eighty cases per term, these lower courts have the final word on the vast majority of cases involving a federal question.

In the waning days of his administration, President Biden vetoed bipartisan legislation to increase the number of federal judges. The Judges Act of 2024 was designed to add sixty-six new district court judgeships over the next ten years—spread out so as minimize the opportunity for any one president to fill them all—because the number of federal judges has, in recent years, failed to keep pace with caseload.[87] Congress used to increase the number of judges more routinely to avert that problem, but—stymied by partisan politics amid an increasingly politicized judicial appointment process—the last meaningful increase in the number of federal judges came in 1990, when the Judicial Improvements Act created sixty-one new federal district court judgeships and eleven new court of appeals judgeships.[88]

The Senate unanimously passed the Judges Act in August 2024, but the Republican-controlled House of Representatives—determined not to give President Biden any opportunity to appoint more federal judges—delayed voting on the bill until after Trump had won the election. It then passed the bill by a vote of 236 to 173, with 171 of the negative votes now coming from Democrats.[89] Although President Biden's veto killed the Judges Act of 2024, President Trump came to office with Republican control of both the House and Senate. Thus, new legislation could emerge.

There is yet another way that courts arguably influenced the 2024 elections. In 2019, the Supreme Court ruled, in a 5–4 decision split along partisan lines, that federal courts cannot hear cases involving partisan gerrymandering.[90] As a result of that decision, voters who wanted to challenge partisan gerrymandering turned to state constitutions and filed cases in state courts. By the start of 2024, such challenges to legislative maps drawn as part of the latest redistricting cycle had been filed in 18 states.[91]

Among these cases, one in North Carolina likely determined which party controlled the House of Representatives in the 119th Congress. In 2022, the North Carolina Supreme Court ordered the Republican-controlled state legislature to redraw maps that the court said had been drawn for unfair partisan advantage. In a challenge to that ruling, the U.S. Supreme Court rejected a controversial argument known as the "independent state legislature theory," which argued that not even state courts could review election laws enacted by state legislatures.[92]

North Carolina judges—including those who sit on its supreme court—are chosen in partisan elections. Following the court's 2022 ruling, voters elected a new conservative majority to the Supreme Court. This new majority—prior to the U.S. Supreme Court's ruling—reversed its earlier ruling. Although the U.S. Supreme Court concluded that this did not moot the challenge to the earlier case and proceeded to reject the independent state legislature theory, a panel of three North Carolina judges ultimately dismissed the challenge to the maps in June 2024.[93] That decision was consequential. Arguably, the Republican-drawn maps that were allowed to stand flipped three House seats from the Democratic column to the Republican column. If true, the ruling turned what would have been a 218–217 Democratic majority in the House into a 220–215 Republican majority.

On December 20, 2024, President Biden reached a major milestone. The Senate confirmed the 235th federal judge that he had nominated—one more than the number that the Senate had confirmed during President Trump's first term and more than the Senate had confirmed during any single term since the 1980s. Commemorating the milestone, President Biden issued a statement. In it, he said, "Judges matter."[94] Indeed, they do.

Notes

1. Bush v. Gore, 531 U.S. 98 (2000).
2. Mary Clare Jaloick, "Republican Lawmakers React with Fury to Trump Verdict and Rally to His Defense," Associated Press, May 30, 2024, https://apnews.com/article/trump-verdict-republicans-guilty-reaction-congress-election-c8193404866565c55b093086890cbef8.
3. Julia Ingram and Jacob Rosen, "Trump Campaign Says It Raised $52.8 Million After Guilty Verdict in Fundraising Blitz," CBS News, May 31, 2024, https://www.cbsnews.com/news/trump-fundraising-guilty-verdict-new-york-conviction/.
4. Shane Goldmacher and Ruth Igielnik, "Republicans Rally Behind Trump After Conviction, Times/Siena Poll Finds," New York Times, July 3, 2024, https://www.nytimes.com/2024/06/26/us/politics/trump-poll-hush-money-conviction.html.
5. Mandy Taheri, "Donald Trump's Trial is a 'Win-Win' For Him, Mitt Romney Says," Newsweek, May 15, 2024, https://www.newsweek.com/donald-trump-trial-win-win-mitt-romney-1901191.
6. Jeffrey M. Jones, "Party Divisions in Views of Supreme Court Keeps Ratings Low," Gallup, October 3, 2024, https://news.gallup.com/poll/651527/party-divisions-views-supreme-court-keep-ratings-low.aspx.
7. Lawrence Hurley, "Biden Warns of 'Unconstitutional Chaos' Due to Texas Abortion Ban," Reuters, September 3, 2021, https://www.reuters.com/world/us/us-supreme-court-declines-block-texas-abortion-ban-2021-09-02/; Megan Brenan, "Views of Supreme Court Remain Near Record

Lows," Gallup, September 29, 2023, https://news.gallup.com/poll/511820/views-supreme-court-remain-near-record-lows.aspx.

8. Dobbs v. Jackson Women's Health Organization, 597 U.S. 215 (2022).

9. Brenan, "Views of the Supreme Court Remain Near Record Lows."

10. Benedict Vigers and Lydia Saad, "Americans Pass Judgment on Their Courts," Gallup, December 17, 2024, https://news.gallup.com/poll/653897/americans-pass-judgment-courts.aspx.

11. Burgess Everett and Glenn Thrush, "McConnell Throws Down the Gauntlet: No Scalia Replacement Under Obama," *Politico*, February 13, 2016, http://www.politico.com/story/2016/02/mitch-mcconnell-antonin-scalia-supreme-court-nomination-219248.

12. Seung Min Kim et al., "Senate GOP Goes 'Nuclear' on Supreme Court Filibuster," *Politico*, April 6, 2017, https://www.politico.com/story/2017/04/senate-neil-gorsuch-nuclear-option-236937.

13. Lee Epstein and Eric Posner, "If the Supreme Court Is Nakedly Political, Can It Be Just?," *New York Times*, July 9, 2018.

14. Epstein and Posner, "If the Supreme Court?"

15. Lee Epstein, "Partisanship 'All the Way Down' on the U.S. Supreme Court," *Pepperdine Law Review* 51 (2024): 503–504.

16. Ruth Marcus, "Justice Sotomayor Drops the S-Bomb," *Washington Post*, December 3, 2021.

17. Alison Durkee, "Clarence Thomas: Here Are All the Ethics Scandals Involving the Supreme Court Justice amid New Ginni Thomas Report," *Forbes*, September 4, 2024; Alison Durkee, "Clarence Thomas Has Reportedly Been Accepting Gifts from Republican Meagadonor Harlan Crow for Decades—and Never Disclosed It," *Forbes*, April 6, 2023; Justin Elliott et al., "Billionaire Harlan Crow Bought Property from Clarence Thomas. The Justice Didn't Disclose Deal," *ProPublica*, April 13, 2023, https://www.propublica.org/article/clarence-thomas-harlan-crow-real-estate-scotus.

18. Brian Slodysko and Eric Turner, "Supreme Court Justice Sotomayor's Staff Prodded Colleges and Libraries to Buy Her Books," Associated Press, July 11, 2023, https://apnews.com/article/supreme-court-sotomayor-book-sales-ethics-colleges-b2cb93493f927f995829762cb8338c02.

19. Jane Mayer, "Is Ginni Thomas a Threat to the Supreme Court?," *New Yorker*, January 21, 2022.

20. Melissa Quinn, "Flags Outside of Alito's Houses Spark Political Backlash as Supreme Court Nears End of Term," CBS News, May 24, 2024, https://www.cbsnews.com/news/flags-alitos-houses-political-backlash-supreme-court-nears-end-of-term/.

21. Joe A. DelReal and Katie Zezima, "Trump's Personal, Racially Tinged Attacks on Federal Judge Alarm Legal Experts," *Washington Post*, June 1, 2016.

22. Fred Barbash and Deanna Paul, "The Real Reason the Trump Administration Is Constantly Losing in Court," *Washington Post*, March 19, 2019.

23. "In His Own Words: The President's Attacks on the Courts," Brennan Center for Justice, June 5, 2017, https://www.brennancenter.org/our-work/research-reports/his-own-words-presidents-attacks-courts.

24. Adam Liptak, "Chief Justice Defends Judicial Independence After Trump Attacks 'Obama Judge,'" *New York Times*, November 21, 2018.

25. Eli Watkins and Joan Biskupic, "Trump Slams Chief Justice After Roberts Chides the President," CNN, November 21, 2018, https://www.cnn.com/2018/11/21/politics/supreme-court-john-roberts-trump/index.html.

26. "In His Own Words."

27. Kate Plummer, "Donald Trump Rages at 'Animal' Judge," *Newsweek*, January 15, 2024.

28. Ryan J. Reilly et al., "Trump Calls Judge Overseeing His Jan 6 Case 'the Most Evil Person,'" NBC News, October 18, 2024, https://www.nbcnews.com/politics/justice-department/trump-calls-judge-overseeing-jan-6-case-evil-person-rcna176112.

29. Ewan Palmer, "Donald Trump Rages at 'Bully' Judge Kaplan," *Newsweek*, January 31, 2024.

30. Jonah E. Bromwich and Ben Protess, "Judge Rules Trump Committed Fraud, Stripping Control of Key Properties," *New York Times*, September 26, 2023.

31. Alex Isenstadt, "Trump Attacks Daughter of Judge Overseeing Hush Money Case," *Politico*, March 28, 2024, https://www.politico.com/news/2024/03/28/trump-attacks-daughter-of-judge-hush-money-case-00149656.

32. Peter Eisler et al., "Trump Blasts His Trial Judges. Then His Fans Call for Violence," Reuters, May 14, 2024, https://www.reuters.com/investigates/special-report/usa-election-threats-courts/.

33. Michael D. Shear, "Biden Criticizes Supreme Court Rulings, but Not the Court," *New York Times*, July 13, 2023.

34. Students for Fair Admissions v. Harvard, 600 U.S. 181 (2023); Niels Lesniewski, "Biden Blasts Supreme Court as Not 'Normal' After Affirmative Action Ruling," Roll Call, June 29, 2023, https://rollcall.com/2023/06/29/biden-blasts-supreme-court-as-not-normal-after-affirmative-action-ruling/.

35. Bernd Debusmann Jr. and Rachel Looker, "Biden Criticizes 'Extreme' Supreme Court in Push for Reform," BBC, July 29, 2024, https://www.bbc.com/news/articles/cw4yz3nwovyo.

36. Trump v. Anderson, 601 U.S. 100 (2024).

37. Franita Tolson, "What Is Abridgement? A Critique of Two Section Twos," *Alabama Law Review* 67 (2015): 434. Today, rather than being used to promote the right to vote, section 2 is used by some to justify limiting it.

They point to section 2 as a textual authorization for states to disenfranchise felons, since the clause makes an exception for "participation in rebellion, or other crime." Gabriel J. Chin, "Reconstruction, Felon Disenfranchisement, and the Right to Vote: Did the Fifteenth Amendment Repeal Section 2 of the Fourteenth Amendment?," *Georgetown Law Journal* 92 (2004): 259.

38. Harvard Law professor Laurence H. Tribe, for example, argued that once Congress passed legislation incurring debt, it could not impose a ceiling to prevent payment of those debts without violating the public debt clause. Laurence H. Tribe, "Why I Changed My Mind on the Debt Limit," *New York Times*, May 7, 2023. The Supreme Court only ruled on the public debt clause once, in a plurality decision in *Perry v. United States* (1935). That ruling concluded that the language of the public debt clause ("The validity of the public debt of the United States, authorized by law . . . shall not be questioned") protects the public debt of the United States, no matter when that debt was issued (as opposed to just the public debt incurred during the Civil War). Perry v. United States, 294 U.S. 330, 354 (1935). Nonetheless, scholars were divided over how the Supreme Court would respond to efforts to use the public debt clause as a solution to Congress's failure to raise the debt ceiling. In the end, Congress raised the debt ceiling, so President Biden never had the opportunity to test the limits of the clause.

39. Ann Gerhart, "Election Results Under Attack: Here Are the Facts," *Washington Post*, last updated March 11, 2024, https://www.washingtonpost .com/elections/interactive/2020/election-integrity/.

40. Rosalind S. Helderman and Elise Viebeck, "'The Last Wall': How Dozens of Judges Across the Political Spectrum Rejected Trump's Efforts to Overturn the Election," *Washington Post*, December 12, 2020.

41. See, for example, a detailed report by political conservatives John Danforth, Benjamin Ginsberg, Thomas B. Griffith, David Hoppe, J. Michael Luttig, Michael W. McConnell, Theodore B. Olson (who argued on behalf of George W. Bush in *Bush v. Gore*), and Gordon H. Smith, "Lost, Not Stolen: The Conservative Case That Trump Lost and Biden Won the 2020 Presidential Election," July 2022, https://www.documentcloud .org/documents/25116913-lost-not-stolen-the-conservative-case-that -trump-lost-and-biden-won-the-2020-presidential-election-july-2022. See also Walter Olson, "Trump's 2020 Stolen Election Claims Are Wrong on the Merits," Cato Institute, September 16, 2024, https://www.cato .org/blog/trumps-2020-stolen-election-claims-are-wrong-merits.

42. Indictment, United States v. Trump, 1:23-cr-00257 (D.D.C. August 1, 2023), https://www.justice.gov/storage/US_v_Trump_23_cr_257.pdf.

43. "Read Pence's Full Letter Saying He Can't Claim 'Unilateral Authority' to Reject Electoral Votes," *PBS News*, January 6, 2021, https://www.pbs.org

/newshour/politics/read-pences-full-letter-saying-he-cant-claim
-unilateral-authority-to-reject-electoral-votes.

44. "Transcript of Trump's Speech at Rally Before US Capitol Riot," Associated Press, January 13, 2021, https://apnews.com/article/election-2020-joe
-biden-donald-trump-capitol-siege-media-e79eb5164613d6718e9f45
02eb471f27.

45. Spencer S. Hsu et al., "As Rioters Stormed Capitol with Pence Inside,
Trump Allegedly Said 'So What?,'" *Washington Post*, October 2, 2024.

46. "43 Months Since the Jan. 6 Attack on the Capitol," United States Attorney's Office, District of Columbia, August 6, 2024, https://www.justice.gov
/usao-dc/43-months-jan-6-attack-capitol.

47. "The Trump Disqualification Tracker," *Lawfare*, last updated March 4,
2024, https://www.lawfaremedia.org/projects-series/the-trump-trials
/section-3-litigation-tracker.

48. For an article about the lead plaintiff in the case, Norma Anderson, see
Patrick Marley, "The 91-Year-Old Republican Suing to Kick Donald
Trump Off the Ballot," *Washington Post*, February 5, 2024.

49. Anderson v. Griswold, 2023 CO 63 (2023), https://law.justia.com/cases
/colorado/supreme-court/2023/23sa300.html.

50. Ibid., 71.

51. Ibid., 71.

52. Ibid., 72.

53. Ibid., 132.

54. Mark Walsh, "A Packed Courtroom for the Trump Ballot Case," *SCOTUS-
blog*, February 8, 2024, https://www.scotusblog.com/2024/02/a-packed
-courtroom-for-the-trump-ballot-case/.

55. Trump v. Anderson, 601 U.S. 100, 110–112 (2024), https://www.supreme
court.gov/opinions/23pdf/601us1r06_m6hn.pdf.

56. Ibid., 116–117.

57. Ibid., 118–119.

58. Ibid., 117–118.

59. Larry Neumeister et al., "Jury Finds Trump Liable for Sexual Abuse,
Awards Accuser $5M," Associated Press, May 9, 2023, https://apnews.com
/article/trump-rape-carroll-trial-fe68259a4b98bb3947d42af9ec83d7db.

60. Bromwich and Protess, "Judge Rules."

61. Kate Christobek, "The Civil Fraud Ruling on Donald Trump, Annotated,"
New York Times, February 16, 2024.

62. For an overview of all the criminal cases against Trump, see Amy O'Kruk
and Curt Merrill, "Donald Trump's Criminal Cases, in One Place," CNN,
updated November 25, 2024, https://www.cnn.com/interactive/2023/07
/politics/trump-indictments-criminal-cases/.

63. Brief of Petitioner—President Donald J. Trump, Trump v. United States,
No. 23-939 (March 19, 2024), https://www.supremecourt.gov/DocketPDF

/23/23-939/303418/20240319150454815_23-939%20-%20Brief%20for%20 Petitioner.pdf.

64. The quotes from Trump's lawyers are quoted in Justice Sotomayor's dissent in *Trump v. United States*, 603 U.S. 593, slip opinion at 10 (2024), https://www.supremecourt.gov/opinions/23pdf/23-939_e2pg.pdf.

65. Alan Feuer, "Trump's Lawyers Seek April 2026 Start to Jan. 6 Trial," *New York Times*, August 17, 2023.

66. Bart Jansen, "Trump's Election Interference Trial Set for March 4 Is Postponed Pending Decision on Immunity," *USA Today*, February 2, 2024.

67. Lydia Wheeler and Kimberly Strawbridge Robinson, "DC Circuit Gives Supreme Court Easy Out of Trump Immunity Fight," *Bloomberg Law*, February 7, 2024, https://news.bloomberglaw.com/us-law-week/dc-circuit -gives-supreme-court-easy-out-of-trump-immunity-fight. For the full text of the ruling, see Charlie Savage, "The Trump Election Immunity Ruling, Annotated," *New York Times*, February 6, 2024.

68. Amy Howe, "Supreme Court Takes Up Trump Immunity Appeal," *SCOTUSblog*, February 28, 2024, https://www.scotusblog.com/2024/02 /supreme-court-takes-up-trump-immunity-appeal/.

69. *Trump*, 603 U.S. 593, majority opinion, at 9–15 of slip opinion.

70. Ibid., 18.

71. Ibid., 20–21.

72. Indictment, *Trump*, 1:23-cr-00257 at 26.

73. *Trump*, 603 U.S. 593, majority opinion, at 24.

74. For example, indictment, *Trump*, 1:23-cr-00257 at 27–29.

75. *Trump*, 603 U.S. 593, Sotomayor dissent, at 4 of slip opinion.

76. Ibid., 10–11.

77. Ibid., 18.

78. Ibid., 16.

79. Ibid., 11–12.

80. Ibid., 29–30 (citations omitted).

81. Ibid., majority opinion, at 39–40 (citations omitted).

82. Ibid., Barrett concurrence, at 3–4.

83. Ibid., Jackson dissent, at 4, 9.

84. Amy Howe, "Supreme Court Allows Virginia to Remove Suspected Non-citizens from Voter Rolls," *SCOTUSblog*, October 30, 2024, https://www .scotusblog.com/2024/10/supreme-court-allows-virginia-to-remove -suspected-non-citizens-from-voter-rolls/. See also "Beals v. Virginia Coalition for Immigrant Rights," *SCOTUSblog*, accessed February 18, 2025, https://www.scotusblog.com/case-files/cases/beals-v-virginia-coalition -for-immigrant-rights/.

85. Susie Coen, "Trump Speech: 'If They Can Do This to Me They Can Do This to Anyone,'" *The Telegraph*, May 31, 2024, https://www.telegraph.co

.uk/us/politics/2024/05/31/donald-trump-convicted-felon-us-election
-presidential-race/.

86. Sam Cabral, "US Supreme Court Justice Sotomayor Ignores Pressure to Retire," BBC News, November 10, 2024, https://www.bbc.com/news /articles/cvg4n2rdjp6o.

87. Nate Raymond and Dan Burns, "Biden Delivers on Threat to Veto Bill to Expand US Judiciary, Reuters, December 24, 2024, https://www.reuters .com/world/us/biden-vetoes-bill-adding-new-judges-courts-following -trumps-win-2024-12-24/.

88. Maggie Jo Buchanan and Stephanie Wylie, "It Is Past Time for Congress to Expand the Federal Courts," Center for American Progress, July 27, 2021, https://www.americanprogress.org/article/past-time-congress -expand-lower-courts/.

89. S.4199—Judges Act of 2024, https://www.congress.gov/bill/118th-congress /senate-bill/4199/all-actions.

90. Rucho v. Common Cause, 588 U.S. 684 (2019). Justice Roberts wrote the majority opinion, joined by Thomas, Alito, Gorsuch, and Kavanaugh. Justice Kagan wrote the dissent, joined by Ginsburg, Breyer, and Sotomayor.

91. Yurij Rudensky, "Status of Partisan Gerrymandering Litigation in State Courts," Brennan Center for Justice, December 19, 2023, https://www .brennancenter.org/our-work/analysis-opinion/status-partisan-gerry mandering-litigation-state-courts.

92. Moore v. Harper, 600 U.S. 1 (2023).

93. Rachel Selzer and Madeleine Greenberg, "State Court Rejects Challenge to Unfair North Carolina Legislative and Congressional Maps," *Democracy Docket*, June 28, 2024, https://www.democracydocket.com/news -alerts/north-carolina-voters-launch-first-state-level-challenge-to-new -republican-drawn-maps/.

94. "Statement from President Joe Biden on Securing 235 Judicial Confirmations," December 20, 2024, https://www.whitehouse.gov/briefing-room /statements-releases/2024/12/20/statement-from-president-joe-biden-on -securing-235-judicial-confirmations/.

The Meaning of the Election

REALITY CHECK

ANDREW RUDALEVIGE

IT WAS A "RESOUNDING MARGIN," a "landslide" win in a "dominating and historic fashion," "an unprecedented and powerful mandate."[1] At least that was what president-elect Donald J. Trump and his team claimed as the dust settled on the 2024 presidential election. A few weeks later, Trump tried to specify the history involved: "I won the biggest mandate in 129 years," he declared. "The mandate was massive."[2]

It wasn't clear what benchmark for mandates had been established in 1895, though the new mayor of Philadelphia did win handily that year. In any case, Trump's 2024 win had plenty of precedent—as one of the many close elections in American political history.[3] Trump captured just 49.8 percent of the popular vote nationally, beating his Democratic opponent, Vice President Kamala Harris, by less than 1.5 percentage points.[4] That was the smallest margin since the contest between George W. Bush and Al Gore in 2000 and in fact narrower than in all but four presidential elections *since* 1895.[5]

Trump's Electoral College win was more robust: He captured 312 votes to Harris's 226, comfortably above the 270 needed for victory, and one state better than his 2016 tally. But this was, again, a worse-than-average margin, hardly a "dominating" result: It ranked forty-fourth of the sixty presidential elections to date in terms of the percentage of the Electoral College won. Thirty-three of those elections occurred after 1895, and Trump's 2024 result trailed twenty-five of them. An objective definition of a "landslide" is hard to come by, but a tally of 312 electoral votes (of 538) compares poorly with Richard Nixon's 520 in 1972, Ronald Reagan's 525 in 1984, and even Barack Obama's 365 in 2008.[6] Further, Harris lost each of the "blue wall" states—Michigan, Wisconsin, and Pennsylvania—by less than 1.75 percentage points. If she had won them (flipping just 115,000 total votes of more than 16 million cast across the three states), she would have won the election with exactly 270 electoral votes.

To be sure, although Trump's win was shallow, it was quite wide—at least compared with his 2016 (and of course 2020) performance. In 2024 he won a plurality of the popular vote for the first time, driven largely by improving his standing in states he still lost. In fact he did better than in 2020 in all fifty states—but did so most dramatically in blue enclaves like New York (up 5.4 percentage points, even as Harris won the state 56–43 percent), New Jersey (+4.6), and California (+4.0). He also made surprising gains among Black and especially Latino men.

Even so, Trump's claim of a mandate was just one of many components of the 2024 campaign to succumb to a reality check. It was a year in which an all-but-nominated candidate was forced from the field just one hundred days before the election. A year in which the winning candidate—convicted criminally and through civil suits of fraud and worse—frequently proclaimed falsehoods and congratulated cinematic cannibal Hannibal Lecter.[7] It was a year in which the facts of policy often diverged from public perceptions of those facts, when people found it agreeable to believe the unreal. Yet even unreality is important when it shapes electoral decision-making. The election of 2024 had no mandates, but it had many meanings.

One of those meanings was quite simple. For the third presidential election in a row, a dissatisfied electorate dismissed an unpopular incumbent administration. The new president had promised drastic policy shifts and a range of authoritarian tactics to take "retribution" against his enemies and the immigrants he said were "poisoning the blood" of the nation.[8] Perhaps an undramatic cause, then, but one that could lead to very dramatic results—depending on how much of the campaign's rhetoric did make its way into reality.

The Most Uniquely Horrible Choice

Nine of the ten biggest box-office hits of 2024 were sequels.[9] But despite their ubiquity, movie sequels don't tend to get much artistic respect. For every *Godfather II*, there are multiples of *Grease, Jaws*, or *Caddyshack*, summed up by one critic's take on *Exorcist II*: "inane, imbecilic . . . farcically stupid and . . . absolutely unforgiveable."[10]

Political sequels are less common. National parties tend to discard losing presidential candidates because they are, well, losers—here, for every William Jennings Bryan (the Democratic nominee in 1896, 1900, and 1908) or Thomas Dewey (the GOP choice in 1944 and 1948), there are many more Al Gores, who despite winning the national popular vote in 2000 quickly faded from future consideration.[11] The last back-to-back elections featuring the same major party nominees were 1952 and 1956, when Illinois Governor Adlai Stevenson II was twice beaten by Dwight D. Eisenhower. And the last time a defeated former president even won his party's nomination was in 1892, when Grover Cleveland bounced back to defeat Benjamin Harrison, who had narrowly ousted Cleveland in 1888.[12]

For much of the 2024 electoral cycle, though, a rerun of the 2020 contest seemed inevitable, even preordained. Yet, at the same time, the studio seemed to have neglected its audience research. The available evidence suggested that *Trump–Biden: The Revenge*—perhaps *Grumpier Old Men* was the better title—would give *Exorcist II*'s critical legacy a run for its money.[13] "For as long as public polling on the 2024 presidential race has been available," *Politico* reported in late 2023, "it's been clear that most Americans don't want Trump vs. Biden II."[14] One Maine voter called it "probably the most uniquely horrible choice I've had in my life."[15]

Indeed, in a flurry of surveys, large majorities rejected each candidate and said they wanted different choices; only a quarter of respondents said they were "enthusiastic" about a rematch.[16] The results were even worse in key swing states: Only 18 percent of Michigan voters wanted Trump to run again, and just 17 percent hoped Biden would do so.[17]

But these aggregate results concealed highly polarized partisans inside them—and American presidential nominations are driven by primary voters, not weighted polls. While a gap in enthusiasm was evident, both parties' activists were largely on board with the top of their ticket. To be sure, Trump's hold on the Republican Party seemed briefly shaken by his 2020 defeat and his indictable—indeed, impeachable—response to it. Within nine months of the January 6, 2021, assault on the U.S. Capitol, however, close to 80 percent of Republicans wanted Trump to run again.[18] The party's elected officials had long since followed their base voters back into the fold. Reflecting that, Trump's renomination, though not formally uncontested, was largely a formality; he won over three-quarters of the GOP primary vote and over 95 percent of pledged delegates to the Republican National Convention.[19] Only Vermont Republican voters (by 4 percentage points) picked another nominee, former South Carolina Governor Nikki Haley. She proved Trump's strongest competitor, while candidates urging a completely Trump-free direction for the party—such as ex–New Jersey Governor Chris Christie and Trump's own former vice president, Mike Pence—were notably unsuccessful in attracting support. Pence withdrew from the race in October 2023, long before primary balloting even started. Christie won 0.63 percent of the total primary vote.

For his part, Joe Biden had described himself as "a bridge" to younger leaders, "not as anything else," during the 2020 campaign.[20] He would be eighty-six by the time a second term ended, and already seemed occasionally frail in public; the proverbial person on the street, asked for key words describing the likely nominees, was prone to label Biden "old," "confused," and "outdated."[21] But as early as March 2021, the president said that his "plan [was] to run for reelection," hoping to elongate his bridge by another four years.[22]

Democratic elites knew of the public's worries about Biden's age and capacity—many party leaders shared them. But if they were not excited about their standard-bearer, neither did he elicit strong negative emotions among the party faithful. Indeed, Biden was something of a lowest common denominator in Democratic politics, with a knack for occupying the party's policy median for five decades even as the party's platform tacked left or right. And for 2024, who else was there? Biden had already beaten Trump once and was thoroughly vetted, unlike most of the governors and senators who might jump into a potentially divisive open nominating contest. Vice President Kamala Harris was then regarded as a weak candidate, but to displace Harris would be to shove aside the first woman, and the first woman of color, to hold national office. That would itself be risky, given that Black women were the Democrats' most reliable voters. On top of everything else, Biden's record in office was certainly defensible. He could point to a massive COVID-19 vaccination program (started more or less from scratch at the beginning of his term), a host of legislative accomplishments, promising economic indicators, and far better than expected midterm results for his party in November 2022.

Thus Biden was the safe choice—the "don't-change-horses-in-midstream" choice—and by the fall of 2022, polling reported that "Democrats increasingly believe Biden should run in 2024."[23] He attracted no serious opposition within the party; in an organizational show of strength, he even won as a write-in candidate in the New Hampshire primary. Biden's biggest obstacle came from activists on the Democratic left, most prominently those angry at his support of Israel as it conducted a retaliatory war against Hamas in the Gaza Strip.[24] These activists roiled college campuses across the nation with pro-Palestinian protests and organized "uncommitted" campaigns in various presidential nominating contests; in Michigan, with its sizable Arab American community, about 13 percent of the primary vote went this way. But while this result attracted outsize news coverage, it was barely higher than the 11 percent of Michigan voters who made the same choice against an unopposed Barack Obama in 2012. Uncommitted delegates numbered just thirty-six of the five thousand delegates voters chose for the Democratic National Convention.

In a close race, of course, every vote was key, but Biden expected reluctant Democratic voters to return to the fold by November. Party allegiance would presumably prevail, if only as a matter of self-interest. Surely student protesters and their allies would realize that withholding a vote for Biden would only help Trump. Surely they would understand that Trump was worse on every policy position they cared about, including the conflict in Gaza. Surely.

More broadly, Biden and his team assumed that the traditional "fundamentals" of presidential elections would ultimately win out. Incumbents seeking a second term normally hold an advantage—only George H. W. Bush and Trump himself had been denied reelection in the past forty years. Economic conditions, as measured by growth in gross domestic product (GDP), are normally correlated with electoral outcomes as well, and the news there seemed good too. In the fall of 2022, a *Bloomberg* survey of economists had unanimously predicted a sharp downturn ("Forecast for U.S. Recession Within Year Hits 100% in Blow to Biden," blared the *Bloomberg* website)[25]—but those economists were unanimously wrong. Growth in 2023 weighed in at a healthy 2.5 percent overall, and well above that in the third and fourth quarters of the year.

But as the nomination campaign wore on, the fundamentals seemed fallible. For one thing, how did the factor of incumbency work when there were two incumbents? Having already served as president, Trump had no need to introduce himself to the electorate; and though the forty-fifth president had left office with a 34 percent Gallup approval rating, voters viewed his performance far more favorably in retrospect. Biden's own approval rating—another good predictor of the vote for the party in power—was mired in the high 30s by early 2024.[26]

One reason for that comparison was the two economies that went with the two incumbents. To be sure, by many measures Biden had been a successful steward of the national economy. After some postpandemic jitters, starting in the third quarter of 2022 growth in the GDP had ticked up consistently, reaching an impressive 4.9 percent in the third quarter of 2023. In the second quarter of 2024, the period normally used in predictive statistical models of the November elections, GDP growth came in at a solid 3.0 percent.[27] Trump had warned in July 2020 that "a vote for the Radical Left Do Nothing Democrats and Corrupt Joe Biden" would cause "your 401k's and stocks . . . to disintegrate and disappear."[28] But in fact stock indices soared under Biden, consistently hitting new record highs; between January 20, 2021, and the last trading day of June 2024, for example, the S&P 500 rose by 42 percent.

Monthly job creation figures were even more impressive, averaging more than four hundred thousand per month into early 2024, and the unemployment rate—6.4 percent when Biden took office (after peaking just under 15 percent in April 2020 as the pandemic took hold)—had been cut nearly in half by the spring of 2023 and then stabilized at 4 percent a year later.[29] Inflation had surged as the pandemic receded, briefly reaching 9.1 percent in June 2022, but it had itself receded to 3.0 percent exactly one year later, ticking further down to 2.5 percent by the summer of 2024, a far cry from the sustained "stagflation" of the late 1970s and early 1980s.[30] These results suggested that the Biden administration and the Federal Reserve Board had managed to pull off an elusive "soft landing," taming inflation without triggering a new recession; certainly the United States demonstrated far stronger postpandemic economic results than peer nations.[31]

The American public, though, proved largely uninterested in global or historical bragging rights. For economists, inflation is a nominal measure; for voters, it is an everyday experience.[32] And that experience remained quite negative for many households. While the *rate* of inflation had dramatically diminished, that just meant prices were rising more slowly than before—and even those increases were building on the higher prices driven by the higher inflation of the years prior, a nastier version of compound interest. Perhaps most relevant to oft-invoked "kitchen table" issues, grocery items were a full 25 percent more expensive in 2023 than in 2019. Insurance costs piled on, reacting to huge payoffs from the floods and wildfires made more frequent by climate change; insurers even exited some badly affected states.[33] And energy prices shot up too as the Russian invasion of Ukraine affected world markets and as gasoline prices began to reflect renewed demand after the enforced immobility of the pandemic. It didn't help that the COVID-19 stimulus money cushioning consumer spending was not renewed. Growth slowed dramatically in the first half of 2022.[34]

The standard macroeconomic response to rising inflation is to increase interest rates—and the Federal Reserve did just that. The "Fed Funds" rate that affects private lending rose from effectively zero during the pandemic to over 2 percent by mid-2022, peaking at 5.25 percent in August 2023. The rate remained there for a full year, lasting into the summer of 2024. As with inflation, this was not onerous by historical standards—in June 1981 the equivalent rate was an astonishing 19 percent—but it helped to raise credit card debt as well as the cost of mortgages, exacerbating existing problems with housing affordability.

Reliance on the economic fundamentals–based election models carried another risk, too—it seemed such models had contracted their own case of long COVID. In 2020, as the pandemic locked down commercial activity, GDP fell sharply: On an annualized basis, the economy shrunk by close to a third in the second quarter alone.[35] Plugging that number into predictive models suggested Trump would garner just 31 percent of the two-party vote in November 2020. That truly would have been "dominating and historic," but it was never likely. Given the emergency that prompted the sharp downturn, voters rarely attributed the pandemic's economic distress to the Trump administration. Indeed, Trump wound up taking credit for the low prices that cratering demand prompted on some items—gasoline, notably—but avoided blame for the economic crash that caused those low prices in the first place.

That double standard hinted at a new but quickly entrenched feature of American politics: the application of negative, polarized partisanship even to empirical assessment. In 2024, attitudes about the economy often outpaced facts—and those attitudes were frequently driven by one's partisan affiliation. Democrats and Republicans viewed the same events very differently. The former complained that the latter were viewing the Trump economy through rose-colored glasses and the Biden economy through distorting lenses. This will be discussed later in more detail and in the wider context of the general election campaign. But it appears two important elements of the economy—one tangible, one "vibes" based—helped hold Biden's approval and polling numbers below their 2020 levels. First, despite the array of impressive statistics, the rising tide had not lifted all boats. But equally clearly, the captains of some vessels that were rising believed, or claimed to believe, that they were still mired in the mud.

To be sure, Trump had his own liabilities. The Supreme Court's 2022 decision in the *Dobbs v. Jackson Women's Health Organization* case, overturning the constitutional guarantee for abortion rights enshrined by *Roe v. Wade* in 1973, was anchored by the three new justices appointed by Trump to the court in his first term.[36] Trump had imposed an anti-*Roe* litmus test on those nominations, and at first bragged that "I was able to kill *Roe v. Wade*"—before realizing the ruling was hugely unpopular.[37] More generally the salience of the renewed presidential campaign helped remind the public of their doubts about Trump. He had won 46 percent of the 2016 popular vote, then averaged just 41 percent approval in the Gallup poll during his four years in office—never reaching the 50 percent mark in that survey—and then lost reelection with 47 percent of the 2020 vote. While his support clearly had a high floor, reinforced by his most fervent fans, it seemed to have a low ceiling as well. It was hard to predict why someone who had not voted for him before would do so in 2024: As one veteran observer of the presidency put it during Trump's first term, "Never in modern times has an occupant of the Oval Office seemed to reject so thoroughly the nostrum that a president's duty is to bring the country together."[38]

Trump never conceded losing the 2020 election, and even though his fact-free allegations of fraud were in turn denied in dozens of courtrooms, those "false claims provoked his supporters to violence," as a House investigatory committee concluded after rioters attacked the U.S. Capitol on January 6, 2021.[39] One week later, Trump's actions led to his second impeachment by the House of Representatives, charging him with "incitement of insurrection" and having "acted in a manner grossly incompatible with self-government and the rule of law." Fifty-seven senators agreed, falling just ten votes short of the two-thirds required to convict him. For his part Trump continued to argue that he should be restored to office via "the termination of all rules, regulations, and articles, even those found in the Constitution."[40] Opponents said he posed a threat to democracy itself.[41] Indeed, officials in three states (though not, ultimately, the Supreme Court) determined that he was ineligible to serve as president under section 3 of the Fourteenth Amendment, which bars from office anyone who has "engaged in insurrection . . . against" or "given aid or comfort to the enemies of" the Constitution.[42]

One could see why Trump might want to terminate rules and regulations—after leaving office, he was formally accused of violating a wide range of them. The Trump Organization was found civilly liable for financial fraud and fined more than $350 million, having variously inflated and deflated its books to obtain loans and avoid taxes. Trump himself was found to have sexually assaulted and then defamed a woman who accused him of rape in a New York department store dressing room in the mid-1990s; juries awarded her $5 million in damages and then an additional $83.3 million when he continued to call her a liar after the first verdict confirmed she was not.[43] And Trump faced criminal charges as well, at both the state and federal levels. More than eighty counts mounted up: for his actions to overturn the results of the 2020 election, for Espionage Act violations (he had stolen and hidden classified documents when his term ended), and for paying hush money through his business to a former mistress in violation of campaign finance and public accounting laws.[44]

Trump claimed that these prosecutions had nothing to do with his actions but were examples of the justice system being "weaponized" against him—"I'm being indicted for you," he told his supporters.[45] But early indications were that voters outside his base were not convinced; more than half of swing-state respondents told pollsters in early 2024 that they could not vote for a convicted felon.[46] And even many of those surveyed who worried about Biden's age saw Trump (himself seventy-eight years old) as "corrupt," "dishonest," and a "crazy" "loudmouth."[47]

As the race entered a sort of calcified stasis by the spring of 2024, the polling wove together all these strands. Trump tended to replicate his 2020 standing nationally and in key states, his projected vote somewhere in the mid- to high 40s. Biden, for his part, was underperforming his 2020 vote share, and Democratic leaders began to worry that recalcitrant Democratic voters would prefer a losing but more leftist campaign to the status quo. Biden had performed well in his March 7, 2024, State of the Union address— the Trump camp was so taken aback by his energy that evening that it claimed Biden was "higher than a kite" on amphetamines—but even so, independent voters' concerns about his age were proving hard to assuage.[48]

Something was needed to shake up the race, Bidenworld thought. Something to show that Biden was up to the job, and to shine a national spotlight on Trump's weaknesses. Something to make the election a referendum on Trump rather than on Biden. That something was an unprecedentedly early presidential debate—to be held on June 27, even before either candidate had been formally nominated by their party.

Plot Twists

The June debate did shake up the race, but not in the way Biden had banked on. Instead, in an extraordinary plot twist, a month later the sequel became a spin-off.

Certainly neither performance on the debate stage was likely to win an Oscar. Trump's answers were frequently false or misleading as he rambled through a series of greatest-hit grievances, from immigration statistics to his ongoing criminal trials to the 2020 election.[49] But this attracted little notice because, as *Politico* summed up the general sentiment, "Joe Biden face-planted in one of the highest stakes moments of his political life. . . . Debating former President Donald Trump with a raspy voice, wandering eyes, pallid complexion and a halting delivery, Biden's performance was at times unintelligible."[50] At one point, Biden answered a question about abortion with an answer about immigration, and at another proudly mumbled that "we finally beat Medicare."[51] Asked to respond to another of Biden's answers, Trump said he could not. "I really don't know what he said at the end of that sentence," the former president replied. "I don't think he does either."[52]

Biden's performance ignited panic within the Democratic Party and fierce pressure to withdraw from the race. Among others, the actor and political donor George Clooney and the *New York Times* editorial board took it upon themselves to intone that Biden, "the shadow of a great public servant," should leave the race "to serve his country."[53] Given Biden's near-unanimous lock on pledged delegates to the impending national convention, it would be hugely difficult to deny him the Democratic nomination without his consent. Biden's defenders argued the president had just had a bad night, hampered by a cold and jet lag from recent travel. A week after the debate, in a nationally televised interview, Biden was asked whether he would "stand down." His response: "If the Lord Almighty comes down and tells me that, I might do that."[54]

This did not quiet either the angst or the speculation about who could serve as a substitute nominee. Some argued for a short flurry of debates in which candidates could make their case to delegates; others, for an open convention, albeit one without smoke-filled rooms (and probably with more cappuccino than Cutty Sark). Vice President Harris, who, as the understudy to an aging president, had received increasing attention as the campaign went on, remained the obvious alternative. But doubts still remained about her leadership and electability.[55] If the choice was limited to Biden or Harris, some party elders favored sticking with Biden.

But others did not agree; and it turned out that former Speaker of the House Nancy Pelosi was the closest thing Democrats had to "the Lord Almighty." She helped orchestrate a series of private and public signals from fellow party leaders who were unconvinced that Biden was up to the rigors of another four years in office—or to beating Trump in the much nearer term.[56] The question was forced by another bolt of divine-adjacent intervention when "God saved me," as (the notoriously nonreligious) Trump told a hushed crowd at the Republican National Convention.[57] On July 13, a would-be assassin opened fire from a rooftop near an outdoor Trump rally in Butler, Pennsylvania, killing one and injuring two others in the crowd. A bullet grazed the top of Trump's ear, causing blood to spurt but without serious damage.[58] Trump stood up from behind the podium, raised his fist, and shouted "fight, fight" to the shocked crowd. The immediately iconic photo provided a stark if exaggerated contrast between Trump's strength and Biden's fragility. Quarantined in Delaware, coughing through a second bout of COVID-19, on July 21 Biden announced that he would not seek another term after all.

This decision had no precedent. Certainly other presidents had chosen not to seek another term for which they were eligible, and still others had been denied renomination by their party. The closest analogue was Lyndon B. Johnson's announcement in 1968 that he would not seek reelection that November, citing his desire to seek an end to the Vietnam War without the distraction of a political campaign. But even that came on March 31, in the midst of a primary season with serious competitors already seeking the Democratic nomination, including Senators Eugene McCarthy and Robert F. Kennedy. Biden gave no detailed reasons for his change of heart—simply that his decision was "in the best interest of my party and of the country."[59] By all accounts, he didn't believe the consistently unpromising poll numbers and was still convinced he would win.[60] But the party had decided, however late, and throughout a fifty-two-year national political career Joe Biden had always been a party man above all.

At that point Harris's ascension to the top of the ticket proved surprisingly undramatic. Whatever doubts party leaders still harbored were quickly cast aside, given the late hour and the problematic optics of jettisoning not just Biden but the woman of color he had chosen in 2020 and now endorsed as his presumed successor. Further, because she was already on the ticket, she was also on the ballot and had unquestioned legal access to the $95 million the Biden–Harris campaign had on hand.[61] Potential rivals in the party's gubernatorial ranks, along with the Congressional Black Caucus and Democratic luminaries ranging from Bill and Hillary Clinton to Alexandria Ocasio-Cortez, endorsed her. Ocasio-Cortez noted that after all the turmoil, the party was in "disconcerting levels of array."[62]

Democratic voters now seemed newly re-arrayed as well. In July, before Biden's withdrawal, just 28 percent of voters had said they were satisfied with their choices—that jumped to 44 percent a month later with Harris as the nominee, including 60 percent of Democrats, up from a very tepid 20 percent in July. Sixty-two percent of Harris voters said they supported her "strongly," while only 34 percent of Biden voters had said the same the month before.[63] Eighty-five percent of Democrats said they were "excited" about the race, up from just 46 percent in June.[64] Another indicator of enthusiasm was Democratic fundraising, which quickly shot to record levels. Before Biden dropped out, the campaign had raised about $1.5 million per day in July (down by some 25 percent since the debate). Harris, by contrast, raised more than $180 million in the final eleven days of July, averaging $16.6 million per day.[65]

In short, in another sudden shift of narrative, Democrats were abruptly optimistic. "America is ready for a new chapter," former

President Barack Obama gushed to the convention crowd. "America is ready for a better story."[66]

New Horse . . . Same Stream

And yet America proved *not* quite ready for Harris's nomination to be the final plot twist. Why not? There are many reasons, but it's worth exploring two in particular. If these expand on the preceding discussion about the shackles weighting down Biden when he was the presumptive Democratic candidate, that should not be surprising—because the first reason was that in 2024 incumbency, even by extension, was a poisoned chalice.

That truth was not limited to the United States. The COVID-19 era seemed to have spread dissatisfaction with governance like, well, a virus: In the fifty-four elections in Western countries from the start of 2020 through the end of 2024, incumbents were removed from office in forty.[67] And not just in the West. In 2024 alone, over fifty countries went to the polls, from Belgium to Botswana, India to Indonesia. Every governing party lost vote share that year, no matter their place on the political spectrum—the first time in the postwar era that had ever happened.[68] Robert Wike of the Pew Research Center noted "a sense of frustration with political elites, viewing them as out of touch, that cuts across ideological lines."[69]

In the United States, the electorate certainly shared that frustration. Pollsters frequently ask whether people think the country is "on the right track" or not—the answer during 2024 was clearly "not." RealClearPolitics, aggregating surveys of this type, put the "wrong track" figure at 67 percent at the start of the year and still in the mid-60s by late October.[70] And in exit polls on Election Day, some 73 percent of voters said they were "dissatisfied" or even "angry" about the direction the United States was going, a number that was even higher in swing states.[71]

This came against a backdrop of even deeper dissatisfaction with the political process generally. A comprehensive study by Pew in 2023 found fewer than 5 percent of Americans expressing strong confidence in the "future of the U.S. political system," against six in ten expressing little or no confidence. More than half said they were often or always "angry" when they thought about politics—only 4 percent said they were "excited."[72] The RealClearPolitics figures show the "wrong track" tally fell below 50 percent only briefly during Biden's presidency (and then only to 49.8 percent), during the narrow window in the late spring of 2021 when pandemic vaccinations were in full swing and the virus's variants had not yet emerged as a continuing threat. By July 2022 that relative optimism had faded and this measure of pessimism had risen to an astonishing 75 percent.

Voters' views of the economy—the top issue for a plurality of those at the polls—were largely negative as well. Three-quarters of respondents to exit polls said that inflation had caused them hardship—nearly a quarter said that hardship had been "severe." Only 31 percent thought the nation's economic status quo was good or excellent. Those voters broke overwhelmingly for Harris. But 70 percent of the remaining 70 percent voted for Trump.[73]

Not surprisingly, then, as Election Day approached, Gallup found that just 41 percent of the public thought President Biden was doing a good job—and that was on one of his better polling days.[74] Every previous president who was that unpopular had either lost their reelection bid or seen their parties lose instead—with Jimmy Carter, George H. W. Bush, and Trump (in 2020) in the first category and Harry Truman, Lyndon Johnson, and George W. Bush in the second.[75]

Kamala Harris was certainly not Joe Biden. Biden was a white man from the fading industrial Northeast who, born in 1943, was too old even to be a baby boomer and had served in federal office since his vice president was eight years old. Harris was the daughter of a South Asian mother and Caribbean father, raised largely by the former in Northern California, and a graduate of a prestigious historically Black university. She had been a local prosecutor and then state attorney general before winning a California Senate seat in 2016, serving in the Senate for just four years before Biden made her his running mate and then the first woman, and first woman of color, to serve as vice president.

In these ways, Harris presented a candidacy that was shiny and new. A reset for the Democrats seemed possible. After a well-received speech at the Democratic National Convention, where Minnesota Governor Tim Walz joined the ticket, Harris erased Biden's deficit in the national polls. A *Washington Post* survey released on August 18 even showed Harris beating Trump by 49 to 45 percent.[76]

But that was where the needle stuck. Poll after poll, whether nationally or in swing states, showed a very close race, nearly always within the margin of error of a given survey. A very successful debate with Trump on September 10 sent Democrats into ecstasies but didn't shift wider opinion. In the end Harris did not, perhaps could not, push back on the "historically ferocious headwinds" her campaign faced.[77] For one thing, despite her nearly four years as vice president—or perhaps because of it—the wider public was mostly unfamiliar with Harris as either politician or person. To the extent they were aware of her record, it was either from negative coverage of the party's initial doubts about her or from her handful of publicized roles in the administration, for instance as point person urging Latin American nations to reduce the problems pushing people to emigrate to the United States. Her own approval as vice president was just 36 percent when Biden left the race.[78] The truncated campaign—there were only 106 days between Biden's choice to leave the race and Election Day on November 5—left little time for Harris to define herself as a person and candidate. She tried to do so in her convention speech, and early advertising downplayed identity politics in favor of centering on her single mother and prosecutorial chops.

That approach was successful, to a degree—Harris's approval rose well above Biden's. But her efforts had to compete with the Trump campaign's competing attempts to fix her in the public mind: mostly as Black, a woman, and practically a communist—as a prototypical San Franciscan concerned only about "them" (and "they/them"), not "us." Harris was a "DEI hire" who would never have been nominated for vice president or president except for her race and gender, Trump allies said; Trump himself called her "stupid," "lazy as hell," "low IQ."[79] (How he lost a debate so decisively to such a person was never quite explained.) Harris's failed campaign for president in 2019, when she had lurched leftward in search of primary votes, was thoroughly exhumed.

Mostly, the Trump campaign and its allies harped on her connection to and responsibility for the nation's "wrong track." Trump rebranded Harris's diplomatic role as "Biden's border czar" and accused her of committing "the most heinous crimes ever committed by any administration in American history" by "allowing these millions of people—millions and millions of people to come through our border and make our civilization very unsafe." As Senator Ted Cruz (R-TX) said in October, it was fine to vote for Democrats—"if you like Kamala Harris's open borders, if you like Kamala Harris's inflation, if you like Kamala Harris letting criminals out of jail and the crime that comes with it."[80]

To be sure, it wasn't possible for Harris to completely dissociate herself from the Biden administration. But she didn't really try to do so. In a friendly interview with ABC's *The View*, for instance, asked what she would have done differently from Biden during the past four years, she replied, "There is not a thing that comes to mind." Indeed, she added, "I've been a part of most of the decisions that have had impact."[81]

At the same time, though, and tellingly, the Harris campaign didn't provide a robust defense of those decisions. Many of its advertisements sought to change the subject to abortion rights, one of Trump's weaker points. But others conceded significant substantive ground to her opponent. The Harris–Walz campaign's most frequently run positive ad said that "fixing the border is tough," even as it touted Harris's experience as a "border state prosecutor" and her promise to hire thousands of additional border agents. Another featured Harris pledging that "bringing down the cost of living will be a defining goal of my administration" and urging voters to "focus on the future."[82] Indeed, even her debate performance began with an odd unwillingness to defend her administration's performance. The first question from moderator David Muir was an old reliable: "Do you believe Americans are better off than they were four years ago?" The answer, for candidates of the party in power, has to be "yes." And in fact, in September 2020, four years before, more than one thousand Americans a day died of COVID-19, a total exacerbated by the Trump administration's mismanagement of pandemic response.[83] If prices were lower in 2020, it was because no one could buy anything. But Harris's response was not "yes." Instead, it was, "So, I was raised as a middle-class kid," before pivoting to her proposals to reduce housing costs.[84]

That approach undermined Harris's "There is not a thing that comes to mind"—a sound bite that quickly appeared in Trump attack ads. The situation seemed an intriguingly distorted echo of 1960, when the Kennedy campaign seized on a quote from President Dwight Eisenhower. Eisenhower had been asked about his own vice president, then running for the top job against John F. Kennedy. What was Nixon's role in the White House? a reporter wondered. Could the president give an example of Nixonian leadership? "If you give me a week," Ike replied, "I might think of one."[85] Nixon was desperate to be seen as a key player in the still-popular Eisenhower administration, only to be rebuffed; Harris could have benefited from such a rebuff but instead grasped the nettle of incumbency all the more tightly.

One can sympathize: Harris was being attacked both for doing nothing and for being all-powerful. It wasn't irrational to assert her own experience in national office and her importance to the White House in which she served. But doing so undermined her parallel efforts to position herself as the "change" candidate in the race and to define the contest as a referendum on Trump rather than on Biden and her. In the end, more than a quarter of voters said that a candidate's most important attribute was to "bring needed change"—only 24 percent of those who said so voted for Harris.[86] That included many who didn't like Trump but voted for him anyway—53 percent of those in the exit poll said Trump was "too extreme," and more than one in ten of them still picked him.[87] Trump's support included a majority of women who fully supported abortion rights but who also felt the economy was doing poorly.[88] It included many of those taking in the firehose of racism and misogyny at Trump's capstone rally at Madison Square Garden on October 27.[89] As Harris campaign mandarin David Plouffe concluded, "What overwhelmed that [rally] was just people's unhappiness with the current situation and wanting change."[90] The horse was less the problem than the stream itself.

Reality Check

A second key to understanding the election lies in how people justify their decisions to themselves. Political psychologist Jon Krosnick gives the short answer: "What we do is we make up stories."[91] But where do these come from? Will Stancil argues that the public's perception of reality is formed through social consensus, rather than a mechanical reflection of each individual's material well-being. Put another way, "Everyone assumes that people think the economy is bad because *they're* miserable. But it's because they're hearing *other people* are miserable!"[92]

A swath of political science similarly concludes that broad economic indicators are a better predictor of the vote than the voter's personal economic situation.[93] In that research, the way people hear about the wider economic situation is through media coverage of those statistical indicators. But in 2024, that didn't seem to be the case: As noted earlier, those statistics should largely have been cause for optimism rather than despair. As Mark Copelovitch and Michael Stern argued, "Most Americans are better off on almost every metric (wages, income, consumption), than four years ago, even controlling for inflation," yet more than half of those polled (mostly in October 2024) said the economy had gotten worse even in the last year. Forty percent, a plurality, said the United States was *currently* in recession, despite nearly four consecutive years of job growth and a 4.1 percent unemployment rate.[94] This suggested not *recession* but *vibe*cession, as Kyla Scanlon and others dubbed the phenomenon.[95]

Copelovitch and Stern concluded that the story of a poor economy was just that—a narrative, and one presented not just by right-wing media but across the journalistic universe. They found that since January 2021, headlines from the entire Nexis Uni database featured the word *inflation* more than 10,000 times, and the word *recession* twice as often as *recovery*—which itself featured in just 1,250 headlines (and in fewer than 100 after the end of 2022). "To update James Carville's famous chestnut, it appears to be the 'information economy, stupid,'" they concluded. "Americans have overwhelmingly heard that the US economy is terrible, and . . . taken it out on the incumbent political party."[96] It goes too far to say that economic perceptions were wholly divorced from families' facts. But it turned out soon after the election that "lots of Republicans suddenly think the economy wasn't that bad after all," as a *Washington Post* headline put it: Now that Trump was president-elect, there was a dramatic positive shift in GOP voters' attitudes between an October 22 poll and another on November 19. Similarly, the month before the election, a plurality of people told the Michigan Consumer Survey that they were worse off than five years ago—after the election, a near-identical plurality told the same survey they were actually better off.[97]

Nor was the economy the only place where fact and belief arguably diverged, or where communal narrative drove out statistical realities. Some of this was a result of common cognitive biases, such as remembering Trump's tenure in office far more fondly than assessments at the time (most ex-presidents get some benefit from this). But other misinformation was more carefully curated. If you attended a Trump rally, you would be told, "We're losing 300,000 people a year to fentanyl that comes through our border." But opioid overdose deaths were a quarter of that figure and had fallen sharply in both 2023 and 2024.[98] If you attended a Trump rally, you would be told that crime was "through the roof"—indeed, that "you can't walk across the street to get a loaf of bread: you get shot, you get mugged, you get raped, you get whatever it may be." But murders, and violent crimes generally, were down in 2024, dramatically so from 2020, the last year of Trump's first presidency.[99] An Ipsos study in October found clear links between media consumption and public opinion about specific issues like crime, immigration, and the economy. Sometimes that link was downright dangerous: After two massive hurricanes hit the southeastern United States in quick succession in the fall, Trump claimed that FEMA's response was hampered because it had already spent its reserve funds to benefit illegal immigrants. Fewer than 20 percent of conservative news consumers, Ipsos found, knew (or conceded) these claims were false.[100]

As with the FEMA story, Trump often amplified narratives that originated in right-wing social media, bringing them to a much wider audience motivated to believe them. Attacks on migrants and immigrants were particularly common—most famously perhaps in his debate with Harris, when he doubled down on a lie about Haitians living (legally) in Springfield, Ohio. "They're eating the dogs!" he shouted. "The people that came in, they're eating the cats. They're eating—they're eating the pets of the people that live there!"[101] Copelovitch argued that departure from reality was itself "fundamental" to U.S. politics in 2024: "Large swathes of the electorate simply believe (or is willing to vote as if it believes) objectively, empirically false things."[102] Trump's brand of identity politics, that centered on white masculinity, ratcheted up tribal fears of threat in ways keenly relevant to this.[103] Adam Serwer, reporting from a number of Trump rallies, concluded that compared with 2016, his supporters "were far more deeply embedded in an unreality carefully molded by the Trump campaign and right-wing media to foment a sense of crisis" serious enough to justify the retaliatory measures Trump threatened to unleash against his (and, they felt, their) enemies.[104]

At the same time, many in Trump's audience did not believe that his most authoritarian pledges would be carried out. Others cheered for his promised tariffs and mass deportations—both likely to be massively inflationary—even as they said that lowering consumer prices was their main priority. Still others, having decided they would vote against the status quo, tuned out any information that might cause them to doubt their choice. A Democratic think tank trying to influence moderate white women concluded, for example, that those in that group who decided that Trump would be a better manager of the economy simply chose to believe that "anything that felt extreme [was] disinformation or hyperbole, even if he said he would do it."[105] It was more comfortable to accept that "all legal scholars" supported overturning *Roe v. Wade*, or that Trump had never heard of *Project 2025*, a collation of controversial policy and personnel blueprints developed by conservative activists for his benefit.[106] Avoiding cognitive dissonance meant creating an alternative reality. "The paradox of running a campaign against Donald Trump," David Graham has observed, "is that you have to convince voters that he is both a liar and deadly serious."[107] It was a challenge the Harris campaign didn't ultimately meet.

The election results themselves produced other wish lists of alternative facts, this time on the Democratic side. Some argued the party needed to tack left toward radical progressivism, others that it needed to tack right, and rural, instead.[108] But there were perhaps only two what-ifs that might have turned the race into an adjacent parallel universe. One hinged on Biden's decision to run again in the first place: What if he had retired from the field by 2023? There would have been risks, and potential rifts, in an open nominating contest. If nothing else, the Israel–Gaza war would have cast a huge shadow over the Democrats' slate of primaries. And there would have been uncomfortable discussions of the "electoral tax" seemingly imposed on female candidates, and how it could be overcome. But since "change" was the key, a convincing argument for change required a wider debate over the direction of the party—even if it had still resulted in a Harris–Walz ticket.

Another and perhaps more plausible development would have been a full sequence of Trump criminal trials. As it was, Trump was elected president as a convicted felon awaiting sentencing.[109] But the trials that would have publicly litigated his role in the January 6 insurrection and the state-level attempts to overturn the 2020 election, as well as his reckless possession and use of boxes of classified documents after he left the presidency, never happened. For her part Harris, perhaps fearing accusations of politicizing the Justice Department, barely spoke about these matters. Even January 6 received very little airtime in her campaign's advertisements.[110]

Trump's base readily accepted his claims that the charges were completely politicized already, that they were "sham lawfare attacks."[111] But a full accounting of his actions—likely live streamed day after day—would have posed huge risks to his candidacy with undecided voters. Instead, Trump's legal team successfully negotiated delay after delay, helped along by both prosecutorial caution and extraordinary judicial decisions.[112] The Supreme Court, for its part, produced an astonishingly broad decision granting criminal immunity for presidents' "official" acts and limiting the use of evidence in other prosecutions.[113] This required prosecutors to rework the January 6 charges over the summer of 2024. The classified documents case, which dealt with postpresidential actions, was also derailed when district court Judge Aileen Cannon discarded an array of higher-court precedent to decide that the special prosecutor bringing the case had been unconstitutionally appointed. The election took place before the Justice Department's appeal of that ruling was heard. And since Justice Department policy is that sitting presidents cannot be prosecuted, after Trump's win all of the federal cases were suspended. Thus did Trump both counter the facts and conquer the counterfactuals.

Reality Revealed: "A Snarly Sort of Politics"

Those counterfactuals do suggest an interesting thought experiment for path dependence in 2024: Given the choices they had on their ballots, voters chose to reject the party in power. But there were places along the way where a new path could have been blazed. The Senate could very plausibly have disqualified Trump from office after finding him guilty in his second impeachment trial in 2021. The courts could have upheld the text of the post–Civil War guardrails against insurrection in the Fourteenth Amendment, or decided that presidents were not in fact above the law. An aging incumbent could have set his ego aside gracefully and chosen to rest on his laurels. And the party system, on both sides of the aisle, could have asserted more authority, earlier, over who carried their banners. In this telling it is elites, not voters, who fostered a polarized, divisive reality.

That done, though, in the end, Harris's deputy campaign manager was right: "The undecideds that we felt would break for us ultimately broke for Trump. And that is what did it."[114] Still, this is a definition of defeat, not an explanation for it. Was it simply a question of punishing an incumbent for a disappointing economy, or do matters hinge on how that disappointment was derived, indeed induced? Surely the reality check matters as well as the reality, in terms of its implications for trust in government and governance moving forward. "Effective policy can only be created out of the material our politics provides," Richard Neustadt wrote in the last chapter of his classic *Presidential Power* in 1960. "It is not very promising material." That was in part because he foresaw "a snarly sort of politics."[115]

Neustadt was surely right about the snarly, then and now. But if the snarliness has reemerged more than sixty years later, it is for a very different reason. Neustadt worried about "party followings more likely to be brittle and unstable than secure"; instead, it is partisanship's iron rule of faith over reason that has brought American politics uncomfortably close to George Orwell's *1984* credo that the Party's "most essential command" was "to reject the evidence of your eyes and ears."[116]

Evidence rejected for whatever reason, one immediate, intriguing reaction to the 2024 election was from Trump supporters hoping that he had been neither serious nor literal during the campaign. "After Backing Trump, Low-Income Voters Hope He Doesn't Slash Their Benefits," read one headline; "Latino Trump Supporters Believe He Won't Deport 'Good' Families," read another.[117] Farmers and contractors warned of workforce shortages; corporate leaders feared retaliatory tariffs; tech magnates pleaded the case for additional visas. The stock market dropped when the Federal Reserve put a hold on future interest rate reductions, warning that Trump's planned tax, trade, and immigration policies were inflationary. Polls showed that substantial majorities opposed Trump's more authoritarian pledges, ranging from politicizing the Department of Justice and FBI to using the military to round up migrants or suppress domestic dissent.[118]

There is an analogue here to the old cliché "Be careful what you wish for"—or perhaps to the Old Testament story of the prophet Samuel, who had no obviously worthy successor as he aged. The people had an answer: "Give us a king!" And despite Samuel's long and detailed warnings—a king will take your sons as cannon fodder for his wars; he'll make your daughters his courtesans; he'll hand over your property to his officers and courtiers; and "you shall be his slaves"—they responded again, "We are determined to have a king over us." God told Samuel, well, you tried—give them a king.[119] Reality revealed is not always a pretty sight.

Ironically—or bizarrely, given the history of the American Revolution—in mid-February 2025 the White House posted images of Trump in regal robes on social media, boasting "long live the king!"[120] The good news for American politics is that institutional, constitutional, and even geographic levers still remain in place to hamper kingship—even a "dictator for a day."[121] As noted at the outset of this chapter, the 2024 election is hard to spin as a popular mandate: It concluded with George W. Bush's 2004 status intact as the only Republican presidential candidate to win more than 50 percent of the national popular vote since his father did so in 1988. Nor did Trump have coattails: House Republicans lost three seats, and while Republicans did recapture the Senate, GOP candidates ran well behind Trump in key swing states, where only one Democratic incumbent was defeated.[122] Trump's grandiose promises during the campaign seemed likely to collide with the realities of narrow majorities and of separated institutions sharing powers.[123]

But those powers require activation. They require other political actors, especially in Congress, to rediscover their Constitutional oaths and institutional pride. They especially challenge the president's copartisans to act not as helpless underlings to executive ambition but as guardians of a coequal branch of government specifically vested with the power of the purse and the duty of deliberation.

That challenge is all the greater in a "snarly" world—but American politics has always required realities to be realigned toward the greater truths of the American creed. As John F. Kennedy wrote, in a speech he planned to deliver on November 22, 1963, it is not too late to be "guided by the lights of learning and reason."[124]

Notes

1. Peter Baker, "The 'Landslide' That Wasn't," *New York Times*, November 22, 2024.
2. Truth Social post, December 17, 2024, https://truthsocial.com/@realDonaldTrump/posts/113671384956576189; "Full Transcript of Donald Trump's 2024 Person of the Year Interview," *Time*, December 12, 2024. He also evoked the "129 years" figure in the *Time* interview.
3. See, for instance, Andrew Rudalevige, "The Meaning of the 2016 Election: The President as Minority Leader," in *The Elections of 2016*, ed. Michael Nelson (Sage/CQ Press, 2017).

4. "2024 Presidential General Election Results," Dave Leip's Atlas of U.S. Presidential Elections, accessed December 22, 2024, https://uselectionatlas .org/RESULTS/.

5. One of those four was his own 2016 win, when he lost the popular vote by 2.1 percent but won the Electoral College. The other margins smaller than Trump's 2024 win in that time frame were in 1960, 1968, and 2000. See Peter Gattuso, "Assessing Claims About Trump's Margin of Victory," *Dispatch*, December 19, 2024, https://thedispatch.com/article/assessing -claims-about-trumps-margin-of-victory/.

6. Not to mention Franklin Roosevelt's 472 in 1932, 523 in 1936, and 449 in 1940, in elections when there were only 531 total electoral votes.

7. Peter Baker, "Trump's Wild Claims, Conspiracies and Falsehoods Redefine Presidential Bounds," *New York Times*, November 3, 2024; David Jackson, "Un-Silence of the Lambs: Donald Trump (Again) Praises Fictional Cannibal Hannibal Lecter," *USA Today*, May 13, 2024.

8. David Smith, "'I Am Your Retribution': Trump Rules Supreme at CPAC as He Relaunches Bid for White House," *Guardian*, March 5, 2023; Michael C. Bender and Michael Gold, "Trump's Dire Words Raise New Fears About His Authoritarian Bent," *New York Times*, November 20, 2023; Charlie Savage et al., "Why a Second Trump Presidency May Be More Radical Than His First," *New York Times*, December 4, 2023.

9. Natalie Issa, "2024 Was the Year of Sequels," Yahoo, December 25, 2024, https://www.yahoo.com/entertainment/2024-sequels-does-mean-movie -040000891.html.

10. Mark Kermode, quoted in "Twelve Film-Lovers Pick Their Most Hated Movies of All Time," *Guardian*, July 1, 2004.

11. In 2024, Gore (b. 1948) was still younger than Joe Biden or Donald Trump.

12. Martin Van Buren, defeated for reelection as a Democrat in 1840, was the Free Soil Party nominee in 1848, winning just over 10 percent of the national popular vote but no electoral votes.

13. As Dave Barry might stress, I am not making this up. *Grumpier Old Men* was the unloved sequel to 1993's *Grumpy Old Men*, while *Jaws: The Revenge* (1987) was the fourth installment of the *Jaws* franchise.

14. Calder McHugh, "Voters Don't Want a Biden-Trump Rematch. This Is Why," *Politico*, December 20, 2023, https://www.politico.com/news /magazine/2023/12/20/biden-trump-2024-presidential-race-no-one -wants-00132791.

15. Quoted in "Few U.S. Adults Want a Biden-Trump Rematch in 2024, AP-NORC Poll Shows," *PBS News Hour*, December 14, 2023, https://www .pbs.org/newshour/politics/few-u-s-adults-want-a-biden-trump -rematch-in-2024-ap-norc-poll-shows.

16. Poll results for December 2023 in "Jump in Enthusiasm for 2024 Race," Monmouth University, August 14, 2024, https://www.monmouth.edu

/polling-institute/reports/monmouthpoll_us_081424/. See also "Few U.S. Adults"; Mark Niquette, "Most Americans in Poll Don't Want Biden or Trump to Run in 2024," *Bloomberg*, July 20, 2022, https://www.bloomberg .com/news/articles/2022-07-20/poll-finds-most-americans-don-t-want -biden-or-trump-to-run-again, citing a Quinnipiac University poll; Steven Liesman, "Majority of Americans Don't Want Biden or Trump to Run Again in 2024, CNBC Survey Shows," CNBC, December 9, 2022, https:// www.cnbc.com/2022/12/09/majority-of-americans-dont-want-biden-or -trump-to-run-again-in-2024-cnbc-survey-shows.html; and Jason Lange, "Trump vs. Biden: The Rematch Many Americans Don't Want," Reuters, January 25, 2024, https://www.reuters.com/world/us/americans-dismayed -by-biden-trump-2024-rematch-reutersipsos-poll-finds-2024-01-25/.

17. Rachel Van Gilder and Rick Albin, "Poll: Low Interest in Biden-Trump Rematch in 2024," Wood TV (Grand Rapids, MI), December 9, 2022, https://www.woodtv.com/news/national/poll-low-interest-in-biden -trump-rematch-in-2024/, reporting on an EPIC-MRA poll.

18. "78% of Republicans Want to See Trump Run for President in 2024, Quinnipiac University National Poll Finds; Americans Now Split on Border Wall as Opposition Softens," Quinnipiac University, October 19, 2021, https://poll.qu.edu/poll-release?releaseid=3825.

19. "2024 Republican Party Presidential Primaries," Wikipedia, last updated February 18, 2025, https://en.wikipedia.org/wiki/2024_Republican_Party _presidential_primaries.

20. Zeke Miller, "Biden Announces 2024 Reelection Bid: 'Let's Finish This Job,'" Associated Press, April 25, 2023, https://apnews.com/article/joe -biden-election-2024-president-democrats-trump-9c72115656855da89a41 cac3f79aa65b.

21. "Americans Offer Unflattering Assessments of Both Biden and Trump in Latest AP-NORC Poll," *PBS News Hour*, August 28, 2023, https://www.pbs .org/newshour/politics/americans-offer-unflattering-opinions-on-both -biden-and-trump-in-latest-ap-norc-poll.

22. Steve Peoples, "Biden: 'My Plan Is to Run for Reelection' in 2024," Associated Press, March 25, 2021, https://apnews.com/article/joe-biden -5a8fd26a4a9ffa9b47c5de52fface72d. The official announcement followed in late April 2023.

23. Eli Yokley, "Democrats Increasingly Believe Biden Should Run in 2024— but If He Doesn't, Harris Remains the Slight Favorite," Morning Consult, September 28, 2022, https://pro.morningconsult.com/instant-intel/demo crats-believe-biden-should-run-2024-primary-harris.

24. In October 2023 Hamas terrorists came across the Israeli border and murdered 1,200 Israeli civilians, an attack that also featured widespread rape and the taking of some 250 hostages. Israel responded with a military campaign against Hamas-controlled Gaza that proved deadly not

just to Hamas fighters but to thousands of Palestinian noncombatants of all ages.

25. Josh Wingrove, "Forecast for U.S. Recession Within Year Hits 100% in Blow to Biden," *Bloomberg*, October 17, 2022, https://www.bloomberg.com /news/articles/2022-10-17/forecast-for-us-recession-within-year-hits-100 -in-blow-to-biden.

26. See "Presidential Job Approval Center," Gallup, accessed February 19, 2025, https://news.gallup.com/interactives/507569/presidential-job-approval -center.aspx.

27. "Annualized Growth of Real GDP in the United States from the Third Quarter of 2013 to the Third Quarter of 2024," Statista, November 4, 2024, https://www.statista.com/statistics/188185/percent-change-from -preceding-period-in-real-gdp-in-the-us/.

28. Quoted in Matt Egan, "Biden Is Beating Trump on Stocks," CNN, November 1, 2024, https://www.cnn.com/2024/11/01/investing/stock-market-biden -trump-democrats-republicans/index.html.

29. Lori Robertson, "Biden's Job Growth Chart Ignores Impact of Pandemic," FactCheck.org, February 9, 2024, https://www.factcheck.org/2024/02 /bidens-job-growth-chart-ignores-impact-of-pandemic/.

30. "Current US Inflation Rates: 2000–2025," US Inflation Calculator, accessed February 19, 2025, https://www.usinflationcalculator.com/inflation/cur rent-inflation-rates/; Tim McMahon, "Historical Inflation Rate," Inflation Data.com, February 12, 2025, https://inflationdata.com/Inflation/Inflation _Rate/HistoricalInflation.aspx. Inflation was at 13.6 percent for the entirety of 1980, for example.

31. Bryan Mena, "America's Economy Just Achieved the Rare Feat of a Soft Landing," CNN, October 30, 2024, https://www.cnn.com/2024/10/30 /economy/us-economy-gdp-q3/index.html; "GDP Issue Brief," Council of Economic Advisers, October 30, 2024, https://bidenwhitehouse.archives .gov/cea/written-materials/2024/10/30/gdp-issue-brief/. The White House even created a new website to tout its view of the administration's achievements: "The Biden Economy: Building Back from a Financial Crisis to the Strongest Economy in the World," accessed March 11, 2025, https:// bidenwhitehouse.archives.gov/economy/.

32. Paraphrasing Harvard economist Stefanie Stantcheva, quoted in Lauren Aratani, "If the US Is Heading for a Soft Landing, Why Do People Feel So Hard Up?," *Guardian*, November 4, 2024.

33. Scott Cohn, "Insurance Crisis That Started in Florida, California Is Spreading," CNBC, July 2, 2024, https://www.cnbc.com/2024/07/02 /florida-california-insurance-crisis-spreading-your-state-next.html.

34. In 2022 the first estimates of GDP growth showed that the U.S. economy fell 1.6 percent in the first quarter and 0.6 percent in the second quarter— recessionary results—before recovering strongly to post overall growth

of 1.94 percent for the year. However, later revisions to the GDP estimates suggested the second quarter did in fact post slight (+0.3 percent) positive growth: see the Bureau of Economic Analysis, National Data, Table 1.1.1 ("Percent Change from Preceding Period in Real Gross Domestic Product"), revisions as of February 27, 2025, https://apps.bea.gov /iTable/?reqid=19&step=2&isuri=1&categories=survey&_gl=1*qp9i2c* _ga*MTczNjA5MjY5Mi4xNzQxMzIzNjY4*_ga_J4698JNNFT*MTcoMT MyMzY2OC4xLjEuMTcoMTMyNDA1NS4zOS4wLjA.#eyJhcHBpZCI6 MTksInNoZXBzIjpbMSwyLDNdLCJkYXRhIjpbWyJjYXRlZ29yaWV V-zIiwiU3VydmV5IlosWyJOSVBBX1RhYmxlXoxpc3c3QiLCIxIl1dfQ==.

35. For more detail, see Andrew Rudalevige, "The Meaning of the Election: Fundamentally Divided," in *The Elections of 2020*, ed. Michael Nelson (University of Virginia Press, 2021).

36. Dobbs v. Jackson Women's Health Organization, 597 U.S. ___ (2022), decided June 24, 2022; for the opinion and oral arguments, see https:// www.oyez.org/cases/2021/19-1392.

37. Sahil Kapur, "Trump: 'I Was Able to Kill Roe v. Wade,'" NBC News, May 17, 2023, https://www.nbcnews.com/politics/donald-trump/trump -was-able-kill-roe-v-wade-rcna84897.

38. Peter Baker, "A Divider, Not a Uniter, Trump Widens the Breach," *New York Times*, September 24, 2017.

39. "January 6 Committee Executive Summary," as reprinted in the *New York Times*, December 19, 2022.

40. Kristen Holmes, "Trump Calls for the Termination of the Constitution in Truth Social Post," CNN, December 3, 2022, https://edition.cnn.com /2022/12/03/politics/trump-constitution-truth-social/index.html.

41. Biden devoted a September 2022 speech at Independence Hall in Philadelphia to the dangers of the "ultra MAGA" movement, while within the Republican ranks Christie accused Trump of putting "himself first before this country," adding that "anyone who is unwilling to say that he is unfit to be president of the United States is unfit themselves to be president of the United States." Quoted in Michael C. Bender, "Chris Christie Goes Down Swinging at Trump and Pleading with His Party," *New York Times*, January 10, 2024; for Biden, see "Remarks by President Biden on the Continued Battle for the Soul of the Nation," Office of the White House Press Secretary, September 1, 2022, https://bidenwhite house.archives.gov/briefing-room/speeches-remarks/2022/09/01 /remarks-by-president-bidenon-the-continued-battle-for-the-soul-of -the-nation/.

42. In *Trump v. Anderson*, decided on March 4, 2024, the Court did not exonerate Trump, but nor did it want to decide the merits of the case; instead, the justices decided that Congress, not individual states, would have to set up the standards for enforcing the terms of the amendment. (If read

literally, the court's reasoning would also make it impossible for a state to bar a twenty-year-old, or an incumbent running for a third term, from appearing on its presidential ballots.) See Carrie Johnson, "A Unanimous Supreme Court Restores Trump to the Colorado Ballot," NPR, March 4, 2024, https://www.npr.org/2024/03/04/1230453714/supreme-court-trump-colorado-ballot.

43. The statute of limitations had expired for criminal charges to be brought on the rape charge, hence the civil suits. See Associated Press et al., "Jury Says Donald Trump Must Pay an Additional $83.3 Million to E. Jean Carroll in Defamation Case," WHYY, PBS, January 26, 2024, https://whyy.org/articles/jury-donald-trump-must-pay-additional-83-million-e-jean-carroll-defamation-case/; Aaron Blake, "Judge Clarifies: Yes, Trump Was Found to Have Raped E. Jean Carroll," *Washington Post*, July 19, 2023.

44. David Graham, "The Cases Against Trump: A Guide," *Atlantic*, November 25, 2024.

45. Nick Corasaniti and Trip Gabriel, "Trump Tells Supporters His Criminal Indictments Are About 'You,'" *New York Times*, August 8, 2023.

46. Lauren Irwin, "Majority of Swing-State Voters in New Poll Wouldn't Vote for Trump If Convicted," *Hill*, January 31, 2024, https://thehill.com/homenews/campaign/4439535-swing-state-voters-trump-convicted-2024/.

47. "Americans Offer Unflattering Assessments."

48. Sara Dorn, "Trump Suggests—Without Evidence—Biden Was 'Higher Than a Kite' During State of the Union," *Forbes*, April 4, 2024.

49. Michael Gold, "Trump's Debate Performance: Relentless Attacks and Falsehoods," *New York Times*, June 28, 2024.

50. Adam Wren et al., "Democrats Really Have No Way to Spin This. We Break Down Biden's Disastrous Debate," *Politico*, June 28, 2024, https://www.politico.com/news/2024/06/28/trump-biden-debate-result-takeaways-00165701.

51. Eric Bradner et al., "Takeaways from CNN's Presidential Debate with Biden and Trump," CNN, June 27, 2024, https://www.cnn.com/2024/06/27/politics/takeaways-biden-trump-debate/index.html.

52. Instead of "Medicare" Biden presumably meant "Big Pharma." Trump's response was, "Well, he's right: he did beat Medicare. He beat it to death."

53. Quotes from Editorial Board, "To Serve His Country, President Biden Should Leave the Race," *New York Times*, June 28, 2024. See also Reid J. Epstein, "George Clooney, a Major Biden Fund-Raiser, Urges Him to Drop Out," *New York Times*, July 10, 2024.

54. Alexandra Hutzler, "Biden Dismisses Concerns About Mental Fitness," ABC News, July 5, 2024, https://abcnews.go.com/Politics/biden-dismisses-concerns-mental-fitness-hed-drop-lord/story?id=111695174.

55. Christopher Cadelago, "New Poll Goes Deep on Kamala Harris' Liabilities and Strengths as a Potential President," *Politico*, June 12, 2024,

https://www.politico.com/news/2024/06/12/kamala-harris-favorability
-poll-00162093.

56. Scott Wong and Ali Vitali, "As Biden Dug In on Continuing His Campaign, Nancy Pelosi Kept the Pressure On," NBC News, July 22, 2024,
https://www.nbcnews.com/politics/2024-election/nancy-pelosi-helped
-pressure-joe-biden-end-2024-campaign-rcna162943.

57. "Read the Transcript of Donald J. Trump's Convention Speech," *New York
Times*, July 19, 2024.

58. In fact it was not clear whether the blood on Trump's ear was caused by
a bullet or by shrapnel—Trump and his team insisted it was the former
but never released any medical records from the incident.

59. "Read Biden's Letter Withdrawing from the Race," *New York Times*,
July 21, 2024, https://www.nytimes.com/interactive/2024/07/21/us/biden
-withdraw-letter.html.

60. Michael D. Shear et al., "He Still Thought He Could Win: Inside Biden's
Decision to Drop Out," *New York Times*, August 15, 2024.

61. Jessica Piper and Hailey Fuchs, "Kamala Harris Takes Over War Chest
as Biden Campaign Becomes Harris for President," *Politico*, July 21, 2024,
https://www.politico.com/news/2024/07/21/kamala-harris-biden
-campaign-funds-00170136.

62. Quoted in Julia Azari, "Kamala Harris' Rise to the Nomination Shows Both
That the Process Works and Its Institutional Weaknesses," USAPP blog,
London School of Economics, August 14, 2024, https://wp.me/p3I2YF-ecI.

63. These are all from Dan Balz et al., "Harris Holds Slight National Lead over
Trump, Post-ABC-Ipsos Poll Finds," *Washington Post*, August 18, 2024.

64. "Jump in Enthusiasm for 2024 Race," Monmouth University, August 14,
2024, https://www.monmouth.edu/polling-institute/reports/monmouth
poll_us_081424/.

65. Theodore Schleifer, "Donations Soared for Harris After Biden Dropped
Out," *New York Times*, August 21, 2024.

66. Barack Obama, "Our Remarks at the 2024 Democratic National Convention," Medium, August 20, 2024, https://barackobama.medium.com/our
-remarks-at-the-2024-democratic-national-convention-4b1f8a9dce8c.

67. The figure comes from Steven Levitsky, cited in David Rising et al., "The
'Super Year' of Elections Has Been Super Bad for Incumbents," Associated Press, November 17, 2024, https://apnews.com/article/global-elections
-2024-incumbents-defeated-c80fbd4e667de86fe08aac025b333f95.

68. John Burns-Murdoch, "Democrats Join 2024's Graveyard of Incumbents,"
Financial Times, November 7, 2024.

69. Quoted in Rising et al., "'Super Year' of Elections."

70. Calculated from "Direction of Country," RealClear Polling, accessed
February 19, 2025, https://www.realclearpolling.com/polls/state-of-the
-union/direction-of-country.

71. "Election 2024: Exit Polls," CNN, updated December 13, 2024, https:// www.cnn.com/election/2024/exit-polls/national-results/general/presi dent/0.

72. "Americans' Dismal Views of the Nation's Politics," Pew Research Center, September 19, 2023, https://www.pewresearch.org/politics/2023/09/19 /americans-dismal-views-of-the-nations-politics/.

73. Emily Guskin et al., "Exit Polls from the 2024 Presidential Election," *Washington Post*, December 2, 2024, https://www.washingtonpost.com /elections/interactive/2024/exit-polls-2024-election/; Jennifer De Pinto et al., "How Trump Won the 2024 Election—CBS News Exit Poll Results," CBS News, November 8, 2024, https://www.cbsnews.com/news/exit-polls -2024-presidential-election/. For what voters identified as key issues, see the AP VoteCast survey: Humera Lodhi et al., "AP VoteCast: How America Voted in 2024," Associated Press, accessed February 19, 2025, https:// apnews.com/projects/election-results-2024/votecast/. This is somewhat different from the national exit poll, which included "the state of democracy" in its possible list of issues.

74. October 14–27 poll by Gallup, reported in "Presidential Job Approval Center." Biden's approval in the national exit poll was 40 percent. A concurrent YouGov survey put Biden's reelection approval a tick below 30 percent, with 54 percent disapproval. Only 9.6 percent approved "strongly." See Mark Copelovitch and Michael Wagner, "The Anti-Incumbent Wave Is Real. But It's Not (Really) About Inflation," *Econbrowser*, November 18, 2024, https://econbrowser.com/archives/2024/11/guest-contribution-the -anti-incumbent-wave-is-real-but-its-not-really-about-inflation.

75. This list only includes presidents since the start of consistent polling on presidential approval in the 1940s.

76. Balz et al., "Harris Holds Slight National Lead."

77. Harris adviser David Plouffe, quoted in Ronald Brownstein, "Why They Lost," *Atlantic*, December 2, 2024.

78. Brownstein, "Why They Lost."

79. Natalie Burke, "The Real Reason Team Trump Keeps Trying to Call Kamala Harris a 'DEI Hire,'" MSNBC, August 3, 2024, https://www .msnbc.com/opinion/msnbc-opinion/team-trump-calls-kamala-harris -dei-hire-rcna164117; Ashley Parker, "Trump Keeps Calling Harris 'Stupid,'" *Washington Post*, October 21, 2024.

80. "Speech: Donald Trump Holds a Campaign Rally in Prairie du Chien, Wisconsin—September 28, 2024," Roll Call Factbase, https://rollcall.com /factbase/trump/transcript/donald-trump-speech-campaign-rally -prairie-du-chien-wisconsin-september-28-2024/; Cruz quoted in Bayliss Wagner, "Donald Trump, Alexis Nungaray Slam Kamala Harris over Border Security in Austin Speech," *Austin American-Statesman*, October 25, 2024.

81. "'The View' Host Asks Harris What She Would Have Done Differently Than Biden," CNN, October 8, 2024, https://www.cnn.com/2024/10/08 /politics/video/kamala-harris-the-view-interview-ana-navarro-digvid.

82. Ad data from the Wesleyan Media Project; thanks to Mike Franz for providing access.

83. See, e.g., James Fallows, "The Three Weeks That Changed Everything," *Atlantic*, June 29, 2020; and Bob Woodward, *Rage* (Simon and Schuster, 2020).

84. Riley Hoffman, "READ: Harris-Trump Presidential Debate Transcript," ABC News, September 10, 2024, https://abcnews.go.com/Politics/harris -trump-presidential-debate-transcript/story?id=113560542.

85. David Graham, "'If You Give Me a Week, I Might Think of One,'" *Atlantic*, May 27, 2016.

86. Guskin et al., "Exit Polls."

87. "Election 2024: Exit Polls," CNN.

88. Brownstein, "Why They Lost."

89. Maggie Haberman et al., "Trump at the Garden: A Closing Carnival of Grievances, Misogyny and Racism," *New York Times*, October 27, 2024.

90. Brownstein, "Why They Lost."

91. "What Drives Voter Behavior? With Jon Krosnick, PhD," *Speaking of Psychology* (podcast), American Psychological Association, October 2020, https://www.apa.org/news/podcasts/speaking-of-psychology/voter -behavior.

92. Quoted in David Klion, "Who Is Will Stancil? And Why Is He in Your Feed?," *New York Magazine*, April 24, 2024. Also see Will Stancil (@whstancil), "'Stancil thought' means 'Politics is guided by a public perception of reality formed through social consensus, rather than by individuals in observing their material conditions and reacting mechanistically.' Media plays a big role in social consensus, it is not the whole thing," X, February 13, 2024, https://x.com/whstancil/status/17574408 02303660158.

93. See the summary of the literature in Andrew Rudalevige, "Revisiting Midterm Loss: Referendum Theory and State Data," *American Politics Quarterly* 29, no. 1 (2001): 29–46.

94. Copelovitch and Wagner, "Anti-Incumbent Wave." See also Mark Copelovitch and Michael Wagner, "The Information Economy: Media Usage, Political Talk Networks, and Public Attitudes Toward Inflation, Unemployment, and Recession," working paper (SSRN, June 2024), https://ssrn .com/abstract=4876787.

95. See Paul Krugman, "A Win for the Vibecession Story," Substack, December 21, 2024, https://paulkrugman.substack.com/p/a-win-for-the-vibe cession-story.

96. Copelovitch and Wagner, "Anti-Incumbent Wave."

97. Philip Bump, "Lots of Republicans Suddenly Think the Economy Wasn't That Bad After All," *Washington Post*, November 21, 2024; Krugman, "Vibecession Story."

98. KFF Health News, "Trump Drastically Inflates Annual Fentanyl Death Numbers," News-Medical.Net, August 23, 2024, https://www.news-medical.net/news/20240823/Trump-drastically-inflates-annual-fentanyl-death-numbers.aspx; Brandon Drenon, "Experts Hopeful as US Drug Overdose Deaths Fall Below 100,000," BBC, November 14, 2024, https://www.bbc.com/news/articles/c8ek5lo4yy70.

99. Isabelle Taft and Kate Selig, "The Number of Murders Kept Falling This Year, but Fear of Crime Persists," *New York Times*, December 30, 2024; David Moye, "Trump's Latest Claim About Crime Is a Real Doozy," *Yahoo! News*, August 20, 2024, https://www.yahoo.com/news/trumps-latest-claim-crime-real-224038664.html. Bonus fact: There were far more murders in Oklahoma City than in San Francisco in both 2023 and 2024—see Major Cities Chiefs Association, *Violent Crime Survey* (November 6, 2024), https://majorcitieschiefs.com/wp-content/uploads/2024/11/MCCA-Violent-Crime-Report-2024-and-2023-January-to-September.pdf.

100. Clifford Young et al., "The Link Between Media Consumption and Public Opinion," Ipsos, October 18, 2024, https://www.ipsos.com/en-us/link-between-media-consumption-and-public-opinion; Bill Barrow and Michelle L. Price, "Trump Makes More Debunked Claims About FEMA as He Surveys Storm Damage in North Carolina," Associated Press, October 21, 2024, https://apnews.com/article/kamala-harris-donald-trump-2024-north-carolina-2dea5d3130416a56f21a5c22ce2e4386.

101. Jazmine Ulloa, "'They're Eating the Cats': Trump Repeats False Claims About Immigrants," *New York Times*, September 10, 2024.

102. Mark Copelovitch (@mcopelov.bsky.social), Bluesky, December 14, 2024, https://bsky.app/profile/mcopelov.bsky.social/post/3ldbznpeoos22.

103. See Kelly Ditmar, "Trump's Reentrenchmen of White and Masculine Dominance," in *The Trump First Term: Appraisals and Aftermath*, ed. Julia Azari et al. (University Press of Kansas, forthcoming).

104. Adam Serwer, "Trump's Followers Are Living in a Dark Fantasy," *Atlantic*, November 4, 2024. See also Baker, "Trump's Wild Claims." Those fondest of proclaiming that "facts don't care about your feelings" were most prone to feeling that false facts were true.

105. Jackie Payne of Galvanize Action, quoted in Brownstein, "Why They Lost."

106. Daniel Dale, "Fact Check: Trump Makes Wildly Inaccurate Claim That 'All Legal Scholars' on 'Both Sides' Wanted Roe Overturned," CNN, April 8, 2024, https://www.cnn.com/2024/04/08/politics/fact-check-trump-abortion-roe-overturned-legal-scholars/index.html.

107. David Graham, "The Trump Believability Gap," *Atlantic*, October 9, 2024.

108. Interestingly, far more voters thought Harris was too liberal than saw Trump as too conservative, perhaps a holdover from her 2019 campaign positions edited and rebroadcast by the Trump campaign, as a *New York Times* poll found in August. See Jonathan Weisman and Ruth Igielnik, "Trump and Harris Neck and Neck After Summer Upheaval, Times/Siena Poll Finds," *New York Times*, September 8, 2024. But Ronald Reagan received more favorable attention at the Democratic National Convention than at the Republican National Convention.

109. Sentencing had been scheduled for July 11, then September 18, then November 26, and finally took place on January 10, 2025. While the conviction remained on the books, no jail time or probation was imposed given Trump's looming return to the White House.

110. It was mentioned in only 11 of the 339 ads coded by the Wesleyan Media Project.

111. See Trump spokesman Steven Cheung, quoted in Kevin Breuninger, "Trump Hush Money Sentencing Delayed Indefinitely," CNBC, November 22, 2024, https://www.cnbc.com/2024/11/22/trump-hush-money -sentencing-delayed-indefinitely.html.

112. As well as by an ill-considered prosecutorial romance in Georgia that opened the door for Trump's lawyers to claim a conflict of interest and delay those proceedings too.

113. *Trump v. United States*, 603 U.S. 593 (2024). See also Andrew Rudalevige, "The Supreme Court's Immunity Decision Sidesteps History," *Good Authority*, July 4, 2024, https://goodauthority.org/news/immunity-supreme -court-scotus-president-trump-july1-ruling/.

114. Quentin Fulks, principal deputy campaign manager, quoted in Brownstein, "Why They Lost."

115. Richard E. Neustadt, *Presidential Power* (John Wiley and Sons, 1960), 192.

116. George Orwell, *Nineteen Eighty-Four* (Clarendon Press, 1984), 226.

117. Tim Craig, "After Backing Trump, Low-Income Voters Hope He Doesn't Slash Their Benefits," *Washington Post*, December 26, 2024; Sam Seder, "Latino Trump Supporters Believe He Won't Deport 'Good' Families," *Majority Report*, YouTube video, 12 min., 21 sec., posted November 11, 2024, https://www.youtube.com/watch?v=QqCyRTsO960.

118. Colby Itkowitz et al., "Majority of Americans Oppose Trump's Proposals to Test Democracy's Limits," *Washington Post*, December 18, 2024. However, a majority of Republican identifiers did support at least some of these.

119. 1 Samuel 8:1–22.

120. Benjamin Oreskes, "'Long Live the King': Trump Likens Himself to Royalty on Truth Social," *New York Times*, February 19, 2025.

121. Jill Colvin and Bill Barrow, "Trump's Vow to Only Be a Dictator on 'Day One' Follows Growing Worry over His Authoritarian Rhetoric," Associated Press, December 7, 2023, https://apnews.com/article/trump-hannity

-dictator-authoritarian-presidential-election-f27e7e9d7c13fabbe3ae7
dd7f1235c72.

122. Senator Robert Casey (D-PA) lost to challenger David McCormick by just over sixteen thousand votes statewide (a margin of 0.24 percentage points, while Trump won the state by 1.7 percentage points). Democrats held Senate seats in Michigan, Wisconsin, Arizona, and Nevada. Two other Democratic incumbents lost, but in less swingy Ohio and Montana— Trump won those states by 11 and 20 percentage points, respectively.

123. This is of course Neustadt's phrase.

124. Talking about the conspiracy theories of the day—from the John Birch Society and the like—he added, "We can hope that fewer people will listen to nonsense." John F. Kennedy, "Remarks Prepared for Delivery at the Trade Mart in Dallas, TX, November 22, 1963 (Undelivered)," John F. Kennedy Presidential Library and Museum, https://www.jfklibrary.org/archives/other-resources/john-f-kennedy-speeches/dallas-tx-trade-mart-undelivered-19631122.

Conclusion

THE UNCERTAIN FUTURE OF AMERICAN DEMOCRACY

GERALD M. POMPER

> The order is rapidly fadin'
> And the first one now will later be last
> For the times, they are a-changin'
> —Bob Dylan, "The Times They Are A-Changin'"

IT WAS SURELY STRANGE.

The presidential election of 2024 defied precedent, prediction, and, possibly, explanation.

In historical perspective, it was rare as a repetition of the last national contest, pitting incumbent President Joseph Biden against former President Donald Trump. Precedents could be found in the successive races between John Adams and Thomas Jefferson (1796, 1800) and Dwight Eisenhower and Adlai Stevenson (1952, 1956). Trump's three successive candidacies matched only the precedent set by Grover Cleveland (1884, 1888, 1892). He also replicated Cleveland's record: win, loss, win—the last two races against the same opponent, Benjamin Harrison.

Substantively, the three elections culminating in 2024 raised serious doubts about the legitimacy and continuity of the electoral process of American democracy (or the republic) itself. In 2016, Trump lost the popular vote to Hillary Clinton but gained office through the nonmajoritarian Electoral College. In 2020, he lost to Biden on both counts but falsely claimed electoral fraud and countenanced a violent invasion of the U.S. Capitol to overturn the results. In 2024, he came within a rounding error of a popular majority, gaining a slight popular vote margin of 1.6 percent over Kamala Harris and a clearer majority in the Electoral College (six more votes than in 2016). But his campaign rhetoric was frightening—including threats of "retribution" against his opponents and an offhand statement of his intention to be a "dictator," at least in his first day in office.

In this volume, we analyze the shocking events involving the candidates and the voters. The full story of the peaceful transfer of power awaits in the near future of 2028.

Nominating the Candidates

The 2024 campaign saw an astonishing sequence of events. Trump had lost the previous contest, held no office, and had a popularity rating under 40 percent. Yet he dominated the partly machinery and easily dispatched his disparate and uninspiring critics. Biden, aged eighty-one, had previously described himself as a bridge to a new generation of Democratic leaders. Although burdened by low public ratings and media critiques, he resolved to seek reelection.

The stage appeared set for a rematch of the 2020 contest. Confident of his control of the political environment, Biden became the presumptive nominee of his party without serious competition on March 12. He then set the rules for the looming contest with Trump. There would be only two presidential debates, to be held in June and early September, after the final selection of delegates to the party conventions. This schedule foreclosed any intraparty challenge to the president, but it also meant the debates would occur before the voters were fully engaged, enabling Biden to dominate the news and campaign agenda.

While the political calendar advanced, simultaneous events unfolded in the courts. Trump had never accepted his defeat by Biden in 2020, claiming he had been victimized by electoral fraud even after losing sixty court cases rejecting his arguments. Unbending, Trump urged his supporters to protest the outcome, leading to a violent invasion at the Capitol on the day established to certify the results, January 6, 2021. Trump's conduct quickly led to his second impeachment by the U.S. House of Representatives, principally by the votes of Democrats along with ten Republicans. The charges were then adjudicated by the U.S. Senate, where fifty-seven Senators (including seven Republicans) voted to convict, short of the constitutional requirement of a two-thirds majority—and only a week before Trump would leave the White House.

The spring of 2024 featured a string of legal problems for Trump. He was indicted by the Justice Department for interference with the election process, and separately for illegally removing government documents from the White House for his personal use. In independent actions in state courts, he faced multiple counts of election interference in Georgia and thirty-four counts of violations associated with an effort to pay hush money to a former lover. Trump's worst day came on May 30, when the New York jury found him guilty of all thirty-four charges.

But the wheels of justice do not always turn unimpeded in the same direction. Trump made the impeachment votes in Congress a test of personal and party loyalty. Of the ten House members supporting his impeachment, only two survived past the next election. Of the seven Republican senators taking that position, four retired before facing the voters again.

When Trump won in 2024, the principal federal case was put on hold until the end of his term in 2029. Sentencing in the New York case was similarly delayed. The second federal case was dismissed by the presiding judge, an appointee of Trump. The Georgia case was suspended because of charges of improper conduct by the lead prosecutor. Most significantly for the future, the Supreme Court on July 1 changed the basic constitutional rules. After withholding a decision for four months, the six Republican justices—three appointed by Trump—created a startling new constitutional power, granting Trump and future presidents "absolute immunity from criminal prosecution for actions within his conclusive and preclusive constitutional authority. And he is entitled to at least presumptive immunity from prosecution for all his official acts."[1]

Back to politics. Biden's planned campaign strategy collapsed at the first debate, held on June 27. He appeared uncertain, hesitant, and basically too old to serve another term in the White House. Trump was belligerent, repetitious, and evasive—yet fully in control and ready to promote his aggressive agenda. Panicked Democratic leaders and press columnists began to call for Biden's withdrawal, but the beleaguered president held to his own counsel and intentions.

The year's next incredible act came when Trump held a series of outdoor rallies as he traveled toward the Republican convention in Milwaukee. While Trump was speaking to enthusiastic supporters in Butler, Pennsylvania, on July 13, a lone gunman, evading security personnel, fired a single shot that grazed Trump's ear as the candidate fortuitously turned away from the bullet. The shooter was immediately killed on his perch. Trump was pushed to the ground by his guards but rose quickly, blood dripping onto his face, and defiantly shouted, "Fight, fight, fight," an iconic image soon imprinted on campaign sweatshirts. Two months later, another assassination attempt was foiled when more alert security guards captured another gunman hiding in trees at Trump's golf club in Florida.

Trump totally dominated the Republican convention a month after the first attack. Relying primarily on the advice of his family, he designated Ohio Senator J. D. Vance, a stalwart of the Make America Great Again movement, as his vice-presidential running mate and presumptive heir of Republican Party leadership. Formal nomination of the ticket was virtually unnoticed on the first day of the conclave, while many of the four thousand delegates were still registering. The four-day program featured celebrities of entertainment and sports more than politicians, with unstinted praise of Trump their common theme.

The highlight of the convention was Trump's rapturous appearance and acceptance speech on Thursday night. He began effectively with a replay of the first assassination attack, and his conviction that he had been saved by "the hand of God." Dramatically, he kissed a memorial bust of a citizen killed in the Butler shooting while covering and protecting his family in the audience. He then spoke for a total of ninety-five minutes, concluding after midnight on the East Coast. His recurrent themes were praise of his own first term ("We never got credit for our accomplishments") combined with policy goals for the future ("We were a great nation, we're going to be a great nation again") and criticism of the Biden administration's record on the "worst ever" inflation, control of the "greatest invasion" of illegal immigrants, and the decline of "a great military with fools on top."

Biden remained resistant to fellow Democrats' desperate pleas to withdraw as Trump seemed invincible. He waited until the morning after the Republican convention, July 21, and then announced his withdrawal from the race. Ten minutes later, he announced his preference for a replacement—Vice President Kamala Harris. To choose the new nominee, various schemes were offered, including a quick national primary open to registered Democrats, an electronic poll over the web of all interested people, or an "open convention" in Chicago of the chosen delegates and ex officio party leaders. None of these plans were feasible or easily defensible as legitimate. Instead the Democrats created an online electronic ballot of the selected delegates. In the single week provided for their decisions, Harris drew the support of party leaders and almost all of the delegates chosen for the party's national convention, a result that was then ratified when the convention occurred.

Harris quickly took control of the convention, after choosing Minnesota Governor Tim Walz as the candidate to replace her as vice president. The speakers at the proceedings included many politicians, as well as some celebrities. President Biden was accorded much praise on the first night, then was succeeded by noted figures such as former President Barack Obama and Michelle Obama, Oprah Winfrey, and other liberal entertainers.

As in the Republican convention, the highlight came on Thursday evening, when Harris gave her acceptance speech, which lasted only forty minutes, including the extensive applause. She hit at Trump as "not a serious man" who "tried to throw away your vote" and an "anti-abortion coordinator," while focusing on what she termed "a new way forward." Her major appeal, however, was to the moderate center of the electorate. As two liberal writers parsed her speech, "The terms America, American, Americans were uttered 34 times; country or nation, 20 times; freedom, 12 times; opportunity, 6 times; Democrats or Democratic party, o times."[2]

The party conventions together provided one basic meaning for the future of American politics, the culmination of an evolution readily apparent since the advent of television, and then computers. The conventions served no more than formal functions, having lost all real power. In earlier history, "brokered" conventions were true representations of the contests and the bargaining among politicians. The selection of the vice-presidential nominee was an essential part of this bargaining. Perhaps the last pure example came in 1932, when Franklin D. Roosevelt won party leadership only after four nominating ballots and his acceptance of John N. Garner for vice president.

The locus of decision changed from the convention floor to the White House, where incumbent chief executives could easily seek a second term (Biden), or to the strategists planning their leader's spots and speeches in decisive state primaries (Trump). As the nation embraced the new media of radio and television, the conventions became locations for celebrations and revelry, drawing thousands of partisan participants—too many for serious bargaining. Candidates might attend preprimary debates, but public attention was limited.

Not coincidentally, the last conventions with multiple nominating ballots for president came in 1952, the first year of extensive television coverage. By 2024, conventions had evolved to be more like wedding celebrations than political contests. The winner/bride is known in advance, she alone chooses her life mate, any previous rivals for her hand are only obedient ushers, and all speeches are fulsome in praise of the happy couple. A "brokered" convention today would require that the "brokers" adopt behaviors absent from their memories and experiences, and vainly act roles in an unrehearsed historical revival.

The Campaign

At first, the replacement of Harris for Biden appeared to succeed brilliantly. Trump had been leading the incumbent president by 5–6 percent in national polls. Harris soon erased the deficit when she won the nomination, and acclaim for her quick control of the convention and acceptance speech allowed her to surge to a polling lead of about 3 percent. She performed well at the only scheduled television debate with Trump on September 10, and two-thirds of viewers rated her the "winner."

The race appeared stable over the next month even as Trump gradually drew nearer, and the polls predicted a close election in the national popular vote and the focus turned to only seven states with critical blocs of electoral votes. Three formed the Midwest's "blue wall" that had narrowly gone for Trump in 2016 and Biden in 2020: Pennsylvania (19 votes), Michigan (15), and Wisconsin (10). Two had switched from Trump in 2016 to Biden in 2020: Arizona (11) and Georgia (16), while two others had stayed with the same candidate both years: Nevada (6) for the Democrat; North Carolina (16) for the Republican.

Political scientists and mathematicians delved into possible outcomes. They could imagine a tied vote of 269–269 in the Electoral College, which had a total even number of 538. Politicians fretted about outliers Nebraska and Maine, which awarded electoral votes by congressional districts, rather than by the winner-take-all rule used in the other states and the District of Columbia. Little attention was given to the remaining forty-three states in the union, which seemed to be safe for either Harris or Trump. Campaign appearances, rallies, direct mail, mass media and online advertising, turnout drives—and sweat and blood—all focused on the seven critical states.

In their efforts, the candidates operated based on different models of the campaign. Campaigns can be described as presenting the election as either a choice or a referendum. A choice election focuses on the contemporary candidates—it's Harris versus Trump. A referendum campaign asks voters to make their judgments by looking back to the previous actions of the incumbent candidate or her or his party—it's Biden *and* Harris versus Trump. In reality, both models exist in the voters' minds, but the candidates can stress one or the other. Harris leaned into the choice model, Trump into the referendum construct.

Trump hewed close to the referendum model. In the single debate with Harris, as in his acceptance speech, he repeatedly identified her with Biden, the unpopular incumbent. Many of his answers to the diffuse questions came back to attacks on their record on immigration policy, combined with derision toward the illegal immigrants whom Biden and Harris had permitted to enter.

Yet Trump also partially framed the election as a matter of choice. In his speeches and text messages, he attacked Harris roundly, even viciously. He commented critically on her looks, intelligence, purported sexual activity, record as attorney general of California and U.S. senator, even her racial identity as Black rather than (Asian) Indian.

Still, the basic Trump message for the election remained the frame of referendum. In his concluding remarks in their "debate," he returned to this theme: "They have had three and a half years, they haven't done it. We're in serious decline. We have no idea what's going on."[3]

Harris wanted voters to use the alternative frame, choice. She knew that Biden had unfavorable ratings for most of his presidential term, so a referendum election was perilous. She knew that Trump had never achieved a majority favorability rating—and early comparisons of his and her own ratings gave her a 10–15 percent lead if favorability could be made the basis for the eventual ballots. In the debate, she emphasized their "two different views" and voiced the voters' presumed hope for "somebody who is better than this."

But Harris, as vice president, had a basic problem. The office was a difficult launchpad for a presidential campaign. Only two party nominees had ever ascended directly from one rung to the other: Martin Van Buren in 1836 and George H. W. Bush in 1988. Other skilled politicians had tried and failed—Richard Nixon in 1960, Hubert Humphrey in 1968, Al Gore in 2000. Harris, like these predecessors, needed to choose between contradictory strategies.

If she wanted to demonstrate her fitness for the highest office, she could claim she had been an important player in the current administration with a major role in its policies and executive actions. Or she could try to establish her independence from the White House, casting herself as a fresh face. She could not do both. The first self-portrait played into Trump's referendum strategy. The second offered a choice frame but also might alienate Biden and his many friends.

The two candidates also employed different tactics. Harris's effort tried to develop a mass movement, while Trump's managers focused on selected targets. Democrats raised an incredible level of contributions—$1.5 billion, $100 million for each of the fifteen weeks after Harris clinched the party nomination. The Democrats focused this spending on established means to increase turnout, door-to-door canvassing as well as phone messaging and advertising on personal websites and advertising on social media such as Facebook, TikTok, and Twitter/X. But in a society now focused on personal security, it was difficult to fully engage through these conversations. The turnout campaign brought millions of volunteer contacts, including millions on the final weekend in critical Pennsylvania, but no evidence that any minds were changed, or actually mobilized.

Republicans, with weaker local organizations ready for local canvassing, used ample financial support from multimillion-dollar donors to respond through streaming television sites, direct mail, and an array of podcasters, commentators, and conservative advocates on such sites as Turning Point USA and YouTube. The targets were previous nonvoters, disaffected, with limited interest in politics. Particularly effective was an advertisement repeatedly inserted on programs such as the baseball World Series. It began with a 2019 clip of Harris supporting mandatory government payment for prisoners seeking gender-affirming operations. The ad ended with an odd emphasis on pronouns to foster voter resentment: "Kamala is for they/them; Donald Trump is for you." Harris made no rebuttal, even though only two such operations were ever done.

As the campaigns became ever noisier and apparently tighter, however, they were irrelevant in many respects. From the time of the first academic studies of voting behavior, we have known that campaigns activate and reinforce the choices of 80 percent of voters, with only 20 percent (an admittedly important share) open to persuasion.[4]

In 2024, the proportion of persuadable voters was likely to be considerably lower. The candidates were established figures, particularly Trump; after Biden withdrew, the proportion of "double-hater" voters who disdained both candidates shrank to 10 percent, and campaign events such as the Harris–Trump debate created only short-lived perturbations, not a consistent trend. Moreover, the persuadable electorate was rapidly shrinking as almost 70 percent of ballots were cast through pre–Election Day modes such as early voting and mail balloting.

Even for those still "undecided" in polls, there was good reason to consider the holdouts not as undecided but as simply undeclared. There was a surfeit of information available for people who claimed they wanted to know more about the "policies" of the candidates, as if they were searching for the details of Trump's proposed revisions of Obamacare or Harris's views on abortion rights, or the late-breaking decision of the Federal Reserve governors on long-term interest rates. More accurately, these voters were exhausted by rather than absorbed with the campaign, cringing rather than reveling in their choice of their next national leader.

The 2024 presidential campaign was not a model of civic life. It ideally would have been a careful comparison between two competent aspirants. Even setting aside reservations about either or both Trump and Harris, there were few forums for comparison. Some television and print journalists conducted parallel interviews, which became contests for dominance between the host and the candidate. Party platforms were available online but scarcely downloaded.

The debates were really jousting contests, not political discussions, with the partial exception of the vice-presidential meeting of Senator Vance and Governor Walz. But 2024 will be remembered as the best evidence of the defects of the concept. The most important effect came in the Biden–Trump debate, driving Biden from the race. The only other presidential debate, between Harris and Trump, was essentially an opportunity for them to show their combat skills.

But even at their best, television debates are seriously flawed. Two-minute answers on complex policy matters are inherently meaningless. Changing subjects incoherently further muddles any serious talk. The voters may gain some sense of the character of the contestants, but these impressions are as superficial and contrived as those of rehearsed contestants on a game show. But winning the presidency is a bigger prize than winning *Wheel of Fortune*. Voters need more than the last person left as the champion of World Wrestling Entertainment.

The Vote

Explaining the vote is a form of intellectual activity for many people— barbers, bartenders, dinner guests, voters, abstainers, pundits, and political scientists—including the experts assembled in this volume. While academicians for many years saw the electorate as limited in its understanding, events and party strategies changed this perspective.

The events of the 1960s brought new groups into politics, changed alliances, and altered party positions. In 1964, Arizona Senator Barry Goldwater urged Republicans to offer the nation "a choice, not an echo." Soon there would be unforeseen events altering the parties: the 1963 March on Washington for civil rights; the women's liberation movement; the agonies of Vietnam; the assassinations of John Kennedy, Martin Luther King Jr., and Robert Kennedy; and urban riots and student marches.

As Southern conservatives departed and Black voters joined, the Democratic Party moved to the left. As northeastern liberals departed and

Southerners joined, the Republican Party moved to the right. The parties have sorted themselves ideologically. In 1972, self-identified liberals were 4 percent of Republicans, conservatives were 27 percent; by 2016, the proportions were 2 percent liberal, 45 percent conservative. Democrats went from 8 percent conservative and 26 percent liberal to 3 percent conservative and 45 percent liberal.

Conceptions of electoral behavior also changed. Voters did not become ideologues, but they did become responsive. In the 2024 election, aside from a small proportion obsessing about Trump or Harris, they did not devote the fall months to political discussion and discourse. They took a more sensible course. The past is more known than the future, so voters rely on retrospective evaluation. They exercise "democratic realism," where "most voters make choices based on longstanding group identities and vague, short-term assessments of their well-being."[5]

Such behavior is quite reasonable in the real world. It is obvious that individual voters will not affect the outcome when over 150 million others will cast ballots. For their personal well-being, they are better off spending their limited time in jobs, close relationships, and leisure activities. Politics is complicated and uncertain in its results. In making political decisions, voters will use clues from the past, such as their party identification and their retrospective judgments on the personal impact of past government policies. If they want to be "good citizens" as this year's vote nears, they will look for easy cues—perhaps an ad on television, an endorsement from their union, the lead of a "smart" friend or relative, or some handy index of "the nature of the times."

The voters of 2024 were not unusual in seeking shortcuts. Reflecting their parties' slogans, Republicans readily emphasized the economy and immigration as major issues, while Democrats stressed democracy and abortion. But the Republican emphases set the national agenda. The impact of the economy on the election was also evident in responses to a neutral question, "How are things going in the United States?" Only 7 percent were "enthusiastic," another 19 percent "satisfied." The outcome of the election could be quickly foretold by the larger groups "dissatisfied" (43 percent, of whom 54 percent favored the Republicans) or "angry" (29 percent, of whom 71 percent supported Trump). The issue of "the economy" was also most important to 39 percent of an authoritative national sample, followed by immigration, chosen by 20 percent.[6] The same outcome built on Biden's poor ratings. On Election Day, his approval rating was down to 40 percent, almost all support coming from Democrats. He was downgraded by

58 percent among all voters, but Democrats now composed a sixth of the critics.

Furthermore, Harris lost support among many demographic groups, when compared with Biden's win in 2020. The most significant declines came from Hispanic voters (−25 percentage points), concentrated among Hispanic men (−33 percent); white voters without a college degree (−4 percent); young women (−3 percent); and first-time voters (−19 percent). She obviously failed to build a winning coalition. Her support did continue among Black voters and college graduates, but this was inadequate.[7]

The loss was not only, perhaps not even predominantly, about specific issues but perhaps more about fundamental party ideology and orientation to politics. The Democrats had gained dominance on the basis of economic policies and an egalitarian concern for the working and middle classes, as pursued by Franklin Roosevelt's New Deal and Harry Truman's Fair Deal. This emphasis on increased opportunity later won support among Black voters and other racial minorities. Trump tried to disrupt this coalition by espousing a populist attack on the privileged (and Democratic) "establishment," elites primarily in government, but occasionally even scorning some of his own rich colleagues.

Democrats abetted his attacks when they widened the meaning of opportunity to expand attention to an increasing variety of groups, such as Native Americans, single-sex couples, and transgender people. All of these efforts were decent and justifiable, but elections are not won by appearing to give these groups priority over others struggling to make their way in a contentious economy and often a bewildering world of changing technology and displacement.

The Democratic Party could be attacked as having a "woke agenda" that prioritized "politically correct" themes over the needs of ordinary voters. As a Republican columnist (who voted for Harris) wrote, the party "increasingly stands for the imposition of bizarre cultural norms on hundreds of millions of Americans who want to live and let live but don't like being told how to speak or what to think."[8] In keeping with this sentiment, the notorious "they/them" ad did arouse feelings of resentment—but not necessarily arising from hostility toward transgender people, a very small group probably unknown to most Americans. It worked because it aroused the sense of an unforeseen threat in a world of uncertainty.

Trump succeeded by defining the election as a referendum, a concept easily grasped by the typical voter. That concept was reinforced by Biden's fundamental error, insisting on renomination so long that Democrats could not restructure the race. Biden validated the referendum construct, Harris was trapped in it, and Trump seized the advantage.

Biden might have withdrawn earlier, perhaps in the State of the Union speech in March, as Lyndon Johnson did in the same situation in 1968. That drama would have won praise for Biden, while affording Democrats the opportunity for an open nominating contest, bringing public attention to their leaders and away from Trump. If Harris had won the open contest, she would have been battle-tested, legitimized, and better able, if needed, to separate from the Biden administration. She might then have emphasized the party's traditional concerns for class equality, reviving its previous coalition.[9]

For the longer run, the election results also carried a graphic warning to the Democratic Party in the geography of the vote. The "blue" areas were almost entirely on the periphery of the nation, the Northeast and the Pacific Coast. In the broad central expanses of the country, the party carried only two states in the Midwest, two in the Rocky Mountain region, and only Virginia in the South. Trump carried all of the seven battleground states. Down-ballot results also brought Republican control of both the House and Senate. Despite Trump's boasts, there was no "mandate" in his thin 1.6 percent margin over Harris, only half of Biden's lead in 2020. What he did win was more important. He had *power*, reinforced by his domination of the Supreme Court. In his rapid nominations of extreme conservatives to executive positions, he showed his uncompromising intentions to use that power for his own purposes.

The election results carried worrisome portents for the Democratic future. They lost votes from 2020 to 2024 in every state other than Colorado, and these losses were especially galling in their one-time redouts such as Illinois, Massachusetts, and New York. Many of their friendly states were losing population compared with such "red" states as Florida and Texas. For the first time in nearly a century, declared Republicans outnumbered Democrats. The fundamental character of the long-standing New Deal coalition was undermined by the loss of white working-class support.[10] Trump's gains were most evident among evangelicals, but he also gained 8 percent among white nonevangelicals and 19 percent among male nonevangelicals who did not hold a college degree.[11] Democratic turnout also fell in areas of traditionally large and decisive turnout in such major cities as Detroit and Philadelphia, facilitating Harris's loss in critical states.[12]

Most basically, the party needed to remember an adage, that "parties are judged not by what they are for, but by who they are with."[13] The loss of working-class voters and Latinos and the limited attention to economic appeals must be repaired. If Democrats forget this dictum, they will lose again.

Consequences

The significance of the presidential election goes beyond the 2024 hoopla and the impending upheavals in the reborn Trump government. We must worry not only about the fates of parties and individual politicians but about the condition of the American nation, a divided country on a troublesome course.

David French, a conservative, warns, "There is not a single important cultural, religious, political or social force that is pulling Americans together more than it is pushing us apart."[14] The nation is divided not only by politics but by residence, sports favorites, entertainment programs, and religious affiliation.

Democrats and Republicans now regard each other as wrong not only in their views but in their basic character. As recently as the year 2000, partisans were mutually tolerant; only 20 percent had dim views of their opponents. By 2022, 62 percent of Republicans had very unfavorable views of Democrats, while 54 percent of Democrats reciprocated with the same negative views about Republicans. Moreover, 53 percent of Republicans endorsed at least four of these descriptions of Democrats: closed-minded, dishonest, immoral, unintelligent, lazy. And 43 percent of Democrats had the same dim judgments of Republicans.[15] Partisan divides now extend even to the most intimate matters. Over a third of Americans would be unhappy if a family member married a person from the opposite party, twice the proportion objecting a decade earlier.[16]

More directly in politics, the political divisions are stark in America. In the three Trump elections, party identification was almost a perfect predictor of presidential vote. The different 2024 result came from independent or uncertain voters, not defecting Republicans following Liz Cheney or the disappearing Dixie Democrats. As the colors on the electoral map vividly show, red and blue states are almost two separate nations. At the more local level, "landslide counties" now constitute 60 percent of the United States, as do thirty-seven states. The national results may add up to a close contest, but the race is only close in the few battlegrounds.

The 2024 election is very different from those of earlier times. A vivid contrast is evident in 1960, the very close contest between John Kennedy and Richard Nixon. That election was close overall, but it was close throughout the country, so that it was a coherent national decision. The margin of victory was under 6 percent in twenty-three of the fifty states, with close results evident in all regions from New Jersey to Hawaii. In 2024, the overall result was again close, but it was not national in scope: The margin of victory was under 6 percent in only eleven states.[17]

Another major difference of 2024 from past elections is the size of the victory. Trump, like other victors, boasted of a "mandate" for important policy changes, but a true mandate requires a landslide electoral victory in the popular vote and more than four hundred tallies in the Electoral College. Once common, landslides have become rare. After Franklin Roosevelt's second contest, the only instances in twenty-two races were Eisenhower's sweeps in 1952 and 1956; the reelections of Lyndon Johnson, Richard Nixon, and Ronald Reagan; and the election of Reagan's successor, George H. W. Bush, in 1988.

True mandates can provide energy in government, a grounding for coherence in public policy. Instead, recent battle lines mark hardened entrenchments between impassioned foes, with neither party able to achieve coherent policy goals. Republicans have not won an overall popular majority in eight of the past nine elections, Democrats have won but one convincing victory—by Obama in 2008—though not a mandate. There have been shifts in power, even midterm reversals of party control in the House in 2018 by Democrats and 2022 by Republicans.

Yet these shifts have hardened differences, adding institutional conflict between the executive and legislative branches to party conflicts deepened by ideological shifts within the parties. Republicans are now in thrall to their dominant right wing as Democrats uneasily seek unity between their moderates and progressives. Even the most basic task, adoption of the national budget, is repeatedly delayed, while legislative activity is subordinated to committee investigations and party grandstanding. The compromises necessary for effective government wither, giving voters ever more reason to disdain their elected leaders.

The citizenry shows its own distemper. After voting reached its highest level in a century in 2020, it declined slightly in 2024, particularly among racial minorities. More broadly, citizen activity continued its long-term decline. Americans no longer merited Alexis de Tocqueville's praise: "To have a hand in the government of society, and to talk about it is the most important business and, so to speak, the only pleasure an American knows. . . . If an American were to be reduced to minding only his own business, he would be deprived of half his existence."[18]

In reality, the opportunities and the exercise of such activity have been severely reduced in American politics. The electorate has fewer opportunities to gain objective news about its political world, as the local press has withered, national evening newscasts are challenged by ideological channels, and personal communications are privatized on partisan or nonpolitical sites and streams. Political "rallies" are forums for entertainers, not candidates, while prospective voters are there to cheer, not to speak. Even the uplifting community ritual of Election Day balloting may soon disappear, replaced by early voting, mail ballots, perhaps even internet email.

The final meaning of this election is not yet written. That meaning and value would come in the peaceful transfer of power, the foundation of a democratic polity. Its hallmark is not the winning of elections—autocrats do that, ceremoniously. Its true character is shown when parties *lose* elections and willingly leave power to their victorious opponents. That transfer was the heritage of John Adams and Thomas Jefferson, when they changed control of the presidency. Their example was controlling for Abraham Lincoln, who prepared a secret concession accepting the secession of the Confederacy and the loss of the Civil War if, as he feared, he lost the wartime election of 1864. Trump in 2020 did not show similar deference to this tradition, but Biden did in 2024. Trump did promise to abide by the result of "a free election" in 2024, but he did not pledge to accept a second defeat by Biden and had aroused, praised, and said he would pardon those who invaded the Capitol in 2021.

I reiterate my initial words: The full story of the peaceful transfer of power awaits in the near future of 2028.

Notes

1. Trump v. United States, 603 U.S. ___ (2024), Docket No. 23-939.
2. William Kristol and Andrew Egger, "Is That—Is That—Optimism We Feel?," *Bulwark*, August 23, 2024, https://www.thebulwark.com/p/is-thatis-thatoptimism-we-feel. As pioneered at the University of Michigan, in the magisterial work by Angus Campbell et al., *The American Voter* (John Wiley, 1960), voters were seen as limited in capability; only 15 percent could apply ideological thinking to evaluations of the parties and candidates.
3. "Kamala Harris vs. Donald Trump Full Presidential Debate: Best from the Sept. 10 War of Words," November 5, 2024, by Oneindia News, YouTube, 1 hour, 32 min., 20 sec., https://www.youtube.com/watch?v=lAH6KUOiSB8.
4. Paul Lazarsfeld et al., *The People Elect a President* (Columbia University Press, 1944).

5. Jack Lucas et al., "Politicians' Theories of Voting Behavior," *American Political Science Review*, published ahead of print, November 2024, https://doi.org/10.1017/S0003055424001060, drawing on Christopher Achen and Larry Bartels, *Democracy for Realists* (Princeton University Press, 2016).

6. "Impact of Anti-Institutional Attitudes," Monmouth University Poll, July 11, 2024, https://www.monmouth.edu/polling-institute/reports /monmouthpoll_us_071124/.

7. Linley Sanders, "How Five key Demographic Groups Voted in 2024: AP Votecast," Associated Press, November 7, 2024, https://apnews.com/article /election-harris-trump-women-latinos-black-voters-0f3fbda3362f3d cfe41aa6b858f22d12.

8. Bret Stephens, "A Party of Prigs and Pontificators Suffers a Humiliating Defeat," *New York Times*, November 6, 2024.

9. Nate Silver, probably the leading mathematical analyst of elections, concludes that 80 percent of the blame for the Democratic loss should be attributed to Biden, 20 percent to Harris: Nate Silver, "Kamala Harris Was a Replacement-Level Candidate," *Silver Bulletin*, November 15, 2024, https://www.natesilver.net/p/kamala-harris-was-a-replacement-level.

10. "Interactive: How Key Groups of Americans Voted in 2024," *PBS News*, November 7, 2024, https://www.pbs.org/newshour/politics/interactive-how -key-groups-of-americans-voted-in-2024-according-to-ap-votecast.

11. John J. Dilulio Jr., "The Four Working-Class Votes," Brookings, December 2, 2024, https://www.brookings.edu/articles/the-four-working-class -votes/.

12. Michael C. Bender, "Many Democrats Sat Out Election at Cost to Harris," *New York Times*, November 12, 2024.

13. This brilliant insight of the late Wilson Carey McWilliams is developed in Gerald Pomper, *The Election of 1976* (Chatham House, 1977), chap. 7, "The Meaning of the Election."

14. David French, *Divided We Fall* (St. Martin's Griffin, 2020), 1.

15. "Rising Partisan Antipathy; Widening Party Gap in Presidential Job Approval," Pew Research Center, August 9, 2022, https://www.pewresearch .org/politics/2022/08/09/rising-partisan-antipathy.

16. "How Would You Feel with a Trump or Biden Voter as a New In-Law?," Monmouth University, May 22, 2024, https://www.monmouth.edu /polling-institute/reports/monmouthpoll_us_052224/.

17. "2024 Presidential General Election Results," Dave Leip's Atlas of U.S. Presidential Elections, accessed December 22, 2024, https://uselectionatlas .org/RESULTS/.

18. Alexis de Tocqueville, *Democracy in America* (Penguin Classics, 2003), vol. 1, pt. 2, chap. 6, p. 284.

CONTRIBUTORS

MICHAEL NELSON is the Fulmer Professor of Political Science at Rhodes College. His book *Resilient America: Electing Nixon in 1968, Channeling Dissent, and Dividing Government* won the American Political Science Association's Richard E. Neustadt Award for the outstanding book on the presidency and executive politics published in 2014, and the Southern Political Science Association conferred its 2009 V. O. Key Award for outstanding book on Southern politics on Nelson and coauthor John Lyman Mason for *How the South Joined the Gambling Nation: The Politics of State Policy Innovation*.

MARJORIE RANDON HERSHEY is professor emerita of political science and philanthropic studies at Indiana University. Among her books and articles about political parties and elections, her book *Party Politics in America* is now in its nineteenth edition.

MARC J. HETHERINGTON is Raymond Dawson Bicentennial Professor of Political Science at the University of North Carolina–Chapel Hill. His research centers on public opinion, with particular focus on polarization and trust in government.

CHARLES R. HUNT is an associate professor of political science at Boise State University and the author of *Home Field Advantage: Roots, Reelection, and Representation in the Modern Congress* and *Congress Explained*. His research focuses on congressional elections, representation, and campaign finance.

GARY C. JACOBSON is Distinguished Professor of Political Science Emeritus at the University of California, San Diego. He specializes in the study of U.S. elections, parties, interest groups, public opinion, and Congress. His most recent book is *Presidents and Parties in the Public Mind* (2019).

JOHN ANTHONY MALTESE is university professor and associate dean of the School of Public and International Affairs at the University of Georgia. His books include *Spin Control: The White House Office of Communications and the Management of Presidential News*, *The Selling of Supreme Court Nominees*, and (with Joseph A. Pika and Andrew Rudalevige) *The Politics of the Presidency*, currently in its eleventh edition.

WILLIAM G. MAYER is professor of political science at Northeastern University. He is the author or coauthor of twelve books, including *The Uses and Misuses of Politics: Karl Rove and the Bush Presidency.*

GERALD M. POMPER is Board of Governors Professor of Political Science (Emeritus) at Rutgers University. His twenty-one books include *Ordinary Heroes and American Democracy, Voters' Choice, Elections in America, Passions and Interests,* and collaborations on studies of presidential elections from 1976 to 2024.

PAUL J. QUIRK holds the Phil Lind Chair in U.S. Politics and Representation at the University of British Columbia. He has published widely on the presidency, Congress, public opinion, and public policy and has won the Louis Brownlow Book Award from the National Academy of Public Administration and the Aaron Wildavsky Enduring Contribution Award from the Public Policy Section of the American Political Science Association.

ANDREW RUDALEVIGE is Thomas Brackett Reed Professor of Government at Bowdoin College and a nonresident faculty senior fellow at the Miller Center at the University of Virginia. His books include *The New Imperial Presidency, The Politics of the Presidency,* and *By Executive Order,* as well as edited volumes on the George W. Bush and Obama administrations.

MILLER CENTER STUDIES ON THE PRESIDENCY